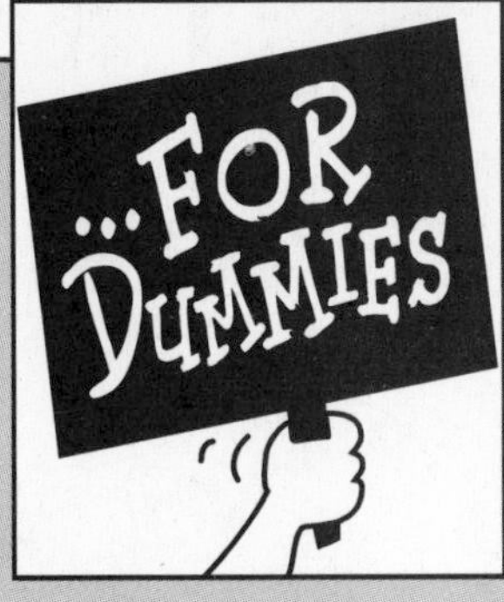

References for the Rest of Us!®

BESTSELLING BOOK SERIES

Are you intimidated and confused by computers? Do you find that traditional manuals are overloaded with technical details you'll never use? Do your friends and family always call you to fix simple problems on their PCs? Then the For Dummies® computer book series from Hungry Minds, Inc. is for you.

For Dummies books are written for those frustrated computer users who know they aren't really dumb but find that PC hardware, software, and indeed the unique vocabulary of computing make them feel helpless. For Dummies books use a lighthearted approach, a down-to-earth style, and even cartoons and humorous icons to dispel computer novices' fears and build their confidence. Lighthearted but not lightweight, these books are a perfect survival guide for anyone forced to use a computer.

"I like my copy so much I told friends; now they bought copies."
— Irene C., Orwell, Ohio

"Quick, concise, nontechnical, and humorous."
— Jay A., Elburn, Illinois

"Thanks, I needed this book. Now I can sleep at night."
— Robin F., British Columbia, Canada

Already, millions of satisfied readers agree. They have made For Dummies books the #1 introductory level computer book series and have written asking for more. So, if you're looking for the most fun and easy way to learn about computers, look to For Dummies books to give you a helping hand.

1/01

by Janet Valade

Best-Selling Books • Digital Downloads • e-Books • Answer Networks • e-Newsletters • Branded Web Sites • e-Learning

New York, NY ◆ Cleveland, OH ◆ Indianapolis, IN

PHP & MySQL™ For Dummies®

Published by
Hungry Minds, Inc.
909 Third Avenue
New York, NY 10022
www.hungryminds.com
www.dummies.com

Library of Congress Control Number: 2002100239

ISBN: 0-7645-1650-7

Printed in the United States of America

10 9 8 7 6 5 4 3 2 1

1B/RT/QU/QS/IN

Distributed in the United States by Hungry Minds, Inc.

Distributed by CDG Books Canada Inc. for Canada; by Transworld Publishers Limited in the United Kingdom; by IDG Norge Books for Norway; by IDG Sweden Books for Sweden; by IDG Books Australia Publishing Corporation Pty. Ltd. for Australia and New Zealand; by TransQuest Publishers Pte Ltd. for Singapore, Malaysia, Thailand, Indonesia, and Hong Kong; by Gotop Information Inc. for Taiwan; by ICG Muse, Inc. for Japan; by Intersoft for South Africa; by Eyrolles for France; by International Thomson Publishing for Germany, Austria and Switzerland; by Distribuidora Cuspide for Argentina; by LR International for Brazil; by Galileo Libros for Chile; by Ediciones ZETA S.C.R. Ltda. for Peru; by WS Computer Publishing Corporation, Inc., for the Philippines; by Contemporanea de Ediciones for Venezuela; by Express Computer Distributors for the Caribbean and West Indies; by Micronesia Media Distributor, Inc. for Micronesia; by Chips Computadoras S.A. de C.V. for Mexico; by Editorial Norma de Panama S.A. for Panama; by American Bookshops for Finland.

For general information on Hungry Minds' products and services, please contact our Customer Care Department within the U.S. at 800-762-2974, outside the U.S. at 317-572-3993 or fax 317-572-4002.

For sales inquiries and reseller information, including discounts, premium and bulk quantity sales, and foreign-language translations, please contact our Customer Care Department at 800-434-3422, fax 317-572-4002, or write to Hungry Minds, Inc., Attn: Customer Care Department, 10475 Crosspoint Boulevard, Indianapolis, IN 46256.

For information on licensing foreign or domestic rights, please contact our Sub-Rights Customer Care Department at 212-884-5000.

For information on using Hungry Minds' products and services in the classroom or for ordering examination copies, please contact our Educational Sales Department at 800-434-2086 or fax 317-572-4005.

For press review copies, author interviews, or other publicity information, please contact our Public Relations Department at 317-572-3168, or fax 317-572-4168.

For authorization to photocopy items for corporate, personal, or educational use, please contact Copyright Clearance Center, 222 Rosewood Drive, Danvers, MA 01923, or fax 978-750-4470.

About the Author

Janet Valade has 20 years experience in the computing field. Most recently, she worked as a Web designer and programmer in a Unix/Linux environment for 4 years. Prior to that, Janet worked for 13 years in a university environment, where she was a systems analyst. During her tenure, she supervised the installation and operation of computing resources, designed and developed a data archive, supported faculty and students in their computer usage, wrote numerous technical papers, and developed and presented seminars on a variety of technology topics. Janet has authored and revised chapters for Linux books and for a Certified Internet Webmaster (CIW) book. To keep in touch, see `janet.valade.com`.

Author's Acknowledgments

First, I wish to express my appreciation to the entire Open Source community. Without those who give their time and talent, there would be no cool PHP and MySQL for me to write about. Furthermore, I never would have learned this software without the lists where people generously spend their time answering foolish questions from beginners.

I want to thank my mother for passing on a writing gene, along with many other things. And my children always for everything. My thanks to my friends Art, Dick, and Marge for responding to my last minute call for help. I particularly want to thank Sammy, Dude, Spike, Lucky, Upanishad, Sadie, and E.B. for their important contributions.

And, of course, I want to thank the professionals who made it all possible. Without my agent and the people at Hungry Minds, Inc., this book would not exist. Because they all do their jobs so well, I can contribute my part to this joint project.

Publisher's Acknowledgments

We're proud of this book; please send us your comments through our Hungry Minds Online Registration Form located at www.dummies.com.

Some of the people who helped bring this book to market include the following:

Acquisitions, Editorial, and Media Development

Project Editor: Paul Levesque

Acquisitions Editor: Bob Woerner

Senior Copy Editor: Kim Darosett

Technical Editor: Allen L. Wyatt

Editorial Manager: Leah P. Cameron

Permissions Editor: Laura Moss

Media Development Specialist: Greg Stephens

Media Development Manager: Laura VanWinkle

Media Development Supervisor: Richard Graves

Production

Project Coordinator: Regina Snyder

Layout and Graphics: Brian Drumm, Joyce Haughey, Jackie Nicholas, Brent Savage, Jacque Schneider, Ron Terry, Erin Zeltner, Jeremey Unger

Proofreaders: Andy Hollandbeck, Linda Quigley, TECHBOOKS Production Services

Indexer: TECHBOOKS Production Services

Special Help

Nicole Laux, Jean Rogers, Barry Childs-Helton

General and Administrative

Hungry Minds Technology Publishing Group: Richard Swadley, Vice President and Executive Group Publisher; Bob Ipsen, Vice President and Group Publisher; Joseph Wikert, Vice President and Publisher; Barry Pruett, Vice President and Publisher; Mary Bednarek, Editorial Director; Mary C. Corder, Editorial Director; Andy Cummings, Editorial Director

Hungry Minds Manufacturing: Ivor Parker, Vice President, Manufacturing

Hungry Minds Marketing: John Helmus, Assistant Vice President, Director of Marketing

Hungry Minds Production for Branded Press: Debbie Stailey, Production Director

Hungry Minds Sales: Michael Violano, Vice President, International Sales and Sub Rights

Contents at a Glance

Cartoons at a Glance

By Rich Tennant

page 7

page 107

page 343

page 251

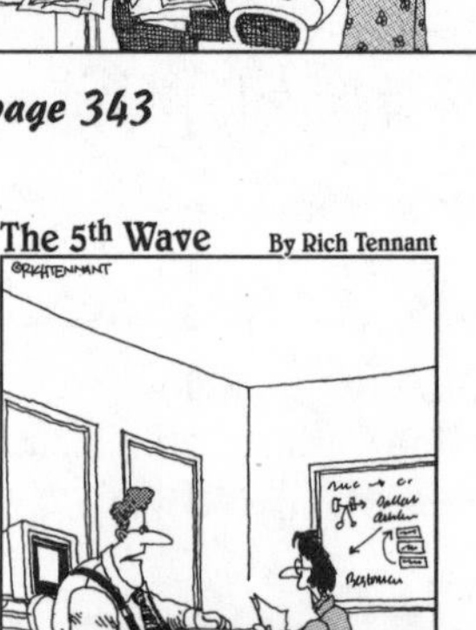

page 61

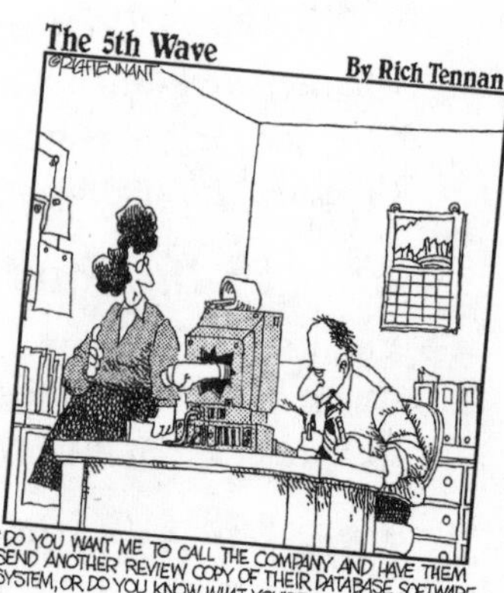

page 325

Cartoon Information:
Fax: 978-546-7747
E-Mail: richtennant@the5thwave.com
World Wide Web: www.the5thwave.com

Table of Contents

Introduction

Welcome to the exciting world of Web database applications. This book provides the basic techniques to build any Web database application, but I certainly recommend that you start with a fairly simple one. In this book, I develop two sample applications, chosen to represent two types of applications frequently encountered on the Web: product catalogs and customer-/member-only sites that require the user to register and login with a password. The sample applications are complicated enough to require more than one program and to use a variety of data and data manipulation techniques, but simple enough to be easily understood and adapted to a variety of Web sites. After you master the simple applications, you can expand the basic design to include all the functionality you can think of.

About This Book

Think of this book as your friendly guide to building a Web database application. This book is designed as a reference, not as a tutorial, so you don't have to read this book from cover to cover, unless you want to. You can start reading at any point in the book — in Chapter 1, Chapter 9, wherever. I divide the task of building a Web database application into manageable chunks of information, so check out the Table of Contents and locate the topic that you're interested in. If you need to know information from another chapter to understand the chapter you're reading, I reference that chapter number.

Here's a sample of some of the topics I discuss in this book:

- Building and using a MySQL database
- Adding PHP to HTML files
- Using the features of the PHP language
- Using HTML forms to collect information from users
- Showing information from a database in a Web page
- Storing information in a database

Conventions Used in This Book

This book includes many examples of PHP programming statements, ranging from a line or two to complete PHP programs. PHP statements in this book are shown in a different typeface that looks like the following line:

```
A PHP program statement
```

In addition, PHP is sometimes shown in the text of a paragraph. When it is, the PHP in the paragraph is also shown in the example typeface, different than the paragraph typeface. For instance, `this text` is an example of a PHP statement, showing the `exact text`, within the paragraph text.

In examples, you will often see some words in italics. Italicized words are general types that need to be replaced with the specific name appropriate for your data. For instance, when you see an example like the following

```
SELECT field1,field2 FROM tablename
```

you know that *field1*, *field2*, and *tablename* need to be replaced with real names because they are in italics. When you use this statement in your program, you might use it in the following form:

```
SELECT name,age FROM Customer
```

In addition, you might see three dots (...) following a list in an example line. You don't need to type the three dots. The three dots just mean that you can have as many items in the list as you want. For instance, when you see the following line

```
SELECT field1,field2,... FROM tablename
```

you don't need to include the three dots in the statement. The three dots just mean that your list of fields can be longer than two. It means you can go on with `field3`, `field4`, and so forth. For example, your statement might be:

```
SELECT name,age,height,shoesize FROM Customer
```

What You're Not to Read

Some information in this book is flagged as *Technical Stuff* with an icon. Sometimes technical stuff is in a sidebar. Technical stuff is information that you don't need to read in order to create a Web database application. Technical stuff may contain a further look under the hood or may describe a technique that requires more technical knowledge to execute. Some readers may be interested in the extra technical information or techniques, but feel free to ignore them if you don't find them interesting or useful.

Foolish Assumptions

To write a focused book, rather than an encyclopedia, I need to assume some background for you, the reader. I am assuming that you know HTML and have created Web sites using HTML. Consequently, although I use HTML in many examples, I do not explain the HTML. If you don't have an HTML background, this book will be more difficult for you to use. I suggest you read an HTML book — such as *HTML 4 For Dummies* by Ed Tittel, Natanya Pitts, and Chelsea Valentine, or *HTML 4 For Dummies, Quick Reference*, by Deborah S. Ray and Eric J. Ray — and build some practice Web pages before you start this book. In particular, some background in HTML forms and tables is useful. However, if you're the impatient type, I won't tell you it's impossible to proceed without knowing HTML. You may be able to glean enough HTML from this book to build your particular Web site. If you choose to proceed without knowing HTML, I would suggest that you have an HTML book by your side to assist you when you need to figure out some HTML that isn't explained in this book.

If you are proceeding without any experience with Web pages, you may not know some basics that are required. You must know how to create and save plain text files, using an editor such as Notepad, or saving the file as plain text from your word processor (not in the word processor format). You also must know where to put the text files containing the code (HTML or PHP) for your Web pages so that the Web pages are available to all users with access to your Web site, and you must know how to move the files to the appropriate location.

You do not need to know how to design or create databases or how to program. All the information you need to know about databases and programming is included in this book.

How This Book Is Organized

This book is divided into six parts, with several chapters in each part. The content ranges from an introduction to PHP and MySQL to installation to creating and using databases to writing PHP programs.

Part I: Developing a Web Database Application Using PHP and MySQL

This part provides an overview of using PHP and MySQL to create a Web database application. It describes and gives the advantages of PHP, of MySQL, and of their use together. You find out how to get started, including what you need, how to get access to PHP and MySQL, and how to test your software. You then find out about the process of developing the application.

Part II: MySQL Database

This part provides the details of working with MySQL databases. You find out how to create a database, change a database, and move data in and out of a database.

Part III: PHP

This part provides the details of writing PHP programs that enable your Web pages to insert new information, update existing information, or remove information from a MySQL database. You find out how to use the PHP features that are used for database interaction and forms processing.

Part IV: Applications

Part IV describes the Web database application as a whole. You find out how to organize the PHP programs into a functioning application that interacts with the database. Two complete sample applications are provided, described, and explained.

Part V: The Part of Tens

This part provides some useful lists of important things to do and not to do when developing a Web database application.

Part VI: Appendixes

This part provides instructions for installing PHP and MySQL for those who need to install the software themselves. Appendix C describes the contents of the CD included with this book.

Icons Used in This Book

Tips provide extra information for a specific purpose. Tips can save you time and effort, so they're worth checking out.

You should always read warnings. Warnings emphasize actions that you must take or must avoid to prevent dire consequences.

This icon flags information and techniques that are more technical than other sections of the book. The information here can be interesting and helpful, but you don't need to understand it to use the information in the book.

This icon is a Post-It note of sorts, highlighting information that's worth committing to memory.

Where to Go From Here

This book is organized in the order in which things need to be done. If you are a total newbie, you probably need to start with Part I, which describes how to get started, including how to design the pieces of your application and how the pieces will interact. When implementing your application, you need to create the MySQL database first, so I discuss MySQL before PHP. After you understand the details of MySQL and PHP, you need to put them together into a complete application, which is described in Part IV. If you already are familiar with any part of the book, you can go directly to the part you need. For instance, if you're familiar with database design, you can go directly to Part II, which describes how to implement the design in MySQL. Or if you know MySQL well, you can just read about PHP in Part III.

Part I

Developing a Web Database Application Using PHP and MySQL

"Look, I've already launched a search for 'reanimated babe cadavers' three times and nothing came up!"

In this part . . .

In this part, I provide an overview. I describe PHP and MySQL, how each one works, and how they work together to make a Web database application possible. After describing the tools, I show you how to set up your working environment. I present your options for accessing PHP and MySQL and point out what to look for in each environment.

After describing the tools and the options for your development environment, I provide an overview of the development process. I discuss planning, designing, and building your application.

Chapter 1

Introduction to PHP and MySQL

In This Chapter

- Finding out what a Web database application is
- Taking a look at PHP
- Discovering how MySQL works
- Finding out how PHP and MySQL work together

So you need to develop an interactive Web site. Perhaps your boss just put you in charge of the company's online product catalog. Or you want to develop your own Web business. Or your sister wants to sell her paintings online. Or you volunteered to put up a Web site open only to members of your circus acrobats' association. Whatever your motivation may be, you can see that the application needs to store information (for instance, information about products, information about paintings, member passwords), thus requiring a database. You can also see that the application needs to interact dynamically with the user (for instance, the user selects a product to view, the user enters membership information). This type of Web site is called a *Web database application*.

You have created static Web pages before, using HTML, but creating an interactive Web site is a new challenge, as is designing a database. You asked three computer gurus you know what you should do. They said a lot of things you didn't understand, but among the technical jargon, you heard "quick" and "easy" and "free" mentioned in the same sentence as PHP and MySQL. Now you want to know more about using PHP and MySQL to develop the Web site you need.

PHP and MySQL work together very well. It's a dynamic partnership. In this chapter, you find out the advantages of each, how each one works, and how they work together to produce a dynamic Web database application.

What Is a Web Database Application?

An *application* is a program or a group of programs designed for use by an end user (for example, customers, members, circus acrobats, and so on). If the end user interacts with the application using a Web browser, the application is a Web-based or *Web application*. If the Web application requires the long-term storage of information, using a database, it is a *Web database application*. This book provides you with the information you need to develop a Web database application that can be accessed using Web browsers such as Internet Explorer and Netscape.

A Web database application is designed to help a user accomplish a task. It can be a simple application that displays information in a browser window (for example, it displays current job openings when the user selects a job title) or a complicated program with extended functionality (for example, the book-ordering application at Amazon or the bidding application at eBay).

Not surprisingly, a Web database application consists of an application and a database — just two pieces:

- **The database is the long-term memory of your Web database application.** The application can't fulfill its purpose without the database. However, the database alone is not enough.
- **The application piece is the program or group of programs that perform the tasks.** Programs create the display that the user sees in the browser window; they make your application interactive by accepting and processing information the user typed in the browser window; and they store information in the database and get information out of the database. The database is useless unless you can move data in and out.

The Web pages you have previously created using HTML alone are *static,* meaning the user can't interact with the Web page. All users see the same Web page. *Dynamic* Web pages, on the other hand, allow the user to interact with the Web page. Different users might see different Web pages. For instance, one user looking at a furniture store's online product catalog might choose to view information about the sofas, whereas another user might choose to view information about coffee tables. To create dynamic Web pages, you must use another language, in addition to HTML.

One language widely used to make Web pages dynamic is JavaScript. JavaScript is useful for several purposes, such as mouseovers (for example, to highlight a navigation button when the user moves the mouse pointer over it) or accepting and validating information that users type into a Web form. However, it is not useful for interacting with a database. You would not use JavaScript to move the information from the Web form into a database. PHP is a language that is particularly well suited to interacting with databases. PHP can accept and validate the information that users type into a Web form and can also move the information into a database. The programs in this book are written using PHP.

The database

The core of a Web database application is the database, the long-term memory that stores information for the application. A database is an electronic file cabinet that stores information in an organized manner so that you can find it when you need it. After all, storing information is pointless if you can't find it. A database can be small, with a simple structure — for example, a database containing the titles and authors' names of all the books you own. Or a database can be huge, with an extremely complex structure — such as the database Amazon must have to hold all its information.

The information you store in the database comes in many varieties. A company's online catalog requires a database to store information about all the company's products. A membership Web site requires a database to store information about members. An employment Web site requires a database (or perhaps two databases) to store information about job openings and information from resumes. The information you plan to store may be similar to information that is stored by Web sites all over the Internet — or information that is unique to your application.

Technically, the term *database* refers to the file or group of files that holds the actual data. The data is accessed using a set of programs called a Database Management System (DBMS). Almost all DBMSs these days are Relational Database Management Systems (RDBMSs), in which data is organized and stored in a set of related tables.

In this book, MySQL is the RDBMS used because it is particularly well suited for Web sites. MySQL and its advantages are discussed in the section, "MySQL, My Database," later in this chapter. You can find out about how to organize and design a MySQL database in Chapter 3.

The application: Moving data in and out of the database

For the database to be useful, you need to be able to move data into and out of it. Programs are your tools for this. Programs interact with the database to store and retrieve data. A program connects to the database and makes a request: "Take this data and store it in the specified location." Another program makes the request: "Find the specified data and give it to me." The application programs that interact with the database run when the user interacts with the Web page. For instance, when the user clicks the Submit button after filling in a Web form, a program processes the information in the form and stores it in a database.

E-mail discussion lists

Good technical support is available from e-mail discussion lists. E-mail discussion lists are groups of people discussing specific topics via e-mail. E-mail lists are available for pretty much any subject you can think of: Powerball, ancient philosophy, cooking, the Beatles, Scottish terriers, politics, and so on. The discussion takes place via e-mail. The *list manager* maintains a distribution list of e-mail addresses for anyone who wants to join the discussion. When you send a message to the discussion list, your message is sent to the entire list so that everyone can see it. Thus, the discussion is a group effort, and anyone can respond to any message that interests him or her.

E-mail discussion lists are supported by various sponsors. Any individual or organization can run a list. Most software vendors run one or more lists devoted to their software. Universities run many lists for educational subjects. In addition, some Web sites manage discussion lists, such as Yahoo! Groups and Topica. Users can create a new list or join an existing list via the Web application.

Software-related e-mail lists are a treasure trove of technical support. Anywhere from a hundred to several thousand users of the software subscribe to the list. Many have extensive experience with the software. Often the developers, programmers, and technical support staff for the software vendor are on the list. Whatever your question or problem, someone on the list probably knows the answer or the solution. You are unlikely to be the first person to ever experience your problem. When you post a question to an e-mail list, the answer usually appears in your inbox within minutes. In addition, most lists maintain an archive of previous discussions so that you can search for answers to your specific problem. When you're new to any software, you can learn a great deal simply by joining the discussion lists for the software and reading the messages for a few days.

Of course, PHP and MySQL have e-mail discussion lists. Actually, each has several discussion lists for special topics, such as *databases and PHP*. You can find the names of the mailing lists and instructions for joining them on the PHP and MySQL Web sites.

MySQL, My Database

MySQL is a fast, easy-to-use RDBMS used for databases on many Web sites. Speed was the developers' main focus from the beginning. In the interest of speed, they made the decision to offer fewer features than their major competitors (for instance, Oracle and Sybase). However, even though MySQL is less full-featured than its commercial competitors, it has all the features needed by the large majority of database developers. It is easier to install and use than its commercial competitors, and the difference in price is strongly in MySQL's favor.

MySQL is developed, marketed, and supported by MySQL AB, a Swedish company. The company licenses it two ways:

- **Open source software:** MySQL is available via the GNU General Public License (GPL) for no charge. Anyone who can meet the requirements of the GPL can use the software for free. If you're using MySQL as a database on a Web site (the subject of this book), you can use MySQL for free, even if you're making money with your Web site.
- **Commercial license:** MySQL is available with a commercial license for those who prefer it to the GPL. If a developer wants to use MySQL as part of a new software product and wants to sell the new product, rather than release it under the GPL, the developer needs to purchase a commercial license. The fee is very reasonable.

Finding technical support for MySQL is not a problem. You can join one of several e-mail discussion lists offered on the MySQL Web site at `www.mysql.com`. You can even search the e-mail list archives, which contain a large knowledge base of MySQL questions and answers. If you're more comfortable getting commercial support, MySQL AB offers technical support contracts — five support levels, ranging from direct e-mail support to phone support, at five price levels.

Advantages of MySQL

MySQL is a popular database with Web developers. Its speed and small size make it ideal for a Web site. Add to that the fact that it's open source, which means free, and you have the foundation of its popularity. Here is a rundown of some of its advantages:

- **It's fast:** The main goal of the folks who developed MySQL was speed. Consequently, the software was designed from the beginning with speed in mind.
- **It's inexpensive:** MySQL is free under the open source GPL license, and the fee for a commercial license is very reasonable.
- **It's easy to use:** You can build and interact with a MySQL database using a few simple statements in the SQL language, the standard language for communicating with RDBMSs. Check out Chapter 4 for the lowdown on the SQL language.
- **It can run on many operating systems:** MySQL runs on a wide variety of operating systems — Windows, Linux, Mac OS, most varieties of Unix (including Solaris, AIX, and DEC Unix), FreeBSD, OS/2, Irix, and others.
- **Technical support is widely available:** A large base of users provides free support via mailing lists. The MySQL developers also participate in the e-mail lists. You can also purchase technical support from MySQL AB for a very small fee.

- **It's secure:** MySQL's flexible system of authorization allows some or all database privileges (for example, the privilege to create a database or delete data) to specific users or groups of users. Passwords are encrypted.
- **It supports large databases:** MySQL handles databases up to 50 million rows or more. The default file size limit for a table is 4GB (gigabytes), but you can increase this (if your operating system can handle it) to a theoretical limit of 8 million terabytes.
- **It's customizable:** The open source GPL license allows programmers to modify the MySQL software to fit their own specific environments.
- **It's memory-efficient:** MySQL is written and thoroughly tested to prevent memory leaks.

How MySQL works

The MySQL software consists of the MySQL server, several utility programs that assist in the administration of MySQL databases, and some supporting software that the MySQL server needs, but that you don't need to know about. The heart of the system is the MySQL server.

The MySQL server is the manager of the database system. It handles all your database instructions. For instance, if you want to create a new database, you send a message to the MySQL server that says "create a new database and call it *newdata.*" The MySQL server then creates a subdirectory in its data directory, names the new subdirectory *newdata,* and puts the necessary files with the required format into the *newdata* subdirectory. In the same manner, to add data to that database, you send a message to the MySQL server, giving it the data and telling it where you want the data to be added. You find out how to write and send messages to MySQL in Part II of this book.

Before you can pass instructions to the MySQL server, it must be running. The MySQL server is usually set up so that it starts when the computer starts and continues running all the time. This is the usual setup for a Web site. However, it's not necessary to set it up to start when the computer starts. If you need to, you can start it manually whenever you want to access a database. When it's running, the MySQL server listens continuously for messages that are directed to it.

Communicating with the MySQL server

All your interaction with the database is done by passing messages to the MySQL server. You can send messages to the MySQL server several ways, but this book focuses on sending messages using PHP. The PHP software has specific statements that you use to send instructions to the MySQL server.

The MySQL server must be able to understand the instructions that you send it. You communicate using the Structured Query Language (SQL), a standard language understood by many RDBMSs. The MySQL server understands SQL. PHP does not understand SQL, but it doesn't need to. PHP just establishes a connection with the MySQL server and sends the SQL message over the connection. The MySQL server interprets the SQL message and follows the instructions. The MySQL server sends a return message, stating its status and what it did (or reporting an error if it was unable to understand or follow the instructions). For the lowdown on how to write and send SQL messages to MySQL, check out Part II of this book.

PHP, a Data Mover

PHP is a *scripting language* designed specifically for use on the Web. PHP is your tool for creating dynamic Web pages. As a special-purpose language, PHP does not need to include many of the features required in a general, all-purpose programming language. Consequently, it is much simpler than many languages, such as C or Java, and contains only the features that are most useful for Web sites.

PHP stands for PHP: Hypertext Preprocessor. In its early development by a guy named Rasmus Lerdorf, it was called Personal Home Page tools. When it developed into a full-blown language, the name was changed to be more in line with its expanded functionality.

The PHP language's syntax is similar to the syntax of C, so if you have experience with C, you will be comfortable with PHP. PHP is actually simpler than C because it doesn't use some of the more difficult concepts of C. PHP also doesn't include the low-level programming capabilities of C because PHP is designed to program Web sites and doesn't require those capabilities.

PHP is particularly strong in its ability to interact with databases. PHP supports pretty much every database you've ever heard of (and some you haven't). PHP handles connecting to the database and communicating with it. You don't need to know the technical details for connecting to a database or for exchanging messages with it. You tell PHP the name of the database and where it is, and PHP handles the details. It connects to the database, passes your instructions to the database, and returns the database response to you.

Technical support is available for PHP. You can join one of several e-mail discussion lists offered on the PHP Web site (`www.php.net`), including a list for *databases and PHP.* In addition, a Web interface to the discussion lists is available at `news.php.net`, where you can browse or search the messages.

Advantages of PHP

The popularity of PHP is growing rapidly because of its many advantages:

- **It's fast:** Because it is embedded in HTML code, the response time is short.
- **It's inexpensive — free, in fact:** PHP is proof that free lunches do exist and that you can get more than you paid for.
- **It's easy to use:** PHP contains only the elements of a programming language needed to create dynamic Web pages. The PHP language is designed to be included easily in an HTML file.
- **It can run on many operating systems:** It runs on a wide variety of operating systems — Windows, Linux, Mac OS, and most varieties of Unix.
- **Technical support is widely available:** A large base of users provides free support via e-mail discussion lists.
- **It's secure:** The user does not see the PHP code.
- **It is designed to support databases:** PHP includes functionality designed to interact with specific databases. It relieves you of the need to know the technical details required to communicate with a database.
- **It's customizable:** The open source license allows programmers to modify the PHP software, adding or modifying features as needed to fit their own specific environments.

How PHP Works

PHP is an *embedded scripting language*. This means that PHP code is embedded in HTML code. You use HTML tags to enclose the PHP language that you embed in your HTML file, the same way you would use other HTML tags. You create and edit Web pages containing PHP the same way you create and edit regular HTML pages.

The PHP software works in conjunction with the Web server. The Web server is the software that delivers Web pages to the world. When you type a URL into your Web browser, you are sending a message to the Web server at that URL, asking it to send you an HTML file. The Web server responds by sending the requested file. Your browser reads the HTML file and displays the Web page. You also request the Web server to send you a file when you click a link in a Web page. In addition, the Web server processes a file when you click a Web page button that submits a form.

When PHP is installed, the Web server is configured to expect certain file extensions to contain PHP language statements. Often the extension is `.php` or `.phtml`, but any extension can be used. When the Web server gets a request for a file with the designated extension, it sends the HTML statements as is, but PHP statements are processed by the PHP software before they're sent to the requester.

When PHP language statements are processed, the output is HTML statements. The PHP language statements are not included in the HTML sent to the browser, so the PHP code is secure and transparent to the user. For instance, in this simple PHP statement:

```
<?php echo "<p>Hello World"; ?>
```

`<?php` is the PHP opening tag and `?>` is the closing tag. `echo` is a PHP instruction that tells PHP to output the upcoming text as plain HTML code. The PHP software processes the PHP statement and outputs this:

```
<p>Hello World
```

which is a regular HTML statement. This HTML statement is delivered to the user's browser. The PHP statement is not delivered to the browser, so the user never sees any PHP statements.

PHP and the Web server must work closely together. PHP is not integrated with all Web servers, but works with many of the most popular Web servers. PHP is developed as a project under the Apache software group — consequently it works best with Apache. PHP also works with Microsoft IIS/PWS, iPlanet (formerly Netscape Enterprise Server), and others.

Although PHP works with several Web servers, it works best with Apache. If you can select or influence the selection of the Web server used in your organization, select Apache. By itself, Apache is a good choice. It is free, open source, stable, and popular. It currently powers 60 percent of all Web sites, according to the Web server survey at `www.netcraft.com`. It runs on Windows, Linux, Mac OS, and most flavors of Unix. Apache is not quite as perfect for Windows as it is for Linux/Unix. If you expect a lot of traffic on your Web site, IIS might be a better choice. Still, although Apache runs better on Linux/Unix than on Windows, the Windows version is improving all the time and may be the best choice for Windows by the time you're ready to select a Web server for your dynamic Web site.

MySQL and PHP, the Perfect Pair

MySQL and PHP are frequently used together. They are often called the dynamic duo. MySQL provides the database part and PHP provides the application part of your Web database application.

Advantages of the relationship

MySQL and PHP as a pair have several advantages:

- **They're free:** It's hard to beat free for cost effective.
- **They're Web-oriented:** Both were designed specifically for use on Web sites. Both have a set of features that are focused on building dynamic Web sites.
- **They're easy to use:** Both were designed for the purpose of getting a Web site up quickly.
- **They're fast:** Both were designed with speed as a major goal. Together they provide one of the fastest ways to deliver dynamic Web pages to users.
- **They communicate well with one another:** PHP has built-in features for communicating with MySQL. You don't need to know the technical details; just leave it to PHP.
- **A wide base of support is available for both:** Both have large user bases. Because they are often used as a pair, they often have the same user base. There are a lot of people available to help, including on e-mail discussion lists, that have experience using MySQL and PHP together.
- **They're customizable:** Both are open source, allowing programmers to modify the PHP and MySQL software to fit their own specific environments.

How they work together

PHP provides the application part and MySQL provides the database part of a Web database application. You use the PHP language to write the programs that perform the application tasks. PHP is flexible enough to perform all the tasks your application requires. It can be used for simple tasks, such as displaying a Web page, or for complicated tasks, such as accepting and verifying data that a user typed into an HTML form. One of the tasks your application must do is move data into and out of the database — and PHP has built-in features to use when writing programs that move data into and out of a MySQL database.

PHP statements are embedded in your HTML files with PHP tags. When the task to be performed by the application requires storing or retrieving data, you use specific PHP statements designed to interact with a MySQL database. You use one PHP statement to connect to the correct database, telling PHP where the database is located, its name, and the password needed to connect to it. The database doesn't need to be on the same machine as your Web site; PHP can communicate with a database across a network. You use another PHP statement to send instructions to MySQL. You send a SQL message across the connection, giving MySQL instructions for the task that you want done. MySQL returns a status message that shows whether it successfully performed the task. If there was a problem, it returns an error message. If your SQL message asked to retrieve some data, MySQL sends the data that you asked for, and PHP stores it in a temporary location where it is available to you.

You then use one or more PHP statements to complete the application task. For instance, you may use PHP statements to display data you retrieved. Or you may use PHP statements to display a status message in the browser, informing the user that the data was saved.

As an RDBMS, MySQL can store very complex information. As a scripting language, PHP can perform very complicated manipulation of data, either data that you need to modify before saving it in the database or data that you retrieved from the database and need to modify before displaying or using it for another task. Together, PHP and MySQL can be used to build a Web database application that has a very sophisticated and complicated purpose.

Chapter 2

Setting Up Your Work Environment

In This Chapter

- Getting access to PHP and MySQL through company Web sites and Web hosting companies
- Building your own Web site from scratch
- Testing PHP and MySQL

After you have decided to use PHP and MySQL, your first task is to get access to them. A work setting already set up for Web application development may be ready and waiting for you with all the tools you need. On the other hand, it may be part of your job to set up this work setting yourself. Perhaps your job is to create a whole new Web site where none existed before. In this chapter, I describe the tools you need and how to get access to them.

The Required Tools

To put up your dynamic Web site, you need to have access to the following three software tools:

- **A Web server:** The software that delivers your Web pages to the world
- **MySQL:** The RDBMS (Relational Database Management System) that will store information for your Web database application
- **PHP:** The scripting language you'll use to write the programs that provide the dynamic functionality for your Web site

These three tools are described in detail in Chapter 1.

Finding a Place to Work

To create your dynamic Web pages, you need access to a Web site that provides your three software tools (see the preceding section). All Web sites include a Web server, but not all Web sites provide MySQL and PHP. These are the most common environments in which you can develop your Web site:

- **A Web site put up by a company on its own computer:** The company — usually the company's Information Technology (IT) department — installs and administers the Web site software. Your job, for the purposes of this book, is to program the Web site, either as an employee of the company or as a contractor.
- **A Web site that is hosted by a Web hosting company:** The Web site is located on the Web hosting company's computer. The Web hosting company installs and maintains the Web site software and provides space on its computer where you can install the HTML files for a Web site.
- **A Web site that does not yet exist:** You plan to install and maintain the Web site software yourself. It may be a Web site of your own that you're building on your own computer, or it may be a Web site you're installing for a client on the client's computer.

How much you need to understand about the administration and operation of the Web site software depends on the type of Web site access you have. In the next few sections, I describe these environments in more detail and explain how you gain access to PHP and MySQL.

A company Web site

When the Web site is run by the company, you don't need to understand the installation and administration of the Web site software at all. The company is responsible for the operation of the Web site. In most cases, the Web site already exists, and your job is to add to, modify, or redesign the existing Web site. In a few cases, the company may be installing its first Web site, and your job is to design the Web site. In either case, your responsibility is to write and install the HTML files for the Web site. You are not responsible for the operation of the Web site.

You access the Web site software through the company's Information Technology (IT) department. The name of this department can vary in different companies, but its function is the same: It keeps the company's computers running and up-to-date.

If PHP and/or MySQL are not available on the company's Web site, IT needs to install them and make them available to you. PHP and MySQL have many options, but IT may not understand the best options — and may have options set in ways that are not well suited for your purposes. If you need PHP or MySQL options changed, you need to request that IT make the change; you won't be able to make the change yourself. For instance, PHP must be installed with MySQL support enabled, so if PHP is not communicating correctly with MySQL, IT may have to reinstall PHP with MySQL support enabled.

In order for the world to see the company's Web pages, the HTML files must be in a specific location on the computer. The Web server that delivers the Web pages to the world expects to find the HTML files in a specific directory. The IT department should provide you with access to the directory where the HTML files need to be installed. In most cases, you develop and test your Web pages in a test location and transfer the completed files to their permanent home. Depending on the access that IT gives you, you might copy the files from the test location to the permanent location, or you might transfer the files via FTP (a method of copying a file from one computer to another on a network). In some cases, for security reasons, the IT folks won't give you access to the permanent location, preferring to install the files in their permanent location themselves.

In order to use the Web software tools and build your dynamic Web site, you need the following information from IT:

- **The location of Web pages:** You need to know where to put the files for the Web pages. IT needs to provide you with the name and location of the directory where the files should be installed. Also, you need to know how to install the files — copy them, FTP them, or use other methods. You may need a user ID and password in order to install the files.
- **The default file name:** When users point their browsers at a URL, a file is sent to them. The Web server is set up to send a file with a specific name when the URL points to a directory. The file that is automatically sent is called the *default* file. Very often the default file is named `index.htm` or `index.html`, but sometimes other names are used, such as `default.htm`. Ask IT what you should name your default file.
- **A MySQL account:** Access to MySQL databases is controlled through a system of account names and passwords. IT sets up a MySQL account for you that has the appropriate permissions, and gives you the MySQL account name and password. (MySQL accounts are explained in detail in Chapter 5.)
- **The location of the MySQL databases:** MySQL databases need not be located on the same computer as the Web site. If the MySQL databases are located on a computer other than that of the Web site, you need to know the hostname (for example, `thor.companyname.com`) under which the databases can be found.
- **The PHP file extension:** When PHP is installed, the Web server is instructed to expect PHP statements in files with specific extensions. Frequently, the extensions used are `.php` or `.phtml`, but other extensions can be used. PHP statements in files that do not have the correct extension won't be processed. Ask IT what extension to use for your PHP programs.

Domain names

Every Web site needs a unique address on the Web. The unique address used by computers to locate a Web site is the *IP address.* It is a series of four numbers between 0 and 255, separated by dots — for example, `172.17.204.2` or `192.163.2.33`.

Because IP addresses are made up of numbers and dots, they're not easy to remember. Fortunately, most IP addresses have an associated name that is much easier to remember. Some examples include `amazon.com`, `www.irs.gov`, or `mycompany.com`. A name that is an address for a Web site is called a *domain name.* A domain can be one computer or many connected computers. When a domain refers to several computers, each computer in the domain may have its own name. A name that includes an individual computer name, such as `thor.mycompany.com`, identifies a *subdomain.*

Each domain name must be unique in order to serve as an address. Consequently, a system of registering domain names ensures that no two locations use the same domain name. Anyone can register any domain name, as long as the name is not already taken. You can register a domain name on the Web. First, you enter your potential domain name to find out whether it is available. If it's available, you register it in your name or a company name and pay the fee. The name is then yours to use, and no one else can use it. The standard fee for domain name registration is $35.00 per year. You should never pay more, but bargains are often available.

Many Web sites provide the ability to register a domain name, including the Web sites of many Web hosting companies. A search at Google (`www.google.com`) for *domain name register* results in over 700,000 hits. Shop around to be sure you find the lowest price. Also, many Web sites allow you to enter a domain name and see who it is registered to. These Web sites do a domain name database search using a tool called *whois.* A search at Google for *domain name whois* results in 200,000 hits. A couple of places where you can do a whois search are Allwhois.com (`www.allwhois.com`) and BetterWhois.com (`www.betterwhois.com`).

You will interact with the IT folks frequently as needs arise. For example, you may need options changed, you may need information to help you interpret an error message, or you may need to report a problem with the Web site software. So a good relationship with the IT folks will make your life much easier. Bring them tasty cookies and doughnuts often.

A Web hosting company

A *Web hosting company* provides everything you need to put up a Web site, including the computer space and all the Web site software. You just create the files for your Web pages and move them to a location specified by the Web hosting company.

About a gazillion companies offer Web hosting services. Most charge a monthly fee, often quite small, and some are even free. (Most, but not all, of the free ones require you to display advertising.) Usually, the monthly fee varies, depending on the resources provided for your Web site. For instance, a Web site with 2MB (megabytes) of disk space for your Web page files would cost less than a Web site with 10MB of disk space.

When looking for a place to host your Web site, make sure that the Web hosting company offers the following:

- **PHP and MySQL:** Not all companies provide these tools. You may have to pay more for a site with access to PHP and MySQL, and sometimes, you have to pay an additional fee for MySQL databases.
- **Access to PHP 4:** Sometimes the PHP versions offered are not the most recent versions. In particular, don't consider a Web site that has access only to PHP 3; you want PHP 4.

Other considerations when choosing a Web hosting company are

- **Reliability:** You need a Web hosting company that you can depend on — one that won't go broke and disappear tomorrow and one that isn't running on old computers, held together by chewing gum and baling wire, with more downtime than uptime.
- **Speed:** Web pages that download slowly are a problem because users will get impatient and go elsewhere. Slow pages may be a result of a Web hosting company that started its business on a shoestring and has a shortage of good equipment — or the Web hosting company may be so successful that its equipment is overwhelmed by new customers. Either way, Web hosting companies that deliver Web pages too slowly are unacceptable.
- **Technical support:** Some Web hosting companies have no one available to answer questions or troubleshoot problems. Technical support is often provided through e-mail only, which can be acceptable if the response time is short. Sometimes you can test the quality of the company's support by calling the tech support number, or test the e-mail response time by sending an e-mail.
- **The domain name:** Each Web site has a domain name that Web browsers use to find the site on the Web. Each domain name is registered, for a small yearly fee, so that only one Web site can use it. Some Web hosting companies allow you to use a domain name that you have registered independently of the Web hosting company, some assist you in registering and using a new domain name, and some require you to use their domain name. For instance, suppose your name is Lola Designer and you want your Web site to be named LolaDesigner. Some Web hosting companies will allow your Web site to be `LolaDesigner.com`, but some will require that your Web site be

named `LolaDesigner.webhostingcompanyname.com`, or `webhostingcompanyname.com/~LolaDesigner`, or something similar. In general, your Web site will look more professional if you use your own domain name.

- **Backups:** Backups are copies of your Web page files and your database that are stored in case your files or database are lost or damaged. You want to be sure that the company makes regular, frequent backup copies of your application. You also want to know how long it would take for backups to be put in place to restore your Web site to working order after a problem.
- **Features:** Select features based on the purpose of your Web site. Usually a hosting company bundles features together into plans — more features = higher cost. Some features to consider are
  - **Disk space:** How many MB/GB (gigabytes) of disk space will your Web site require? Media files, such as graphics or music files, can be quite large.
  - **Data transfer:** Some hosting companies charge you for sending Web pages to users. If you expect to have a lot of traffic on your Web site, this cost should be a consideration.
  - **E-mail addresses:** Many hosting companies provide you with a number of e-mail addresses for your Web site. For instance, if your Web site is `LolaDesigner.com`, you could allow users to send you e-mail at `me@LolaDesigner.com`.
  - **Software:** Hosting companies offer access to a variety of software for Web development. PHP and MySQL are the software discussed in this book. Some hosting companies might offer other databases, and some might offer other development tools such as FrontPage extensions, shopping cart software, credit card validation, and other tools.
  - **Statistics:** Often you can get statistics regarding your Web traffic, such as the number of users, time of access, access by Web page, and so on.

One disadvantage of hosting your site with a commercial Web hosting company is that you have no control over your development environment. The Web hosting company provides the environment that works best for it. The Web hosting company probably sets up the environment for ease of maintenance, low cost, and minimal customer defections. Most of your environment is set by the company, and you can't change it. You can only beg the company to change it. The company will be reluctant to change a working setup, fearing a change may cause problems for the company's system or for other customers.

Access to MySQL databases is controlled via a system of accounts and passwords that must be maintained manually, causing extra work for the hosting company. For this reason, many hosting companies either don't offer MySQL or charge extra for it. Also, PHP has a myriad of options that can be set, unset, or given various values. The hosting company decides the option settings based on its needs, which may or may not be ideal for your purposes.

It's pretty difficult to research Web hosting companies from a standing start — a search at Google.com for *Web hosting* results in almost a million and a half hits. The best way to research Web hosting companies is to ask for recommendations from people who have experience with those companies. People who have used a hosting company can warn you if the service is slow or the computers are down often. After you have gathered a few names of Web hosting companies from satisfied customers, you can narrow the list to the one that is best suited to your purposes and most cost-effective.

Setting up and running your own Web site

If you're starting a Web site from scratch, you need to understand the Web site software fairly well. You have to make several decisions regarding hardware and software. You have to install a Web server, PHP, and MySQL, as well as maintain, administer, and update the system yourself. Taking this route requires more work and more knowledge. The advantage is that you have total control over the Web development environment.

Here are the general steps that lead to your dynamic Web site (these steps are explained in more detail in the next few sections):

1. **Set up the computer.**
2. **Install the Web server.**
3. **Install MySQL.**
4. **Install PHP.**

If you're starting from scratch, with nothing but an empty space where the computer will go, start at Step 1. If you already have a running computer but no Web software, start at Step 2. Or if you have an existing Web site that does not have PHP and MySQL installed, start with Step 3.

Setting up the computer

Your first decision is to choose which hardware platform and operating system to use. In most cases, you will choose a PC with either Linux or Windows as the operating system. Here are some advantages and disadvantages of these two operating systems:

- **Linux:** Linux is open source, so it's free. It also has advantages for use as a Web server — it runs for long periods without needing to be rebooted, and Apache, the most popular Web server, runs better on Linux than Windows. Running Linux on a PC is the lowest cost option. The disadvantage of running Linux is that many people find Linux more difficult to install, configure, administer, and install software on than Windows.

- **Windows:** Unlike Linux, Windows is not free. However, the advantages are that most people feel that Windows is easier to use, and because it's widely used, many people can help you if you have problems.

I assume you're buying a computer with the operating system and software installed, ready to use. It is easier to find a computer that comes with Windows installed on it than with Linux, but Linux computers are available. For instance, at this time, Dell, IBM, and HP offer computers with Linux installed.

If you're building your own hardware, you need more information than I have room to provide in this book. If you have the hardware and plan to install an operating system, Windows is easier to install, but Linux is getting easier all the time. You can install Linux from a CD, like Windows, but you often must provide information or make decisions that require more knowledge about your system. If you already know how to perform system administration tasks — such as installing software and making backups — in Windows or in Linux, the fastest solution is to use the operating system you already know.

For using PHP and MySQL, you should seriously consider Linux. PHP is a project of the Apache Software Foundation, so it runs best with the Apache server. And Apache runs better on Linux than on Windows. Therefore, if all other things are equal and the computer is mainly for running a Web site with a Web database application, Linux is well suited for your purposes.

Other solutions besides a PC with Windows or Linux are available, but they're less popular:

- Other free, Unix-based operating systems are available for PCs, such as FreeBSD (which some people prefer to Linux) or a version of Solaris provided by Sun for free download.
- Mac computers can be used as Web servers, but installing the software is not as easy as installing it on a Windows or Linux machine — and it's usually the last to be upgraded. Unless you need the Mac for other purposes, it is probably not your best choice for a Web server.

Installing the Web server

After you set up the computer, you need to decide which Web server to install. The answer is almost always Apache. Apache offers the following advantages:

- **It's free:** What else do I need to say?
- **It runs on a wide variety of operating systems:** Apache runs on Windows, Linux, Mac OS, FreeBSD, and most varieties of Unix.

- **It's popular:** Approximately 60 percent of Web sites on the Internet use Apache, according to surveys at `www.netcraft.com/survey` and at `www.securityspace.com/s_survey/data/`. This wouldn't be true if it didn't work well. Also, this means that a large group of users can provide help.
- **It's reliable:** After Apache is up and running, it should run as long as your computer runs. Emergency problems with Apache are extremely rare.
- **It's customizable:** The open source license allows programmers to modify the Apache software, adding or modifying modules as needed to fit their own specific environment.
- **It's secure:** Free software is available that runs with Apache to make it into a secure SSL server. Security is an essential issue if you're using the site for e-commerce.

Apache is automatically installed when you install most Linux distributions. For most other Unix flavors, you have to download the Apache source code and compile it yourself, although some *binaries* (programs that are already compiled for specific operating systems) are available. For Windows, you need to install a binary file — preferably on Windows NT/2000, although Apache also runs on Windows 95/98/ME. (The Apache Web site does not yet mention Windows XP.) As of this writing, Apache 1.3.23 is the current stable release, but Apache 2 is released in beta and will be preferable when it has a stable release. See the Apache Web site (`httpd.apache.org`) for information, software downloads, documentation, and installation instructions for various operating systems. The Web site provides extensive documentation that is improving all the time.

Other Web servers are available. Microsoft offers Internet Information Server (IIS), the second most-popular Web server on the Internet with approximately 27 percent of Web sites. If you're expecting to have a lot of traffic on your Web site, IIS might perform better in a Windows environment than Apache, although the Windows version of Apache is getting better all the time. Sun offers iPlanet (formerly Netscape Enterprise Server), which serves less than 5 percent of the Internet. Other Web servers are available, but they have even smaller user bases.

Installing MySQL

After setting up the computer and installing the Web server, you're ready to install MySQL. You need to install MySQL before installing PHP because you need to provide the path to the MySQL software when you install PHP.

But before installing MySQL, be sure that you actually need to install it. It may already be running on your computer. Or it may be installed but not running. For instance, many Linux distributions automatically install MySQL. Here's how to check whether MySQL is currently running:

- **Linux/Unix:** Type the following:

  ```
  ps -ax
  ```

  In the list of programs that appears, look for one called mysqld.
- **Windows:** If MySQL is running, you should see it in your system tray at the bottom of your screen, possibly as a traffic signal with a green light If you cannot find an icon for it, then it probably is not running.

Even if MySQL is not currently running, it might be installed, just not started. Here's how to check to see whether MySQL is installed on your computer:

- **Linux/Unix:** Type the following:

  ```
  find / -name "mysql*"
  ```

  If a directory named mysql is found, MySQL has been installed.
- **Windows:** Look for a program called WinMySQLadmin, which starts and stops MySQL, among other functions. You may be able to find it on the Start menu (choose Start⇨Programs). If not, look for it in a MySQL directory, which is probably at `c:\mysql\bin`.

If MySQL is installed, but not started, here's how to start it:

- **Linux/Unix:**
  1. **Change to the directory mysql/bin.**

     This is the directory that you should have found when you were checking whether MySQL was installed.
  2. **Type** `safe_mysqld &`.

     When this command finishes, the prompt is displayed.
  3. **Check that the MySQL server started by typing** `ps -ax`.

     In the list of programs that appears, look for one called mysqld.
- **Windows:**
  1. **Start the WinMySQLadmin program.**

     If you can't find it on the menu, navigate to the program, which is probably at `c:\mysql\bin\winmysqladmin.exe`, and then double-click it.
  2. **Right-click in the WinMySQLadmin window.**

     A submenu appears.
  3. **Select the menu item for your operating system — Win 9x or Win NT (which includes Win 2000 and XP).**
  4. **Click Start the Server.**

If MySQL is not installed on your computer, you need to download it and install it from www.mysql.com. The Web site provides all the information and software you need. Also, the MySQL software is included on the CD with this book. (You can find detailed installation instructions in Appendix A.)

Installing PHP

After you install MySQL, you're ready to install PHP. As I mention earlier, you must install MySQL before you install PHP because you need to provide the path to the MySQL software when you install PHP. If PHP is not compiled with MySQL support when it is installed, it won't communicate with MySQL.

Before you install PHP, check whether it's already installed. For instance, some Linux distributions automatically install PHP. To see whether PHP is installed, search your disk for any PHP files:

- **Linux/Unix:** Type the following:

```
find / -name "php*"
```

- **Windows:** Use the Find feature (choose Start➪Find) to search for *php**.

If you find PHP files, PHP is already installed, and you may not need to reinstall it. For instance, even if you installed MySQL yourself after the PHP was installed you may have installed it in the location where PHP is expecting it. Better safe than sorry, however: Perform the testing described in the next section to see whether MySQL and PHP are working correctly together.

If you don't find any PHP files, PHP is not installed. In order to install PHP, you need access to the Web server for your site. For instance, when you install PHP with Apache, you need to edit the Apache configuration file. All the information and software you need is provided on the PHP Web site (www.php.net). The PHP software is also included on the CD, and detailed installation instructions are provided in Appendix B.

Testing, Testing, 1, 2, 3

Suppose you believe that PHP and MySQL are available for you to use, for one of the following reasons:

- The IT department at your company or your client company gave you all the information you asked for and told you that you are good to go.
- The Web hosting company gave you all the information you need and told you that you are good to go.
- You followed all the instructions and installed PHP and MySQL yourself.

Now you need to test to make sure PHP and MySQL are working correctly.

PHP

To test whether PHP is installed and working, follow these steps:

1. **Create the following file somewhere in your Web space with the name `test.php`.**

```
<html>
<head>
<title>PHP Test</title>
</head>
<body>
<p>This is an HTML line
<p>
<?php
   echo "This is a PHP line";
   phpinfo();
?>
</body>
</html>
```

2. **Point your browser at the file `test.php` created in Step 1.**

   You should see the following in the Web browser:

```
This is an HTML line
This is a PHP line
```

   Below these lines, you should see a large table, which shows all the information associated with PHP on your system. It shows PHP information, path and file names, variable values, and the status of various options.

3. **Check the PHP values for the values you need.**

   For instance, you need MySQL support enabled. Looking through the listing, find the section for MySQL and make sure that MySQL support is On. Also, for the programs in this book, you need register_globals set to on.

4. **Change values if necessary.**

   If you do not have administrative access to PHP, you have to ask the administrator to change any values that need changing. If you installed PHP yourself and/or have administrative access to PHP, you can change the values yourself. (Changing PHP settings is discussed in Appendix B.)

MySQL

After you know that PHP is running okay, you can test whether you can access MySQL by using PHP. Just follow these steps:

1. **Create the following file somewhere in your Web space with the name** `mysql_up.php`**. You can copy the file from the CD.**

```
<html>
<head>
<title>Test MySQL</title>
<body>
<!-- mysql_up.php -->
<?php
$host="hostname";
$user="mysqlaccount";
$password="mysqlpassword";

mysql_connect($host,$user,$password);
$sql="show status";
$result = mysql_query($sql);
if ($result == 0)
   echo("<b>Error " . mysql_errno() . ": " . mysql_error() . "</b>");
elseif (mysql_num_rows($result) == 0)
   echo("<b>Query executed successfully!</b>");
else
{
?>
<!-- Table that displays the results -->
<table border="1">
  <tr><td><b>Variable_name</b></td><td><b>Value</b></td></tr>
  <?php
    for ($i = 0; $i < mysql_num_rows($result); $i++) {
      echo("<TR>");
      $row_array = mysql_fetch_row($result);
      for ($j = 0; $j < mysql_num_fields($result); $j++) {
        echo("<TD>" . $row_array[$j] . "</td>");
        }
        echo("</tr>");
    }
  ?>
</table>
<?php } ?>
</body>
</html>
```

2. **Lines 7, 8, and 9 of the program need to be changed. These lines are**

```
$host="host";
$user="mysqlaccount";
$password="mysqlpassword";
```

Change *`host`* to the name of the computer where MySQL is installed — for example, `databasehost.mycompany.com`. If the MySQL database is on the same computer as your Web site, you can use `localhost` as the hostname.

Change *`mysqlaccountname`* and *`mysqlpassword`* to the appropriate values. (MySQL accounts and passwords are discussed in Chapter 5.) If your MySQL account does not require a password, type nothing between the quotes, as follows:

```
$password="";
```

3. **Point your browser at `mysql_up.php`.**

   You should see a table with a long list of variable names and values. You don't want to see an error message or a warning message. Don't worry about the contents of the table. It's only important that the table is displayed so that you know your connection to MySQL is working correctly.

   If no error or warning messages are displayed, MySQL is working fine. If you see an error or a warning message, you need to fix the problem that's causing the message.

Error and warning messages are usually fairly clear. The following is a common error message:

```
MySQL Connection Failed: Access denied for user: 'user73@localhost' (Using
          password: YES)
```

This message means that MySQL did not accept your MySQL account number or your MySQL password. Notice the message says `YES` for `Using password`, but does not show the actual password you tried for security reasons. If you tried with a blank password, the message would say `NO`.

If you receive an error message, double-check your account number and password. Remember that this is your MySQL account number, not your account number to log on to the computer. If you can't connect with the account number and password you have, you may need to contact the IT department or Web hosting company that gave you the account number. (For a further discussion of MySQL accounts and passwords, see Chapter 5.)

Chapter 3

Developing a Web Database Application

In This Chapter

- Planning your application
- Selecting and organizing your data
- Designing your database
- Overview of building your database
- Overview of writing your application programs

Developing a Web database application involves more than just storing data in MySQL databases and typing in PHP programs. Development has to start with planning. Building the application pieces comes after planning. The development steps are

1. **Develop a plan, listing the tasks your application will perform.**
2. **Design the database needed to support your application tasks.**
3. **Build the MySQL database, based on the database design.**
4. **Write the PHP programs that perform the application tasks.**

These steps are discussed in detail in this chapter.

Planning Your Web Database Application

Before you ever put finger to keyboard to write a PHP program, you need to *plan* your Web database application. This is possibly the most important step in developing your application. It's painful to discover, just after you finish the last program for your application, that you left something out and have to start over from the beginning. It's also hard on your computer when you take out your frustrations by drop-kicking it across the room.

Good planning prevents such painful backtracking. In addition, it keeps you focused on the functionality of your application, preventing you from writing pieces for the application that do really cool things but turn out to have no real purpose in the finished application. And if more than one person is working on your application, planning ensures that all the pieces will fit together in the end.

Identifying what you want from the application

The first step in the planning phase is to identify exactly why you're developing your application and what you want from it. For example, your main purpose may be to

- Collect names and addresses from users so that you can develop a customer list.
- Deliver information about your products to users, as in a customer catalog.
- Sell products online.
- Provide technical support to people who already own your product.

After you've clearly identified the general purpose of your application, make a list of exactly what you want that application to do. For instance, if your goal is to develop a database of customer names and addresses for marketing purposes, the application's list of required tasks is fairly short:

- Provide a form for customers to fill out.
- Store the customer information in a database.

If your goal is to sell products online, the list is a little longer:

- Provide information about your products to the customer.
- Motivate the customer to buy the product.
- Provide a way for the customer to order the product online.
- Provide a method for the customer to pay for the product online.
- Validate the payment so that you know you will actually get the money.
- Send the order to whoever is responsible for filling it and sending the product to the customer).

At this point in the planning process, the tasks you want your application to perform are still pretty general. You can accomplish each of these tasks many different ways. So now you need to examine the tasks closely, and detail exactly how the application will accomplish them. For instance, if your goal is to sell products online, you might expand the previous list like this:

- Provide information about products to the customer.
  - Display a list of product categories. Each category is a link.
  - When the customer clicks a category link, the list of products in that category is displayed. Each product name is a link.
  - When a customer clicks a product link, the description of the product is displayed.
- Motivate the customer to buy the product.
  - Provide well-written descriptions of the products that communicate their obviously superior qualities.
  - Use flattering pictures of the products.
  - Make color product brochures available online.
  - Offer quantity discounts.
- Provide a way for customers to order the product online.
  - Provide a button that customers can click to indicate their intention to buy the product.
  - Provide a form that collects necessary information about the product the customer is ordering, such as size, color, and so on.
  - Compute and display the total cost for all items in the order.
  - Compute and display the shipping costs.
  - Compute and display the sales tax.
  - Provide forms for customers to enter shipping and billing addresses.
- Provide a method for customers to pay for the product online.
  - Provide a button that customers can click to pay with a credit card.
  - Display a form that collects customers' credit card information.
- Validate the payment so that you know you will actually get the money.
  - The usual method is to send the customer's credit card information to a credit card processing service.
- Send the order to whoever is responsible for filling it and sending the product to the customer.
  - E-mailing order information to the shipping department should do it.

At this point, you should have a pretty clear idea of what you want from your Web database application. However, this doesn't mean that your goals can't change. (In fact, your goals *are* very likely to change as you develop your Web database application and discover new possibilities.) At the onset of the project, it's important to start with as comprehensive a plan as possible to keep you focused so that you avoid running into a dead end or getting sidetracked.

Taking the user into consideration

Identifying what *you* want your Web database application to do is only one aspect of planning. You must also consider what your users will want from it. For example, say your goal is to gather a list of customer names and addresses for marketing purposes. Will customers be willing to give up that information?

Your application needs to fulfill a purpose for the users, as well as for you. Otherwise, they'll just ignore it. Before users will be willing to give you their names and addresses, for example, they need to perceive that they will benefit in some way from giving you this information. Here are a few examples of why users might be willing to register their names and addresses at your site:

- **To receive a newsletter.** To be perceived as valuable, the newsletter should cover an industry related to your products. It should offer news and spot trends, not just serve as marketing material about your products.
- **To enter a sweepstakes for a nice prize.** Who can turn down a chance to win an all-expense-paid vacation to Hawaii or a brand-new Ford Explorer?
- **To receive special discounts.** For example, you can periodically e-mail special discount opportunities to customers.
- **To be notified about new products or product upgrades when they become available.** For example, customers may be interested in being notified when a software update is available for downloading.
- **To get access to valuable information.** For instance, you must register at the New York Times Web site in order to gain access to its articles online.

Now add the customer tasks to your list of tasks that you want the application to perform. For instance, consider this list of tasks you identified for setting up an online retailer:

- Provide a form for customers to fill out.
- Store the customer information in a database.

If you take the customer's viewpoint into account, the list expands a bit:

- Present a description of the advantages customers receive by registering with the site.
- Provide a form for customers to fill out.
- Add customers' e-mail addresses to the newsletter distribution list.
- Store the customer information in a database.

After you have a list of tasks you want and tasks your users want, you have a plan for a Web application that is worth your time to develop and worth your users' time to use.

Making the site easy to use

In addition to planning what your Web application is going to do, you need to consider how it is going to do it. Making your application easy to use is important. If customers can't find your products, they aren't going to buy them. And if customers can't find the information they need in a pretty short time, they will go look elsewhere. On the Web, it is always easy for customers to go elsewhere.

Making your application easy to use is called *usability engineering*. Web usability includes such issues as:

- **Navigation:** What is on your site and where it is located should be immediately obvious to a user.
- **Graphics:** Graphics make your site attractive, but graphic files can be slow to display.
- **Access:** Some design decisions can make your application accessible or not accessible to users who have disabilities such as impaired vision.
- **Browsers:** Different browsers (even different versions of the same browser) may display the same HTML file differently.

Web usability is a large and important subject, and delving into the topic more deeply is beyond the scope of this book. But fear not, you can find lots of helpful information on Web usability on — you guessed it — the Web. Be sure to check out the Web sites of usability experts Jakob Nielsen (`www.useit.com`) and Jarod Spool (`world.std.com/~uieweb/`). Vincent Flanders also has a fun site full of helpful information about Web design at `WebPagesThatSuck.com`. And books on the subject can be very helpful, such as *Web Design For Dummies* by Lisa Lopuck (Hungry Minds, Inc.).

Leaving room for expansion

One certainty about your Web application is that it will change over time. Down the line, you may think of new functions for it or just simply want to change something about it. Or maybe Web site software improves so that your Web application can do things that it couldn't do when you first put it up. Whatever the reason, your Web site will change. So when you plan your application, you need to keep future changes in mind.

You can design your application in steps, taking planned change into account. You can develop a plan in which you build an application today that meets your most immediate needs and make it available as soon as it's ready. Your plan can include adding functions to the application as quickly as you can develop them. For instance, you can build a product catalog and publish it on your Web site as soon as it is ready. You can then begin work on an online ordering function for the Web site, which you will add when it is ready.

You can't necessarily foresee all the functions that you might want in your application in the future. For instance, you may design your travel Web site with sections for all possible destinations today, but the future might surprise you. Trips to Mars? Alpha Centauri? An alternate universe? Plan your application with the flexibility needed to add functionality in the future.

Writing it down

Write your plan down. You will hear this often from me. I speak from the painful experience of not writing it down. When you develop your plan, it is foremost in your mind and perfectly clear. But in a few short weeks, you will be astonished to discover that it has gone absolutely hazy while your attention was on other pressing issues. Or you will want to make some changes in the application a year from now and won't remember exactly how the application was designed. Or you are working with a partner to develop the application and will be surprised to discover that your partner misunderstood your verbal explanation and developed functions for the application that don't fit in your plan. You can avoid these types of problems by writing everything down.

Looking at the two examples used in this book

In the next two sections, I introduce the two example Web database applications that I created for this book. I refer to these examples throughout the book to demonstrate aspects of application design and development.

Stuff for Sale

The first example is an online product catalog. You're the owner of a pet store, and you want your catalog to provide customers with information about the pets that are for sale. Selling the pets online is not feasible, although you're toying with the idea of allowing customers to reserve pets online — before they come into the store to purchase them. Currently, the application is simply an online catalog. Customers can look through the catalog online and then come into the store to buy the pet. The information about all the pets is stored in a database, and customers can search the database for information on specific pets or types of pets.

Here is your plan for this application:

- Allow customers to select which pet they want to see information about.

  Offer two selection methods:

  - **Selecting from a list of links:** Display a list of links that are pet categories (for example, dog, cat, dinosaur, and so on). When the customer clicks a category link, a list of pets is displayed. Each pet in the list is a link to a description of the pet.
  - **Typing in search terms:** Display a search form in which customers can type words that describe the type of pet they're looking for. The application searches the database for matching words and displays the pet information for any pets that match the search words. For example, a customer can type **cat** to see a list of all available cats. Each cat in the list is a link to a description of that cat.

- Display a description of the pet when the customer clicks the link. The description is stored in a database.

Members Only

The second example Web database application is related to the preceding pet store example. In addition to the online catalog, you also want to put up a section on your pet store Web site *for members only*. In order to access this area of the site, customers have to register — providing their names and addresses. In this Members Only section, customers can order pet food at a discount, find out about pets that are on order but haven't arrived yet, and gain access to articles with news and information about pets and pet care.

This is your plan for this application:

- Display a description of what special features and information are available in the Members Only section.
- Provide an area where customers can register for the Members Only section.

- Provide a link to the registration area.
- In the registration area, display a form where customers can type their registration information. The form should include space for a user login name and password, as well as the information you want to collect.
- Validate the information that the user entered (for example, verify that the zip code is the correct length, the e-mail address is in the correct format, and so on).
- Store the information in the database.

- Provide a login section for customers who are already registered for the Members Only section.
    - Display a login form that asks for the customer's user name and password.
    - Compare the user name and password that are entered with the user names and passwords in the database. If no match is found, display an error message.
- Display the Members Only Web page after the customer has successfully logged in.

Designing the Database

After you determine exactly what the Web database application is going to do (see the beginning part of this chapter if you haven't done this yet), you're ready to design the database that holds the information needed by the application. Designing the database includes identifying the data that you need — and organizing the data in the way required by the database software.

Choosing the data

First, you must identify what information belongs in your database. Look at the list of tasks you want the application to perform and determine what information you need to complete each of those tasks.

Here are a few examples:

- An online catalog needs a database containing product information.
- An online order application needs a database that can hold customer information and order information.
- A travel Web site needs a database with information on destinations, reservations, fares, schedules, and so on.

In many cases, your application may include a task that collects information from the user. You will have to balance your urge to collect all the potentially useful information that you can think of against your users' reluctance to give out personal information — as well as their avoidance of forms that look too time-consuming. One compromise is to ask for some optional information. The users who don't mind can enter it, but users who object can leave it blank. Another possibility is to offer an incentive. The longer the form is, the stronger the incentive you'll need to motivate the user to fill out the form. A user might be willing to fill out a very short form to enter a sweepstakes that offers two sneak-preview movie tickets for a prize. But if the form is long and complicated, the prize needs to be more valuable, such as a free trip to California and a tour of a Hollywood movie studio.

In the first example application, your customers search the online catalog for information on pets they may want to buy. You want customers to see information that will motivate them to buy a pet. The information that you want to have available in the database for the customer to see is

- The name of the pet — for example, poodle, unicorn, and so on
- A description of the pet
- A picture of the pet
- The cost of the pet

In the second example application, the Members Only section, you want to store information about registered members. The information that you want to store in the database is

- Member name
- Member address
- Member phone number
- Member fax number
- Member e-mail address

Take the time to develop a comprehensive list of the information to be stored in your database. Although you can change and add information to your database after it's developed, it's easier to include the information from the beginning. Also, if you add information to the database later — after it's in use — the first users in the database will have incomplete information. For example, if you change your form halfway through so that it now asks for the user's age, you won't have the age for the people who already filled out the form and are already in the database.

Organizing the data

MySQL is a Relational Database Management System (RDBMS), which means that the data is organized into tables. (See Chapter 1 for more on MySQL.) You can establish relationships between the tables in the database.

Organizing data in tables

RDBMS tables are organized like other tables you're used to — in rows and columns, as shown in Figure 3-1. The place where a particular row and column intersect, the individual cell, is called a *field.*

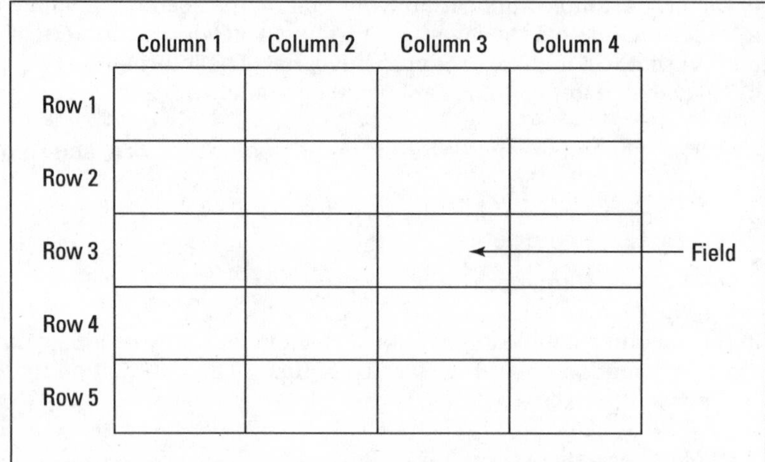

Figure 3-1: MySQL data is organized into tables.

The focus of each table is an *object* (a thing) that you want to store information about. Here are some examples of objects:

- Customers
- Products
- Companies
- Animals
- Cities
- Rooms
- Books
- Computers
- Shapes

- Documents
- Projects
- Weeks

You create a table for each object. The table name should clearly identify the objects it contains. The name must be one word, with no spaces in it. It's customary to name the table in the singular. Thus, a name for a table of customers might be Customer, and a table containing customer orders might be named CustomerOrder.

In database talk, an object is called an *entity,* and an entity has *attributes*. In the table, each row represents an entity, and the columns contain the attributes of each entity. For instance, in a table of customers, each row contains information for a single customer. Some of the attributes contained in the columns might be first name, last name, phone number, age, and so on.

Here are the steps for organizing your data into tables:

1. **Name your database.**

   Assign a name to the database for your application. For instance, a database containing information about households in a neighborhood might be named HouseholdDirectory.

2. **Identify the objects.**

   Look at the list of information you want to store in the database (if you haven't done this yet, check out the section, "Choosing the data," earlier in this chapter). Analyze your list and identify the objects. For instance, the HouseholdDirectory database may need to store the following:

   - Name of each family member
   - Address of the house
   - Phone number
   - Age of each household member
   - Favorite breakfast cereal of each household member

   When you analyze this list carefully, you realize that you're storing information about two objects: the household and household members. That is, the address and phone number are for the household in general, but the name, age, and favorite cereal are for a particular household member.

3. **Define and name a table for each object.**

   For instance, the HouseholdDirectory database needs a table called Household and a table called HouseholdMember.

4. **Identify the attributes for each object.**

   Analyze your information list and identify the attributes you need to store for each object. Break the information to be stored into its smallest reasonable pieces. For instance, when storing the name of a person in a table, you can break down the name into first name and last name. Doing this enables you to sort by the last name, which would be more difficult if the first and last name were stored together. In fact, you can even break down the name into first name, middle name, and last name, although not many applications need to use the middle name separately.

5. **Define and name columns.**

   Define and name columns for each separate item of information that you identified in Step 4. Give each column a name that clearly identifies the information in that column. The column names should be one word, with no spaces. For instance, you might have columns named firstName and lastName or first_name and last_name.

6. **Identify the primary key.**

   Each row in a table must have a unique identifier. No two rows in a table can be exactly the same. When you design your table, you decide which column holds the unique identifier, called the *primary key*. The primary key can be more than one column combined. In many cases, your object attributes will not have a unique identifier. For instance, a customer table may not have a unique identifier because two customers can have the same name. When there is no unique identifier column, you need to add a column specifically to be the primary key. Frequently, a column with a sequence number is used for this purpose. For example, in Figure 3-2, the primary key is the cust_id field because each customer has a unique ID number.

7. **Define the defaults.**

   You can define a default that MySQL will assign to a field when no data is entered into the field. A default is not required, but is often useful. For instance, if your application stores an address that includes a country, you can specify US as the default. If the user does not type a country, US will be entered.

8. **Identify columns with required data.**

   You can specify that certain columns are not allowed to be empty. For instance, the column containing your primary key can't be empty. You may consider other columns to be in error if they are blank.

Well-designed databases store each piece of information in only one place. Storing it in more than one place is inefficient and creates problems if information needs to be changed. If you change information in one place but forget to change it in another place, your database can have serious problems.

If you find that you're storing the same data in several rows, you probably need to reorganize your tables. For example, suppose you're storing data about books, including the publisher's address. When you enter the data, you realize that you're entering the same publisher's address in many rows. A more efficient way to store this data would be to store the book information in one table and the book publisher information in a separate table. You can define two tables: Book and BookPublisher. In the Book table, you would have the columns title, author, pub_date, and price. In the BookPublisher table, you would have columns such as name, streetAddress, city, and so on.

Creating relationships between tables

Some tables in a database are related to one another. Most often, a row in one table is related to several rows in another table. A column is needed to connect the related rows in different tables. In many cases, you include a column in one table to hold data that matches data in the primary key column of another table.

A common application that needs a database with two related tables is a customer order application. For example, one table contains the customer information, such as name, address, phone, and so on. Each customer can have from zero to many orders. You could store the order information in the table with the customer information, but a completely new row would be created each time the customer placed an order, and each new row would contain all the customer's information. It would be much more efficient to store the orders in a separate table. The Order table would have a column that contains the identifying information for a customer so that the order is related to the correct row of the Customer table. The relationship is shown in the tables in Figures 3-2 and 3-3.

The Customer table in this example looks like Figure 3-2. Notice the unique cust_id for each customer.

cust_id	first_name	last_name	phone
27895	John	Smith	555-5555
44555	Joe	Lopez	555-5553
23695	Judy	Chang	555-5552
27822	Jubal	Tudor	555-5556
29844	Joan	Smythe	555-5559

Figure 3-2: A sample from the Customer table.

The related Order table is shown in Figure 3-3. Notice that it has the same cust_id column that appears in the Customer table. In this way, the order information in the Order table is connected to the related customer's name and phone number in the Customer table.

Order_no	cust_id	item_num	cost
87-222	27895	cat-3	200.00
87-223	27895	cat-4	225.00
87-224	44555	horse-1	550.00
87-225	44555	dog-27	210.00
87-226	27895	bird-1	50.00

Figure 3-3: A sample from the Order table.

In this example, the columns that relate the Customer table and the Order table have the same name. They could have different names, as long as the data in the columns is the same.

Designing the sample databases

In the following two sections, I design the two databases for the two example applications used in this book.

Pet Catalog

You want to display the following list of information when customers search your pet catalog:

- The name of the pet — for example, poodle, unicorn, and so on
- A description of the pet
- A picture of the pet
- The cost of the pet

In the Pet Catalog plan, a list of pet categories is displayed. This requires that each pet be classified into a pet category and that the pet category be stored in the database.

You design the Pet Catalog database by following the steps presented in the "Organizing data in tables" section, earlier in this chapter:

1. **Name your database.**

   The database for the Pet Catalog is named PetCatalog.

2. **Identify the objects.**

   The information list is

   - The name of the pet — for example, poodle, unicorn, and so on
   - A description of the pet
   - A picture of the pet
   - The cost of the pet
   - Category for the pet

   All this information is about pets, so the only object for this list is pet.

3. **Define and name a table for each object.**

   The Pet Catalog application needs a table called Pet.

4. **Identify the attributes for each object.**

   Now you look at the information in detail:

   - **Name of the pet:** A single attribute — for example, poodle, unicorn, and so on.
   - **Description of the pet:** This breaks down into two attributes: the written description of the pet as it would appear in a printed catalog and the color of the pet.
   - **Picture of the pet:** A path name to a graphic file containing a beautiful picture of the pet.
   - **Cost of the pet:** The dollar amount that the store is asking for the pet.
   - **Category for the pet:** This breaks down into two attributes: a category name that includes the pet — for example, dog, horse, dragon — and a description of the category.

   It would be inefficient to include two types of information in the Pet table:

   - The category information includes a description of the category. Because each category can include several pets, including the category description in the Pet table would result in the same description appearing in several rows. It is more efficient to define Pet Category as an object with its own table.

- If the pet comes in several colors, then all the pet information will be repeated in a separate row for each color. It is more efficient to define Pet Color as an object with its own table.

The added tables are named PetType and PetColor.

5. **Define and name columns.**

   The Pet table has one row for each pet. The columns for the Pet table are

   - **petID:** Each pet name is required to be unique.
   - **petType:** The category name. This is the column that connects the pet to the correct row in the PetType table.
   - **petDescription:** The description of the pet.
   - **price:** The price of the pet.
   - **pix:** The file name of a graphics file that contains a picture of the pet.

   The PetType table has one row for each pet category. It has the following columns:

   - **petType:** The login name of the member who logged in. This is the column that links this table to the Member table. This is a unique value in the Member table, but not a unique value in this table.
   - **typeDescription:** The description of the type.

   The PetColor table has one row for each pet color. It has the following columns:

   - **petID:** The name of the pet. This is the column that connects the color row to the correct row in the Pet table.
   - **petColor:** The color of the pet.

6. **Identify the primary key.**

   - The primary key of the Pet table is petID.
   - The primary key of the PetType table is petType.
   - The primary key of the PetColor is petID and petColor together.

7. **Define the defaults.**

   No defaults are defined for either table.

8. **Identify columns with required data.**

   The following columns should never be allowed to be empty:

   - petID
   - petColor
   - petType

   These columns are the primary key columns. A row without these values should never be allowed in the tables.

Members Only

You created the following list of information you want to store when customers register for the Members Only section of your Web site:

- Member name
- Member address
- Member phone number
- Member fax number
- Member e-mail address

In addition, you also would like to collect the date when the member registered and track how often the member actually goes into the Members Only section.

You design the Members Only database by following the steps presented in the "Organizing data in tables" section, earlier in this chapter:

1. **Name your database.**

   The database for the Members Only section is named MemberDirectory.

2. **Identify the objects.**

   The information list is

   - Member name
   - Member address
   - Member phone number
   - Member fax number
   - Member e-mail address
   - Member registration date
   - Member logins

   All this information pertains to members, so the only object for this list is member.

3. **Define and name a table for each object.**

   The MemberDirectory database needs a table called Member.

4. **Identify the attributes for each object.**

   Look at the information list in detail:

   - **Member name:** This breaks down into two attributes: first name and last name.
   - **Member address:** This breaks down into four attributes: street address, city, state, and zip code. Currently, you only have pet

stores in the United States, so you can assume the member address is an address in the U.S. mailing address format.

- **Member phone number:** One attribute.
- **Member fax number:** One attribute.
- **Member e-mail address:** One attribute.
- **Member registration date:** One attribute.

Several pieces of information are related to member logins:

- Logging into the Members Only section requires a login name and a password. These two items need to be stored in the database.
- The easiest way to keep track of member logins is to store the date/time when the user logged into the Members Only section.

Because each member can have many logins, many date/times for logins need to be stored. Therefore, rather than defining the login time as an attribute of the member, define login as an object, related to the member, but requiring its own table.

The added table is named Login. The attribute of a login object is its login time (time includes date).

5. **Define and name columns.**

The Member table has one row for each member. The columns for the Member table are

- loginName

  Each login name must be unique. The programs in the application make sure that no two members ever have the same login name.
- password
- createDate
- firstName
- lastName
- street
- city
- state
- zip
- email
- phone
- fax

The Login table has one row for each *login,* that is, each time a member logs into the Members Only section. It has the following columns:

- **loginName:** The login name of the member who logged in. This is the column that links this table to the Member table. This is a unique value in the Member table but not a unique value in this table.
- **loginNumber:** This is a sequence number for each member login. If this is the first time this member logged in, the value in this column is 1; if this is the second login, the value is 2; and so on.
- **loginTime:** The date and time of login.

6. **Identify the primary key.**
   - The primary key for the Member table is loginName.
   - The primary key for the Login table is loginName and loginNumber together.
7. **Define the defaults.**

   No defaults are defined for either table.
8. **Identify columns with required data.**

   The following columns should never be allowed to be empty:
   - loginName
   - password
   - loginNumber

   These columns are the primary key columns. A row without these values should never be allowed in the tables.

Types of data

MySQL stores information in different formats based on the type of information you tell MySQL to expect. MySQL allows different types of data to be used in different ways. The main types of data are character, numerical, and date/time data.

Character data

The most common type of data is *character* data — data that is stored as strings of characters. It can only be manipulated in strings. Character data can be moved and printed. Two character strings can be concatenated together. A substring can be selected from a longer string. One string can be substituted for another. Most of the information you store will be character data, such as customer name, address, phone number, pet description, and so on.

Character data can be stored in a fixed-length format or a variable-length format. In *fixed-length format,* MySQL reserves a fixed space for the data. If the data is longer than the fixed length, only the characters that fit are stored, and the remaining characters on the end are not stored. If the string is shorter than the fixed length, the extra spaces are wasted. In a *variable-length format*, MySQL stores the string in a field that is the same length as the string. If a character string length varies only a little, use the fixed-length format. For instance, a length of 10 works for all zip codes. If the zip code does not include the zip+4 number, it is only a few characters shorter. However, if your character string can vary more than a few characters, use a variable-length format to save space. For instance, your pet description might be *Small bat* or might run to several lines of description. So it would be better to store this description in a variable-length format.

Numerical data

Another common type of data is *numerical* data — data that is stored as a number. Decimal numbers (for example, 10.5, 2.34567, 23456.7) can be stored, as well as integers (for example, 1, 2, 248). When data is stored as a number, it can be used in numerical operations, such as adding, subtracting, squaring, and so on. If data is not going to be used for numerical operations, it is more efficient to store it as a character string. For instance, you are not likely to want to add up the digits in the users' phone numbers, so phone numbers should be stored as character strings.

MySQL stores positive and negative numbers. You can tell MySQL to store only positive numbers. If the data is not going to be negative, store the data as unsigned. For instance, a city population or the number of pages in a document can never be negative.

Date and time data

A third common type of data is date and time data. Data stored as a date can be displayed in a variety of date formats. It can also be used to determine the length of time between two dates or two times — or between a specific date or time and some arbitrary date or time.

Enumeration data

Sometimes data can have only a limited number of values. For instance, the only possible values for a column might be `yes` or `no`. MySQL provides a data type called *enumeration* for use with this type of data. You tell MySQL what values can be stored in the column (for example, `yes`, `no`), and MySQL will not store any other values in the column.

MySQL data type names

When you create a database, you tell MySQL what kind of data to expect in a particular column by using the MySQL names for data types. Table 3-1 shows the MySQL data types used most often in Web database applications.

Table 3-1 MySQL Data Types

MySQL Data Type	*Description*
`CHAR(length)`	Fixed length character string.
`VARCHAR (length)`	Variable length character string. The longest string that can be stored is `length`, which must be between 1 and 255.
`TEXT`	Variable length character string with a maximum length of 64KB of text.
`INT(length)`	Integer with a range from –2147483648 to +2147483648. The number that can be displayed is limited by `length`. For instance, if `length` is 4, only numbers from –999 to 9999 can be displayed, even though higher numbers are stored.
`INT(length) UNSIGNED`	Integer with a range from 0 to 4294967295. `length` is the size of the number that can be displayed. For instance, if `length` is 4, only numbers up to 9999 can be displayed, even though higher numbers are stored.
`DECIMAL (length,dec)`	Decimal number where `length` is the number of characters that can be used to display the number, including decimal points, signs, and exponents, and `dec` is the maximum number of decimal places allowed. For instance, 12.34 has `length` of 5 and `dec` of 2.
`DATE`	Date value with year, month, and date. Displays the value as YYYY-MM-DD (for example, 2001-04-03).
`TIME`	Time value with hour, minute, and second. Displays as HH:MM:SS.
`DATETIME`	Date and time are stored together. Displays as YYYY-MM-DD HH:MM:SS.
`ENUM ("val1", "val2" ...)`	Only the values listed can be stored. A maximum of 65535 values can be listed.

MySQL allows many other data types, but they're less frequently needed. For a description of all the available data types, see the documentation on the MySQL documentation at `www.mysql.com/doc/C/o/Column_types.html`.

Writing it down

Here's my usual nagging: *Write it down.* You probably spent considerable time making the design decisions for your database. At this point, the decisions are firmly fixed in your mind. You don't believe you can forget them.

However, suppose a crisis intervenes and you don't get back to this project for two months. You will have to analyze your data and make all the design decisions again. You can avoid this by writing the decisions down now.

Document the organization of the tables, the column names, and all other design decisions. A good format is a document that describes each table in table format, with a row for each column and a column for each design decision. For instance, your columns would be *column name*, *data type*, and *description*.

Taking a look at the sample database designs

This section contains the database designs for the two example Web database applications.

Stuff for Sale

The database design for the Pet Catalog application includes three tables: Pet, PetType, and PetColor. Tables 3-2 through 3-4 show the organization of these tables. The table definition is not set in concrete; MySQL allows you to change tables pretty easily. If you set the data type for a variable to `char(20)` and find that isn't long enough, you can easily change the data type.

The database design is as follows:

Database name: PetCatalog

Table 3-2 Database Table 1: Pet

Variable Name	*Type*	*Description*
`petID`	`char(25)`	Name of pet; primary key
`petType`	`char(15)`	Category of pet
`petDescription`	`varchar(255)`	Description of pet
`price`	`decimal(9,2)`	Price of pet
`pix`	`char(15)`	Path name to graphic file that contains picture of pet

Table 3-3 Database Table 2: PetType

Variable Name	Type	Description
petType	char(25)	Name of pet category; primary key
typeDescription	varchar(255)	Description of category

Table 3-4 Database Table 3: PetColor

Variable Name	Type	Description
petID	char(25)	Name of pet (primary key 1)
petColor	char(15)	Color name (primary key 2)

Members Only

The database design for the Members Only application includes two tables named Member and Login. Tables 3-5 and 3-6 document the organization of these tables. The table definition is not set in concrete. MySQL allows you to change tables pretty easily. If you set the data type for a variable to `char(20)` and find that it isn't long enough, it's easy to change the data type.

The database design is as follows:

Database name: MemberDirectory

Table 3-5 Database Table 1: Member

Variable Name	Type	Description
loginName	varchar(20)	User-specified login name (primary key)
password	char(9)	User-specified password
createDate	date	Date member registered and created login account
lastName	varchar(50)	Member's last name
firstName	varchar(40)	Member's first name
street1	varchar(50)	Member's street address

(continued)

Table 3-5 *(continued)*

Variable Name	*Type*	*Description*
`city`	`varchar(40)`	Member's city
`state`	`char(2)`	Member's state
`zip`	`char(10)`	Member's zip code
`email`	`varchar(50)`	Member's e-mail address
`phone`	`char(15)`	Member's phone number
`fax`	`char(15)`	Member's fax number

Table 3-6 Database Table 2: Login

Variable Name	*Type*	*Description*
`loginName`	`char(15)`	Login Name specified by user (primary key 1)
`loginNumber`	`int(4)`	Number of times this user has logged in
`loginTime`	`datetime`	Date and time of login

Developing the Application

After you've developed a plan listing the tasks your application is going to perform and developed a database design, you're ready to create your application. First, you build the database and then you write your PHP programs. You are moments away from a working Web database application. Well, perhaps that's an exaggeration. But you are making progress.

Building the database

Building the database means turning the paper database design into a working database. Building the database is independent of the PHP programs that your application uses to interact with the database. The database can be accessed using programming languages other than PHP, such as Perl, C, or Java. The database stands on its own to hold the data.

You should build the database before writing the PHP programs. The PHP programs are written to move data in and out of the database, so you can't develop and test them until the database is available.

The database design names the database and defines the tables that make up the database. To build the database, you communicate with MySQL using the SQL language. You tell MySQL to create the database and to add tables to the database. You tell MySQL how to organize the data tables and what format to use to store the data. Detailed instructions for building the database are provided in Chapter 4.

Writing the programs

Your programs perform the tasks for your Web database application. They create the display that the user sees in the browser window. They make your application interactive by accepting and processing information typed in the browser window by the user. They store information in the database and get information out of the database. The database is useless unless you can move data in and out of it.

The plan that you developed (as discussed in the earlier sections in this chapter) outlines the programs you need to write. In general, each task in your plan calls for a program. If your plan says that your application will display a form, you need a program that displays a form. If your plan says that your application will store the data from a form, you need a program that gets the data from the form and puts it in the database.

The PHP language was developed specifically to write interactive Web applications. It has the built-in functionality needed to make writing application programs as painless as possible. It has methods that were included in the language specifically to access data from forms. It has methods to put data into a MySQL database, and it has methods to get data from a MySQL database. Detailed instructions for writing PHP programs are provided in Part III of this book.

Part II

MySQL Database

"Our automated response policy to a large company-wide data crash is to notify management, back up existing data, and sell 90% of my shares in the company."

In this part . . .

This part provides the details of working with a MySQL database. You find out how to use SQL to communicate with MySQL. In addition, you discover how to create a database, change a database, and move data in and out of a database.

Chapter 4

Building the Database

In This Chapter

- Using SQL to make requests to MySQL
- Creating a new database
- Adding information to an existing database
- Looking at information in an existing database
- Removing information from an existing database

After completing your database design (see Chapter 3 if you haven't done this yet), you're ready to turn it into a working database. In this chapter, you find out how to build a database based on your design — and how to move data in and out of it.

The database design names the database and defines the tables that make up the database. In order to build the database, you must communicate with MySQL, providing the database name and the table structure. Later on, you must communicate with MySQL to add data to (or request information from) the database. The language you use to communicate with MySQL is SQL. This chapter explains how to create SQL queries and use them to build new databases and interact with existing databases.

Communicating with MySQL

The MySQL server is the manager of your database:

- It creates new databases.
- It knows where the databases are stored.
- It stores and retrieves information, guided by the requests (called *queries*) that it receives.

To make a request that MySQL can understand, you build an SQL query and send it to the MySQL server. (For a more complete description of the MySQL server, see Chapter 1.) The next two sections detail how to do this.

Building SQL queries

SQL (Structured Query Language) is the computer language you use to communicate with MySQL. SQL is almost English; it is made up largely of English words, put together into strings of words that sound similar to English sentences. In general (fortunately), you don't need to understand any arcane technical language to write SQL queries that work.

The first word of each query is its name, which is an action word, a verb, that tells MySQL what you want to do. The queries that I discuss in this chapter are `CREATE`, `DROP`, `ALTER`, `SHOW`, `INSERT`, `LOAD`, `SELECT`, `UPDATE`, and `DELETE`. This basic vocabulary is sufficient to create — and interact with — databases on Web sites.

The query name is followed by words and phrases — some required and some optional — that tell MySQL how to perform the action. For instance, you always need to tell MySQL what to create, and you always need to tell it which table to insert data into or select data from.

The following is a typical SQL query. As you can see, it uses English words:

```
SELECT lastName FROM Member
```

This query retrieves all the last names stored in the table named Member. Of course, more complicated queries (such as the following) are less English-like:

```
SELECT lastName,firstName FROM Member WHERE state="CA" AND
       city="Fresno" ORDER BY lastName
```

This query retrieves all the last names and first names of members that live in Fresno and puts them in alphabetical order by last name. This query is less English-like but still pretty clear.

Here are some general points to keep in mind when constructing an SQL query, as illustrated in the preceding sample query:

- **Capitalization:** In this book, I put the SQL language words in all caps; items of variable information (such as column names) are usually given labels that are all or mostly lowercase letters. I did this to make it easier for you to read, not because MySQL needs this format. The case of the SQL words doesn't matter; *select* is the same as *SELECT,* and *from* is the same as *FROM*, as far as MySQL is concerned. On the other hand, the case of the table names, column names, and other variable information does matter if your operating system is Unix and Linux. When using Unix or Linux, MySQL needs to match the column names exactly, so the case for the column names has to be correct — *lastname* is not the same as *lastName*. Windows, however, isn't as picky as Unix and Linux; from its point of view, *lastname* and *lastName* are the same.

- **Spacing:** SQL words need to be separated by one or more spaces. It doesn't matter how many spaces you use; you could just as well use 20 spaces or just 1 space. SQL also doesn't pay any attention to the end of the line. You can start a new line at any point in the SQL statement or write the entire statement on one line.
- **Quotes:** Notice that `CA` and `Fresno` are enclosed in double quotes (") in the preceding query. CA and Fresno are series of characters called *text strings* or *character strings*. (Strings are explained in detail later in this chapter.) You are asking MySQL to compare the text strings in the SQL query with the text strings already stored in the database. Text strings are enclosed in quotes. When you compare numbers, such as integers, stored in numeric columns, you do not enclose the numbers in quotes. (Chapter 3 explains the types of data that can be stored in a MySQL database.)

Sending SQL queries

This book is about PHP and MySQL as a pair. Consequently, I don't describe the multitude of ways in which you can send SQL queries to MySQL, many of which have nothing to do with PHP. Rather, I provide a simple PHP program that you can use to execute SQL queries. (For the lowdown on PHP and how to write PHP programs, check out Part III of this book.)

The program `mysql_send.php` has one simple function: to execute queries and display the results. Copy the program from the CD into the directory where you are developing your Web application, change the information in lines 11–13, and point your browser at the program. Listing 4-1 shows the program, in case you want to type it in yourself.

Listing 4-1: PHP Program for Sending SQL Queries to MySQL

```
<!-- Program Name:  mysql_send.php
     Description: PHP program that sends an SQL query to the
                  MySQL server and displays the results.
-->
<html>
<head>
<title> SQL Query Sender</title>
</head>
<body>
<?php
 $user="mysqlaccountname";
 $host="hostname";
 $password="mysqlpassword";

 /* Section that executes query */
 if (@$form == "yes")
 {
   mysql_connect($host,$user,$password);
```

(continued)

Listing 4-1 ***(continued)***

```
   mysql_select_db($database);
   $query = stripSlashes($query) ;
   $result = mysql_query($query);
   echo "Database Selected: <b>$database</b><br>
         Query: <b>$query</b>
         <h3>Results</h3>
         <hr>";
   if ($result == 0)
     echo("<b>Error ".mysql_errno().": ".mysql_error()."</b>");
   elseif (@mysql_num_rows($result) == 0)
      echo("<b>Query completed. No results returned.</b><br>");
   else
   {
     echo "<table border="1">
           <thead>
            <tr>";
             for ($i = 0; $i < mysql_num_fields($result); $i++)
             {
                 echo("<th>" . mysql_field_name($result,$i) . "</th>");
             }
     echo "</tr>
           </thead>
           <tbody>";
             for ($i = 0; $i < mysql_num_rows($result); $i++)
             {
                echo "<tr>";
                $row = mysql_fetch_row($result);
                for ($j = 0; $j < mysql_num_fields($result); $j++)
                {
                  echo("<td>" . $row[$j] . "</td>");
                }
                echo "</tr>";
             }
             echo "</tbody>
                 </table>";
   }
   echo "<hr><br>
         <form action=$PHP_SELF method=post>
          <input type=hidden name=query value=\"$query\">
          <input type=hidden name=database value=$database>
          <input type=submit name=\"queryButton\" value=\"New Query\">
          <input type=submit name=\"queryButton\" value=\"Edit Query\">
         </form>";
   unset($form);
   exit();
 }

 /* Section that requests user input of query */
 @$query = stripSlashes($query);
 if (@$queryButton != "Edit Query")
 {
   $database = " ";
   $query = " ";
 }
?>

<form action=<?php echo $PHP_SELF ?>?form=yes method="post">
 <table>
  <tr>
   <td align="right"><b>Type in database name</b></td>
   <td>
```

```
    <input type=text name="database" value=<?php echo $database ?> >
    </td>
   </tr>
   <tr>
    <td align="right" valign="top"><b>Type in SQL query</b></td>
    <td><textarea name="query" cols="60" rows="10"><?php echo $query ?>
        </textarea>
    </td>
   </tr>
   <tr>
    <td colspan="2" align="center"><input type="submit" value="Submit
              Query"></td>
   </tr>
  </table>
</form>
</body>
</html>
```

You need to change lines 11, 12, and 13 of the program before you can use it. These lines are

```
$host="hostname";
$user="mysqlaccountname";
$password="mysqlpassword";
```

Change *hostname* to the name of the computer where MySQL is installed, for example, databasehost.mycompany.com. If the MySQL database is installed on the same computer as your Web site, you can use localhost as the hostname.

Change *mysqlaccountname* and *mysqlpassword* to the account name and password that you were given by the MySQL administrator to use to access your MySQL database. If you installed MySQL yourself, an account named root with no password is automatically installed. Sometimes an account with a blank account name and password is installed. You can use either the root or the blank account, but it is much better if you install an account specifically for use with your Web database application. (MySQL accounts and passwords are discussed in detail in Chapter 5.)

An account named root with no password is not secure. You should give it a password right away. An account with a blank account name and password is even less secure. Anyone can access your database without needing to know an account name or password. You should delete this account if it exists.

If your MySQL account does not require a password, type nothing between the double quotes, as follows:

```
$password="";
```

After you have entered the correct hostname, account name, and password in mysqlsend.php, these are the general steps you follow to execute an SQL query:

1. **Point your browser at mysql_send.php.**

   You see the Web page shown in Figure 4-1.

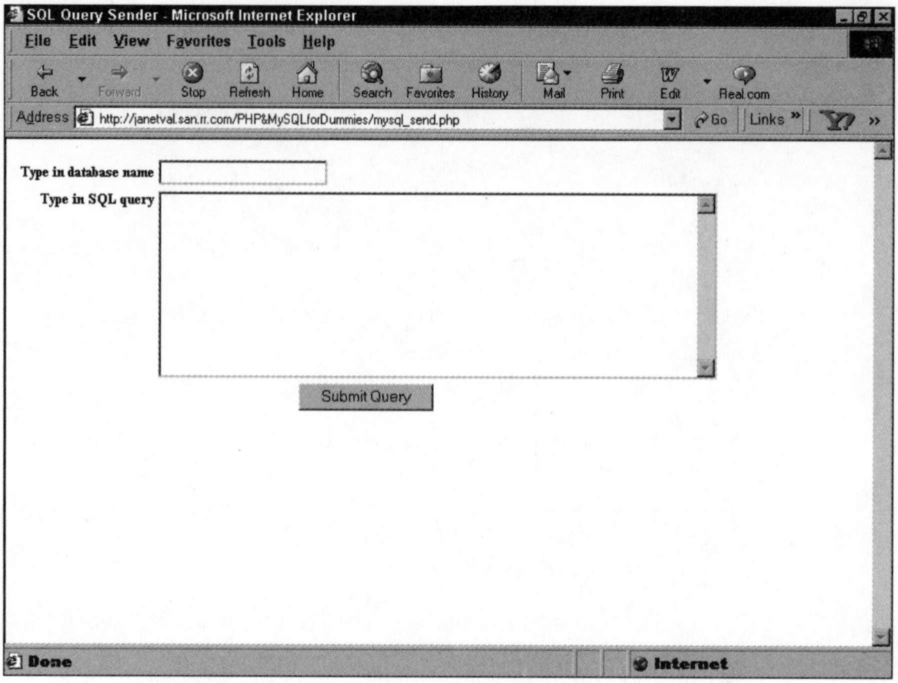

Figure 4-1: An SQL query Web page produced by `mysql_send.php`.

2. **Type the SQL query in the large text box.**
3. **Enter a database name in the first text box if the SQL query requires one.**

   The details of writing specific SQL queries are explained in the following sections of this chapter.
4. **Click the Submit Query button.**

   The query is executed, and a page is displayed, showing the results of the query. If your query had an error, the error message is displayed.

You can test the `mysql_send.php` program by entering this test query in Step 2 of the preceding steps:

```
SHOW DATABASES
```

This query does not require you to enter a database name, so you can skip Step 3. When you click the Submit Query button in Step 4, a listing of the existing databases is displayed. In most cases, you see a database called Test, which is installed automatically when MySQL is installed. Also, you will probably see a database called MySQL, which MySQL uses to store information it needs, such as account names, passwords, and permissions. Even if there are no existing databases, your SQL query will execute correctly. If a problem occurs, an error message is displayed. MySQL error messages are usually pretty helpful in finding the problem.

A quicker way to send SQL queries to the MySQL server

When MySQL is installed, a simple, text-based program called mysql (or sometimes the *terminal monitor* or the *monitor*) is also installed. Programs that communicate with servers are called *client software*; because this program communicates with the MySQL server, it's a client. When you enter SQL queries in this client, the response is returned to the client and displayed on-screen. The monitor program can send queries across a network; it doesn't have to be running on the machine where the database is stored.

To send SQL queries to MySQL by using the mysql client, follow these steps:

1. **Locate the mysql client.**

   By default, the mysql client program is installed in a subdirectory called bin, under the directory where MySQL was installed. In Unix/Linux, the default is `/usr/local/mysql/bin`. In Windows, the default is `c:/mysql/bin`. However, the client may have been installed in a different directory. Or, if you are not the MySQL administrator, you may not have access to the mysql client. If you don't know where MySQL is installed or can't run the client, ask the MySQL administrator to put the client somewhere where you can run it or to give you a copy that you can put on your own computer.

2. **Start the client.**

   In Unix/Linux, type the path/filename (for example, `/usr/local/mysql/bin/mysql`). In Windows, open a command prompt window and then type the path/filename (for example, `c:\mysql\bin\mysql.exe`). Press Enter after typing the path/filename, unless you are using the parameters shown in Step 3.

3. **If you're starting the mysql client to access a database across the network, use the following parameters after the mysql command:**

   -h host: *host* is the name of the machine where MySQL is located.

   -u user: *user* is your MySQL account name.

   -p: This parameter prompts you for the password for your MySQL account.

   For instance, if you are in the directory where the mysql client is located, the command might look like this:

   ```
   mysql -h mysqlhost.mycompany.com -u root -p
   ```

   Press Enter after typing the command.

4. **Enter your password when prompted for it.**

   The mysql client starts, and you see something similar to this:

   ```
   Welcome to the MySQL monitor. Commands end with ; or \g.
   ```

(continued)

(continued)

```
Your MySQL connection id is 459 to server version: 3.22.20a-log
Type 'help' for help.
mysql>
```

5. **At the mysql prompt, type your SQL query, followed by a semicolon (;), and then press the Enter key.**

   The mysql client continues to prompt for input and does not execute the query until you enter a semicolon. The response to the query is displayed on-screen.

6. **To leave the mysql client, type** quit **at the prompt and then press the Enter key.**

Building a Database

A database has two parts: a structure to hold the data and the data itself. In the following few sections, I explain how to create the database structure. First you create an empty database with no structure at all, and then you add tables to it.

The SQL queries you use to work with the database structure are `CREATE`, `ALTER`, `DROP`, and `SHOW`. To use these queries, you must have a MySQL account that has permission to create, alter, and drop databases and tables. See Chapter 5 for more on MySQL accounts.

Creating a new database

To create a new, empty database, use the following SQL query:

```
CREATE DATABASE databasename
```

where *databasename* is the name you give the database. For instance, these two SQL queries create the sample databases used in this book:

```
CREATE DATABASE PetCatalog
CREATE DATABASE MemberDirectory
```

After you create an empty database, you can add tables to it. To see for yourself that a database was, in fact, created, use this SQL query:

```
SHOW DATABASES
```

You can delete any database with this SQL query:

```
DROP DATABASE databasename
```

Use DROP carefully because it is irreversible. After a database is dropped, it is gone forever. And any data that was in it is gone as well.

Adding tables to a database

You can add tables to any database, whether it is a new, empty database that you just created or an existing database that already has tables and data in it. You use the CREATE query to add tables to a database.

In the sample database designs introduced in Chapter 3, the PetCatalog database is designed with three tables: Pet, PetType, and Color. The MemberDirectory database is designed with two tables: Member and Login. Because a table is created in a database, you must indicate the database name where you want the table created. If you don't, you see the error message No Database Selected.

The query to add a table begins with

```
CREATE TABLE tablename
```

Next comes a list of column names with definitions. The information for each column is separated from the information for the next column by a comma. The entire list is enclosed in parentheses. Each column name is followed by its data type (data types are explained in detail in Chapter 3) and any other definitions required. Here are some definitions that you can use:

- NOT NULL: This column must have a value; it cannot be blank.
- DEFAULT *value*: This value is stored in the column when the row is created if no other value is given for this column.
- AUTO_INCREMENT: You use this definition to create a sequence number. As each row is added, the value of this column increases by one integer from the last row entered. You can override the auto number by assigning a specific value to the column.
- UNSIGNED: You use this definition to indicate that the values for this numeric field will never be negative numbers.

The last item in a CREATE TABLE query indicates which column or combination of columns is the unique identifier for the row, called the *primary key*. Each row of a table must have a field or a combination of fields that is different for each row. No two rows can have the same primary key. If you attempt to add a row with the same primary key as a row that is already in the table, you get an error message, and the row is not added. The database design identifies the primary key (as described in Chapter 3). You specify the primary key by using the following format:

```
PRIMARY KEY(columnname)
```

The *columnname* is enclosed in parentheses. If you're using a combination of columns as the primary key, include all the column names, separated by commas. For instance, you would designate the primary key for the Login table in the MemberDirectory database by using this query:

```
PRIMARY KEY (loginName,loginTime)
```

Listing 4-2 shows the `CREATE TABLE` query used to create the Member table of the MemberDirectory database. You could enter this query on a single line if you wanted to. MySQL doesn't care how many lines you use. However, the format shown in Listing 4-2 makes it easier to read. This human-friendly format also helps you spot typos.

Listing 4-2: An SQL Query for Creating a Table

```
CREATE TABLE Member (
  loginName     VARCHAR(20) NOT NULL,
  createDate    DATE          NOT NULL,
  password      CHAR(255)    NOT NULL,
  lastName      VARCHAR(50),
  firstName     VARCHAR(40),
  street        VARCHAR(50),
  city          VARCHAR(50),
  state         CHAR(2),
  zip           CHAR(10),
  email         VARCHAR(50),
  phone         CHAR(15),
  fax           CHAR(15),
PRIMARY KEY(loginName) )
```

Notice that the list of column names in Listing 4-2 is enclosed in parentheses, one on the first line and one on the last line, and a comma follows each column definition.

Remember not to use any MySQL reserved words for column names, as discussed in Chapter 3. If you do, MySQL gives you an error message that looks like this:

```
You have an error in your SQL syntax near 'order var(20))' at line 1
```

Notice this message shows the column definition that it didn't like and the line where it found the offending definition. However, the message doesn't tell you much about what the problem is. The `error in your SQL syntax` that it refers to is using the MySQL reserved word `order` as a column name.

To see the tables that have been added to a database, use this SQL query:

```
SHOW TABLES
```

You can also see the structure of a table with this query:

```
SHOW COLUMNS FROM tablename
```

You can remove any table with this query:

```
DROP TABLE tablename
```

Use DROP carefully because it is irreversible. After a table is dropped, it is gone forever. And any data that was in it is gone as well.

Changing the database structure

Your database is not written in stone. By using the ALTER query, you can change the name of the table; add, drop, or rename a column; or change the data type or other attributes of the column.

The basic format for this query is ALTER TABLE *tablename*, followed by the specific changes you're requesting. Table 4-1 shows the changes you can make.

Table 4-1 Changes You Can Make with the ALTER Query

Change	*Description*
ADD *columnname definition*	Adds a column; *definition* includes the data type and optional definitions.
ALTER *columnname* SET DEFAULT *value*	Changes the default value for a column.
ALTER *columnname* DROP DEFAULT	Removes the default value for a column.
CHANGE *columnname newcolumnname definition*	Changes the definition of a column and renames the column; *definition* includes the data type and optional definitions.
DROP *columnname*	Deletes a column, including all the data in the column. The data cannot be recovered.
MODIFY *columnname definition*	Changes the definition of a column; *definition* includes the data type and optional definitions.
RENAME *newtablename*	Renames a table.

Changing a database is not a rare occurrence. You may want to change your database for many reasons. For example, suppose you defined the column lastName with VARCHAR(20) in the Member table of the MemberDirectory database. At the time, 20 characters seemed sufficient for a last name. But now you just received a memo announcing the new CEO, John Schwartzheimer-Losertman. Oops. MySQL will truncate his name to the first 20 letters, a less-than-desirable new name for the boss. So you need to make the column wider — pronto. Send this query to change the column in a second:

```
ALTER TABLE Member MODIFY lastName VARCHAR(50)
```

Moving Data In and Out of the Database

An empty database is like an empty cookie jar — it's not much fun. And, searching an empty database is no more interesting or fruitful than searching an empty cookie jar. A database is only useful with respect to the information that it holds.

A database needs to be able to receive information for storage and to deliver information on request. For instance, the MemberDirectory database needs to be able to receive the member information, and it also needs to be able to deliver its stored information when you request it. For instance, if you want to know the address of a particular member, the database needs to deliver that information when you request it.

Your MySQL database responds to four types of requests:

- **Adding information:** Adding a row to a table.
- **Updating information:** Changing information in an existing row. This includes adding data to a blank field in an existing row.
- **Retrieving information:** Looking at the data. This request does not remove data from the database.
- **Removing information:** Deleting data from the database.

Sometimes your question requires information from more than one table. For instance, the question, "How much does a green dragon cost?" requires information from the Pet table and from the Color table. You can ask this question easily in a single `SELECT` query by combining the tables.

The following sections discuss how to receive and deliver information, as well as how to combine tables.

Adding information

Every database needs data. For example, you may want to add data to your database so that your users can look at it — an example of this is the Pet Catalog. Or you may want to create an empty database for users to put data into, making the data available for your eyes only — an example of this is the Member Directory. In either scenario, data will be added to the database.

If your data is still on paper, you can enter it directly into a MySQL database, one row at a time, using an SQL query. However, if you have a lot of data, this process could be tedious and involve a lot of typing. Suppose you have information on 1,000 products that needs to be added to your database. Assuming you are greased lightening on a keyboard and can enter a row per minute, that's 16 hours of rapid typing — well, rapid editing anyway. Not fun, but doable. On the other hand, suppose you need to enter 5,000 members of an organization into a database and it takes five minutes to enter each member. Now you're looking at over 400 hours of typing — who has time for that?

If you have a large amount of data to enter, you may want to consider some alternatives. Sometimes scanning in the data is an option. Or perhaps you need to beg, borrow, or hire some help. In many cases, it may be faster to enter the data into a big text file than to enter each row in a separate SQL query.

There is an SQL query that can read data from a big text file — or even a small text file. So, if your data is already in a computer file, you can work with that file; you don't need to type all the data again. Even if the data is in a format other than a text file (for example, an Excel, Access, or Oracle file), you can usually convert the file to a big text file, which can then be read into your MySQL database. If the data is not yet in a computer file and there's a lot of it, consider the possibility that it might be faster to enter that data into the computer in a big text file and transfer it into MySQL as a second step.

Most text files can be read into MySQL, but some formats are easier than others. If you're planning to enter the data into a big text file, read the section, "Adding a bunch of data," to find the best format for your text file. Of course, if the data is already on the computer, you have to work with the file as it is.

Adding one row at a time

You use the `INSERT` query to add a row to a database. This query tells MySQL which table to add the row to and what the values are for the fields in the row. The general form of the query is

```
INSERT INTO tablename (columnname, columnname,.....,columnname)
     VALUES (value, value,.....,value)
```

The following rules apply to the `INSERT` query:

- **Values must be listed in the same order in which the column names are listed:** The first value in the value list is inserted into the column that's named first in the column list; the second value in the value list is inserted into the column that's named second in the column list, and so on.
- **A partial column list is allowed:** You do not need to list all the columns. Columns that are not listed are given their default value or left blank if no default value is defined.

- **A column list is not required:** If you're entering values for all the columns, you don't need to list the columns at all. If no columns are listed, MySQL will look for values for all the columns, in the order in which they appear in the table.
- **The column list and value list must be the same length:** If the list of columns is longer or shorter than the list of values, you get an error message like this: `Column count doesn't match value count.`

The following `INSERT` query adds a row to the Member table:

```
INSERT INTO Member (loginName,createDate,password,lastName,
                    street,city,state,zip,email,phone,fax)
       VALUES ("bigguy","2001-Dec-2","secret","Smith","Goliath",
               "1234 Happy St","Las Vegas","NV","88888","US",
               "gsmith@GSmithCompany.com","(555) 555-5555","")
```

Notice that firstName is not listed in the column name list. No value is entered into the firstName field. If firstName was defined as `NOT NULL`, MySQL would not allow this, but because firstName is not defined as `NOT NULL`, this is okay. Also, if the definition for firstName included a default, the default value would be entered, but because it doesn't, the field is left blank. Notice that the value for `fax` is empty; MySQL has no problem with empty fields.

To look at the data you entered and ensure that you entered it correctly, use an SQL query that retrieves data from the database. These SQL queries are described in detail in "Retrieving information," later in this chapter. In brief, the following query retrieves all the data in the Member table:

```
SELECT * FROM Member
```

Adding a bunch of data

If you have a large amount of data to enter and it's already in a computer file, you can transfer the data from the existing computer file to your MySQL database. The SQL query that reads data from a text file is `LOAD`. The `LOAD` query requires you to specify a database.

Because data in a database is organized in rows and columns, the text file being read must indicate where the data for each column begins and ends and where the end of a row is. To indicate columns, a specific character separates the data for each column. By default, MySQL looks for a tab character to separate the fields. However, if a tab doesn't work for your data file, you can choose a different character to separate the fields and tell MySQL in the query that a different character than the tab separates the fields. Also by default, the end of a line is expected to be the end of a row — although you can choose a character to indicate the end of a line if you need to. A data file for the Pet table might look like this:

```
Unicorn<TAB>horse<TAB>Spiral horn<Tab>5000.00<Tab>/pix/unicorn.jpg
Pegasus<TAB>horse<TAB>Winged<Tab>8000.00<Tab>/pix/pegasus.jpg
Lion<TAB>cat<TAB>Large, Mane on neck<Tab>2000.00<Tab>/pix/lion.jpg
```

A data file with tabs between the fields is called a *tab delimited* file. Another common format is a *comma delimited* file, where commas separate the fields. If your data is in another file format, you need to convert it into a delimited file.

To convert data in another file format into a delimited file, check the manual for that software or talk to your local expert who understands the data's current format. Many programs, such as Excel, Access, or Oracle, allow you to output the data into a delimited file. For a text file, you may be able to convert it to delimited format by using the *search and replace* function of an editor or word processor. For a truly troublesome file, you may need to seek the help of an expert or a programmer.

The basic form of the `LOAD` query is

```
LOAD DATA INFILE "datafilename" INTO TABLE tablename
```

This basic form may be followed by optional phrases if you want to change a default delimiter. The options are

```
FIELDS TERMINATED BY 'character'
FIELDS ENCLOSED BY 'character'
LINES TERMINATED BY 'character'
```

Suppose you have the data file for the Pet table, shown earlier in this section, except that the fields are separated by a comma rather than a tab. The name of the data file is `pets.dat`, and it's located in the same directory as the database. The SQL query to read the data into the table is

```
LOAD DATA INFILE "pets.dat" INTO TABLE Pet
         FIELDS TERMINATED BY ','
```

To look at the data you loaded, to be sure that it's correct, use an SQL query that retrieves data from the database. These types of SQL queries are described in detail in the next section. In brief, use the following query to look at all the data in the table so you can check it:

```
SELECT * FROM Pet
```

Retrieving information

The only purpose in storing information is to have it available when you need it. A database lives to answer questions. What pets are for sale? Who are the members? How many members live in Arkansas? Do you have an alligator for sale? How much does a dragon cost? What is Goliath Smith's phone number? And on and on. You use the `SELECT` query to ask the database questions.

The simplest, basic `SELECT` query is

```
SELECT * FROM tablename
```

This query retrieves all the information from the table. The asterisk (*) is a wild card meaning *all the columns.*

The SELECT query can be much more selective. SQL words and phrases in the SELECT query can pinpoint exactly the information needed to answer your question. You can specify what information you want, how you want it organized, and what the source of the information is:

- **You can request only the information (the columns) you need to answer your question.** For instance, you can request only the first and last names to create a list of members.
- **You can request information in a particular order.** For instance, you can request that the information be sorted in alphabetical order.
- **You can request information from selected objects (the rows) in your table.** (See Chapter 3 for an explanation of database objects.) For instance, you can request the first and last names for only those members whose addresses are in Florida.

Retrieving specific information

To retrieve specific information, list the columns containing the information you want. For example:

```
SELECT columnname,columnname,columnname,... FROM tablename
```

This query retrieves the values from all the rows for the indicated column(s). For instance, the following query retrieves all the last names and first names stored in the Member table:

```
SELECT lastName,firstName FROM Member
```

In some cases, you don't want to see the values in a column, but you want to know something about the column. For instance, you might want to know the lowest value in the column or the highest value in the column. Table 4-2 lists some of the information that is available about a column.

Table 4-2 Information That Can Be Selected

SQL Format	*Description of Information*
AVG(*columnname*)	Returns the average of all the values in *columnname*
COUNT(*columnname*)	Returns the number of rows in which *columnname* is not blank
MAX(*columnname*)	Returns the largest value in *columnname*
MIN(*columnname*)	Returns the smallest value in *columnname*
SUM(*columnname*)	Returns the sum of all the values in *columnname*

For example, the query to find out the highest price in the Pet table is

```
SELECT MAX(price) FROM Pet
```

SQL words like MAX() and SUM() are called *functions*. SQL provides many functions in addition to those in Table 4-2. Some functions, like those in Table 4-2, provide information about a column. Other functions change each value selected. For example, SQRT() returns the square root of each value in the column, and DAYNAME() returns the name of the day of the week for each value in a date column, rather than the actual date stored in the column. Over 100 functions are available for use in a SELECT query. For descriptions of all the functions, see the MySQL documentation at www.mysql.com/documentation.

Retrieving data in a specific order

You may want to retrieve data in a particular order. For instance, in the Member table, you might want members organized in alphabetical order by last name. Or, in the Pet table, you might want the pets grouped by type of pet.

In a SELECT query, ORDER BY and GROUP BY affect the order in which the data is delivered to you:

- **ORDER BY:** To sort information, use the phrase:

  ```
  ORDER BY columnname
  ```

  The data is sorted by *columnname* in ascending order. For instance, if *columnname* is lastName, the data is delivered to you in alphabetical order by the last name.

  You can sort in descending order by adding the word DESC before the column name. For example:

  ```
  SELECT * FROM Member ORDER BY DESC lastName
  ```

- **GROUP BY:** To group information, use the following phrase:

  ```
  GROUP BY columnname
  ```

  The rows that have the same value of *columnname* are grouped together. For example, use this query to group the rows that have the same value as petType:

  ```
  SELECT * FROM Pet GROUP BY petType
  ```

You can use GROUP BY and ORDER BY in the same query.

Retrieving data from a specific source

Very frequently, you don't want all the information from a table. You only want information from selected database objects, that is *rows.* Three SQL words are frequently used to specify the source of the information:

- **WHERE:** Allows you to request information from database objects with certain characteristics. For instance, you can request the names of members that live in California, or you can list only the pets that are cats.

- `LIMIT`: Allows you to limit the number of rows from which information is retrieved. For instance, you can request all the information from the first three rows in the table.
- `DISTINCT`: Allows you to request information from only one row of identical rows. For instance, in the Login table, you can request the loginName, but specify no duplicate names, thus limiting the response to one record for each member. This would answer the question, "Has the member ever logged in?" rather than the question "How many times has the member logged in?"

The `WHERE` clause of the `SELECT` query enables you to make very complicated selections. For instance, suppose your boss asks for a list of all the members whose last names begin with B, who live in Santa Barbara, and who have an 8 in either their phone or fax number. I'm sure there are many uses for such a list. You can get this list for your boss with a `SELECT` query using a `WHERE` clause.

The basic format of the `WHERE` clause is

```
WHERE expression AND|OR expression AND|OR expression ...
```

`Expression` specifies a value to compare to the values stored in the database. Only the rows containing a match for the expression are selected. You can use as many expressions as needed, each one separated by `AND` or `OR`. When you use `AND`, both of the expressions connected by the `AND` (that is, both the expression before the `AND` *and* the expression after the `AND`) must be true in order for the row to be selected. When you use `OR`, only one of the expressions connected by the `OR` must be true for the row to be selected.

Some common expressions are shown in Table 4-3.

Table 4-3 Expressions for the WHERE Clause

Expression	*Example*	*Result*
column = *value*	zip="12345"	Selects only the rows where 12345 is stored in the column named zip
column > *value*	zip > "50000"	Selects only the rows where the zip code is 50001 or higher
column >= *value*	zip >= "50000"	Selects only the rows where the zip code is 50000 or higher
column < *value*	zip < "50000"	Selects only the rows where the zip code is 49999 or lower
column <= *value*	zip <= "50000"	Selects only the rows where the zip code is 50000 or lower

Expression	Example	Result
column BETWEEN *value1* AND *value2*	zip BETWEEN "20000" AND "30000"	Selects only the rows where the zip code is greater than 19999 but less 30001
column IN (*value 1,value2,...*)	zip IN ("90001", "30044")	Selects only the rows where the zip code is 90001 or 30044
column NOT IN (*value1,value 2,...*)	zip NOT IN ("90001", "30044")	Selects only the rows where the zip code is any zip code except 90001 or 30044
column LIKE *value* — *value* can contain the wildcards % (which matches any string) and _, (which matches any character)	zip LIKE "9%"	Selects all rows where the zip code begins with 9
column NOT LIKE *value* — *value* can contain the wildcards % (which matches any string) and _, (which matches any character)	zip NOT LIKE "9%"	Selects all rows where the zip code does not begin with 9

You can combine any of the expressions in Table 4-3 with ANDs and ORs. In some cases, you need to use parentheses to clarify the selection criteria. For instance, you can use the following query to answer your boss's urgent need to find all the people in the Member Directory whose names begin with B, who live in Santa Barbara, and who have an eight in either their phone or fax number:

```
SELECT lastName,firstName FROM Member
       WHERE lastName LIKE "B%"
         AND city = "Santa Barbara"
         AND (phone LIKE "%8%" OR fax LIKE "%8%")
```

Notice the parentheses in the last line. You would not get the results your boss asked for without the parentheses. Without the parentheses, each connector would be processed in order from the first to the last, resulting in a list that includes all members whose names begin with B and who live in Santa Barbara and whose phone numbers have an 8 in them *and* all members whose fax numbers have an 8 in them, whether they live in Santa Barbara or not and whether their name begins with a B or not. When the last OR is processed, members are selected whose characteristics match the expression before the OR *or* the expression after the OR. The expression before the

OR is connected to previous expressions by the previous ANDs and so does not stand alone, but the expression after the OR does stand alone, resulting in the selection of all members with an 8 in their fax number.

LIMIT specifies how many rows can be returned. The form for LIMIT is

```
LIMIT startnumber,numberofrows
```

The first row you want to retrieve is *startnumber*, and the number of rows you want to retrieve is *numberofrows*. If *startnumber* is not specified, 1 is assumed. To select only the first three members who live in Texas, use this query:

```
SELECT * FROM Member WHERE state="TX" LIMIT 3
```

Some SELECT queries will find identical records, but in this example, you only want to see one, not all, of the identical records. To prevent the query from returning all the identical records, add the word DISTINCT immediately after SELECT.

Combining tables

In the earlier sections of this chapter, I assume that all the information you want is in a single table. However, you may want to combine information from different tables. You can do this easily in a single query. The tables are combined side by side, and the information is retrieved from both tables.

Combining tables is called a *join*. Tables are combined by matching data in a column — the column that they have in common. The combined results table produced by a join contains all the columns from both tables. For instance, if one table has two columns, memberID and height, and the second table has two columns, memberID and weight, a join results in a table with four columns: memberID (from the first table), height, memberID (from the second table), and weight.

There are two types of joins: an *inner join* and an *outer join*. The difference between an inner join and an outer join is in the number of rows included in the results table. The results table produced by an inner join contains only rows that existed in both tables. The combined table produced by an outer join contains all rows that existed in one table with blanks in the columns for the rows that did not exist in the second table. For instance, if table1 contains a row for Joe and a row for Sally, and table2 contains only a row for Sally, an inner join would contain only one row, the row for Sally. However, an outer join would contain two rows, a row for Joe and a row for Sally, even though the row for Joe would have a blank field for weight.

You use different SELECT queries for an inner and an outer join. The following query is an inner join:

```
SELECT columnnamelist FROM table1,table2
                      WHERE table1.col2 = table2.col2
```

And this query is an outer join:

```
SELECT columnnamelist FROM table1 OUTER JOIN table2
                      USING (table1.col1=table2.col2)
```

In both queries, table1 and table2 are the tables to be joined. You can join more than two tables. In both queries, col1 and col2 are the names of the columns that are being matched to join the tables. The tables are matched based on the data in these columns. These two columns can have the same name or different names. The two columns must contain the same type of data.

As an example of an inner and outer join, consider a short form of the Pet Catalog. One table is Pet, with two columns, petName and petType, holding the following data:

```
petName   petType

Unicorn   Horse
Pegasus   Horse
Lion      Cat
```

The second table is Color, with two columns, petName and petColor, holding the following data:

```
petName   petColor

Unicorn   white
Unicorn   silver
```

You need to ask a question that requires information from both tables. If you do an inner join with the following query:

```
SELECT * FROM Pet,Color WHERE Pet.petName = Color.petName
```

you get the following results table with four columns: petName (from Pet), petType, petName (from Color), and petColor.

```
petName   petType   petName  petColor

Unicorn   Horse Unicorn      white
Unicorn   Horse Unicorn      silver
```

Notice that only Unicorn appears in the results table, because only Unicorn was in both of the original tables, before the join. On the other hand, suppose you do an outer join with the following query:

```
SELECT * FROM Pet OUTER JOIN Color USING (Pet.petName=Color.petName)
```

You get the following results table, with the same four columns — petName (from Pet), petType, petName (from Color), and petColor — but with different rows:

```
petName  petType   petName  petColor
Unicorn  Horse     Unicorn  white
Unicorn  Horse     Unicorn  silver
Pegasus  Horse     <blank>  <blank>
Lion     Cat       <blank>  <blank>
```

This table has four rows. It has the same first two rows as the inner join, but it has two additional rows, rows that are in PetType but not in Color. Notice that the columns from the table Color are blank for the last two rows.

Which type of join to use depends on the question you want to ask. If you want a list of pets that come in different colors, use the inner join; only the pets in the Color table will appear in the results. However, if you want a list of all pets, showing whether or not they come in different colors, use an outer join.

Updating information

Changing information in an existing row is called *updating* the information. For instance, you might need to change the address of a member because she has moved, or you might need to add a fax number that a member left blank when he originally entered his information.

The UPDATE query is very straightforward:

```
UPDATE tablename SET column=value,column=value,...  WHERE clause
```

In the SET clause, you list the columns to be updated and the new values to be inserted. List all the columns you want to change in one query. Without a WHERE clause, the values of the column(s) would be changed in all the rows. But with the WHERE clause, you can specify which rows to update. For instance, to update an address in the Member table, use this query:

```
UPDATE Member SET street="3333 Giant St",
                  phone="555-555-5555"
              WHERE loginName="bigguy"
```

Removing information

Keep the information in your database up-to-date by deleting obsolete information. You can remove a row from a table with the DELETE query:

```
DELETE FROM tablename WHERE clause
```

Be extremely careful when using DELETE. If you use a DELETE query without a WHERE clause, it will delete all the data in the table. I mean all the data. I repeat, *all the data.* The data cannot be recovered. This function of the DELETE query is right at the top of my don't-try-this-at-home list.

You can delete a column from a table by using the ALTER query:

```
ALTER TABLE DROP columnname
```

Or, of course, you could remove the whole thing and start over again with:

```
DROP TABLE tablename
```

or

```
DROP DATABASE databasename
```

Chapter 5

Protecting Your Data

In This Chapter

- Understanding MySQL data security
- Adding new MySQL accounts
- Modifying existing accounts
- Changing passwords
- Making backups
- Repairing data
- Restoring data

Your data is essential to your Web database application. Storing and/or presenting data are major activities of your Web database application. You have spent valuable time developing your database, and it contains important information entered by you or by your users. You need to protect it. This chapter shows you how.

Controlling Access to Your Data

You need to control access to the information in your database. You need to decide who can see the data and who can change it. Imagine what would happen if your competitors could change the information in your online product catalog or copy your list of customers — you'd be out of business in no time flat. Clearly, you need to guard your data.

MySQL provides a security system for protecting your data. No one can access the data in your database without an account. Each MySQL account has the following attributes:

- A name
- A hostname — the machine from which the account can access the MySQL server
- A password
- A set of permissions

To access your data, someone must use a valid account name and know the password associated with that account. In addition, that person must be connecting from a computer that is permitted to connect to your database using that specific account.

After the user is granted access to the database, what he or she can do to the data depends on what permissions have been set for the account. Each account is either allowed or not allowed to perform an operation in your database, such as `SELECT`, `DELETE`, `INSERT`, `CREATE`, `DROP`, and so on. The settings that specify what an account can do are called *privileges* or *permissions*. You can set up an account with all permissions, no permissions, or anything in between. For instance, for an online product catalog, you want the customer to be able to see the information in the catalog but not be able to change it.

When a user attempts to connect to MySQL and execute a query, MySQL controls access to the data in two stages:

1. **Connection verification:** MySQL checks the validity of the account name and password and checks whether the connection is coming from a host that is allowed to connect to the MySQL server using the specified account. If everything checks out, MySQL accepts the connection.
2. **Request verification:** After MySQL accepts the connection, it checks to see if the account has the necessary permissions to execute the specified query. If it does, MySQL executes the query.

Any query that you send to MySQL can fail either because the connection is rejected in the first step or because the query is not permitted in the second step. An error message is returned to help you identify the source of the problem.

The following few sections describe accounts and permissions in more detail.

Understanding account names and hostnames

Together, the account name and *hostname* (the name of the computer that is authorized to connect to the database) identify a unique account. Two accounts with the same name but different hostnames can exist — as long as they have different passwords and permissions. However, you *cannot* have two accounts with the same name *and* the same hostname.

The MySQL server will accept connections from a MySQL account only when it is connecting from hostname. When you build the `GRANT` or `REVOKE` query (described later in this chapter), you identify the MySQL account using both the account name and the hostname in the following format: *`accountname@hostname`* (for instance, `root@localhost`).

The MySQL account name is completely unrelated in any way to the Unix/Linux or Windows user name, also sometimes called the *login name*. If you are using an administrative MySQL account named `root`, it is not related to the Unix/Linux `root` login name. Changing the MySQL login name does not in any way affect the Unix/Linux or Windows login name — and vice versa.

MySQL account names and hostnames are defined as follows:

- **An account name can be up to 16 characters long.** You can use special characters in account names, such as a space or hyphen (-). However, you cannot use wildcards in the account name.
- **An account name can be blank.** If an account exists in MySQL with a blank account name, any account name will be valid for that account. A user could use any account name to connect to your database, given the user is connecting from a hostname that is allowed to connect to the blank account name and uses the correct password, if required. You can use an account with a blank name to allow anonymous users to connect to your database.
- **Hostname can be a name or an IP address.** For example, it can be a name such as `thor.mycompany.com` or an IP address such as `192.163.2.33`. The machine on which the MySQL server is installed is called `localhost`.
- **Wild cards can be used in the hostname.** You can use a percent sign (%) as a wild card; `%` matches any hostname. If you add an account for `george@%`, someone using the account named `george` can connect to the MySQL server from any computer.
- **The hostname can be blank.** A blank hostname is the same as using `%` for the hostname.

An account with a blank account name and a blank hostname is possible. Such an account would allow anyone to connect to the MySQL server using any account name from any computer. An account with a blank name and a percent sign (%) for the hostname is the same thing. It is very unlikely that you would want such an account. Such an account is sometimes installed when MySQL is installed, but it's given no privileges, so it can't do anything.

When MySQL is installed, it automatically installs an account with all privileges: `root@localhost`. This account is installed without a password. Anyone who is logged in to the computer on which MySQL is installed can access MySQL and do anything to it by using the account named `root`. (Of course, `root` is a well-known account name, so this account is not very secure. If you are the MySQL administrator, you should add a password to this account immediately.)

On some operating systems, additional accounts besides `root@localhost` are automatically installed. For instance, on Windows, an account called `root@%` might be installed with no password protection. This `root` account with all privileges can be used by anyone from any machine. You should remove this account immediately or, at the very least, give it a password.

Finding out about passwords

A password is set up for every account. If no password is provided for the account, the password is blank, which means that no password is required. MySQL doesn't have any limit for the length of a password, but sometimes other software on your system limits the length to eight characters. If so, any characters after eight are dropped.

For extra security, MySQL encrypts passwords before it stores them. That means passwords are not stored in the recognizable characters that you entered. This security measure ensures that no one can look at the stored passwords and see what they are.

Unfortunately, some bad people out there may try to access your data by guessing your password. They use software that tries to connect rapidly in succession using different passwords, a practice called *cracking*. The following are some recommendations for choosing a password that is as difficult to crack as possible:

- Use 6–8 characters.
- Include one or more of each of the following — uppercase letter, lowercase letter, number, and punctuation mark.
- Do not use your account name or any variation of your account name.
- Do not include any word that is in the dictionary.
- Do not include a name.
- Do not use a phone number or a date.

A good password is hard to guess, does not include any word in any dictionary (including foreign language dictionaries), and is easy to remember. If it is too hard to remember, you may need to write it down, which defeats the purpose of having a password. One way to create a good password is to use the first characters of a favorite phrase. For instance, you could use the phrase "All for one! One for all!" to make this password:

```
Afo!Ofa!
```

This password does not include any numbers, but you can fix that by using the numeral *4,* instead of the letter *f.* Then your password is

```
A4o!O4a!
```

Or you could use the number 1 instead of the letter *o* to represent one. Then the password is

```
A41!14a!
```

This password is definitely hard to guess. Other ways to incorporate numbers into your passwords include substituting 1 (one) for *l* (ell) or substituting zero for the letter *o*.

Taking a look at account permissions

Account permissions are used by MySQL to specify who can do what. Anyone using a valid account can connect to the MySQL server, but he or she can only do those things that are allowed by the permissions for the account. For example, an account may be set up so that users can select data but not insert data or update data.

Permissions can be granted for particular databases, tables, or columns. For instance, an account can be set up that allows the user to select data from all the tables in the database, but insert data into only one table and update on only a single column in a specific table.

Permissions are added by using the `GRANT` query — and removed by using the `REVOKE` query. The `GRANT` or `REVOKE` query must be sent using an account that has permission to execute `GRANT` or `REVOKE` statements in the database. If you attempt to send a `GRANT` query or a `REVOKE` query using an account without grant permission, you get an error message. For instance, if you try to grant permission to use a select command, and you send the query using an account that does not have permission to grant permissions, you might see the following error message:

```
grant command denied
```

Permissions can be granted or removed individually or all at once. Table 5-1 lists the permissions that you might want to assign or remove.

Table 5-1 MySQL Account Permissions

Permission	*Description*
`ALL`	All permissions
`ALTER`	Can alter the structure of tables
`CREATE`	Can create new databases or tables
`DELETE`	Can delete rows in tables
`DROP`	Can drop databases or tables
`GRANT`	Can change the permissions on a MySQL account
`INSERT`	Can insert new rows into tables

(continued)

Table 5-1 *(continued)*

Permission	*Description*
SELECT	Can read data from tables
SHUTDOWN	Can shutdown the MySQL server
UPDATE	Can change data in a table
USAGE	No permissions at all

Granting ALL is not a good idea because it includes permissions for administrative operations, such as shutting down the MySQL server. You are unlikely to want anyone other than yourself to have such sweeping privileges.

Setting Up MySQL Accounts

When creating a new account, you specify the password, the name(s) of the computer(s) allowed to access the database using this account, and the permissions; however, you can change these at any time. All the account information is stored in a database named mysql that is automatically created when MySQL is installed. To add a new account or change any account information, you must use an account that has the proper permissions on the mysql database.

You need at least one account in order to access the MySQL server. When MySQL is installed, it automatically sets up some accounts, including an account called `root` that has all permissions. If you have MySQL access through a company Web site or a Web hosting company, the MySQL administrator for the company should give you the account; the account is probably not named `root`, and it may or may not have all permissions.

The rest of this section describes how to add and delete accounts and change passwords and permissions for accounts. If you have an account that you received from your company IT department or from a Web hosting company, you may receive an error when you try to send any or some of the `GRANT` or `REVOKE` queries described. If your account is restricted from performing any of the necessary queries, you need to request an account with more permissions or ask the MySQL administrator to add a new account or make the changes you need.

The MySQL security database

When MySQL is installed, it automatically creates a database called mysql. All the information used to protect your data is stored in this database, including account names, hostnames, passwords, and permissions.

Permissions are stored in columns. The format of each column name is `permission_priv` where *`permission`* is one of the permissions shown in Table 5-1. For instance, the column containing `ALTER` permissions is named `alter_priv`. The value in each permission column is `Y` or `N`, meaning yes or no. So, for instance, in the user table (described in the following list), there would be a row for an account and there would be a column for `alter_priv`. If the account field for `alter_priv` contains `Y`, the account can be used to execute an `ALTER` query. If `alter_priv` contains `N`, the account does not have permission to execute an `ALTER` query.

The mysql database has five tables:

- **user table:** This table stores permissions that apply to all the databases and tables. It contains a row for each valid account with user name, hostname, and password. The MySQL server will reject a connection for an account that does not exist in this table.
- **db table:** This table stores permissions that apply to a particular database. It contains a row for the database, which gives permissions to an account name and hostname. The account must exist in the user table for the permissions to be granted. Permissions that are given in the user table overrule permissions in this table. For instance, if the user table has a row for the account *designer* that gives insert privileges, designer can insert into all the databases. If a row in the `db` table shows N for insert for the designer account in the PetCatalog database, the user table overrules it, and designer can insert in the PetCatalog database.
- **host table:** This table controls access to a database depending on the host. The host table works with the db table. If a row in the db table has an empty field for the host, MySQL checks the host table to see if the db has a row there. In this way, you can allow access to a db from some hosts but not from others. For instance, say you have two databases: db1 and db2. The db1 database has information that is very sensitive, so you only want certain people to see it. The db2 database has information you want everyone to see. If you have a row in the db table for db1 with a blank host field, you can have two rows for db1 in the host table. One row can give all permissions to users connecting from a specific host, whereas another row can deny privileges to users connecting from any other host.
- **tables_priv table:** This table stores permissions that apply to specific tables.
- **columns_priv table:** This table stores permissions that apply to specific columns.

You can see and change the tables in `mysql` directly if you're using an account that has the necessary permissions. You can use SQL queries such as `SELECT`, `INSERT`, `UPDATE`, and others. If you're accessing MySQL through your employer, a client, or a Web hosting company, it is unlikely that you will be given an account that has the necessary permissions.

Identifying what accounts currently exist

To see what accounts currently exist for your database, you need an account that has the necessary permissions. Try to execute the following query on a database named mysql:

```
SELECT * FROM user
```

You should get a list of all the accounts. However, if you are accessing MySQL through your company or a Web hosting company, you probably don't have the necessary permissions. In that case, you may get an error message like this:

```
No Database Selected
```

This message means that your account is not allowed to select the mysql database. Or you may get an error message saying that you don't have select permission. Even though this message is annoying, it's good in the sense that it's a sign the company has good security measures in place. However, it's bad in the sense that you can't see what privileges your account has. You must ask your MySQL administrator or try to figure it out yourself by trying queries and seeing if you are allowed to execute them.

Adding new accounts and changing permissions

The preferred way to access MySQL from PHP is to set up an account specifically for this purpose with only the permissions that are needed. This section describes how to add new accounts and change permissions. If you are using an account given to you by a company IT department or a Web hosting company, it may or may not have all the permissions needed to create a new account. If it does not, you won't be able to successfully execute the `GRANT` query to add an account and will have to request a second account to use with PHP.

If you need to request a second account, get an account with restricted permission, if at all possible, because your Web database application will be more secure if the account used in your PHP programs doesn't have more privileges than are necessary.

You use the same `GRANT` query to set up a new account or to change the password or add permissions for an existing account. If the account already exists, the `GRANT` query changes the password or adds permissions. If the account does not yet exist, the `GRANT` query adds a new account.

Here is the general format for a `GRANT` query:

```
GRANT permission (columns) ON tablename TO accountname@hostname
  IDENTIFIED BY 'password'
```

You can use this `GRANT` query to create a new account or change an existing account. You need to fill in the following information:

- *`permission (columns)`*: You must list at least one permission. You can limit each permission to one or more columns by listing the column name in parentheses following the permission. If no column name is listed, the permission is granted on all columns in the table(s). You can list as many permission/columns as needed, separated by commas. The possible permissions are listed in Table 5-1. For instance, a `GRANT` query might start with this:

```
GRANT select (firstName,lastName), update, insert (birthdate) ...
```

- *`tablename`*: Indicate which tables the permission is granted on. At least one table is required. You can list several tables, separated by commas. The possible values for *`tablename`* are
    - *`tablename`*: The entire table named *`tablename`* in the current database. You can use an asterisk (*) to mean all tables in the current database. If you use an asterisk and no current database is selected, the privilege will be granted to all tables on all databases.
    - *`databasename.tablename`*: The entire table named *`tablename`* in *`databasename`*. You can use an asterisk (*) for either the database name or the table name to mean *all*. Using `*.*` grants the permission on all tables in all databases.
- *`accountname@hostname`*: If the account already exists, it is given the indicated permissions. If the account doesn't exist, it's added. The account is identified by the *`accountname`* and *`hostname`* as a pair. If an account exists with the specified account name but a different hostname, the existing account is not changed; a new one is created.
- *`password`*: This is the password you are adding or changing. A password is not required. If you do not want to add or change a password for this account, leave out the entire phrase `IDENTIFIED BY '`*`password`*`'`.

The `GRANT` query to add a new account for use in the PHP programs for the PetCatalog database might be

```
GRANT select ON PetCatalog.* TO phpuser@localhost IDENTIFIED BY 'A41!14a!'
```

Adding and changing passwords

You can add or change passwords by using the `GRANT` query. You can include a password requirement when you add a new account, as described in the preceding section. If an account already exists, you can change its password by using the following `GRANT` query:

```
GRANT permission ON * TO accountname@hostname IDENTIFIED BY 'password'
```

You need to fill in the following information:

- *permission*: You must list at least one permission in a GRANT query. If the permission has already been granted, it is not changed.
- *accountname@hostname*: It the account already exists, it's given the indicated permission and password. If the account doesn't exist, the account is added. The account is identified by the *accountname* and *hostname* as a pair. If an account exists with the specified account name but a different hostname, the account is not changed; a new one is created.
- *password*: The password in the GRANT query replaces the existing password. If you supply an empty password using

  ```
  IDENTIFIED BY ''
  ```

  then the existing password is replaced with a blank, leaving the account with no password. For tips on choosing a good password, check out the "Finding out about passwords" section, earlier in the chapter.

Removing permissions

To remove permissions, use the REVOKE query. The general format is

```
REVOKE permission (columns) ON tablename FROM accountname@hostname
```

You need to fill in the following information:

- *permission (columns)*: You must list at least one permission. You can remove each permission from one or more columns by listing the column name in parentheses following the permission. If no column name is listed, the permission is removed from all columns in the table(s). You can list as many permission/columns as needed, separated by commas. The possible permissions are listed in Table 5-1. For instance, a REVOKE query might start like this:

  ```
  REVOKE select (firstName,lastName), update, insert (birthdate) ...
  ```

- *tablename*: Indicate which tables the permission is being removed from. At least one table is required. You can list several tables, separated by commas. The possible values for *tablename* are
  - *tablename*: The entire table named *tablename* in the current database. You can use an asterisk (*) to mean all tables. If you use an asterisk when no current database is selected, the privilege will be revoked on all tables on all databases.
  - *databasename.tablename*: The entire table named *tablename* in *databasename*. You can use an asterisk (*) for either the database name or the table name to mean *all*. Using *.* revokes the permission on all tables in all databases.

- *accountname@hostname*: The account is identified by the *accountname* and *hostname* as a pair. If an account exists with the specified account name but a different hostname, the REVOKE query will fail, and you will receive an error message.

Removing accounts

Removing an account is usually not necessary. If you created an account with permissions you don't want, just change the permissions. If you don't want to use an account, remove all the permissions so the account can't do anything. To remove all the permissions for an account, use a REVOKE query with the following syntax:

```
REVOKE all ON *.* FROM accountname@hostname
```

To actually be able to remove an account, you need an account with the necessary permissions on the mysql database. You need to use a DELETE query on the user table in the mysql database, but be careful using a DELETE query. For more information on the structure of the mysql security database, see "The MySQL security database" sidebar, earlier in this chapter.

Backing Up Your Data

You need to have at least one copy of your valuable database. Disasters occur rarely, but they do occur. The computer where your database is stored can break down and lose your data, the computer file can become corrupted, the building can burn down, and so on. Backup copies of your database guard against data loss from such disasters.

You should have at least one backup copy of your database, stored in a location that is separate from the copy that is currently in use. More than one copy — perhaps as many as three — is usually a good idea.

- Store one copy in a handy location, perhaps even on the same computer, to quickly replace a working database that has been damaged.
- Store a second copy on another computer, in case the computer breaks down and the first backup copy isn't available.
- Store a third copy in a completely different physical location, for that remote chance that the building burns down. If the second backup copy is stored via network on a computer at another physical location, this third copy isn't needed.

If you don't have access to a computer offsite where you can back up your database, you can copy your backup to a portable medium, such as a tape or a CD, and store it offsite. Certain companies will store your computer media at their location for a fee, or you can just put the media in your pocket and take it home.

If you use MySQL on someone else's computer, such as the computer of your employer or a Web hosting company, the people who provide your access are responsible for backups. They should have automated procedures in place that make backups of your database. A good question to ask when evaluating a Web hosting company is what its backup procedures are. You want to know how often backup copies are made and where they are stored. If you aren't confident that your data is safe, you can discuss changes or additions to the backup procedures.

If you are the MySQL administrator, you are responsible for making backups. MySQL provides a program called mysqldump that you can use to make backup copies; mysqldump creates a text file that contains all the SQL statements needed to re-create your entire database. The file contains the `CREATE` statements for each table and `INSERT` statements for each row of data in the tables. You can restore your database by executing the set of MySQL statements. You can restore it in its current location, or you can restore it on another computer if necessary.

Follow these steps to make a backup copy of your database in Linux/Unix:

1. **Change to the bin subdirectory in the directory where MySQL is installed.**

   For instance, type `cd /usr/local/mysql/bin`.

2. **Type the following:**

   ```
   mysqldump --user=accountname --password=password databasename >path/
             backupfilename
   ```

   where

   - *`accountname`* is the name of the MySQL account you are using to back up the database.
   - *`password`* is the password for the account.
   - *`databasename`* is the name of the database you want to back up.
   - *`path/backupfilename`* is the path to the directory where you want to store the backups and the name of the file that the SQL output will be stored in.

   The account you use needs to have select permission. If the account does not require a password, you can leave out the entire password option.

   You can type the command on one line, without pressing Enter. Or you can type a backslash (\), then press Enter, and then continue the command on another line.

For example, to back up the PetCatalog database, the command might be:

```
mysqldump --user=root --password=bigsecret PetCatalog \
>/usr/local/mysql/backups/PetCatalogBackup
```

Note: The Linux/Unix account you are logged into must have permission to write a file into the backup directory.

To make a backup copy of your database in Windows, follow these steps:

1. **Open a command prompt window.**

   For instance, choose Start⇨Programs⇨MS-DOS prompt.

2. **Change to the bin subdirectory in the directory where MySQL is installed.**

   For instance, type `cd c:\mysql\bin`.

3. **Type the following:**

   ```
   mysqldump.exe --user=accountname --password=password databasename
             >path\backupfilename
   ```

   where

   - *`accountname`* is the name of the MySQL account you are using to back up the database.
   - *`password`* is the password for the account.
   - *`databasename`* is the name of the database you want to back up.
   - *`path\backupfilename`* is the path to the directory where you want to store the backups and the name of the file that the SQL output will be stored in.

   The account you use needs to have select permission. If the account does not require a password, you can leave out the entire password option.

   You must type the `mysqldump` command on one line without pressing Enter.

   For example, to back up the PetCatalog database, the command might be:

   ```
   mysqldump.exe --user=root PetCatalog >PetCatalogBackup
   ```

Backups should be made at certain times — at least once per day. If your database changes frequently, you may want to back up more often. For example, you may want to back up to the backup directory hourly, but back up to another computer once a day.

Restoring Your Data

At some point, one of your database tables might become damaged and unusable. It's unusual, but it happens. For instance, a hardware problem or an unexpected shutdown of the computer can cause corrupted tables. Sometimes an anomaly in the data that confuses MySQL can cause corrupt tables. In some cases, a corrupt table can cause your MySQL server to shut down.

Here is a typical error message that signals a corrupted table:

```
Incorrect key file for table: 'tablename'.
```

In some cases, you can repair the corrupted data table(s) by using a repair utility provided with MySQL. If the repair utility doesn't restore the corrupted table(s) to working order, all is not lost — you can replace the corrupted table(s) with the data stored in a backup copy. In some cases, the database may be lost completely. For instance, if the computer where your database resides breaks down and can't be fixed, your current database is lost, but your data isn't gone forever. You can replace the broken computer with a new computer and restore your database from a backup copy.

Repairing tables

Often a damaged database can be fixed. MySQL provides a utility called myisamchk that repairs tables. If you are accessing MySQL on your employer's or client's computer or through a Web hosting company, you need to contact the MySQL administrator to run myisamchk for you.

If you are the MySQL administrator, you can run myisamchk yourself. To use myisamchk on Linux/Unix, follow these steps:

1. **Change to the bin subdirectory in the directory where MySQL is installed.**

   For instance, type `cd /usr/local/mysql/bin`.

2. **Stop the MySQL server by typing this query:**

   ```
   mysqladmin -u accountname -p shutdown
   ```

   where *accountname* is the name of an account.

   The account must have shutdown permission. If the account does not require a password, leave out the `-p`. If you include `-p`, you will be asked for your password.

3. **Type the following:**

   ```
   myisamchk -r path/databasename/tablename.MYI
   ```

   Include the complete path to your data directory, followed by the database name, the table name, and `.MYI`. You can use an asterisk (*) as a wild card. For instance, to repair all the tables in the PetCatalog database, you might type

   ```
   myisamchk -r ../data/PetCatalog/*.MYI
   ```

After you type the statement, you see output on the screen showing which tables are being checked.

4. **Start the MySQL server by typing the following:**

   ```
   mysqladmin -u accountname -p start
   ```

To use myisamchk on Windows, follow these steps:

1. **Open a command prompt window.**

   For instance, choose Start⇨Programs⇨MS-DOS prompt.

2. **Change to the bin subdirectory in the directory where MySQL is installed.**

   For instance, type `cd c:\mysql\bin`.

3. **Stop the MySQL server by typing**

   ```
   mysqladmin.exe -u accountname -p shutdown
   ```

   where *accountname* is the name of an account with shutdown permission. If the account does not require a password, leave out the `-p`. If you include `-p`, you will be prompted for your password.

4. **Type the following:**

   ```
   myisamchk.exe -r path/databasename/tablename.MYI
   ```

   Include the complete path to your data directory, followed by the database name, the table name, and `.MYI`. You can use an asterisk (*) as a wild card. The `-r` option is the recover option. For instance, to repair all the tables in the PetCatalog database, you might type

   ```
   myisamchk.exe -r ..\data\PetCatalog\*.MYI
   ```

   After you enter this statement, you see output on the screen showing which tables are being checked. Wait for myisamchk to finish running.

5. **Start your MySQL server by typing the following:**

   ```
   mysqladmin.exe -u accountname -p start
   ```

   If your table still isn't working after you run this command, try running the myisamchk utility again using the `-o` option instead of the `-r` option. The `-o` option is an older repair process that is much slower than the `-r` option, but it handles some cases the `-r` option can't handle.

Restoring from a backup copy

If repairing your data doesn't return the database to working condition or if your database is completely unavailable, such as in the case of a computer failure, you can replace your current database table(s) with the database stored in a backup copy. The backup copy contains a snapshot of the data as it was at the time the copy was made. Any changes to the database since the backup copy was made are not included; you have to re-create those changes manually.

Again, if you access MySQL through an IT department or through a Web hosting company, you need to ask the MySQL administrator to restore your database from a backup. If you are the MySQL administrator, you can restore it yourself.

As described in Chapter 4, you build a database by creating the database and then adding tables to the database. The backup you create using the mysqldump utility is a file that contains all the SQL statements necessary to rebuild all the tables, but it does not contain the statements needed to create the database.

Your database may not exist at all, or it may exist with one or more corrupted tables. You can restore the entire database or any single table. Follow these steps to restore a single table:

1. **If the table currently exists, delete the table with the following SQL query:**

   ```
   DROP TABLE tablename
   ```

   where *tablename* is the table you want to delete.

2. **Point your browser at `mysql_send.php`.**

   For a description of `mysql_send.php`, see Chapter 4.

3. **Copy the `CREATE` query for the table from the backup file into the form in the browser window.**

   For instance, choose Edit➪Copy and Edit➪Paste.

4. **Type the name of the database in which you are restoring the table.**

   The form shows where to type the database name.

5. **Click Submit.**

   A new Web page shows the results of the query.

6. **Click New Query.**

7. **Copy an `INSERT` query for the table from the backup file into the form in the browser window.**

   For instance, choose Edit➪Copy and Edit➪Paste.

8. **Type the name of the database in which you are restoring the table.**

   The form shows where to type the database name.

9. **Click Submit.**

   A new Web page shows the results of the query.

10. **Click New Query.**

11. **Repeat Steps 7 through 10 until all the `INSERT` queries from the backup file have been sent.**

If there are so many `INSERT` queries for the table that sending them one by one would take forever or if there are just a lot of tables, you can send all the queries in the backup file at once, by following these steps:

1. **If any of the tables in the backup file currently exist, delete them with the following SQL query:**

   ```
   DROP TABLE tablename
   ```

   where *tablename* is the table you want to delete.

2. **Change to the bin subdirectory in the directory where MySQL is installed.**

   On Linux/Unix, do the following:

   Type a cd command to change to the correct directory (for instance, type `cd /usr/local/mysql/bin`).

   On Windows, do as follows:

   1. Open a command prompt window.

      For instance, choose Start➪Programs➪MS-DOS prompt.

   2. Type a `cd` command to change to the correct directory (for instance, type `cd c:\mysql\bin`).

3. **Type the command that sends the SQL queries in the backup file.**

   On Linux/Unix, do as follows:

   Type

   ```
   mysql -u accountname -p databasename < path/backupfilename
   ```

   where *accountname* is an account that has create permission. If the account doesn't require a password, leave out the `-p`. If you use the `-p`, you will be asked for the password. *databasename* is the existing database in which you want to build all the tables. Use the entire path and file name for the backup file. For instance, a command to restore the PetCatalog database might be:

   ```
   mysql -u root -p PetCatalog < /usr/backupfiles/PetCatalog.bak
   ```

   On Windows, do the following:

   Type:

   ```
   mysql.exe -u accountname -p databasename < path\backupname
   ```

   where *accountname* is an account that has create permission. If the account doesn't require a password, leave out the `-p`. If you use the `-p`, you will be asked for the password. *databasename* is the existing database in which you want to build all the tables. Use the entire path and file name for the backup file. For instance, a command to restore the PetCatalog database might be:

   ```
   mysql.exe -u root -p PetCatalog < c:\mysql\bak\PetCatalog.bak
   ```

The tables may take a short time to restore. Wait for the command to finish. If a problem occurs, an error message is displayed. If no problems occur, you see no output. When the command is finished, the prompt appears.

To restore only selected tables using the backup file, make a file that contains only the queries for the selected tables you want to restore. Then follow Steps 1 through 3 in the preceding list. In Step 3, type the path name or file name for the file with the subset of queries you want, instead of the full backup file.

If the database is not there at all, you need to create it before you can use the queries in the backup file to rebuild all the tables. To restore the database when nothing exists, use the following steps:

1. **Add the following two lines to the top of the backup file:**

   ```
   CREATE DATABASE databasename;
   use databasename;
   ```

   where *databasename* is the name of the database you want to restore. For instance, the commands for the PetCatalog database are

   ```
   CREATE DATABASE PetCatalog;
   use PetCatalog;
   ```

   Note: Make sure that you add the semicolons (;) at the end of each line.

2. **Change to the bin subdirectory in the directory where MySQL is installed.**

   On Linux/Unix, do the following:

   Type a `cd` command to change to the correct directory (for instance, type `cd /usr/local/mysql/bin`).

   On Windows, do the following:

   1. Open a command-prompt window.

      For instance, choose Start⇨Programs⇨MS-DOS prompt.

   2. Type a `cd` command to change to the correct directory (for instance, type `cd c:\mysql\bin`).

3. **Type the command that sends the SQL queries in the backup file.**

   On Linux/Unix, do as follows:

   Type this:

   ```
   mysql -u accountname -p < path/backupfilename
   ```

where *accountname* is an account that has create permission. If the account doesn't require a password, leave out the `-p`. If you use the `-p`, you will be asked for the password. *databasename* is the existing database in which you want to build all the tables. Use the entire path and file name for the backup file. For instance, a command to restore the PetCatalog database might be:

```
mysql -u root -p < /usr/backupfiles/PetCatalog.bak
```

On Windows, do as follows:

Type this:

```
mysql.exe -u accountname -p < path\backupfilename
```

where *accountname* is an account that has create permission. If the account doesn't require a password, leave out the `-p`. If you use the `-p`, you will be asked for the password. *databasename* is the existing database in which you want to build all the tables. Use the entire path and file name for the backup file. For instance, a command to restore the PetCatalog database might be:

```
mysql.exe -u root -p < c:\mysql\bak\PetCatalog.bak
```

The tables may take a short time to restore. Wait for the command to finish. If a problem occurs, an error message is displayed. If no problems occur, you see no output. When the command is finished, the prompt appears.

Your database is now restored with all the data that was in it at the time the copy was made. If the data has changed since the copy was made, the changes are lost. For instance, if more data was added after the backup copy was made, the new data is not restored. If you know the changes that were made, you can make them manually in the restored database.

Part III
PHP

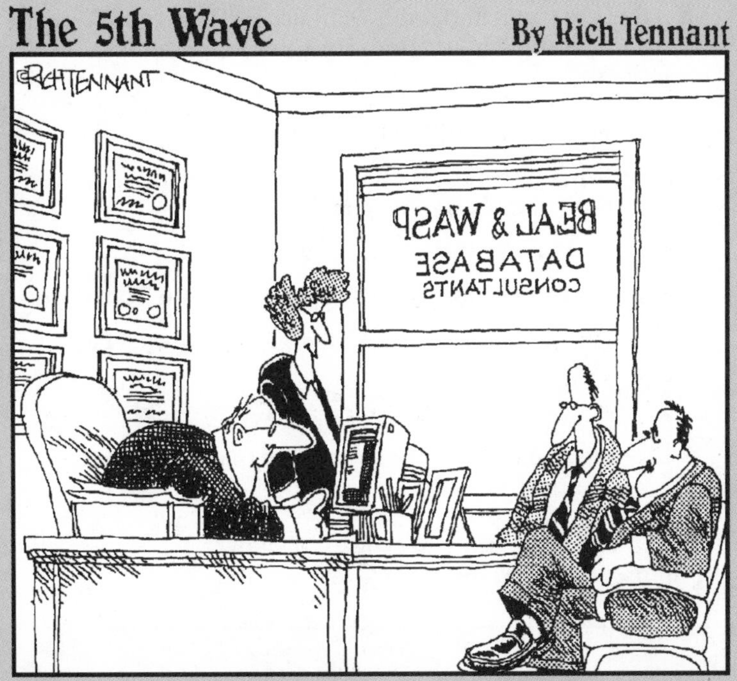

"Your database is beyond repair, but before I tell you our backup recommendation, let me ask you a question. How many index cards do you think will fit on the walls of your computer room?"

In this part . . .

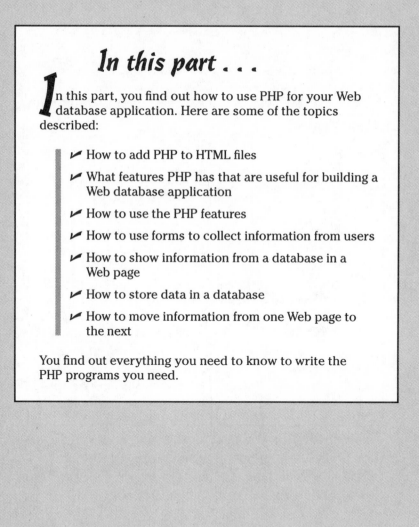

In this part, you find out how to use PHP for your Web database application. Here are some of the topics described:

- How to add PHP to HTML files
- What features PHP has that are useful for building a Web database application
- How to use the PHP features
- How to use forms to collect information from users
- How to show information from a database in a Web page
- How to store data in a database
- How to move information from one Web page to the next

You find out everything you need to know to write the PHP programs you need.

Chapter 6

General PHP

In This Chapter

- Adding PHP sections to HTML files
- Writing PHP statements
- Using PHP variables
- Comparing values in PHP variables
- Documenting your programs

Programs are the application part of your Web database application. Programs perform the tasks. They create and display Web pages, accept and process information from users, store information in the database, get information out of the database, and perform any other necessary tasks.

PHP is the language you use to write your programs. PHP is a scripting language designed specifically for use on the Web. It is your tool for creating dynamic Web pages. It has features designed to aid in programming the tasks needed by dynamic Web applications.

In this chapter, I describe the general rules for writing PHP programs, the rules that apply to all PHP statements. Consider these rules similar to general grammar and punctuation rules. In the remaining chapters in Part III, you find out about specific PHP statements and features and how to write PHP programs to perform specific tasks.

Adding a PHP Section to an HTML Page

PHP is a partner to HTML that extends its abilities. It enables an HTML program to do things it can't do on its own. HTML programs can display Web pages. HTML has features that allow you to format those Web pages. HTML allows you to display graphics in your Web pages and play music files. But HTML alone does not allow you to interact with the person viewing the Web page.

HTML is almost interactive. HTML forms allow users to type information that the Web page is designed to collect. However, you can't access that information without using a language other than HTML. PHP processes form information, without requiring a separate program, and allows other interactive tasks as well.

HTML tags are used to make PHP language statements part of HTML programs. The program file is named with a `.php` extension. (Other extension(s) can be defined by the PHP administrator, such as `.phtml` or `.php4`, but `.php` is the most common. So for this book, I will assume that `.php` is the extension for PHP programs.) The PHP language statements are enclosed in PHP tags with the following form:

```
<?php     ?>
```

Sometimes you can use a shorter version of the PHP tags. You can try using `<?` and `?>`, without the `php`. If short tags are enabled, you can save a little typing.

PHP processes all statements between the two PHP tags. After the PHP section is processed, it's discarded, or, if the PHP statements produce output, the PHP section is replaced by the output. The browser does not see the PHP section, only its output if there is any output. For more on this process, check out the sidebar "How the Web server processes PHP files."

How the Web server processes PHP files

When a browser is pointed to a regular HTML file with an `.html` or `.htm` extension, the Web server sends the file, as is, to the browser. The browser processes the file and displays the Web page that is described by the HTML tags in the file. When a browser is pointed to a PHP file, with a `.php` extension, the Web server looks for PHP sections in the file and processes them, instead of just sending them as is to the browser. The steps the Web server uses to process a PHP file are as follows:

1. The Web server starts scanning the file in HTML mode. It assumes that the statements are HTML and sends them to the browser without any processing.
2. The Web server continues in HTML mode until it encounters a PHP opening tag (`<?php`).
3. When it encounters a PHP opening tag, the Web server switches into PHP mode. This is sometimes called *escaping from HTML*. It assumes that all statements are PHP statements. It executes the PHP statements. If there is output, the Web server sends the output to the browser.
4. The Web server continues in PHP mode until it encounters a PHP closing tag (`?>`).
5. When the Web server encounters a PHP closing tag, it returns to HTML mode. It resumes scanning, and the cycle continues from Step 1.

As an example, I'll start with a program that displays `Hello World!` in the browser window. It's sort of a tradition that the first program you write in any language is the Hello World program. You may have written a Hello World program when you first learned HTML. Listing 6-1 shows an HTML program that displays `Hello World!` in a browser window.

Listing 6-1: The Hello World HTML Program

```
<html>
<head><title>Hello World Program</title></head>
<body>
<p>Hello World!
</body>
</html>
```

If you point your browser at this HTML program, you see a Web page that displays

```
Hello World!
```

in the browser window.

Listing 6-2 shows a PHP program that does exactly the same thing — it displays `Hello World!` in a browser window.

Listing 6-2: The Hello World PHP Program

```
<html>
<head><title>Hello World Program</title></head>
<body>
<?php>
  echo "<p>Hello World!"
?>
</body>
</html>
```

If you point your browser at this program, it displays exactly the same Web page as the HTML program in Listing 6-1. In this PHP program, the PHP section is

```
<?php
  echo "<p>Hello World!"
?>
```

The PHP tags enclose only one statement — an *echo statement.* The echo statement is a PHP statement that you will use frequently. It simply outputs the text between the double quotes.

There is no rule that says you must enter the PHP on separate lines. You could just as well include the PHP in the file on a single line, like this:

```
<?php echo "<p>Hello World!" ?>
```

When the PHP section is processed, it is replaced with the output. In this case, the output is

```
<p>Hello World!
```

If you replace the PHP section in Listing 6-2 with the preceding output, the program now looks exactly like the HTML program in Listing 6-1. If you point your browser at either program, you see the same Web page. If you look at the source code that the browser sees (in the browser, choose View⇨Source), you see the same source code listing for both programs.

Writing PHP Statements

The PHP section that you add to your HTML file consists of a series of PHP statements. Each PHP statement is an instruction to PHP to do something. In the Hello World program shown in Listing 6-2, the PHP section contains only one PHP statement. The echo statement instructs PHP to output the text between the double quotes.

PHP statements end with a semicolon (;). PHP does not notice white space or the end of lines. It continues reading a statement until it encounters a semicolon or the PHP closing tag, no matter how many lines the statement spans. Leaving out the semicolon is a common error, resulting in an error message that looks something like this:

```
Parse error: expecting `','' or `';'' in c:\hello.php on line 6
```

Notice that the error message gives you the line number where it encountered problems. This information helps you locate the error in your program.

It's a good idea to write your PHP programs using an editor that uses line numbers. If your editor doesn't let you specify which line you want to go to, you have to count the lines manually from the top of the file every time you receive an error message.

Sometimes groups of statements are combined together into a *block*. A block is enclosed by curly braces ({ }). A block of statements execute together. A common use of a block is in a *conditional block,* a block in which statements are executed only when certain conditions are true. For instance, you might want your program to do the following:

```
if (the sky is blue)
{
  put leash on dragon;
  take dragon for a walk in the park;
}
```

These statements are enclosed in curly brackets to ensure they execute as a block. If the sky is blue, both `put leash on dragon` and `take dragon for a walk in the park` are executed. If the sky is not blue, neither statement is executed (no leash; no walk).

If you wanted to, you could write the entire PHP section in one long line, as long as you separated statements with semicolons and enclosed blocks with curly brackets. However, a program written this way would be impossible for people to read. Therefore, you should put statements on separate lines, except for occasional, really short statements.

Error messages and warnings

PHP tries to be helpful when problems arise. It provides error messages and warnings as follows:

- **Error message:** You receive this message when the program has a problem that prevents it from running. The message contains as much information as possible to help you identify the problem. A common error message is

  ```
  Parse error: parse error in c:\
     catalog\test.php on line 6
  ```

  Often, you receive this error message because you've forgotten a semicolon, a parenthesis, or a curly brace.

- **Warning message:** You receive this message when the program sees a problem but the problem is not serious enough to prevent the program from running. Warning messages do not mean the program can't run. The program continues to run. Warning messages just tell you that you are doing something unusual and to take a second look at what you are doing to be sure you really want to do it.

  One common reason you may receive a warning message is if you're echoing variables that don't exist. Here's an example of what you might see in that instance:

  ```
  Warning: Undefined variable: age in
     testing.php on line 9
  ```

Notice that both error and warning messages indicate the file name causing the problem and the line number where the problem was encountered.

PHP has several kinds of error and warning messages. Which kinds are sent depends on the error message level that PHP is set to. You want to see all the error messages, but you may not want to see all the warnings. Often the only problem with a warning is the unsightly warning message. Or, you may want warning messages displayed during development but not after the application is being used by customers.

To change the error message level to show more or fewer messages, you must be the PHP administrator. Edit the `php.ini` file on your system. It contains a section that explains the error message levels and how to set them. Change the line that sets your error message level and save the edited `php.ini` file. You may need to restart your Web server before the changes in the PHP configuration file take effect.

In general, PHP doesn't care whether the statements are in upper- or lowercase. Echo, echo, ECHO, and eCHo are all the same to PHP. The exception to this rule is variable names. For variable names, the case does matter. Variables are explained in detail in the next section.

Using PHP Variables

Variables are containers used to hold information. A variable has a name, and information is stored in the variable. For instance, you might name a variable `$age` and store the number 12 in it. After information is stored in a variable, it can be used later in the program. One of the most common uses for variables is to hold the information that a user types into a form.

Naming a variable

When you're naming a variable, keep the following rules in mind:

- All variable names have a dollar sign ($) in front of them. This tells PHP that it is a variable name.
- Variable names can be any length.
- Variable names can include letters, numbers, and underscores.
- Variable names must begin with a letter or an underscore. They cannot begin with a number.
- Upper- and lowercase letters are not the same. `$firstname` and `$Firstname` are not the same variable. If you store information in `$firstname`, you can't access that information by using the variable name `$firstName`.

When you name variables, use names that make it clear what information is in the variable. Using variable names like `$var1`, `$var2`, `$A`, or `$B` does not contribute to the clarity of the program. Although PHP doesn't care what you name the variable and won't get mixed up, people trying to follow the program will have a hard time keeping track of which variable holds what information. Variable names like `$firstName`, `$age`, and `$orderTotal` are much more descriptive and helpful.

Creating and assigning values to variables

Variables can hold either numbers or strings of characters. You store information in variables by using a single equal sign (=). For instance, the following four PHP statements assign information to variables:

```
$age = 12;
$price = 2.55;
$number=-2;
$name = "Goliath Smith";
```

You can now use any of these variable names in an echo statement to see the value in that variable. For instance, if you use the following PHP statement in a PHP section:

```
echo $age;
```

the output is 12. If you include the following line in an HTML file:

```
<p>Your age is <?php echo $age ?>.
```

the output on the Web page is

```
Your age is 12.
```

Whenever you put information into a variable that did not exist before, you create that variable. For instance, suppose you use the following PHP statement:

```
$firstname = "George";
```

If this statement is the first time you've mentioned the variable `$firstname`, this statement creates the variable and sets it to `"George"`. If you have a previous statement setting `$firstname` to `"Mary"`, this statement changes the value of `$firstname` to `"George"`.

You can also remove information from a variable. For example, the following statement takes information out of the variable `$age`:

```
$age = "";
```

The variable has no value. It does not mean that `$age` is set to 0, because zero is a value. It means that `$age` does not store any information at all.

You can go even further and uncreate the variable by using this statement:

```
unset($age);
```

After this statement is executed, the variable `$age` no longer exists.

A variable keeps its information for the whole program, not just for a single PHP section. If a variable is set to `"yes"` at the beginning of a file, it will still hold `"yes"` at the end of the page. For instance, suppose your file has the following statements:

```
<p>Hello World!
<?php
    $age = 15;
$name = "Harry";
?>
<br>Hello World again!<br>
<?php
    echo $name;
?>
```

The echo statement in the second PHP section will display `Harry`. The Web page resulting from these statements is

```
Hello World!
Hello World again!
Harry
```

Dealing with warning messages

If you use a statement that includes a variable that does not exist, you may get a warning message. It depends on the error message level that PHP is set to. Warning messages are not the same as error messages. Warning messages do not mean the program can't run. The program continues to run. Warning messages just tell you that you are doing something unusual and to take a second look at what you are doing to be sure you really want to do it. For instance, suppose you use the following statements:

```
unset($age);
echo $age;
$age2 = $age;
```

You may see two warnings, one for the second statement and one for the third statement. The warning message will look something like this:

```
Warning: Undefined variable: age in testing.php on line 9
```

Suppose you definitely want to use these statements. The program works exactly the way you want it to. The only problems are the unsightly warning messages. You can prevent warning messages within a program by inserting an at sign (@) at the point where the warning message would be issued. For instance, you can prevent the warnings generated by the preceding statements if you change the statements to this:

```
unset($age);
echo @$age;
$age2 = @$age;
```

If you are the PHP administrator, you can change the error message level so that warning messages are not displayed. For details on how to do this, check out the sidebar, "Error messages and warnings," elsewhere in this chapter.

Using PHP Constants

Constants are very similar to variables. Constants are given a name, and a value is stored in them. However, constants are constant; they can't be changed. After you set the value for a constant, it stays the same. If you used a constant for age and set it to 29, it can't be changed. Wouldn't that be nice — 29 forever?

Constants are used when information is used several places in the program and doesn't change during the program. It's useful to set a constant for the value at the beginning of the program and use it throughout the program. By making it a constant, instead of a variable, you make sure it won't get changed accidentally. By giving it a name, you know what the information is instantly. And by setting a constant once at the start of the program, instead of using the value throughout the program, you can change the value in one place, if it needs changing, instead of hunting for it in many places in the program to change it.

For instance, you might set a constant that is the company name and a constant that is the company address and use them wherever needed. Then, if the company moved, you could just change the value in the company address at the start of the program, instead of having to find every place in your program that echoed the company name to change it.

Constants are set using the define statement. The format is

```
define("constantname","constantvalue");
```

For instance, to set a constant with the company name, use the following statement:

```
define("COMPANY","ABC Pet Store");
```

Now use the constant in your program wherever you need your company name:

```
echo COMPANY;
```

When you echo a constant, you can't enclose it in quotes. If you do, it will echo the constant name, instead of the value. You can echo it without anything, as shown in the preceding example, or enclosed with parentheses.

You can use any name for a constant that you can use for a variable, except constant names do not begin with a dollar sign ($). By convention, constants are given names that are all uppercase, so you can see easily that they're constants. However, PHP itself doesn't care what you name a constant. You can store either a string or a number in it. The following statement is perfectly okay with PHP:

```
define ("AGE",29);
```

Just don't expect Mother Nature to believe it.

Working with Numbers

PHP allows you to do mathematical operations on numbers. You indicate mathematical operations by using two numbers and a mathematical operator. For instance, one operator is the plus (+) sign, so you can indicate a mathematical operation like this:

```
1 + 2
```

Table 6-1 shows the mathematical operators that you can use.

Table 6-1 Mathematical Operators

Operator	Description
+	Add two numbers together.
-	Subtract the second number from the first number.
*	Multiply two numbers together.
/	Divide the first number by the second number.
%	Find the remainder when the first number is divided by the second number. This is called *modulus.* For instance, in `$a = 13 % 4`, `$a` is set to `1`.

You can do several mathematical operations at once. For instance, the following statement performs three operations:

```
$result = 1 + 2 * 4 + 1;
```

The order in which the arithmetic is performed is important. You can get different results depending on which operation is performed first. PHP does multiplication and division first, and then addition and subtraction. If other considerations are equal, PHP goes from left to right. Consequently, the preceding statement sets `$result` to `10`, in the following order:

```
$result = 1 + 2 * 4 + 1   (first, it does the multiplication)
$result = 1 + 8 + 1       (next, it does the leftmost addition)
$result = 9 + 1           (next, it does the remaining addition)
$result = 10
```

You can change the order in which the arithmetic is performed by using parentheses. The arithmetic inside the parentheses is performed first. For instance, you can write the previous statement with parentheses like this:

```
$result = (1 + 2) * 4 + 1;
```

This statement sets `$result` to `13`, in the following order:

```
$result = (1 + 2) * 4 + 1  (first, it does the math in the parentheses)
$result = 3 * 4 + 1        (next, it does the multiplication)
$result = 12 + 1           (next, it does the addition)
$result = 13
```

On the better-safe-than-sorry principle, it's best to use parentheses whenever more than one answer is possible.

Often the numbers you work with are dollar amounts, such as product prices. You want your customers to see prices in the proper format on Web pages. In other words, dollar amounts should always have two decimal places. However, PHP stores and displays numbers in the most efficient format. If the number is 10.00, it is displayed as `10`. To put numbers into the proper format for dollars, you can use *sprintf.* The following statement formats a number into a dollar amount:

```
$newvariablename = sprintf("%01.2f", $oldvariablename);
```

This statement reformats the number in *`$oldvariablename`* and stores it in the new format in *`$newvariablename`*. For example, the following statements display money in the correct format:

```
$price = 25;
$f_price = sprintf("%01.2f",$price);
echo "$f_price<br>";
```

You see the following on the Web page:

```
25.00
```

(sprintf can do more than format decimal places. For more information on using sprintf to format values, see Chapter 14.)

If you want commas to separate thousands in your number, you can use number_format. The following statement creates a dollar format with commas:

```
$price = 25000;
$f_price = number_format($price,2);
echo "$f_price<br>";
```

You see the following on the Web page:

```
25,000.00
```

The 2 in the number_format statement sets the format to two decimal places. You can use any number to get any number of decimal places.

Working with Character Strings

A *character string* is a series of characters. Characters are letters, numbers, and punctuation. When a number is used as a character, it is just a stored character, the same as a letter. It can't be used in arithmetic. For instance, a phone number is stored as a character string because it only needs to be stored, not added or multiplied.

When you store a character string in a variable, you tell PHP where the string begins and ends by using double quotes or single quotes. For instance, the following two statements are the same:

```
$string = "Hello World!";
$string = 'Hello World!';
```

Suppose you wanted to store a string as follows:

```
$string = 'It is Tom's house';
echo $string;
```

These statements won't work because when PHP sees the ' (single quote) after Tom, it thinks this is the end of the string. It displays the following:

```
It is Tom
```

You need to tell PHP to interpret the single quote (') as an apostrophe, not as the end of the string. You can do this by using a backslash (\) in front of the single quote. The backslash tells PHP that the single quote does not have any special meaning; it's just an apostrophe. This is called *escaping* the character. Use the following statements to display the entire string:

```
$string = 'It is Tom\'s house';
echo $string;
```

When you enclose a string in double quotes, you must also use a backslash in front of any double quotes in the string.

Single-quoted strings versus double-quoted strings

Single-quoted and double-quoted strings are handled differently. Single-quoted strings are stored literally, with the exception of \', which is stored as an apostrophe. In double-quoted strings, variables and some special characters are evaluated before the string is stored. Here are the most important differences in the use of double or single quotes when writing programs:

- **Handling variables:** If you enclose a variable in double quotes, PHP uses the value of the variable. However, if you enclose a variable in single quotes, PHP uses the literal variable name. For example, if you use the following statements:

  ```
  $age = 12;
  $result1 = "$age";
  $result2 = '$age';
  echo $result1;
  echo $result2;
  ```

  The output is

  ```
  12
  $age
  ```

- **Starting a new line:** The special characters `\n` tell PHP to start a new line. When you use double quotes, PHP starts a new line at `\n`, but with single quotes, `\n` is a literal string. For instance, using the following statements,

  ```
  $string1 = "String in \ndouble quotes";
  $string2 = 'String in \nsingle quotes';
  ```

  `string1` displays as

  ```
  String in
  double quotes
  ```

  and `string2` displays as

  ```
  String in \nsingle quotes
  ```

- **Inserting a tab:** The special characters `\t` tell PHP to insert a tab. When you use double quotes, PHP inserts a tab at `\t`, but with single quotes, `\t` is a literal string. For instance, using the following statements,

  ```
  $string1 = "String in \tdouble quotes";
  $string2 = 'String in \tsingle quotes';
  ```

  `string1` displays as

  ```
  String in     double quotes
  ```

  and `string2` displays as

  ```
  String in \tsingle quotes
  ```

Joining strings together

You can join strings together, a process called *concatenation*, by using a dot (.). For instance, you can join strings with the following statements:

```
$string1 = 'Hello';
$string2 = 'World!';
$stringall = $string1.$string2;
echo $string;
```

The echo statement outputs:

```
HelloWorld!
```

Notice that no space appears between `Hello` and `World`. That's because no spaces are included in the two strings that are joined. You can add a space between the words by using the following concatenation statement rather than the earlier statement:

```
$stringall = $string1." ".$string2;
```

You can also take strings apart. You can separate them at a given character or look for a substring in a string. You use functions to perform these and other operations on a string. Functions are explained in Chapter 7.

Working with Dates and Times

Dates and times can be important elements in a Web database application. PHP has the ability to recognize dates and times and handle them differently than plain character strings. Dates and times are stored by the computer in a format called a *timestamp*. However, this is not a format in which you or I would want to see the date. PHP converts dates from your notation into a timestamp the computer understands and from a timestamp into a format that is familiar to people. PHP handles dates and times using built-in functions.

The timestamp format is a Unix Timestamp, an integer that is the number of seconds from January 1, 1970 00:00:00 GMT to the time represented by the timestamp. This format makes it easy to calculate the time between two dates — just subtract one timestamp from the other.

Formatting a date

The function you will use most often is `date`. `date` converts a date or time from the timestamp format into a format you specify. The general format is

```
$mydate = date("format",$timestamp);
```

`$timestamp` is a variable with a timestamp stored in it. You previously stored the timestamp in the variable, using a PHP function as described later in this section. If `$timestamp` is not included, the current time is obtained from the operating system and used. Thus, you can get today's date with the following statement:

```
$today = date("yyyy/m/d");
```

If today is January 10, 2002, this statements returns:

```
2002/01/10
```

The *format* is a string that specifies the date format you want stored in the variable. For instance, the format `"yy-m-d"` returns 02-1-15 and `"M.d.yyyy"` returns Jan.15.2002. Table 6-2 lists some of the symbols that you can use in the format string. (For a complete list of symbols, see the documentation at `www.php.net`.) The parts of the date can be separated by hyphens (-), dots (.), slashes (/), or spaces.

Table 6-2 Date Format Symbols

Symbol	*Meaning*
`M`	Month in text, abbreviated, such as Jan
`F`	Month in text not abbreviated, such as January
`m`	Month in numbers with leading zeros, such as 02 or 12
`n`	Month in numbers without leading zeros, such as 1 or 12
`d`	Day of the month; two digits with leading zeros, such as 01 or 14
`j`	Day of the month without leading zeros, such as 3 or 30
`l`	Day of the week in text not abbreviated, such as Friday
`D`	Day of the week in text as an abbreviation, such as Fri
`w`	Day of the week in numbers from 0 (Sunday) to 6 (Saturday)
`Y`	Year in four digits, such as 2002
`y`	Year in two digits, such as 02
`g`	Hour between 0 and 12 without leading zeros such as 2 or 10.
`G`	Hour between 0 and 24 without leading zeros, such as 2 or 15
`h`	Hour between 0 and 12 with leading zeros, such as 01 or 10
`H`	Hour between 0 and 24 with leading zeros, such as 00 or 23
`i`	Minutes, such as 00 or 59
`s`	Seconds, such as 00 or 59
`a`	am or pm in lowercase
`A`	AM or PM in uppercase

Storing a timestamp in a variable

You can assign a timestamp with the current date and time to a variable with the following statements:

```
$today = time();
```

You can store a specific date and time as a timestamp using the function `mktime`. The format is

```
$importantDate = mktime(h,m,s,mo,d,y);
```

where *h* is hours, *m* is minutes, *s* is seconds, *mo* is month, *d* is day, and *y* is year. For instance, you would store the date January 15, 2002 using the following statement:

```
$importantDate = mktime(0,0,0,1,15,2002);
```

If you wanted to know how long ago `$importantDate` was, you could subtract it from `$today`. For instance:

```
$timeSpan = $today - $importantDate;
```

This gives you the number of seconds between the important date and today. Or use the statement

```
$timeSpan =(($today - $importantDate)/60)/60
```

to find out the number of hours since the important date.

Using dates with MySQL

Often you want to store a date in your MySQL database. For instance, you might want to store the date a customer made an order or the time a member logged in. MySQL also recognizes dates and time and handles them differently than plain character strings. However, MySQL handles them differently than PHP. In order to use dates and times in your application, you need to understand both the way PHP handles dates, described in the previous few sections, and the way MySQL handles dates.

I discuss the `DATE` and `DATETIME` data types for MySQL in detail in Chapter 4. The following is a summary:

- `DATE`: MySQL date columns expect dates with the year first, the month second, and the day last. The year can be `yyyy` or `yy`. The month can be `mm` or `m`. The day can be `dd` or `d`. The parts of the date can be separated by a hyphen (-), a slash (/), a dot (.), or a space.

- `DATETIME`: MySQL datetime columns expect both the date and the time. The date is formatted as described in the preceding bullet. The date is followed by the time in the format `hh:mm:ss`.

Dates and times must be formatted in the correct MySQL format to store them in your database. PHP functions can be used for formatting. For instance, you can format today's date into a MySQL format using the statement:

```
$today = ("yyyy-m-d");
```

You can format a specific date using the statement:

```
$importantDate = ("yyyy.m.d",mktime(0,0,0,1,15,2002));
```

You can then store the date in a database with an SQL query like this:

```
UPDATE Member SET createDate="$today"
```

Comparing Values

In programs, you often use *conditional statements.* That is, if something is true, you do one thing, but if something is not true, you do something different. Here are two examples of conditional statements:

```
if user is a child
   show toy catalog
if user is not a child
   show electronics catalog
```

In order to know which conditions exist, the program must ask questions. Your program then performs tasks based on the answers. Some questions you might want to ask are

- Is the customer a child? If so, display a toy catalog.
- Which product has more sales? Display the most popular one first.
- Did the customer enter the correct password? If so, display the Members Only Web page.
- Does the customer live in Ohio? If so, display the map to the Ohio store location.

To ask a question in a program, you form a statement that compares values. The program tests the statement and determines whether the statement is true or false. For instance, you can state the preceding questions as:

- The customer is less that 13 years of age. True or false? If true, display the toy catalog.
- Product 1 sales are higher than product 2 sales. True or false? If true, display product 1 first; if false, display product 2 first.
- The customer's password is *secret.* True or false? If true, show the Members Only Web page.
- The customer lives in Ohio. True or false? If true, display a map to the Ohio store location.

Comparisons can be quite simple. For instance, is the first value larger than the second value? Or smaller? Or equal to? But sometimes you need to look at character strings to see whether they have certain characteristics, instead of looking at their exact values. For instance, you might want to identify strings that begin with *S* or strings that look like phone numbers. For this type of comparison, you compare a string to a pattern, which is described in the section "Matching character strings to patterns," later in this chapter.

Making simple comparisons

Simple comparisons compare one value to another value. PHP offers several ways to compare values. Table 6-3 shows the comparisons that are available.

Table 6-3 Comparing Values

Comparison	*Description*
==	Are the two values equal?
>	Is the first value larger than the second value?
>=	Is the first value larger than or equal to the second value?
<	Is the first value smaller than the second value?
<=	Is the first value smaller than or equal to the second value?
!=	Are the two values not equal to each other?
<>	Are the two values not equal to each other?

You can compare both numbers and strings. Strings are compared alphabetically, with all uppercase characters coming before any lowercase characters. For instance, *SS* comes before *Sa.* Characters that are punctuation also have an order, and one character can be found to be larger than another character. However, comparing a comma to a period doesn't have much practical value.

Strings are compared based on their ASCII code. In the ASCII character set, each character is assigned an ASCII code that corresponds to a decimal number between 0 and 127. When strings are compared, they are compared based on this code. For instance, the number that represents the comma is 44. The period corresponds to 46. Therefore, if a period and a comma are compared, the period is seen as larger.

Comparisons are often used to execute statements only under certain conditions. For instance, in the following example, the block of statements is only executed when the comparison `$weather == "raining"` is true:

```
if ( $weather == "raining" )
{
    put up umbrella;
    cancel picnic;
}
```

PHP checks the variable `$weather` to see if it is equal to `"raining"`. If it is, PHP executes the two statements. If `$weather` is not equal to `"raining"`, PHP does not execute the two statements.

The comparison sign is two equal signs (==). One of the most common mistakes is to use a single equal sign for a comparison. A single equal sign puts the value into the variable. Thus, a statement like `if ($weather = "raining")` would set `$weather` to `raining` rather than check whether it already equaled raining, and would always be true.

For example, here's a solution to the programming problem presented at the beginning of this section. The problem is

```
if user is a child
   show toy catalog
if user is not a child
   show electronics catalog
```

To determine whether a customer is an adult, you compare the customer's age to the age when the customer is considered to be an adult. You need to decide at what age a customer would stop being interested in toy catalogs and start being more interested in electronic catalogs. Suppose you decide that 13 seems like the right age. You then ask whether the customer is younger than 13 by comparing the customer's age to 13. If the age is less than 13, show the toy catalog; if the age is 13 or over, show the electronics catalog. These comparisons would have the following format:

```
$age < 13      (is the customer's age less than 13?)
$age >= 13     (is the customer's age greater than or equal to 13?)
```

One way to program the conditional actions is to use the following statements:

```
if ($age < 13)
     $status = "child";
if ($age >= 13)
     $status = "adult";
```

These statements instruct PHP to compare the customer's age to 13. In the first statement, if the customer's age is less than 13, the customer's status is set to `"child"`. In the second statement, if the customer's age is equal to 13 or greater than 13, the customer's status is set to `"adult"`. You then show the toy catalog to customers whose status is `child` and show the electronic catalog to those whose status is `adult`. Although you can write these if statements in a more efficient way, the statements shown will work. A full description of conditional statements is provided in Chapter 7.

Matching character strings to patterns

Sometimes you need to compare character strings to see whether they fit certain characteristics, rather than to see whether they match exact values. For instance, you might want to identify strings that begin with *S* or strings that have numbers in them. For this type of comparison, you compare the string to a pattern. These patterns are called *regular expressions*.

You have probably used some form of pattern matching in the past. For instance, when you use an asterisk (*) as a wild card when searching for files (`dir s*.doc` or `ls s*.txt`), you are pattern matching. For instance, `c*.txt` is a pattern. Any string that begins with a `c` and ends with the string `.txt`, with any characters in between the `c` and the `.txt`, matches the pattern. The strings `cow.txt`, `c3333.txt`, and `c3c4.txt` all match the pattern. Using regular expressions is just a more complicated variation of using wild cards.

The most common use for pattern matching on Web pages is to check the input from a form. If the information doesn't make sense, it's probably not something you want to store in your database. For instance, if the user types a name into a form, you can check to see if it seems like a real name by matching patterns. You know a name consists mainly of letters and spaces. Other valid characters might be a hyphen (-) — for example, Smith-Kline — and a single quote (') — for example, O'Hara. You can check the name by setting up a pattern that is a string containing only letters, spaces, hyphens, and single quotes and matching the name to the pattern. If the name doesn't match — that is, if it contains characters not in the pattern, such as numerals or a question mark (?) — it's not a real name.

Patterns consist of literal characters and special characters. Literal characters are normal characters, with no special meaning. A *c* is a *c* with no meaning other than it's one of 26 letters in the alphabet. Special characters have special meaning in the pattern, such as the asterisk (*) when used as a wild card. Table 6-4 shows the special characters used in patterns.

Table 6-4 Special Characters Used in Patterns

<table>
<tr><th>Character</th><th>Meaning</th><th>Example</th><th>Match</th><th>Not a Match</th></tr>
<tr><td>^</td><td>Beginning of line</td><td>^c</td><td>cat</td><td>my cat</td></tr>
<tr><td>$</td><td>End of line</td><td>c$</td><td>tic</td><td>stick</td></tr>
<tr><td>.</td><td>Any single character</td><td>..</td><td>me, go</td><td>a, men, mean</td></tr>
<tr><td>?</td><td>The preceding character is optional</td><td>mea?n</td><td>mean, men</td><td>moan</td></tr>
<tr><td>( )</td><td>Groups literal characters into a string that must be matched exactly</td><td>m(ea)n</td><td>mean, mn</td><td>men</td></tr>
<tr><td>[ ]</td><td>Encloses a set of optional literal characters</td><td>m[ea]n</td><td>men, man</td><td>mean</td></tr>
<tr><td>[!]</td><td>Encloses a set of non-matching optional characters</td><td>m[!ea]n</td><td>min, mon</td><td>men, man</td></tr>
<tr><td>-</td><td>Represents all the characters between two characters</td><td>m[a-c]n</td><td>man, mbn, mcn</td><td>mdn, mun</td></tr>
<tr><td>+</td><td>One or more of the preceding items</td><td>door[1-3]+</td><td>door111, door131</td><td>door, door55</td></tr>
<tr><td>*</td><td>Zero or more of the preceding items</td><td>door[1-3]*</td><td>door, door311</td><td>door4, door445</td></tr>
<tr><td>{ , }</td><td>The starting and ending number of a range of repetitions</td><td>[0-9]{2,5}</td><td>123, 145</td><td>1, xx3</td></tr>
<tr><td>\</td><td>The following character is literal</td><td>m*n</td><td>m*n</td><td>men, mean</td></tr>
<tr><td>(| |)</td><td>A set of alternate strings</td><td>(Tom|Tommy)</td><td>Tom, Tommy</td><td>Thomas, Tommie</td></tr>
</table>

Literal and special characters are combined to make patterns, sometimes long complicated patterns. A string is compared to the pattern, and if it matches, the comparison is true. Some example patterns follow, with a breakdown of the pattern and some sample matching and non-matching strings:

- `^[A-Z].*` **— strings that begin with an uppercase letter**
  - `^[A-Z]` — uppercase letter at the beginning of the string
  - `.*` — a string of characters that is one or more characters long

  Strings that match:
  - Play it again, Sam
  - I

  Strings that do not match:
  - play it again, Sam
  - i
- `Dear (son|daughter)` **— two alternate strings**
  - `Dear` — literal characters
  - `(son|daughter)` — either son or daughter

  Strings that match:
  - Dear son
  - My Dear daughter

  Strings that do not match:
  - Dear Goliath
  - son
- `^[0-9]{5,5}(\-[0-9]{4,4})?$` **— any zip code**
  - `^[0-9]{5,5}` — any string of five numbers
  - `\-` — a literal
  - `[0-9]{4,4}` — a string of numbers that is four characters long
  - `( )?` — groups the last two parts of the pattern and makes them optional

  Strings that match:
  - 90001
  - 90002-4323

  Strings that do not match:
  - 9001
  - 12-4321

- **`^.+@.+\.com$` — any string with @ embedded that ends in *.com***
  - `^.+` — any string of one or more characters at the beginning
  - `@` — a literal @ (at sign). @ is not a special character
  - `.+` — any string of one or more characters
  - `\.` — a literal dot
  - `com$` — a literal string *com* at the end of the string

  Strings that match:
  - mary@hercompany.com

  Strings that do not match:
  - mary@hercompany.net
  - @mary.com

You can compare a string to a pattern by using *ereg*. The general format is

```
ereg("pattern",value);
```

For instance, to check the name that a user typed in a form, compare the name to a pattern as follows:

```
ereg("^[A-Za-z' -]+$",$name)
```

When you use a literal hyphen (-) in a set that is enclosed with square brackets, the hyphen must be either the first or last character in the set. Otherwise, if it is between two characters, it will be interpreted as a special character indicating a range between the two characters.

Joining Comparisons with And/Or/Xor

Sometimes one comparison is sufficient to check for a condition, but often, you need to ask more than one question. For instance, suppose your company offers catalogs for different products in different languages. You need to know which product the customer wants to see *and* which language he or she needs to see it in. This is the general format for a series of comparisons:

```
comparison and|or|xor comparison and|or|xor comparison and|or|xor ...
```

Comparisons are connected by one of the three following words:

- `and`: Both comparisons are true.
- `or`: One of the comparisons or both of the comparisons are true.
- `xor`: One of the comparisons is true but not both of the comparisons.

Table 6-5 shows some examples of multiple comparisons.

Table 6-5 Multiple Comparisons

Condition	*Is True If*
`$customer == "Smith" or $customer == "Jones"`	The customer is named either Smith or Jones.
`$customer == "Smith" and $custState =="OR"`	The customer is named Smith *and* the customer lives in Oregon.
`$customer == "Smith" or $custState == "OR"`	The customer is named Smith *or* the customer lives in Oregon *or both.*
`$customer == "Smith" xor $custState == "OR"`	The customer is named Smith or the customer lives in Oregon, but *not both.*
`$customer != "Smith" and $custAge < 13`	The customer is named anything except Smith and is under 13 years of age.

You can string together as many comparisons as necessary. The comparisons using `and` are tested first, the comparisons using `xor` are tested next, and the comparisons using `or` are tested last. For instance, the following is a condition that includes three comparisons:

```
$age == 200 or $age == 300 and $name == "Goliath"
```

If the customer's name is Goliath and he is 300 years old, this statement is true. The statement is also true if the customer is 200 years old, regardless of what his name is. This condition is not true if the customer is 300 years old, but his name is not Goliath. You get these results because the program checks the condition as follows:

1. **The `and` is compared.** The program checks `$age` to see if it equals `300`, and it checks `$name` to see if it equals `Goliath`. If both match, the condition is true, and the program does not need to check `or`. If only one or neither of the variables equal the designated value, the testing continues.
2. **The `or` is compared.** The program checks `$age` to see if it equals `200`. If it does, the condition is true. If it does not, the condition is false.

You can change the order in which comparisons are made by using parentheses. The word inside the parentheses is evaluated first. For instance, you can rewrite the previous statement with parentheses as follows:

```
( $age == 200 or $age == 300 ) and $name == "Goliath"
```

The parentheses change the order in which the conditions are checked. Now the `or` is checked first. This condition is true if the customer's name is Goliath and he is either 200 or 300 years old. You get these results because the program checks the condition as follows:

1. **The `or` is compared.** The program checks `$age` to see if it equals either 200 or 300. If it does, this part of the condition is true. However, the comparison on the other side of the `and` must also be true, so the testing continues.
2. **The `and` is compared.** The program checks `$name` to see if it equals Goliath. If it does, the condition is true. If it does not, the condition is false.

Use parentheses liberally, even when you believe you know the order of the comparisons. Unnecessary parentheses can't hurt, but comparisons that have unexpected results can.

If you are familiar with other languages, such as C, you may have used `||` (for *or*) and && (for *and*) in place of the words. The `||` and && work in PHP as well. The statement `$a < $b && $c > $b` is just as valid as the statement `$a < $b and $c > $b`. The `||` is checked before the word *or,* and the && is checked before the word *and.*

Adding Comments to Your Program

Comments are notes that are embedded in the program itself. Adding comments in your programs that describe their purpose and what they do is essential. It's important for the lottery factor; that is, if you win the lottery and run off to a life of luxury on the French Riviera, someone else will have to finish the application. The new person needs to know what your program is supposed to do and how it does it. Actually, comments benefit you as well. You may need to revise the program next year when the details are long buried in your mind under more recent projects.

Use comments liberally. PHP ignores comments; comments are for humans. You can embed comments in your program anywhere as long as you tell PHP that they are comments. The format for comments is

```
/*  comment text
more comment text  */
```

Your comments can be as long or as short as you need. When PHP sees code that indicates the start of a comment (`/*`), it ignores everything until it sees the code that indicates the end of a comment (`*/`).

The following is one possible format for comments at the beginning of each program:

```
/*  name:        catalog.php
    description: Program that displays descriptions of products. The
                 descriptions are stored in a database. The product
                 descriptions are selected from the database based on
                 the category the user entered into a form.
    written by:  Lola Designer
    created:     2/1/02
    modified:    3/15/02
*/
```

You should use comments throughout the program to describe what the program does. Comments are particularly important when the program statements are complicated. Use comments such as the following frequently:

```
/* Get the information from the database */
/* Check whether the customer is over 18 years old */
/* Add shipping charges to the order total */
```

PHP also has a short comment format. You can specify that a single line is a comment by using the pound sign (#) or two slashes (//) in the following manner:

```
# This is comment line 1
// This is comment line 2
```

You can also use # or // in the middle of a line to signal the beginning of a comment. PHP will ignore everything from the # or // to the end of the line. This is useful for commenting a particular statement, as in the following example:

```
$average = $orderTotal/$nItems     // compute average price per item
```

PHP comments are not included in the HTML code that is sent to the user's browser. The user does not see these comments.

Chapter 7

PHP Building Blocks for Programs

In This Chapter

- Echoing output to Web pages
- Assigning values to variables
- Incrementing variables
- Stopping and breaking out of programs
- Creating and using arrays
- Using conditional statements
- Building and using loops for repeated statements
- Using functions

PHP programs are a series of instructions in a file named with an extension (usually `.php` or `.phtml` but can be anything) that tells the Web server to look for PHP sections in the file. PHP begins at the top of the file and executes each instruction, in order, as it comes to it. Instructions are the building blocks of PHP programs.

The basic building blocks are simple statements — a single instruction followed by a semicolon. A simple program consists of a series of simple statements. For example, the Hello World program discussed in Chapter 6 is a simple program. However, the programs that make up a Web database application are not that simple. They are dynamic and interact with both the user and the database. Consequently, the programs require more complex building blocks.

Here are some common programming tasks that require complex building blocks:

- **Storing groups of related values together.** You often have information that is related, such as the description, picture, and price of a product or a list of customers. Storing this information as a group that you can access under one name is efficient and useful. This PHP feature is called an *array.*

- **Setting up statements that execute only when certain conditions are met.** Programs frequently need to do this. For instance, you may want to display a toy catalog to a child and an electronics catalog to an adult. This type of statement is called a *conditional statement.* The PHP conditional statements are the *if* statement and the *case* statement.
- **Setting up a block of statements that is repeated.** You frequently need to repeat statements. For instance, you may want to create a list of all your customers. To do that, you might use two statements: one that gets the customer row from the database, and one that stores the customer name in a list. You would need to repeat these two statements for every row in the customer database. The feature that enables you to do this is called a *loop*. Three types of loops are *for* loops, *while* loops, and *do..while* loops.
- **Writing blocks of statements that can be reused many times.** Many tasks are performed in more than one part of the application. For instance, you may retrieve product information from the database and display it numerous times in an application. Getting and displaying the information may require several statements. Writing a block of statements that displays the product information and using this block repeatedly is much more efficient than writing the statements over again every time you need to display the product information. PHP allows you to reuse statement blocks by creating a *function*.

In this chapter, you find out how to use the building blocks of PHP programs. I describe the most frequently used simple statements and the most useful complex statements and variables. You find out how to construct the building blocks and what they are used for. Then in Chapter 8, you find out how to use these building blocks to move data in and out of a database.

Useful Simple Statements

A simple statement is a single instruction followed by a semicolon (;). Here are some useful simple statements used in PHP programs:

- **echo statement:** Produces output that browsers handle as HTML.
- **assignment statement:** Assigns values to variables.
- **increment statement:** Increases or decreases numbers in variables.
- **exit statement:** Stops the execution of your program.
- **function call:** Uses stored blocks of statements at any location in a program.

I discuss these simple statements and when to use them in the following few sections.

Using echo statements

You use echo statements to produce output. The output from an echo statement is sent to the user's browser, which handles the output as HTML.

The general format of an echo statement is

```
echo outputitem,outputitem,outputitem...
```

where the following rules apply:

- An `outputitem` can be a string or a variable.
- List as many `outputitem`s as you need.
- Separate each `outputitem` with a comma.
- If an `outputitem` includes a space, enclose it in a double or single quote. The difference between double and single quotes is explained in Chapter 6.
- The output from `outputitem`s is separated by spaces. For instance, the two `outputitem`s, `Hello,World`, would be output as `Hello World`.

Table 7-1 shows some echo statements and their output. For the purposes of the table, assume that `$string1` is set to `Hello` and `$string2` is set to `World!`.

Table 7-1 Echo Statements

Echo Statement	*Output*
`echo Hello;`	`Hello`
`echo Hello,World!;`	`Hello World!`
`echo Hello World!;`	Not valid; results in an error message
`echo "Hello World!";`	`Hello World!`
`echo 'Hello World!';`	`Hello World!`
`echo $string1;`	`Hello`
`echo $string1,$string2;`	`Hello World!`
`echo "$string1 $string2";`	`Hello World!`
`echo "Hello",$string2;`	`Hello World!`
`echo "Hello", "$string2";`	`Hello World!`
`echo '$string1',"$string2";`	`$string1 World!`

Double quotes and single quotes have different effects on variables. When you use single quotes, variable names are echoed as is. When you use double quotes, variable names are replaced by the variable values.

You can separate variable names with curly braces ({}). For instance, the following statements

```
$pet = "bird";
echo "The $petcage has arrived.";
```

will not output `bird` as the `$pet` variable. In other words, the output will not be `The birdcage has arrived.` Rather, PHP will look for the variable `$petcage` and won't be able to find it. You can echo the correct output by using curly braces to separate the `$pet` variable:

```
$pet = "bird";
echo "The {$pet}cage has arrived.";
```

The preceding statement will output:

```
The birdcage has arrived.
```

Echo statements output a line of text that is sent to a browser. The browser considers the text to be HTML and handles it that way. Therefore, you need to make sure that your output is valid HTML code that describes the Web page you want the user to see.

When you want to display a Web page (or part of a Web page) using PHP, you need to consider three stages in producing the Web page:

- **The PHP program:** PHP echo statements that you write.
- **The HTML source code:** The source code for the Web page that you see when you choose View⇨Source in your browser. The source code is the output from the echo statements.
- **The Web page:** The Web page that your users see. The Web page results from the HTML source code.

The echo statements send exactly what you echo to the browser — no more, no less. If you do not echo any HTML tags, none are sent.

PHP allows some special characters that format output, but they are not HTML tags. The PHP special characters only affect the output from the echo statement, not the display on the Web page. For instance, if you want to start a new line in the PHP output, you must include a special character (`\n`) that tells PHP to start a new line. However, this special character just starts a new line in the output; it does *not* send an HTML tag to start a new line on the Web page. Table 7-2 shows examples of the three stages.

Table 7-2 Stages of Web Page Delivery

Echo Statement	*HTML Source Code*	*Web Page Display*
`echo "Hello World!";`	`Hello World!`	`Hello World!`
`echo "Hello World!";` `echo "Here I am!";`	`Hello World!` `Here I am!`	`Hello World!Here I am!`
`echo "Hello World!\n";` `echo "Here I am!";`	`Hello World!` `Here I am`	`Hello World! Here I am!`
`echo "Hello World! \n"` `echo "Here I am!"`	`Hello World! ` `Here I am!"`	`Hello World!` `Here I am!`

Table 7-2 summarizes the differences between the stages in creating a Web page with PHP. To look at these differences more closely, consider the following two echo statements:

```
echo "Line 1";
echo "Line 2";
```

If you put these lines in a program, you might *expect* the Web page to display the following:

```
Line 1
Line 2
```

However, this is *not* the output you would get. The Web page would actually display this:

```
Line 1Line 2
```

If you look at the source code for the Web page, you see exactly what is sent to the browser, which is this:

```
Line 1Line 2
```

Notice that the line that is output and sent to the browser contains exactly the characters that you echoed — no more, no less. The character strings you echoed did not contain any spaces, so no spaces appear between the lines.

Also, notice that the two lines are echoed on the same line. If you want a new line to start, you have to send a signal indicating the start of that a new line. To signal that a new line starts here in PHP, echo the special character `\n`. Change the echo statements to the following:

```
echo "line 1\n";
echo "line 2";
```

Now you get what you want, right? Well, actually no. Now you see the following on the Web page:

```
line 1 line 2
```

If you look at the source code, you see this:

```
line 1
line 2
```

So, the `\n` did its job: It started a new line in the output. However, HTML displays the output on the Web page as one line. If you want HTML to display two lines, you must use a tag, such as the `<br>` tag. So, change the PHP end of line special character to an HTML tag, as follows:

```
echo "line 1<br>";
echo "line 2";
```

Now you see what you want on the Web page:

```
line 1
line 2
```

If you look at the source code for this output, you see this:

```
line 1<br>line 2
```

Use `\n` liberally. Otherwise, your HTML source code will have some really long lines. For instance, if you echo a long form, the whole thing might be one long line in the source code, even though it looks fine in the Web page. Use `\n` to break the HTML source code into reasonable lines. Taking the extra time to add these breaks will pay off if you have to troubleshoot a Web page that does not look the way you expected. It's much easier to examine the source code if it's not one mile-long line.

Using assignment statements

Assignment statements are statements that assign values to variables. The variable name is listed to the left of the equal sign; the value to be assigned to the variable is listed to the right of the equal sign. Here is the general format:

```
$variablename = value;
```

The *value* can be a single value or a combination of values, including values in variables. A variable can hold numbers or characters, but not both at the same time. Therefore, a value cannot be a combination of numbers and characters. The following are valid assignment statements:

```
$number = 2;
$number = 2+1;
$number = (2 - 1) * (4 * 5) -17;
$number2 = $number + 3;
$string = "Hello World";
$string2 = $string." again!";
```

If you combine numbers and strings in a value, you won't get an error message; you'll just get unexpected results. For instance, the following statements combine numbers and strings:

```
$number = 2;
$string = "Hello";
$combined = $number + $string;
$combined2 = $number.$string;
echo $combined;
echo $combined2;
```

The output of these statements is

```
2          ($string is evaluated as 0)
2Hello     ($number is evaluated as a character)
```

Using increment statements

Often a variable is used as a *counter.* For instance, suppose you want to be sure that everyone sees your company logo, so you display it three times. You set a variable to 0. Each time you display the logo, you add 1 to the variable. When the value of the variable reaches 3, you know that it's time to stop showing the logo. The following statements show the use of a counter:

```
$counter=0;
$counter = $counter + 1;
echo $counter;
```

These statements would output `1`. Because counters are used so often, PHP provides shortcuts. The following statements have the same effect as the preceding statements:

```
$counter=0;
$counter++;
echo $counter;
```

This echo statement also outputs `1`, because ++ adds 1 to the current value of `$counter`. Or you can use the following statement:

```
$counter--;
```

This statement subtracts 1 from the current value of `$counter`.

Sometimes you may want to do a different mathematical operation. You can use any of the following shortcuts:

```
$counter=+2;
$counter=-3;
$counter=*2;
$counter=/3;
```

These statements add 2 to `$counter`, subtract 3 from `$counter`, multiply `$counter` by 2, and divide `$counter` by 3, respectively.

Using exit

Sometimes you want the program to stop executing, just stop at some point in the middle of the program. For instance, if the program encounters an error, often you want it to stop, rather than continue with more statements. The exit statement stops the program. No more statements are executed after the exit statement. The format of an exit statement is

```
exit("message");
```

The *`message`* is a message that is output when the program exits. For instance, you might use the statement

```
exit("The program is exiting");
```

You can also stop the program with the die statement, as follows:

```
die("The program is dying");
```

The die statement is the same as the exit statement. Die is just another name for exit. Sometimes it's just more fun to say die.

Using function calls

Functions are blocks of statements that perform certain specified tasks. You can think of functions as mini-programs or sub-programs. The block of statements is stored under a function name, and you can execute the block of statements any place you want by *calling* the function by its name. (For details on how to use functions, check out the section, "Using Functions," later in this chapter.)

You can call a function by listing its name followed by parentheses, like this:

```
functionname();
```

For instance, you might have a function that gets all the names of customers that reside in a certain state from the database and displays the names in a list in the format *last name, first name.* You write the statements that do these tasks and store them as a function under the name `get_names`. Then when you call the function, you need to specify which state. You can use the following statement at any location in your program to get the list of customer names from the given state, which in this case is California:

```
get_names('CA');
```

The value in the parentheses is given to the function so it knows which state you're specifying. This is called *passing* the value. You can pass a list of values.

PHP provides many built-in functions. For example, in Chapter 6 I discuss a built-in function called `unset`. You can uncreate a variable named `$testvar` by using this function call:

```
unset($testvar);
```

Using PHP Arrays

Arrays are complex variables. An *array* stores a group of values under a single variable name. An array is useful for storing related values. For instance, you can store information about a shirt, such as size, color, and cost, in a single array named `$shirtinfo`. Information in an array can be handled, accessed, and modified easily. For instance, PHP has several methods for sorting an array.

The following few sections give you the lowdown on arrays.

Creating arrays

The simplest way to create an array is to assign a value to a variable with square brackets ([ ]) at the end of its name. For instance, assuming that you have not referenced `$pets` at any earlier point in the program, the following statement creates an array called `$pets`:

```
$pets[1] = "dragon";
```

At this point, the array named `$pets` has been created and has only one value — dragon. Next, you use the following statements:

```
$pets[2] = "unicorn";
$pets[3] = "tiger";
```

Now, the array `$pets` contains three values: dragon, unicorn, and tiger.

An array can be viewed as a list of *key/value pairs.* To get a particular value, you specify the *key* in the brackets. In the preceding array, the keys are numbers — 1, 2, and 3. However, you can also use words for keys. For instance, the following statements create an array of state capitals:

```
$capitals['CA'] = "Sacramento";
$capitals['TX'] = "Austin";
$capitals['OR'] = "Salem";
```

You can use shortcuts rather than write separate assignment statements for each number. One shortcut uses the following statements:

```
$pets[] = "dragon";
$pets[] = "unicorn";
$pets[] = "tiger";
```

When you create an array using this shortcut, the values are automatically assigned keys that are serial numbers, starting with the number 0. For example, the following statement:

```
echo "$pets[0]";
```

sends the following output:

```
dragon
```

The first value in an array with a numbered index is 0, unless you deliberately set it to a different number. One common mistake when working with arrays is to think of the first number as 1, rather than 0.

An even better shortcut is to use the following statement:

```
$pets = array ( "dragon","unicorn","tiger");
```

This statement creates the same array as the preceding shortcut. It assigns numbers as keys, starting with 0. You can use a similar statement to create arrays with words as keys. For example, the following statement creates the array of state capitals:

```
$capitals = array ( "CA" => "Sacramento", "TX" => "Austin",
                    "OR" => "Salem" );
```

Removing values from arrays

Sometimes you need to completely remove a value from an array. For example, suppose you have the following array:

```
$pets = array ( "dragon", "unicorn", "tiger", "parrot", "scorpion" );
```

This array has five values. Now you decide that you no longer want to carry scorpions in your pet store, so you use the following statement to try to remove scorpion from the array:

```
$pets[4] = "";
```

Although this statement sets `$pets[4]` to null, it does not remove it from the array. You still have an array with five values, one of the values being null. To totally remove the item from the array, you need to unset it with the following statement:

```
unset($pets[4]);
```

Now your array has only four values in it.

Sorting arrays

One of the most useful features of arrays is that PHP will sort them for you. It sorts in a variety of ways. For example, the following statement sorts the `$pets` array:

```
sort ($pets);
```

This statement sorts by the values and assigns new keys that are the appropriate numbers. The values are sorted with numbers first, uppercase letters next, and lowercase letters last. For instance, consider the `$pets` array created in the preceding section:

```
$pets[0] = "dragon";
$pets[1] = "unicorn";
$pets[2] = "tiger";
```

After the following sort statement,

```
sort ($pets);
```

the array becomes

```
$pets[0] = "dragon";
$pets[1] = "tiger";
$pets[2] = "unicorn";
```

To sort arrays that have words for keys, use the asort statement as follows:

```
asort ($capitals);
```

This statement sorts the capitals by value, but keeps the original key for each value, instead of assigning a number key. For instance, consider the state capitals array created in the preceding section:

```
$capitals['CA'] = "Sacramento";
$capitals['TX'] = "Austin";
$capitals['OR'] = "Salem";
```

After the following sort statement,

```
asort ($capitals);
```

the array becomes

```
$capitals['TX'] = "Austin";
$capitals['CA'] = "Sacramento";
$capitals['OR'] = "Salem";
```

There are several other sort statements that sort in other ways. Table 7-3 lists all the available sort statements.

Table 7-3 Ways You Can Sort Arrays

Sort Statement	*What It Does*
`sort ($arrayname)`	Sorts by value; assigns new numbers as the keys
`asort ($arrayname)`	Sorts by value; keeps the same key
`rsort ($arrayname)`	Sorts by value in reverse order; assigns new numbers as the keys
`arsort ($arrayname)`	Sorts by value in reverse order; keeps the same key
`ksort ($arrayname)`	Sorts by key
`krsort ($arrayname)`	Sorts by key in reverse order
`usort ($arrayname,functionname)`	Sorts by a function (see "Using Functions," later in this chapter)

Getting values from arrays

You can retrieve any individual value in an array by accessing it directly. Here is an example:

```
$CAcapital = $capitals['CA'];
echo $CAcapital ;
```

The output from these statements is

```
Sacramento
```

You can echo an array value like this:

```
echo $capitals['TX'];
```

If you include the array value in a longer echo statement that's enclosed by double quotes, you may need to enclose the array value name in curly braces like this:

```
echo "The capital of Texas is {$capitals['TX']}<br>";
```

You can get several values at once from an array with the *list* statement. The list statement gets values from an array and puts them into variables. The following statements include a list statement:

```
$shirtInfo = array ("large", "blue", 12.00);
sort ($shirtInfo);
list($firstvalue,$secondvalue) = $shirtInfo;
echo $firstvalue,"<br>";
echo $secondvalue,"<br>";
```

The first line creates the `$shirtInfo` array. The second line sorts the array. The third line sets up two variables named `$firstvalue` and `$secondvalue` and copies the first two values in `$shirtInfo` into the two new variables, as if you had used the two statements

```
$firstvalue=$shirtInfo[0];
$secondvalue=$shirtInfo[1];
```

The third value in `$shirtInfo` is not copied into a variable because there are only two variables in the list statement. The output from the echo statements is

```
blue
large
```

Notice that the output is in alphabetical order, not in the order in which the values were entered. It's in alphabetical order because the array is sorted after it is created.

In some cases, you may want to retrieve the key from an array, instead of the value. For instance, the following statements retrieve a key:

```
$shirtInfo = array ("size" => "large", "color" => "blue",
                    "cost" => 12.00);
$value = $shirtInfo['size'];
$key = key($shirtInfo);
echo "$key: $value<br>";
```

The output from these statements is

```
size: large
```

You can retrieve all the values from an array with words as keys using extract. Each value is copied into a variable named for the key. For instance, the following statements get all the information from `$shirtInfo` and echo it:

```
extract($shirtInfo);
echo "size is $size; color is $color; cost is $cost";
```

The output for these statements is

```
size is large; color is blue; cost is 12.00;
```

Walking through an array

You will often want to do something to every value in an array. You may want to echo each value, store each value in the database, or add six to each value in the array. In technical talk, walking through each and every value in an array, in order, is called *iteration*. It is also sometimes called *traversing*. Here are two ways to walk through an array:

- **Manually:** Move a pointer from one array value to another
- **Using foreach:** Automatically walk through the array, from beginning to end, one value at a time

Manually

You can walk through an array manually by using a pointer. To do this, think of your array as a list. Imagine a pointer pointing to a value in the list. The pointer stays on a value until you move it. After you move it, it stays there until you move it again. You can move the pointer with the following instructions:

- `current($`*`arrayname`*`)`: Refers to the value currently under the pointer; does not move the pointer
- `next($`*`arrayname`*`)`: Moves the pointer to the value after the current value
- `previous($`*`arrayname`*`)`: Moves the pointer to the value above the current pointer location
- `end($`*`arrayname`*`)`: Moves the pointer to the last value in the array
- `reset($`*`arrayname`*`)`: Moves the pointer to the first value in the array

The following statements manually walk through an array containing state capitals:

```
$value = current ($capitals);
echo "$value<br>;
$value = next ($capitals);
echo "$value<br>;
$value = next ($capitals);
echo "$value<br>;
```

Using this method to walk through an array, you need an assignment statement and an echo statement for every value in the array — for each of the 50 states. The output is a list of all the state capitals.

This method gives you flexibility. You can move through the array in any manner, not just one value at a time. You can move backwards, go directly to the end, skip every other value by using two next statements in a row, or whatever method is useful. However, if you want to go through the array from beginning to end, one value at a time, PHP provides *foreach,* which does exactly what you need much more efficiently. Foreach is described in the next section.

Using foreach

Foreach walks through the array one value at a time and executes the block of statements using each value in the array. The general format is

```
foreach ( $arrayname as $keyname => $valuename  )
{
    block of statements;
}
```

Fill in the following information:

- `arrayname`: The name of the array that you are walking through.
- `keyname`: The name of the variable where you want to store the key. *`Keyname`* is optional. If you leave out `$keyname =>`, the value is put into `$valuename`.
- `valuename`: The name of the variable where you want to store the value.

For instance, the following foreach statement walks through the sample array of state capitals and echoes a list:

```
$capitals = array ( "CA" => "Sacramento", "TX" => "Austin",
                    "OR" => "Salem" );
ksort ($capitals);
foreach ( $capitals as $state => $city )
{
    echo "$city, $state<br>";
}
```

The preceding statements give the following Web page output:

```
Sacramento, CA
Salem, OR
Austin, TX
```

You can use the following line in place of the foreach line in the previous statements:

```
foreach ( $capitals as $city )
```

The output using this line is

```
Sacramento
Salem
Austin
```

When foreach starts walking through an array, it moves the pointer to the beginning of the array. You don't need to reset an array before walking through it with foreach.

Multidimensional arrays

In the earlier sections of this chapter, I describe arrays that are a single list of key/value pairs. However, on some occasions, you might want to store values with more than one key. For instance, suppose you want to store these product prices together in one variable:

- shirt, 20.00
- pants, 22.50
- blanket, 25.00
- bedspread, 50.00
- lamp, 44.00
- rug, 75.00

You can store these products in an array as follows:

```
$productPrices['shirt'] = 20.00;
$productPrices['pants'] = 22.50;
$productPrices['blanket'] = 25.00;
$productPrices['bedspread'] = 50.00;
$productPrices['lamp'] = 44.00;
$productPrices['rug'] = 75.00;
```

Your program can easily look through this array whenever it needs to know the price of an item. But suppose you have 3,000 products. Your program would need to look through 3,000 products to find the one with *shirt* or *rug* as the key.

Notice that the list of products and prices includes a wide variety of products that can be classified into groups: clothing, linens, and furniture. If you classify the products, then the program would only need to look through one classification to find the correct price. Classifying the products would be much more efficient. You can classify the products by putting the costs in a multidimensional array as follows:

```
$productPrices['clothing']['shirt'] = 20.00;
$productPrices['clothing']['pants'] = 22.50;
$productPrices['linens']['blanket'] = 25.00;
```

```
$productPrices['linens']['bedspread'] = 50.00;
$productPrices['furniture']['lamp'] = 44.00;
$productPrices['furniture']['rug'] = 75.00;
```

This kind of array is called a *multidimensional* array because it's like an array of arrays. Figure 7-1 shows the structure of `$productPrices` as an array of arrays. The figure shows that `$productPrices` has three key/value pairs. The keys are clothing, linens, and furniture. The value for each key is an array with two key/value pairs. For instance, the value for the key *clothing* is an array with the two key/value pairs: *shirt/20.00* and *pants/22.50.*

$productPrices	key	value	
		key	*value*
	clothing	shirt	20.00
		pants	22.50
	linens	blanket	30.00
		bedspread	50.00
	furniture	lamp	44.00
		rug	75.00

Figure 7-1: The structure of `$productPrices`, an array of arrays.

`$productPrices` is a two-dimensional array. PHP can also understand multidimensional arrays that are four, five, six, or more levels deep. However, my head starts to hurt if I try to comprehend an array that is more than three levels deep. The possibility of confusion increases as the number of dimensions increases.

You can get values from a multidimensional array by using the same procedures that you use with a one-dimensional array. For instance, you can access a value directly with this statement:

```
$shirtPrice = $productPrices['clothing']['shirt'];
```

You can also echo the value:

```
echo $productPrices['clothing']['shirt'];
```

However, if you combine the value within double quotes, you need to use curly braces to enclose the variable name. The $ that begins the variable name must follow the { immediately, without a space, as follows:

```
echo "The price of a shirt is \${$productPrices['clothing']['shirt']}";
```

Notice the backslash (\) in front of the first dollar sign ($). The backslash tells PHP that $ is a literal dollar sign, not the beginning of a variable name. The output is

```
The price of a shirt is $20
```

You can walk through a multidimensional array by using foreach statements (described in the preceding section). You need a foreach statement for each array. One foreach statement is inside the other foreach statement. Putting statements inside other statements is called *nesting*.

Because a two-dimensional array, such as `$productPrices`, contains two arrays, it takes two foreach statements to walk through it. The following statements get the values from the multidimensional array and output them in an HTML table:

```
echo "<table border=1>";
foreach ( $productPrices as $category )
{
   foreach ( $category as $product => $price )
   {
     $f_price = sprintf("%01.2f", $price);
     echo "<tr><td>$product:</td><td>\$$f_price</td></tr>";
   }
}
echo "</table>";
```

Figure 7-2 shows the Web page produced with these PHP statements.

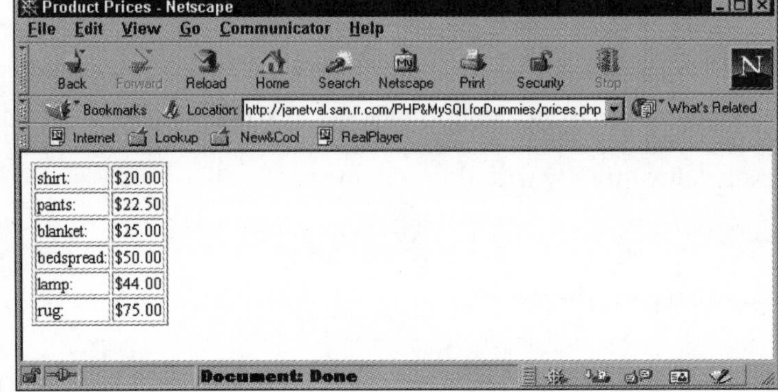

Figure 7-2: The Web page output for the multidimensional array `$productPrices`.

Here is how the program interprets these statements:

1. Outputs the `table` tag.
2. Gets the first key/value pair in the `$productPrices` array and stores the value in the variable `$category`. The value is an array.

3. Gets the first key/value pair in the `$category` array. Stores the key in `$product` and stores the value in `$price`.
4. Formats the value in `$price` into the correct format for money.
5. Echoes one table row for the product and its price.
6. Goes to the next key/value pair in the `$category` array.
7. Formats the price and echoes the next table row for the product and its price.
8. Because there are no more key/value pairs in `$category`, the inner foreach statement ends.
9. Goes to the next key/value pair in the outer foreach statement. Puts the next value in `$category`, which is an array.
10. Repeats the procedure in Steps 2 through 9 until the last key/value pair in the last `$category` array is reached. The inner foreach statement ends. The outer foreach statement ends.
11. Outputs the `/table` tag to end the table.

In other words, the outer foreach starts with the first key/value pair in the array. The key is `clothing`, and the value of this pair is an array that is put into the variable `$category`. The inner foreach then walks through the array in `$category`. When it reaches the last key/value pair in `$category`, it ends. The program is then back in the outer loop, which goes on to the second key/value pair . . . and so on until the outer foreach reaches the end of the array.

Useful Conditional Statements

A *conditional statement* executes a block of statements only when certain conditions are met. Here are two useful types of conditional statements:

- **if statement:** Sets up a condition and tests it. If the condition is true, a block of statements is executed.
- **switch statement:** Sets up a list of alternative conditions. Tests for the condition and executes the appropriate block of statements.

I describe these statements in more detail in the following two sections.

Using if statements

An *if* statement asks whether certain conditions exist. A block of statements executes depending on which conditions are met. The general format of an if conditional statement is

```
if ( condition ... )
{
   block of statements
}
elseif  ( condition ... )
```

```
{
   block of statements
}
else
{
   block of statements
}
```

The if statement consists of three sections:

- **if:** This section is required. It tests a condition.
  - **If condition is true:** The block of statements is executed. After the statements are executed, the program moves to the next instruction following the conditional statement; if the conditional statement contains any elseif or else sections, the program skips over them.
  - **If condition is not true:** The block of statements is not executed. The program skips to the next instruction, which can be an elseif, an else, or the next instruction after the if conditional statement.
- **elseif:** This section is optional. It tests a condition. You can use more than one elseif section if you want.
  - **If condition is true:** The block of statements is executed. After executing the block of statements, the program goes to the next instruction following the conditional statement; if the if statement contains any additional elseif sections or an else section, the program skips over them.
  - **If condition is not true:** The block of statements is not executed. The program skips to the next instruction, which can be an elseif, an else, or the next instruction after the if conditional statement.
- **else:** This section is optional. Only one else section is allowed. This section does not test a condition, rather it executes the block of statements. If the program has entered this section, it means that the if section and all the elseif sections are not true.

Each section of the if conditional statement tests a condition that consists of one or more comparisons. A comparison asks a question that can be true or false. Some conditions are

```
$a == 1;
$a < $b
$c != "Hello"
```

The first comparison asks if `$a` is equal to `1`; the second comparison asks if `$a` is smaller than `$b`; the third comparison asks if `$c` is not equal to

"Hello". You can use two or more comparisons in a condition by connecting the comparisons with and, or, or xor. I discuss comparing values and using more than one comparison in detail in Chapter 6.

The following example uses all three sections of the if conditional statement. Suppose you have a German, French, Italian, and English version of your product catalog. You want your program to display the correct language version, based on where the customer lives. The following statements set a variable to the correct catalog version, depending on the country where the customer lives, and set a message in the correct language. You can then display the appropriate catalog based on the value of the variable $version.

```
if ($country == "Germany" )
{
   $version = "German";
   $message = " Sie sehen unseren Katalog auf Deutsch";
}
elseif ($country == "France" )
{
   $version = "French";
   $message = " Vous verrez notre catalogue en francais";
}
elseif ($country == "Italy" )
{
   $version = "Italian";
   $message = " Vedrete il nostro catalogo in Italiano";
}
else
{
  $version = "English";
  $message = "You will see our catalog in English";
}
echo "$message<br>";
```

The if conditional statement proceeds as follows:

1. **Compares the variable $country to "Germany".** If they are the same, $version is set to "German", $message is set in German, and the program skips to the echo statement. If $country does *not* equal Germany, $version and $message are *not* set, and the program skips to the elseif section.
2. **Compares the variable $country to "France".** If they are the same, $version and $message are set, and the program skips to the echo statement. If $country does *not* equal France, $version and $message are *not* set, and the program skips to the second elseif section.
3. **Compares the variable $country to "Italy".** If they are the same, $version is set to "Italian", and the program skips to the echo statement. If $country does *not* equal Italy, $version and $message are *not* set, and the program skips to the else section.
4. **$version is set to English, and $message is set in English.** The program continues to the echo statement.

When the block to be executed by any section of the if conditional statement contains only one statement, the curly braces are not needed. For instance, if the preceding example only had one statement in the blocks, as follows:

```
if ($country == "France")
{
   $version = "French";
}
```

You could write it as follows:

```
if ($country == "France" )
   $version = "French";
```

This shortcut can save some typing, but when several if statements are used, it can lead to confusion.

You can have an if conditional statement inside another if conditional statement. Putting one statement inside another is called *nesting*. For instance, suppose you need to contact all your customers who live in Idaho. You plan to send e-mail to those who have an e-mail address and send a letter to those who do not have an e-mail address. You can identify the groups of customers using the following nested if statements:

```
if ( $custState == "ID" )
{
   if ( $EmailAdd != "" )
   {
     $contactMethod = "letter";
   }
   else
   {
     $contactMethod = "email";
   }
}
else
{
   $contactMethod = "none needed";
}
```

These statements first check to see if the customer lives in Idaho. If the customer does live in Idaho, the program tests for an e-mail address. If the e-mail address is blank, the contact method is set to letter. If the e-mail address is not blank, the contact method is email. If the customer does not live in Idaho, the else section sets the contact method to indicate that the customer will not be contacted at all.

Using switch statements

For most situations, the if conditional statement works best. However, sometimes you have a list of conditions and want to execute different statements for each of the conditions. For instance, suppose your program computes sales tax. How do you handle the different state sales tax rates? The switch statement was designed for such situations.

The switch statement tests the value of one variable and executes the block of statements for the matching value of the variable. The general format is

```
switch ( $variablename )
{
  case value :
     block of statements;
     break;
  case value :
     block of statements;
     break;
  ...
  default:
     block of statements;
     break;
}
```

The switch statement tests the value of `$variablename`. The program then skips to the case section for that value and executes statements until it reaches a break statement or the end of the switch statement. If there is no case section for the value of `$variablename`, the program executes the default section. You can use as many case sections as you need. The default section is optional. If you use a default section, it's customary to put the default section at the end, but it can go anywhere.

The following statements set the sales tax rate for different states:

```
switch ( $custState )
{
  case "OR" :
     $salestaxrate = 0;
     break;
  case "CA" :
     $salestaxrate = 1.0;
     break;
  default:
     $salestaxrate = .5;
     break;
}
$salestax = $orderTotalCost * $salestaxrate;
```

In this case, the tax rate for Oregon is 0, the tax rate for California is 100 percent, and the tax rate for all the other states is 50 percent. The switch statement looks at the value of `$custState` and skips to the section that matches the value. For instance, if `$custState` is `TX`, the program executes the default section and sets `$salestaxrate` to `.5`. After the switch statement, the program computes `$salestax` at `.5` times the cost of the order.

The break statements are essential in the case section. If a case section does not include a break statement, the program does *not* stop executing at the end of the case section. The program continues executing statements past the end of the case section, on to the next case section, and continues until it reaches the end of the switch statement.

The last case section in a switch statement doesn't actually require a break statement. You can leave it out. However, it's a good idea to include it for clarity.

Using Loops

Loops are used frequently in programs. Loops set up a block of statements that repeat. Sometimes, the loop repeats a specified number of times. For instance, a loop to echo all the state capitals needs to repeat 50 times. Sometimes, the loop repeats until a certain condition exists. For instance, a loop that displays product information for all the products needs to repeat until it has displayed all the products, regardless of how many products there are. Here are three types of loops:

- **basic for loop:** Sets up a counter; repeats a block of statements until the counter reaches a specified number
- **while loop:** Sets up a condition; checks the condition, and if it is true, repeats a block of statements
- **do..while loop:** Sets up a condition; executes a block of statements; checks the condition; if the condition is true, repeats the block of statements

I describe each of these loops in detail in the following few sections.

Using for loops

The most basic *for* loops are based on a counter. You set the beginning value for the counter, set the ending value, and set how the counter is incremented. The general format is

```
for (startingvalue;endingvalue;increment)
{
    block of statements;
}
```

Fill in the following values:

- `startingvalue`: A statement that sets up a variable to be your counter and sets it to your starting value. For instance, the statement `$i=1;` sets `$i` as the counter variable and sets it equal to `1`. Frequently, the counter variable is started at 0 or 1. The starting value can be a combination of numbers (2 + 2) or a variable.
- `endingvalue`: A statement that sets your ending value. As long as this statement is true, the block of statements keeps repeating. When this statement is not true, the loop ends. For instance, the statement `$i < 10;`

sets the ending value for the loop to 10. When `$i` is equal to 10, the statement is no longer true (because `$i` is no longer less than 10), and the loop stops repeating. The statement can include variables, such as `$i < $size;`.

- *`increment`*: A statement that increments your counter. For instance, the statement `$i++;` adds 1 to your counter at the end of each block of statements. You can use other increment statements, such as `$i=+1;` or `$i--;`.

The basic for loop sets up a variable — for example, a variable called `$i` — that is a counter. This variable has a value during each loop. The variable `$i` can be used in the block of statements that is repeating. For instance, the following simple loop displays `Hello World!` three times:

```
for ($i=1;$i<=3;$i++)
{
  echo "$i. Hello World!<br>";
}
```

The statements in the block do not need to be indented. PHP doesn't care whether they're indented. However, indenting the blocks makes it much easier for you to understand the program.

The output from these statements is

```
1. Hello World!
2. Hello World!
3. Hello World!
```

For loops are particularly useful to loop through an array. Suppose you have an array of customer names and want to display them all. You can do this easily with a loop:

```
for ($i=0;$i<100;$i++)
{
  echo "$customerNames[$i]<br>"
}
```

The output displays a Web page with a list of all the customer names, one on each line. In this case, you know you have 100 customer names, but suppose you don't know how many customers are in this list. You can ask PHP how many values are in the array and use that value in your for loop. For example, you can use the following statements:

```
for ($i=0;$i<sizeof($customerNames);$i++)
{
   echo "$customerNames[$i]<br>"
}
```

Notice that the ending value is `sizeof($customerNames)`. This statement finds out the number of values in the array and uses that number. That way, your loop repeats exactly the number of times that there are values in the array.

The first value in an array with a numbered index is 0, unless you deliberately set it to a different number. One common mistake when working with arrays is to think of the first number as 1, rather than 0.

Using while loops

A *while* loop continues repeating as long as certain conditions are true. The loop works as follows:

1. You set up a condition.
2. The condition is tested at the top of each loop.
3. If the condition is true, the loop repeats. If the condition is not true, the loop stops.

Advanced *for* loops

The structure of a for loop is quite flexible and allows you to build loops for almost any purpose. A for loop has this general format:

```
for ( beginning statements;
      conditional statements;
      ending statements)
{
     block of statements;
}
```

Where

- The beginning statements execute once at the start of the loop.
- The conditional statements are tested for each loop.
- The ending statements execute once at the end of the loop.

Each of the statement sections is separated by a semicolon (;). Each section can contain as many statements as needed, separated by commas. Any section can be empty.

The following loop has statements in all three sections:

```
for ($i=0,$j=1;$t<=4;$i++,$j++)
{
  $t = $i + $j;
  echo "$t<br>";
}
```

The output of these statements is

```
1
3
5
```

The loop is executed in the following order:

1. The beginning section containing two statements is executed; `$i` is set to `0`, and `$j` is set to 1.
2. The conditional section containing one statement is evaluated. Is `$t` less than or equal to `4`? Yes, so the statement is true. The loop continues to execute.
3. The statements in the statement block are executed. `$t` becomes equal to `$i` plus `$j`, which is 0 + 1, which equals 1. Then `$t` is echoed to give the output `1`.
4. The ending section containing two statements is executed — `$i++` and `$j++`. One is added to `$i` so it equals 1, and 1 is added to `$j` so that it now equals 2.
5. The conditional section is evaluated. Is `$t` less than or equal to `4`? Because `$t` is equal to 1 at this point, the statement is true. The loop continues to execute.
6. The statements in the statement block are executed. `$t` becomes equal to `$i` plus `$j`, which is 1 + 2, which equals 3. Then `$t` is echoed to give the output `3`.
7. The ending section containing two statements is executed — `$i++` and `$j++`. One is added to `$i` so it equals 2, and 1 is added to `$j` so that it equals 3.
8. The conditional section is evaluated. Is `$t` less than or equal to `4`? Because `$t` now equals 3, the statement is true. The loop continues to execute.
9. The statements in the statement block are executed. `$t` becomes equal to `$i` plus `$j`, which is 2 + 3, which equals 5. Then `$t` is echoed to give the output `5`.
10. The ending section containing two statements is executed — `$i++` and `$j++`. One is added to `$i` so it equals 3, and one is added to `$j` so that it equals 4.
11. The conditional section is evaluated. Is `$t` less than or equal to `4`? Because `$t` now equals 5, the statement is not true. The loop does not continue to execute. The loop ends, and the program continues to the next statement after the end of the loop.

The general format of a while loop is

```
while ( condition )
{
   block of statements
}
```

`Condition` is any expression that can be found to be true or false. Comparisons, such as the following, are often used as conditions. (For detailed information on using comparisons, see Chapter 6.)

```
$test <= 10
$test1 == $test2
$a == "yes" and $b != "yes"
$name != "Smith"
```

As long as the condition is found to be true, the loop will repeat. When the condition tests false, the loop will stop. The following statements set up a while loop that looks through an array for a customer named Smith:

```
$customers = array ( "Huang", "Smith", "Jones" );
$testvar = "no";
$k = 0;
while ( $testvar != "yes" )
{
  if ($customers[$k] == "Smith" )
  {
    $testvar = "yes";
    echo "Smith<br>";
  }
  else
  {
    echo "$customers[$k], not Smith<br>";
  }
  $k++;
}
```

These statements display the following on a Web page:

```
Huang, not Smith
Smith
```

The program executes the previous statements as follows:

1. Sets the variables before starting the loop: `$customers` (an array with three values), `$testvar` (a test variable set to `"no"`), and `$k` (a counter variable set to 0).
2. Starts the loop by testing whether `$testvar != "yes"` is true. Because `$testvar` was set to `"no"`, the statement is true, so the loop continues.
3. Tests the if statement. Is `$customers[$k] == "Smith"` true? At this point, `$k` is `0`, so the program checks `$customers[0]`. Because `$customers[0]` is `"Huang"`, the statement is not true. The statements in the if block are not executed, so the program skips to the else statement.
4. Executes the statement in the else block. The else block outputs the line `"Huang, not Smith"`. This is the first line of the output.
5. Adds one to `$k`, which now becomes equal to 1.
6. Reaches the bottom of the loop.
7. Goes to the top of the loop.

8. Tests the condition again. Is `$testvar != "yes"` true? Because `$testvar` has not been changed and is still set to `"no"`, it is true, so the loop continues.
9. Tests the if statement. Is `$customers[$k] == "Smith"` true? At this point, `$k` is 1, so the program checks `$customers[1]`. Because `$customers[1]` is `"Smith"`, the statement is true. So the loop enters the if block.
10. Executes the statements in the if block. Sets `$testvar` to `"yes"`. Outputs `"Smith"`. This is the second line of the output.
11. Adds one to `$k` which now becomes equal to 2.
12. Reaches the bottom of the loop.
13. Goes to the top of the loop.
14. Tests the condition again. Is `$testvar != "yes"` true? Because `$testvar` has been changed and is now set to `"yes"`, it is *not* true. The loop stops.

It's possible to write a while loop that is infinite — that is, a loop that loops forever. You can easily, without intending to, write a loop in which the condition is always true. If the condition never becomes false, the loop never ends. For a discussion of infinite loops, see the section "Infinite loops," later in this chapter.

Using do..while loops

Do..while loops are very similar to while loops. A do..while loop continues repeating as long as certain conditions are true. You set up a condition. The condition is tested at the bottom of each loop. If the condition is true, the loop repeats. When the condition is not true, the loop stops.

The general format for a do..while loop is

```
do
{
   block of statements
} while ( condition );
```

The following statements set up a loop that looks for the customer named Smith. This program does the same thing as a program in the preceding section using a while loop:

```
$customers = array ( "Huang", "Smith", "Jones" );
$testvar = "no";
$k = 0;
do
```

```
{
  if ($customers[$k] == "Smith" )
  {
    $testvar = "yes";
    echo "Smith<br>";
  }
  else
  {
    echo "$customers[$k], not Smith<br>";
  }
  $k++;
} while ( $testvar != "yes" )
```

The output of these statements in a browser is

```
Huang, not Smith
Smith
```

This is the same output shown for the while loop example. The difference between a while loop and a do..while loop is where the condition is checked. In a while loop, the condition is checked at the top of the loop. Therefore, the loop will never execute if the condition is never true. In the do..while loop, the condition is checked at the bottom of the loop. Therefore, the loop always executes at least once, even if the condition is never true.

For instance, in the preceding loop that checks for the name Smith, suppose the original condition is set to yes, instead of no, using this statement:

```
$testvar = "yes";
```

The condition would test false from the beginning. It would never be true. In a while loop, there would be no output. The statement block would never run. However, in a do..while loop, the statement block would run once before the condition was tested. Thus, the while loop would produce no output, but the do..while loop would produce the following output:

```
Huang, not Smith
```

The do..while loop produces one line of output before the condition is tested. It does not produce the second line of output because the condition tests false.

Infinite loops

You can easily set up loops so that they never stop. These are called *infinite loops.* They repeat forever. However, seldom does anyone create an infinite loop intentionally. It is usually a mistake in the programming. For instance, a slight change to the program that sets up a while loop can make it into an infinite loop.

Here is the program shown in the section, "Using while loops," earlier in this chapter:

```
$customers = array ( "Huang", "Smith", "Jones" );
$testvar = "no";
$k = 0;
while ( $testvar != "yes" )
{
  if ($customers[$k] == "Smith" )
  {
    $testvar = "yes";
    echo "Smith<br>";
  }
  else
  {
    echo "$customers[$k], not Smith<br>";
  }
  $k++;
}
```

Here is the program with a slight change:

```
$customers = array ( "Huang", "Smith", "Jones" );
$testvar = "no";
while ( $testvar != "yes" )
{
  $k = 0;
  if ($customers[$k] == "Smith" )
  {
    $testvar = "yes";
    echo "Smith<br>";
  }
  else
  {
    echo "$customers[$k], not Smith<br>";
  }
  $k++;
}
```

The small change is moving the statement `$k = 0;` from outside the loop to inside the loop. This small change makes it into an endless loop. The output of this changed program is

```
Huang, not Smith
Huang, not Smith
Huang, not Smith
Huang, not Smith
...
```

This will repeat forever. Every time the loop runs, it resets `$k` to 0. Then it gets `$customers[0]` and echoes it. At the end of the loop, `$k` is incremented to 1. However, when the loop starts again, `$k` is set back to 0. Consequently, only the first value in the array, `Huang`, is ever read. The loop never gets to the name Smith, and `$testvar` is never set to `"yes"`. The loop is endless.

Don't be embarrassed if you write an infinite loop. I guarantee that the best programming guru in the world has written many infinite loops. It's not a big deal. If you are testing a program and get output in your Web page repeating endlessly, it will stop by itself in a short time. The default time is 30 seconds, but the timeout period may have been changed by the PHP administrator. You can also click the Stop button on your browser to stop the display in your browser. Then figure out why the loop is repeating endlessly and fix it.

A common mistake that can result in an infinite loop is using a single equal sign (=) when you mean double equal signs (==). The single equal sign stores a value in a variable; the double equal signs test whether two values are equal. If you write the following condition using a single equal sign,

```
while ($testvar = "yes")
```

it is always true. The condition simply sets `$testvar` equal to `"yes"`. This is not a question that can be false. What you probably meant to write is this:

```
while ($testvar == "yes")
```

This is a question asking whether `$testvar` is equal to `"yes"`, which can be answered either true or false.

Another common mistake is to leave out the statement that increments the counter. For instance, in the program earlier in this section, if you leave out the statement `$k++;`, `$k` is always 0, and the result is an infinite loop.

Breaking out of a loop

Sometimes you want your program to break out of a loop. PHP provides two statements for this purpose:

- **break:** Breaks completely out of a loop and continues with the program statements after the loop.
- **continue:** Skips to the end of the loop where the condition is tested. If the condition tests positive, the program continues from the top of the loop.

Break and continue are usually used in a conditional statement. Break, in particular, is used most often in switch statements, as discussed earlier in the chapter.

The following statements show the difference between continue and break:

```
$counter = 0;
while ( $counter < 5 )
{
  $counter++;
```

```
  If ( $counter == 3 )
  {
      echo "break<br>";
      break;
  }
  echo "End of while loop: counter=$counter<br>";
}
echo "After the break loop<p>";
```

```
$counter = 0;
while ( $counter < 5 )
{
  $counter++;
  If ( $counter == 3 )
  {
      echo "continue<br>";
      continue;
  }
  echo "End of while loop: counter=$counter<br>";
}
echo "After the continue loop<br>";
```

These statements build two loops that are the same, except that the first one uses break and the second one uses continue. The output from these statements displays in your browser as follows:

```
End of while loop: counter=1
End of while loop: counter=2
break
After the break loop

End of while loop: counter=1
End of while loop: counter=2
continue
End of while loop: counter=4
End of while loop: counter=5
After the continue loop
```

The first loop ends at the break statement. It stops looping and jumps immediately to the statement after the loop. The second loop does not end at the continue statement. It just stops the third repeat of the loop and jumps back up to the top of the loop. It then finishes the loop, with the fourth and fifth repeats, before it goes to the statement after the loop.

One use for break statements is insurance against infinite loops. The following statements inside a loop can stop it at a reasonable point:

```
$test4infinity++;
if ($test4infinity > 100 )
{
   break;
}
```

If you're sure that your loop should never repeat more than 100 times, these statements will stop the loop if it becomes endless. Use whatever number seems reasonable for the loop you are building.

Using Functions

Applications often perform the same task at different points in the program or in different programs. For instance, your application may display the company logo on several different Web pages or in different parts of the program. Suppose you use the following statements to display the company logo:

```
echo '<hr width="50" align="left">',"\n";
echo '<img src="/images/logo.jpg" width="50" height="50"><br>',"\n";
echo '<hr width="50" align="left"><br>',"\n";
```

You can create a function that contains the preceding statements and name it `display_logo`. Then whenever the program needs to display the logo, you can just call the function that contains the statements with a simple function call, as follows:

```
display_logo();
```

Notice the parentheses after the function name. These are required in a function call because they tell PHP that this is a function.

Using a function offers several advantages:

- **Less typing.** You only have to type the statements once, in the function. Forever after, you just use the function call and never have to type the statements again.
- **Easier to read.** The line `display_logo()` is much easier for a person to understand at a glance.
- **Fewer errors.** After you have written your function and fixed all its problems, it runs correctly wherever you use it.
- **Easier to change.** If you decide to change the way the task is performed, you only need to change it in one place. You just change the function, instead of finding a hundred different places in your program where you performed the task and changing the code a hundred times. For instance, suppose you changed the name of the graphics file that holds the company logo. You just change the file name in one place, the function, and it works correctly everywhere.

You can create a function by putting the code into a function block. The general format is

```
function functionname()
{
   block of statements;
   return;
}
```

For instance, you create the function to display the company logo with the following statements:

```
function display_logo()
{
   echo '<hr width="50" align="left">',"\n";
   echo '<img src="/images/logo.jpg" width="50" height="50"><br>',"\n";
   echo '<hr width="50" align="left"><br>',"\n";
   return;
}
```

The return statement stops the function and returns to the main program. The return statement at the end of the function is not required, but it makes the function easier to understand. The return statement is often used for a conditional end to a function.

Suppose your function displays an electronics catalog. You might use the following statement at the beginning of the function:

```
if ( $age < 13 )
   return;
```

If the customer's age is less than 13, the function stops, and the electronics catalog isn't displayed.

You can put functions anywhere in the program, but the usual practice is to put all the functions together at the beginning or the end of the program file. Functions that you plan to use in more than one program can be in a separate file. Each program accesses the functions from the external file. For more on organizing applications into files and accessing separate files, check out Chapter 10.

Notice that the sample function is quite simple. It doesn't use variables, and it doesn't share any information with the main program. It just performs an independent task when called. You can use variables in functions and pass information between the function and the main program, as long as you know the rules and limitations. The remaining sections in this chapter explain how to use variables and pass values.

Using variables in functions

You can create and use variables that are local to the function. That is, you can create and use a variable inside your function. However, the variable is not available outside of the function; it's not available to the main program. You can make the variable available by using a special statement called *global* that makes a variable available at any location in the program. For instance, the following function creates a variable:

```
function format_name()
{
   $first_name = "Goliath";
   $last_name = "Smith";
   $name = $last_name.", ".$first_name;
}
format_name();
echo "$name";
```

These statements produce no output. In the echo statement, `$name` doesn't contain any value. The variable `$name` was created inside the function, so it doesn't exist outside the function.

You can create a variable inside a function that does exist outside the function by using the global statement. The following statements contain the same function with a global statement added:

```
function format_name()
{
   $first_name = "Goliath";
   $last_name = "Smith";
   global $name;
   $name = $last_name.", ".$first_name;
}
format_name();
echo "$name";
```

The program now echoes this:

```
Smith, Goliath
```

The global statement makes the variable available at any location in the program. You must make the variable global before you can use it. If the global statement follows the `$name` assignment statement, the program does not produce any output.

The same rules apply when you're using a variable that was created in the main program. You can't use a variable in a function that was created outside the function unless the variable is global, as shown in the following statements:

```
$first_name = "Goliath";
$last_name = "Smith";
function format_name()
{
   global $first_name, $last_name;
   $name = $last_name.", ".$first_name;
   echo "$name";
}
format_name();
```

If you don't use the global statement, `$last_name` and `$first_name` inside the function are different variables, created when you name them. They have no values. The program would produce no output without the global statement.

Passing values between a function and the main program

You can pass values into the function and receive values from the function. For instance, you might write a function to add the correct sales tax to an order. The function would need to know the cost of the order and which state the customer resides in. The function would need to send back the amount of the sales tax.

Passing values to a function

You can pass values to a function by putting the values between the parentheses when you call the function, as follows:

```
functionname(value,value,...);
```

For instance, the following function computes the sales tax:

```
function compute_salestax($amount,$custState)
{
  switch ( $custState )
  {
    case "OR" :
      $salestaxrate = 0;
      break;
    case "CA" :
      $salestaxrate = 1.0;
      break;
    default:
      $salestaxrate = .5;
      break;
  }
  $salestax = $amount * $salestaxrate;
  echo "$salestax<br>";
}
$cost = 2000.00;
$custState = "CA";
compute_salestax($cost,$custState);
```

In the last line, the amount of the order and the state in which the customer resides are passed to the function `compute_salestax`. The output from this program is `2000` because the tax rate for California is 100 percent.

You can pass as many values as you need to. Values can be variables or values, including values that are computed. The following function calls are valid:

```
compute_salestax(2000,"CA");
compute_salestax(2*1000,"");
compute_salestax(2000,"C"."A");
```

Values can be passed in an array. The function receives the variable as an array. For instance, the following statements pass an array:

```
$arrayofnumbers = array ( 100, 200);
addnumbers($arrayofnumbers);
```

The function receives the entire array. For instance, suppose the function starts with the following statement:

```
function addnumbers($numbers)
```

The variable `$numbers` is an array. The function can include statements such as:

```
return $numbers[0] + $numbers[1];
```

The values passed are passed by position. That is, the first value in the list you pass is used as the first value in the list the function expects, the second is used for the second, and so forth. If your values aren't in the same order, the function uses the wrong value when performing the task. For instance, for `compute_salestax`, you might call `compute_salestax` passing values in the wrong order as follows:

```
compute_salestax($custState,$orderCost);
```

The function uses the state as the cost of the order, which it sets to 0, because it is a string. It sets the state to the number in `$orderCost`, which would not match any of its categories. The output would be `0`.

If you do not send enough values, the function sets the missing one to 0. If you send too many values, the function ignores the extra values. In most cases, you do not want to pass the wrong number of values, although there are a few rare instances when this would be useful.

If you pass the wrong number of values to a function, you might get a warning message, depending on the error message level that PHP is set to. For the lowdown on error and warning messages, check out Chapter 6.

Getting a value from a function

If you want a function to send a value back to the main program, use the *return* statement. The main program can put the value in a variable or use it in any manner it would use any value.

To return a value from the function, put the return statement in the function. The general format is

```
return value;
```

For instance, in the tax program from the preceding section, I echo the sales tax using the following statements.

```
$salestax = $amount * $salestaxrate;
echo "$salestax<br>";
```

I could return the sales tax to the main program, rather than echoing it, by using the following statement:

```
$salestax = $amount * $salestaxrate;
return $salestax;
```

In fact, I could use a shortcut and send it back to the main program with one statement:

```
return $amount * $salestaxrate;
```

The main program can use the value in any of the usual ways. The following statements use the function call in valid ways:

```
$salestax = compute_salestax($cost,$custState);
```

```
$totalcost = $cost + compute_salestax($cost,$custState);
```

```
if ( compute_salestax($cost,$custState) > 100000.00 )
        $echo "Thank you very, very, very much<br>";
```

```
foreach($customerOrder as $amount)
{
   $total = $amount + compute_salestax($amount,$custState);
   echo "Your total is $total<br>";
}
```

A function can have more than one return statement in it. This is normally used for conditional statements or with loops.

Using built-in functions

PHP's many built-in functions are one reason why PHP is so powerful and useful for Web pages. The functions included with PHP are normal functions. They are no different than functions you create yourself. It's just that PHP has already done all the work for you.

I discuss some of the built-in functions in this chapter and the earlier chapters. For example, see Chapter 6 for more on the functions `unset` and `number_format`. Some very useful functions for interacting with your MySQL database are discussed in Chapter 8. Other useful functions are listed in Part V of this book. And, of course, all the functions are listed and described in the PHP documentation on the PHP Web site at `www.php.net/docs.php`.

Chapter 8

Data In, Data Out

In This Chapter

- Connecting to the database
- Getting information from the database
- Using HTML forms with PHP
- Getting data from an HTML form
- Processing the information users type into HTML forms
- Storing data in the database
- Using functions to move data in and out of the database

PHP and MySQL work very well together. This dynamic partnership is what makes PHP and MySQL so attractive for Web database application development. Whether you have a database full of information that you want to make available to users (such as a product catalog) or a database waiting to be filled up by users (for example, a membership database), PHP and MySQL work together to implement your application.

One of PHP's strongest features is its ability to interact with databases. It provides functions that make communicating with MySQL extremely simple. You use PHP functions to send SQL queries to the database. You don't need to know the details of communicating with MySQL; PHP handles the details. You only need to know the SQL queries and how to use the PHP functions.

Previous chapters in this book describe the tools you use to build your Web database application. You find out how to build SQL queries in Chapter 4, and how to construct and use the building blocks of the PHP language in Chapters 6 and 7. In this chapter, you find out how to use these tools for the specific tasks that a Web database application needs to perform.

Making a Connection

Before you can store any data or get any data, you need to connect to the database. The database may be on the same computer with your PHP programs, or it may be on a different computer. You don't need to know the details of connecting to the database because PHP handles all the details. All you need to know is the name and location of the database. Think of a database connection in the same way you'd think of a telephone connection. You don't need to know the details about how the connection is made, how your words move from your telephone to another telephone. You only need to know the area code and phone number. The phone company handles the details.

After connecting to the database, you send SQL queries to the MySQL database using a PHP function designed specifically for this purpose. You can send as many queries as you need. The connection remains open until you specifically close it or the program ends. In a telephone conversation, the connection remains open until you terminate it by hanging up the phone.

Connecting to the MySQL server

The first step in communicating with your MySQL database is connecting to the MySQL server. To connect to the server, you need to know the name of the computer where the database is located, the name of your MySQL account, and the password to your MySQL account. To open the connection, use the `mysql_connect` function as follows:

```
$connection = mysql_connect("address","mysqlaccountname","password")
     or  die ("message");
```

Fill in the following information:

- *`address`*: The name of the computer where MySQL is installed — for example, `databasehost.mycompany.com`. If the MySQL database is on the same computer as your Web site, you can use `localhost` as the computer name. If this information is blank (" "), PHP assumes localhost.
- *`mysqlaccountname`*: The name of your MySQL account. (MySQL accounts are discussed in detail in Chapter 5.) You can leave this information blank (" "), meaning any account can connect, but this is usually a bad idea for security reasons.
- *`password`*: The password for your MySQL account. If your MySQL account does not require a password, don't type anything between the quotes: " ".
- *`message`*: The message that is sent to the browser if the connection fails. The connection fails if the computer or network is down or if the MySQL server is not running. It also can fail if the information provided isn't correct — for example, there's a typo in the password.

  You may want to use a descriptive *`message`* during development, such as `Couldn't connect to server`, but use a more general message suitable for customers after the application is in use, such as `The Pet Catalog is not available at the moment. Please try again later.`

The *address* includes a port number that is needed for the connection. Almost always, the port number is 3306. On rare occasions, the MySQL administrator needs to set up MySQL to connect on a different port. In these cases, the port number is required for the connection. The port number is specified as: *hostname:portnumber*. For instance, you might use `localhost:8808`.

Using the statements, `mysql_connect` attempts to open a connection to the named computer using the account name and password provided. If the connection fails, the program stops running at this point and sends *message* to the browser.

The following statement connects to the MySQL server on the local computer, using a MySQL account named catalog that does not require a password:

```
$connection = mysql_connect("localhost","catalog","")
     or  die ("Couldn't connect to server.");
```

For security reasons, it's a good idea to store the connection information in variables and use the variables in the connection statement, as follows:

```
$host="localhost";
$user="catalog";
$password="";
$connection = mysql_connect($host,$user,$password)
     or  die ("Couldn't connect to server.");
```

In fact, for even more security, you can put the assignment statements for the connection information in a separate file in a hidden location so that the account name and password are not even in the program. Chapter 10 explains how to do this.

The variable `$connection` contains information that identifies the connection. You can have more than one connection open at a time by using more than one variable name. A connection remains open until you close it or until the program ends. You close a connection as follows:

```
mysql_close($connectionname);
```

For instance, to close the connection in the preceding example, use this statement:

```
mysql_close($connection);
```

Selecting the right database

After the connection to the MySQL server is established and open, you need to tell MySQL which database you want to interact with. Use the `mysql_select_db` function as follows:

```
$db = mysql_select_db("databasename",$connectionname)
      or die ("message");
```

Fill in the following information:

- *databasename*: The name of the database.
- *connectionname*: The variable that contains the connection information. If you don't enter a connection, PHP uses the last connection that was opened.
- *message*: The message that is sent to the browser if the database can't be selected. The selection might fail because the database can't be found, which is usually the result of a typo in the database name.

For instance, you can select the database PetCatalog with the following statement:

```
$db = mysql_select_db("PetCatalog",$connection)
      or die ("Couldn't select database.");
```

Handling MySQL errors

You use the mysql functions of the PHP language, such as `mysql_connect` and `mysql_query`, to interact with the MySQL database. If one of these functions fails to execute correctly, a MySQL error message is returned with information about the problem. However, this error message is not sent to the browser unless the program deliberately sends it. Here are the three usual ways to call the mysql functions:

- **Calling the function without error handling.** The function is called without any statements that provide error messages. For instance, the `mysql_connect` function can be called as follows:

  ```
  $connection = mysql_connect($host,$user,$password);
  ```

  If this statement fails (for instance, the account is not valid), the connection is not made, but the remaining statements in the program continue to execute. In most cases, this is not useful because some of the statements in the rest of the program may depend on having an open connection, such as getting or storing data in the database.

- **Calling the function with a die statement.** The function is called with a *die* statement that sends a message to the browser. For instance, the `mysql_connect` function can be called as follows:

  ```
  $connection = mysql_connect($host,$user,$password)
     or die ("Couldn't connect to server");
  ```

  If this statement fails, the connection is not made, and the die statement is executed. The die statement stops the program and sends the message to the browser. If the connection can't be established, no more statements are executed. You can put any message you want in the die statement.

- **Calling the function in an if statement.** The function is called using an if statement that executes a block of statements if the connection fails. For instance, the `mysql_connection` function can be called as follows:

```
if (!$connection = mysql_connect($host,$user,$password))
{
    $message = mysql_error();
    echo "$message<br>";
    die();
}
```

  If this statement fails, the statements in the if block are executed. The `mysql_error` function returns the mysql error message and saves it in the variable `$message`. The error message is then echoed. The die statement ends the program so that no more statements are executed. Notice the ! (exclamation point) in the if statement. ! means "`not`". In other words, the if statement is true if the assignment statement is not true.

What error handling you want to include in your program depends on what you expect to happen in the program. When you're developing the program, you expect some errors to happen. Therefore, during development, you probably want error handling that is more descriptive, such as the third method in the preceding list. For instance, suppose you're using an account called `root` to access your database, and you make a typo using the following statements:

```
$host = "localhost";
$user = "rot";
$password = "";
if (!$connection = mysql_connect($host,$user,$password))
    {
        $message = mysql_error();
        echo "$message<br>";
        die();
    }
```

Because you typed "`rot`" instead of "`root`", you would see an error message similar to the following one:

```
Access denied for user: 'rot@localhost' (Using password: NO)
```

This error message has the information you need to figure out what the problem is; it shows your account name with the typo. However, after your program is running and customers are using it, you probably don't want your users to see a technical error message like the preceding one. Instead, you probably want to use the second method with a general statement in the die message, such as `The Pet Catalog is not available at the moment. Please try again later.`

If `mysql_select_db` is unable to select the database, the program stops running at this point, and the message `Couldn't select database.` is sent to the browser.

For security reasons, it is a good idea to store the database name in a variable and use the variable in the connection statement, as follows:

```
$database = "PetCatalog";
$db = mysql_select_db($database,$connection)
      or die ("Couldn't select database.");
```

In fact, for even more security, you can put the assignment statement for the database name in a separate file in a hidden location — as suggested for the assignment statements for the connection information — so that the database name is not even in the program. Chapter 10 explains how to do this.

The database stays selected until you explicitly select a different database. To select a different database, just use a new `mysql_select_db` function statement.

Sending SQL queries

After you have an open connection to the MySQL server and PHP knows which database you want to interact with, you send your SQL query. The query is a request to the MySQL server to store some data, update some data, or retrieve some data. (See Chapter 4 for more on the SQL language and how to build SQL queries.)

To interact with the database, put your SQL query into a variable and send it to the MySQL server using the function `mysql_query` as in the following example:

```
$query = "SELECT * FROM Pet";
$result = mysql_query($query)
     or    die ("Couldn't execute query.");
```

The query is executed on the currently selected database for the last connection that you opened. If you need to — if you have more than one connection open, for instance — you can send the query to a specific database server like this:

```
$result = mysql_query($query,$connection)
     or    die ("Couldn't execute query.");
```

The variable `$result` holds information on the result of executing the query. The information depends on whether or not the query gets information from the database:

- **For queries that don't get any data:** The variable `$result` contains information on whether the query executed successfully or not. If it's successful, `$result` is set to 1; if it's not successful, `$result` is set to the message in the die function. Some queries that don't return data are `INSERT` and `UPDATE`.

- **For queries that return data:** The variable `$result` contains a pointer to where the returned data is located, not the returned data itself. Some queries that do return data are `SELECT` and `SHOW`.

The use of single and double quotes can be a little confusing when assigning the query string to `$query`. You are actually using quotes on two levels: the quotes needed to assign the string to `$query` and the quotes that are part of the SQL language query itself. The following rules will help you avoid any problems with quotes:

- Use double quotes at the beginning and end of the string.
- Use single quotes before and after variable names.
- Use single quotes before and after any literal values.

The following are examples of assigning query strings:

```
$query = "SELECT firstName FROM Member";
$query = "SELECT firstName FROM Member WHERE lastName='Smith'";
$query = "UPDATE Member SET lastName='$last_name'";
```

The query string itself does not include a semicolon (;), so don't put a semicolon inside the final quote. The only semicolon is at the very end; this is the PHP semicolon that ends the statement.

Getting Information from a Database

Getting information from a database is a common task for Web database applications. Here are two common uses for information from the database:

- **Use the information to conditionally execute statements.** For instance, you might get the state of residence from the Member Directory and send different messages to members who live in different states.
- **Display the information in a Web page.** For instance, you might want to display product information from your database.

In order to use the database information in a program, you need to put the information in variables. Then you can use the variables in conditional statements, echo statements, or other statements. Getting information from a database is a two-step process:

1. **You build a `SELECT` query and send the query to the database. When the query is executed, the selected data is stored in a temporary location.**
2. **You move the data from the temporary location into variables and use it in your program.**

Sending a SELECT query

You use the SELECT query to get data from the database. SELECT queries are written in the SQL language. (The SELECT query is discussed in detail in Chapter 4.)

To get data from the database, build the SELECT query you need, storing it in a variable, and send the query to the database. The following statements select all the information from the Pet table in the PetCatalog database:

```
$query = "SELECT * FROM Pet";
$result = mysql_query($query)
     or    die ("Couldn't execute query.");
```

The mysql_query function gets the data requested by the SELECT query and stores it in a temporary location. You can think of this data as being stored in a table, similar to a MySQL table, with the information in rows and columns.

The function returns a pointer to the temporary location where the data is stored. In the preceding statements, the pointer is put into the variable $result. The next step after executing the function is to move the data from its temporary location into variables that can be used in the program.

Getting and using the data

You use the mysql_fetch_array function to get the data from the temporary location. The function gets one row of data from the temporary location. You may have selected only one row of data, but most likely, you selected more than one row of data. You use the function in a loop when you need to get more than one row of data.

Getting one row of data

To move the data from its temporary location and put it into variables that you can use in your program, you use the PHP function mysql_fetch_array. The general format for the mysql_fetch_array function is

```
$row = mysql_fetch_array($resultpointer,typeofarray);
```

This statement gets one row from the data table in the temporary location and puts it in an array variable called $row. Fill in the following information:

- *resultpointer*: The variable that points to the temporary location of the results.

- *typeofarray*: The type of array the results are put into. It can be one of two types of arrays or both types. Use one of the following values:
  - MYSQL_NUM: An array with a key/value pair for each column in the row using numbers as keys.
  - MYSQL_ASSOC: An array with a key/value pair for each column in the row using the column names as keys.
  - MYSQL_BOTH: An array with both types of keys. In other words, the array has two key/value pairs for each column, one with a number as the key and one with the column name as the key. If no array type is given in the function call, MYSQL_BOTH is assumed.

The mysql_fetch_array function gets one row of data from the temporary location. In some cases, one row is all you selected. For instance, to check the password entered by a user, you only need to get the user's password from the database and compare it with the password that the user entered. The following statements check a password:

```
$userEntry = "secret";   // password user entered into an HTML form
$query = "SELECT password FROM Member WHERE loginName='gsmith'";
$result = mysql_query($query)
     or    die ("Couldn't execute query.");
$row = mysql_fetch_array($result,MYSQL_ASSOC);
if ( $userEntry == $row['password'] )
{
    echo "Login accepted<br>";
    statements that display Members Only Web pages
}
else
{
    echo "Invalid password<br>";
    statements that allow user to try another password
}
```

Note the following points about the preceding statements:

- The SELECT query requests only one field (password) from one row (row for gsmith).
- The mysql_fetch_array function returns an array called $row with column names as keys.
- The if statement compares the password that the user typed in ($userEntry) to the password obtained from the database ($row ['password']) to see if they are the same using two equal signs (==).
- If the comparison is true, the passwords match, and the if block, which displays the Members Only Web pages, is executed.
- If the comparison is not true, the user did not enter a password that matches the password stored in the database, and the else block is executed. The user sees an error message stating that the password is not correct and is returned to the login Web page.

PHP provides a shortcut that is convenient for using the variables retrieved with the `mysql_fetch_array` command. You can use the `extract` function, which splits the array into variables that have the same name as the key. For instance, you can use the extract function to rewrite the previous statements that test the password. Here's how:

```
$userEntry = "secret";   // password user entered into an HTML form
$query = "SELECT password FROM Member WHERE loginName='gsmith'";
$result = mysql_query($query)
     or    die ("Couldn't execute query.");
$row = mysql_fetch_array($result,MYSQL_ASSOC);
extract($row);
if ( $userEntry == $password )
{
    echo "Login accepted<br>";
    statements that display Members Only Web pages
}
else
{
    echo "Invalid password<br>";
    statements that allow user to try another password
}
```

Using a loop to get all the rows of data

If you selected more than one row of data, use a loop to get all the rows from the temporary location. The loop statements in the loop block get one row of data and process it. The loop repeats until all rows have been retrieved. You can use a while loop or a for loop to retrieve this information. (For more on while loops and for loops, check out Chapter 7.)

The most common way to process the information is to use a while loop as follows:

```
while ( $row = mysql_fetch_array($result))
{
   block of statements
}
```

This loop repeats until it has fetched the last row. If you just want to echo all the data, for example, you would use a loop similar to the following:

```
while ( $row = mysql_fetch_array($result))
{
   extract($row);
   echo "$petType: $petID<br>";
}
```

Now, take a look at an example of how to get information for the Pet Catalog application. Assume the Pet Catalog has a table called Pet with four columns: petID, petType, petDescription, and price. Table 8-1 shows a sample set of data in the Pet table.

Table 8-1 Sample Data in Pet Table

petID	*petType*	*petDescription*	*price*
Unicorn	Horse	Spiral horn centered in forehead	10000
Pegasus	Horse	Flying; wings sprouting from back	15000
Pony	Horse	Very small; half the size of standard horse	500
Asian dragon	Dragon	Serpentine body	30000
Medieval dragon	Dragon	Lizard-like body	30000
Lion	Cat	Large; maned	2000
Gryphon	Cat	Lion body; eagle head; wings	25000

The `petdisplay.php` program in Listing 8-1 selects all the horses from the Pet table and displays the information in an HTML table in the Web page. The variable `$pettype` contains information that a user typed into a form.

Listing 8-1: Displays Items from the Pet Catalog

```
<html>
<head><title>Pet Catalog</title></head>
<body>
<?php
  $user="catalog";
  $host="localhost";
  $password="";
  $database = "PetCatalog";
  $connection = mysql_connect($host,$user,$password)
       or die ("couldn't connect to server");
  $db = mysql_select_db($database,$connection)
       or die ("Couldn't select database");
  $pettype = "horse";  //horse was previously typed in a form by user
  $query = "SELECT * FROM Pet WHERE petType='$pettype'";
  $result = mysql_query($query)
       or die ("Couldn't execute query.");

  /* Display results in a table */
  echo "<h1>Horses</h1>";
  echo "<table cellspacing='15'>";
  echo "<tr><td colspan='3'><hr></td></tr>";
  while ($row = mysql_fetch_array($result))
  {
     extract($row);
     $f_price = number_format($price,2);
      echo "<tr>\n
           <td>$petID</td>\n
           <td>$petDescription</td>\n
           <td align='right'>\$$f_price</td>\n
           </tr>\n";
```

(continued)

Listing 8-1 *(continued)*

```
      echo "<tr><td colspan='3'><hr></td></tr>\n";
   }
   echo "</table>\n";
?>
</body>
</html>
```

Figure 8-1 shows the Web page displayed by the program in Listing 8-1. The Web page shows the Pet items for the petType `horse`, with the display formatted in an HTML table.

The program in Listing 8-1 uses a while loop to get all the rows from the temporary location. In some cases, you may need to use a for loop. For instance, if you need to use a number in your loop, a for loop is more useful than a while loop.

To use a for loop, you need to know how many rows of data were selected. You can find out how many rows are in the temporary storage by using the PHP function `mysql_num_rows` as follows:

```
$nrows = mysql_num_rows($result);
```

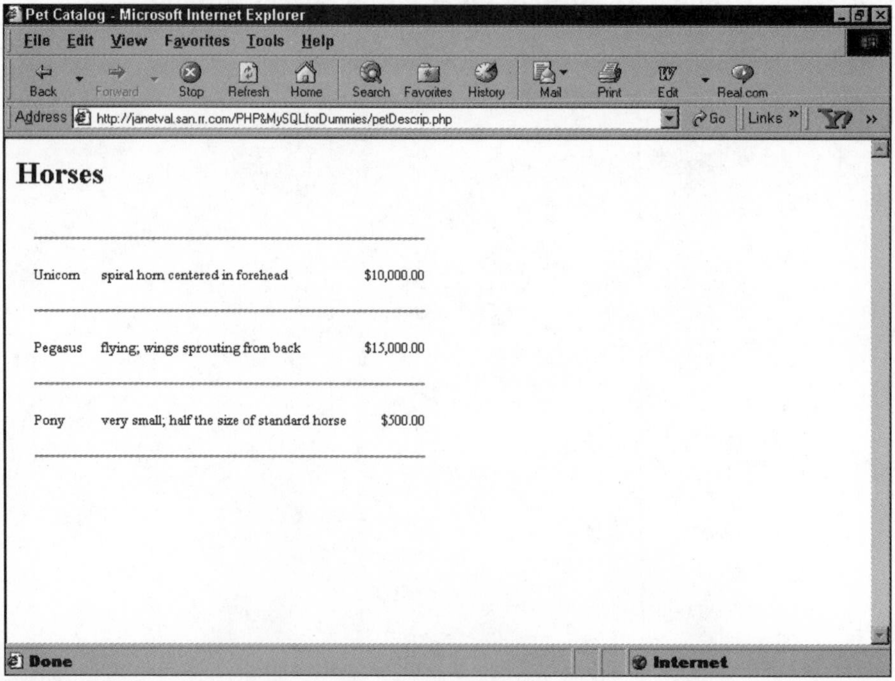

Figure 8-1: The Web page resulting from `petdisplay.php`.

The variable `$nrows` contains the number of rows in the temporary storage location. Using this number, you can build a for loop to get all the rows, as follows:

```
for ($i=0;$i<$nrows;$i++)
{
   $row = mysql_fetch_array($result))
   block of statements;
}
```

For instance, the program in Listing 8-1 displays the Pet items of the type `horse`. Suppose you want to number each item. Listing 8-2 shows a program, `petDescripFor.php`, that displays a numbered list by using a for loop.

Listing 8-2: Displays Numbered List of Items from the Pet Catalog

```
<html>
<head><title>Pet Catalog</title></head>
<body>
<?php
  $user="catalog";
  $host="localhost";
  $password="";
  $database = "PetCatalog";
  $connection = mysql_connect($host,$user,$password)
       or die ("couldn't connect to server");
  $db = mysql_select_db($database,$connection)
       or die ("Couldn't select database");
  $pettype = "horse";  //horse was previously typed in a form by user
  $query = "SELECT * FROM Pet WHERE petType='$pettype'";
  $result = mysql_query($query)
       or die ("Couldn't execute query.");
  $nrows = mysql_num_rows($result);

  /* Display results in a table */
  echo "<h1>Horses</h1>";
  echo "<table cellspacing='15'>";
  echo "<tr><td colspan='4'><hr></td></tr>";
  for ($i=0;$i<$nrows;$i++)
  {
     $n = $i + 1;    //add 1 so that numbers don't start with 0
     $row = mysql_fetch_array($result);
     extract($row);
     $f_price = number_format($price,2);
      echo "<tr>\n
           <td>$n.</td>\n
           <td>$petID</td>\n
           <td>$petDescription</td>\n
           <td align='right'>\$$f_price</td>\n
           </tr>\n";
     echo "<tr><td colspan='4'><hr></td></tr>\n";
  }
  echo "</table>\n";
?>
</body>
</html>
```

Figure 8-2 shows the Web page that results from using the for loop in this program. Notice that a number appears before the listing for each Pet item on this Web page.

Using functions to get data

In most applications, you get data from the database. Often you get the data in more than one location in your program or more than one program in your application. *Functions* — blocks of statements that perform certain specified tasks — are designed for such situations. (Functions are explained in detail in Chapter 7.)

A function to get data from the database can be really useful. Whenever the program needs to get data, you call the function. Not only do functions save you a lot of typing, but they also make the program easier for you to follow.

For example, consider a product catalog, such as the Pet Catalog. You will need to get information about a specific product many times. You can write a function that gets the data and then use that function whenever you need data.

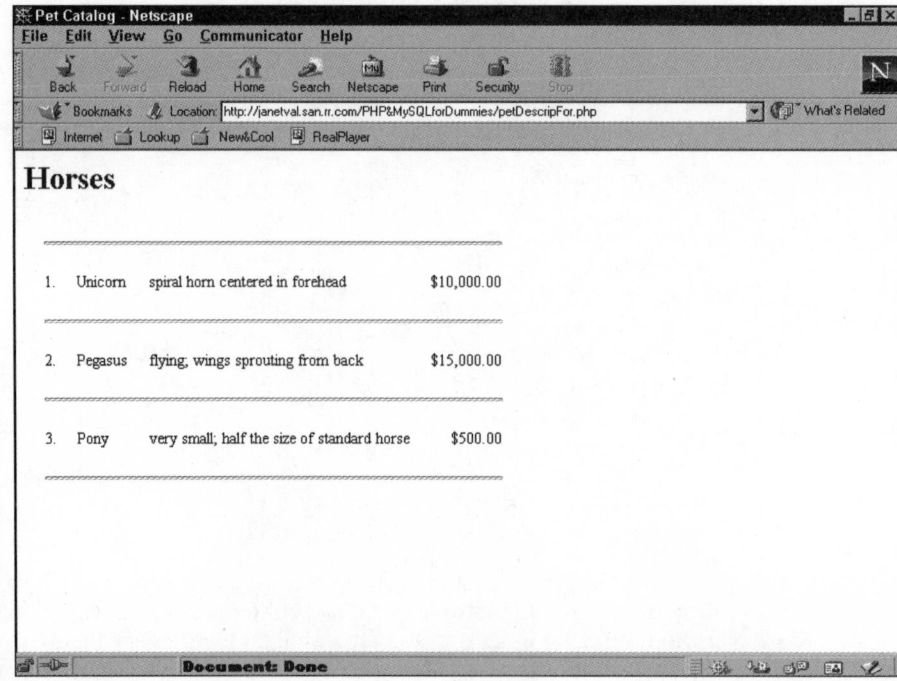

Figure 8-2: The Web page resulting from `petDescripFor.php`.

Listing 8-3 for program `getdata.php` shows how to use a function to get data. The function in Listing 8-3 will get the information for any single pet in the Pet Catalog. The pet information is put into an array, and the array is returned to the main program. The main program can then use the information any way it wants. In this case, it echoes the pet information to a Web page.

Listing 8-3: Gets Data from Database Using a Function

```
<html>
<head><title>Pet Catalog</title></head>
<body>
<?php
  $user="catalog";
  $host="localhost";
  $password="";
  $connection = mysql_connect($host,$user,$password)
       or die ("Couldn't connect to server");

  $petInfo = getPetInfo("Unicorn");                //call function

  $f_price = number_format($petInfo['price'],2);  //format as money
  echo "<p><b>{$petInfo['petID']}</b><br>\n
        Description: {$petInfo['petDescription']}<br>\n
        Price: {$petInfo['price']}\n"
?>
</body>
</html>

<?php
function getPetInfo($petID)
{
  $db = mysql_select_db("PetCatalog")
       or die ("Couldn't select database");
  $query = "SELECT * FROM Pet WHERE petID='$petID'";
  $result = mysql_query($query)
       or die ("Couldn't execute query.");
  return mysql_fetch_array($result,MYSQL_ASSOC);
}
?>
```

The Web page displays:

```
Unicorn
Description: spiral horn centered in forehead
Price: $10,000.00
```

Notice the following about the program in Listing 8-3:

- The program is easier to read with the function call than it would be if all the function statements were in the main program.
- You can connect to the MySQL server once in the main program and call the function many times to get data. If the connection were in the function rather than the main program, it would connect every time you called the function. Because every connection slows down your server, it's better to connect only once if possible.

- If you only have one connection, mysql_select_db will use that connection. If you have more than one connection, you can pass the connection and use it in your mysql_select_db function call. If your application only uses one database, you can select that database once in the main program instead of selecting it in the function.
- The function call sends the string "Unicorn". In most cases, the function call will use a variable name.
- The program creates the variable $petInfo to receive the data from the function. $petInfo is an array because the information stored in it is an array.

The preceding function is very simple — it returns one row of the results as an array. But functions can be more complex. The preceding section provides a program to get all the pets of a specified type. The program getPets.php in Listing 8-4 uses a function for the same purpose. The function returns a multidimensional array with the pet data for all the pets of the specified type.

Listing 8-4: Displays Numbered List of Items from the Pet Catalog

```
<html>
<head><title>Pet Catalog</title></head>
<body>
<?php
  $user="catalog";
  $host="localhost";
  $password="";
  $connection = mysql_connect($host,$user,$password)
       or die ("couldn't connect to server");

  $petInfo = getPetsOfType("horse");                //call function

  /* Display results in a table */
  echo "<h1>Horses</h1>";
  echo "<table cellspacing='15'>";
  echo "<tr><td colspan='4'><hr></td></tr>";
  for ($i=1;$i<=sizeof($petInfo);$i++)
  {
      $f_price = number_format($petInfo[$i]['price'],2);
      echo "<tr>\n
           <td>$i.</td>\n
           <td>{$petInfo[$i]['petID']}</td>\n
           <td>{$petInfo[$i]['petDescription']}</td>\n
           <td align='right'>\$$f_price</td>\n
           </tr>\n";
     echo "<tr><td colspan='4'><hr></td></tr>\n";
  }
  echo "</table>\n";
?>
</body>
</html>

<?php
function getPetsOfType($petType)
{
```

```
   $db = mysql_select_db("PetCatalog")
        or die ("Couldn't select database");
   $query = "SELECT * FROM Pet WHERE petType='$petType'";
   $result = mysql_query($query)
        or die ("Couldn't execute query.");

   $j = 1;
   while ($row=mysql_fetch_array($result,MYSQL_ASSOC))
   {
     foreach ($row as $colname => $value)
     {
        $array[$j][$colname] = $value;
     }
     $j++;
   }
   return $array;
}
?>
```

The program in Listing 8-4 proceeds as follows:

1. Connects to the MySQL server in the main program.
2. Calls the function `getPetsOfType`. Passes `"horse"` as a character string. Sets up `$petInfo` to receive the data returned by the function.
3. The function selects the database PetCatalog.
4. The function sends a query to get all the rows with `horse` in the petType column. The data is stored in a table in a temporary location. The variable `$result` points to the location of the temporary table.
5. Sets up a counter. `$j` is a counter that is incremented in each loop. It starts at 1 before the loop.
6. Starts a while loop. The function attempts to get a row from the temporary data table and is successful. If there were no rows to get in the temporary location, the while loop would end.
7. Starts a foreach loop. The loop walks through the row, processing each field.
8. Stores values in the array. `$petInfo` is a multidimensional array. Its first key is a number, which is set by the counter. Because this is the first time through the while loop, the counter, `$j`, is now equal to 1. All the fields in the row are stored in `$petInfo` with the column name as the key. (Multidimensional arrays are explained in detail in Chapter 7.)
9. Increments the counter. `$j` is incremented by 1.
10. Reaches the end of the while loop.
11. Returns to the top of the while loop.
12. Repeats Steps 6 through 11 for every row in the results.

13. Returns `$array` to the main program. `$array` contains all the data for all the selected rows.
14. `$petInfo` receives data from the function. All the data is passed. Figure 8-3 shows the structure of `$petInfo` after the function has finished executing.
15. The main program sends Pet Descriptions to the browser in an HTML table. The appropriate data is inserted from the `$petInfo` array.

```
petInfo  [1]  [petID]            =  Unicorn
              [petDescription]   =  spiral horn centered in forhead
              [price]            =  10000

         [2]  [petID]            =  Pegasus
              [petDescription]   =  flying; wings sprouting from back
              [price]            =  15000

         [3]  [petID]            =  Pony
              [petDescription]   =  very small; half the size of a standard horse
              [price]            =  500
```

Figure 8-3: The structure of the multidimensional array `$petInfo`.

The Web page that results from the program in Listing 8-4 is identical to the Web page shown in Figure 8-2, which is produced by a program that does not use a function. Functions do not produce different output. Any program you can write using a function, you can also write without using a function. Functions just make programming easier.

Getting Information from the User

Many applications are designed to ask questions that users answer by typing information. Sometimes the information is stored in a database; sometimes the information is used in conditional statements to deliver an individual Web page. Some of the most common application tasks that require users to answer questions are

- **Online ordering.** Customers need to select products and enter shipping and payment information.
- **Registering.** Many sites require users to provide some information before they receive certain benefits, such as access to special information or downloadable software.
- **Logging in.** Many sites restrict access to their pages. Users must enter an account name and password before they can see the Web pages.

- **Viewing selected information.** Many sites allow users to specify what information they want to see. For instance, an online catalog might allow users to type the name of the product or select a product category that they want to see.

You ask questions by displaying HTML forms. The user answers the questions by typing information into the form and clicking a button to submit the form information. In the next few sections, I do not tell you about the HTML required to display a form; I assume you already know HTML. (If you don't know HTML or need a refresher, check out *HTML 4 For Dummies,* by Ed Tittel, Natanya Pitts, and Chelsea Valentine.) What I do tell you is how to use PHP to display HTML forms and to process the information that users type into the form.

Using HTML forms

HTML forms are very important for interactive Web sites. If you are unfamiliar with HTML forms, you need to read the forms section of an HTML book. To display a form using PHP, you can do one of the following:

- **Use echo statements to echo the HTML for a form.** For example:

  ```
  echo "<form action='processform.php' method='post'>\n
       <input type='text' name='name'>\n
       <input type='submit' value='Submit Name'>\n
       </form>\n";
  ```

- **Use plain HTML outside the PHP sections.** For a plain static form, there is no reason to include it in a PHP section. For example:

  ```
  <?php
     statements in PHP section
  ?>
  <form action="processform.php" method="post">
  <input type="text" name="fullname">
  <input type="Submit Name">
  </form>
  <?php
    statements in PHP section
  ?>
  ```

Either of these methods produces the form displayed in Figure 8-4.

When the user clicks the submit button, the information in the input field(s) is stored in a variable given the name `"fullname"` and sent to the program listed as the action target in the form tag. For instance, if the user typed *Goliath Smith* in the input field shown in Figure 8-4 and clicked the submit button, a variable is created as follows:

```
$name  = "Goliath Smith";
```

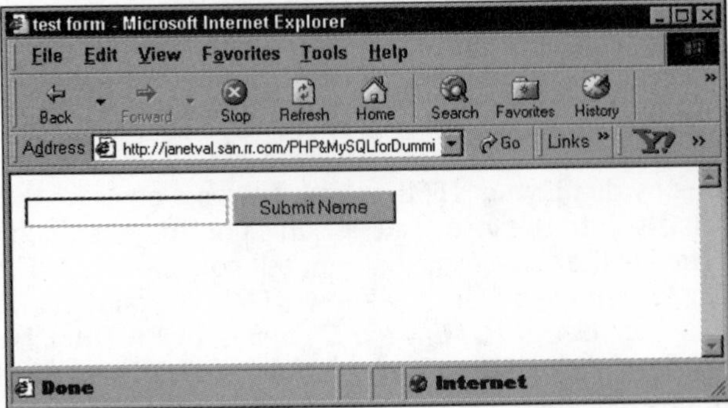

Figure 8-4: A form produced by HTML statements.

and the program `processform.php` runs, allowing you to access the information from the form. For more on how to process the information from forms, read the section "Using the information from the form," later in this chapter.

PHP brings new capabilities to HTML forms. Because you can use variables in PHP forms, your forms can now be dynamic. Here are the major capabilities that PHP brings to forms:

- Using variables to display information in input text fields
- Using variables to build dynamic lists for users to select from
- Using variables to build dynamic lists of radio buttons
- Using variables to build dynamic lists of check boxes

Displaying dynamic information in form fields

When you display a form on a Web page, you can put information into the fields, rather than just display a blank field. For example, if most of your customers live in the United States, you might automatically enter *US* in the country field when you ask customers for their address. If the customer does indeed live in the United States, you've saved the customer some typing. And if the customer doesn't live in the US, he or she can just replace US with the appropriate country. Also, if the program automatically enters US as the value in the field, you know that the information doesn't have any errors in it.

To display a text field that contains information, you use the following format for the input field HTML statements:

```
<input type="text" name="country" value="US">
```

Using PHP, you can use a variable to display this information, by using either of the following statements:

```
<input type="text" name="country" value="<?php echo $country ?>">
```

```
echo "<input type='text' name='country' value='$country'>";
```

The first example creates an input field in an HTML section, using a short PHP section for the value only. The second example creates an input field using an echo statement inside a PHP section. If you are using a long form with only an occasional variable, it is more efficient to use the first format. If your form uses many variables, it is more efficient to use the second format.

If you have user information stored in a database, you might want to display the information from the database in the form fields. For instance, you might show the information to the user so that he or she can make any needed changes. Or you might display the shipping address for the customer's last online order so he or she doesn't need to type the address again. Listing 8-5 shows the program `showForm.php`, which displays a form with information from the database.

Listing 8-5: Program to Display HTML Form

```
<html>
<head><title>Member address</title></head>
<body>
<?php
  $user="admin";
  $host="localhost";
  $password="";
  $database = "MemberDirectory";
  $loginName = "gsmith";     // user login name

  $connection = mysql_connect($host,$user,$password)
       or die ("couldn't connect to server");
  $db = mysql_select_db($database,$connection)
       or die ("Couldn't select database");
  $query = "SELECT * FROM Member WHERE loginName='$loginName'";
  $result = mysql_query($query)
       or die ("Couldn't execute query.");
  $row = mysql_fetch_array($result);
  extract($row);

  /* Display user address in a form */
  echo "<h1 align='center'>Address for $loginName</h1>\n";
  echo "<br><p align='center'>
       <font size='+1'><b>Please check the information below and change
          any information that is incorrect.</b></font>
       <hr>
       <form action='processForm.php' method='post'>
       <center>
       <table width='95%' border='0' cellspacing='0' cellpadding='2'>
       <tr><td align='right'><B>First Name:</br></td>
           <td><input type='text' name='firstName' size='65' maxlength='65'
              value='$firstName' > </td>
```

(continued)

Listing 8-5 ***(continued)***

```
        </tr>
        <tr><td align='right'><B>Last Name:</B></td>
            <td> <input type='text' name='lastName' size='65' maxlength='65'
                value='$lastName'> </td>
        </tr>
        <tr><td align='right'><B>Street Address:</B></td>
            <td> <input type='text' name='street' size='65' maxlength='65'
                value='$street'> </td>
        </tr>
        <tr><td align='right'><B>City:</B></td>
            <td> <input type='text' name='city' size='65' maxlength='65'
                value='$city'>
            </td>
        </tr>
        <tr><td align='right'><B>State:</B></td>
            <td><input type='text' name='state' size='4' maxlength='4'
                value='$state'>
               <B>Zipcode:</B>
             <input type='text' name='zip' size='14' maxlength='14' value='$zip'>
               <B>Country:</B>
             <input type='text' name='country' size='26' maxlength='26'
                value='$country'> </td>
       </tr>
       </table>
       <p align='center'>
         <input type='submit' value='Submit Address'>
       </form>";
?>
</center>
</body>
</html>
```

Notice the following in the program in Listing 8-5:

- **The form statement transfers the action to the program** `processForm.php`. This program processes the information in the form and updates the database with any information that the user changed. Checking data in a form and saving information in the database are discussed later in this chapter.
- **The fields in the form are formatted in an HTML table.** Tables are an important part of HTML. If you are not familiar with HTML tables, you should read the tables section of an HTML book.
- **Each input field in the form is given a name.** The information in the input field is stored in a variable that has the same name as the input field.
- **The program gives the field names in the form the same names as the columns in the database.** This simplifies moving information between the database and the form, requiring no transfer of information from one variable to another.

For security reasons, always include *maxlength* in your HTML statement. Maxlength defines the number of characters a user is allowed to type into the field. If the information is going to be stored in a database, set maxlength to the same number as the width of the column in the database table.

Figure 8-5 shows the Web page resulting from the program in Listing 8-5. The information in the form is the information that is stored in the database.

Building selection lists

One type of field you can use in an HTML form is a *selection list.* Instead of typing into a field, your users select from a list. For instance, in a product catalog, you might provide a list of categories from which users select what they want to view. Or the form for users' addresses might include a list of states users can select. Or users might enter a date by selecting a month, day, and year from a list.

Use selection lists whenever feasible. When the user selects an item from a list, you can be sure that the item is accurate, with no misspelling, odd characters, or other problems introduced by users' typing errors.

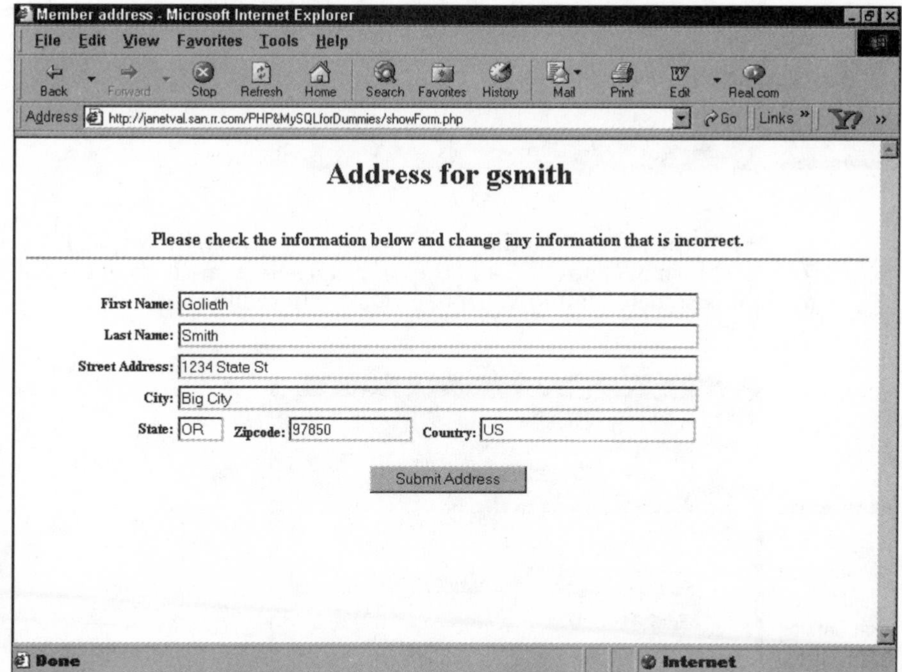

Figure 8-5: A form showing the user's address.

An HTML selection list for the categories in the Pet Catalog is formatted as follows:

```
<form action="processform.php" method="post">
<select name="petType">
  <option value="horse">horse
  <option value="cat" selected>cat
  <option value="dragon">dragon
</select>    
<input type="submit" value="Select Type of Pet">
</form>\n";
```

Figure 8-6 shows the selection list that these HTML statements produce. Notice that *cat* is the choice that is selected when the field is first displayed. You determine this default selection by including `selected` in the option tag.

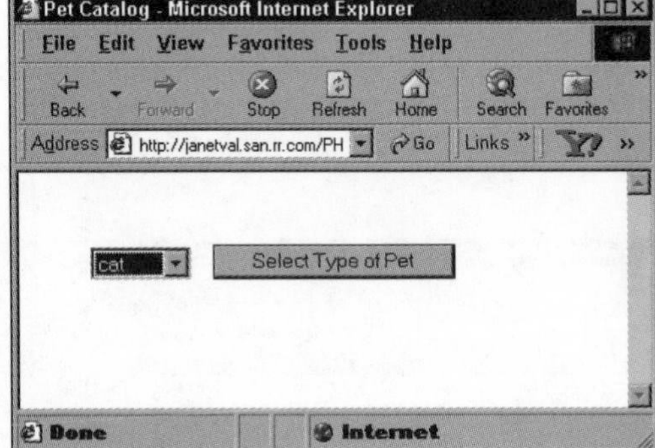

Figure 8-6: A selection field for the Pet Catalog.

When the user clicks the arrow on the select box, the whole list drops down, as shown in Figure 8-7, and the user can select any item in the list. Notice that cat is selected until the user selects a different item.

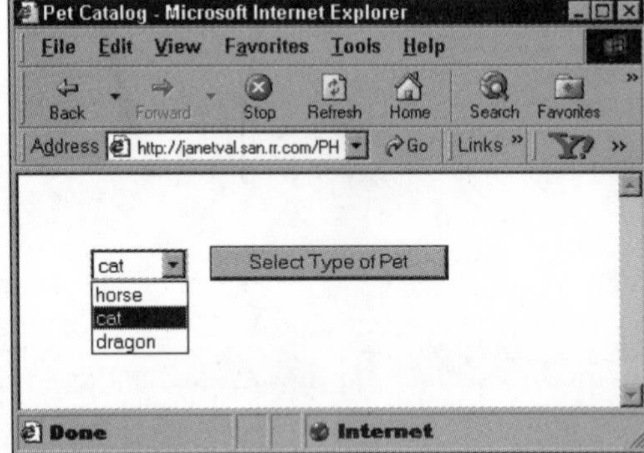

Figure 8-7: A selection field for the Pet Catalog with a drop-down list.

Using PHP, your options can be variables. This capability allows you to build dynamic selection lists. For instance, you must maintain the static list of pet categories shown in the preceding example. If you add a new pet category, you must add an option tag manually. However, with PHP variables, you can build the list dynamically from the categories in the database. When you add a new category to the database, the new category is automatically added to your selection list without your having to change your PHP program. Listing 8-6 for program `buildSelection.php` builds a selection list of pet categories from the database.

Listing 8-6: Program to Build a Selection List

```
<html>
<head><title>Pet Types</title></head>
<body>
<?php
  $user="catalog";
  $host="localhost";
  $password="";
  $database = "PetCatalog";

  $connection = mysql_connect($host,$user,$password)
       or die ("couldn't connect to server");
  $db = mysql_select_db($database,$connection)
       or die ("Couldn't select database");
  $query = "SELECT DISTINCT petType FROM Pet ORDER BY petType";
  $result = mysql_query($query)
       or die ("Couldn't execute query.");

  /* create form containing selection list */
  echo "<form action='processform.php' method='post'>
        <select name='petType'>\n";

  while ($row = mysql_fetch_array($result))
  {
     extract($row);
     echo "<option value='$petType'>$petType\n";
  }
  echo "</select>\n";
  echo "<input type='submit' value='Select Type of Pet'>
        </form>\n";
?>
</body>
</html>
```

Notice the following in the program in Listing 8-6:

- **Using `DISTINCT` in the query:** `DISTINCT` causes the query to get each pet type only once. Without `DISTINCT`, the query would return each pet type several times if it appeared several times in the database.
- **Using `ORDER BY` in the query:** The pet types are sorted alphabetically.
- **Echo statements before the loop:** The form and select tags are echoed before the while loop starts because they are echoed only once.

- **Echo statements in the loop:** The option tags are echoed in the loop, one for each pet type in the database. No item is marked as *selected,* so the first item in the list is selected automatically.
- **Echo statements after the loop:** The end form and select tags are echoed after the loop because they are echoed only once.

The selection list produced by this program is initially the same as the selection list shown in Figure 8-6, with cat selected. However, cat is selected in this program because it is the first item in the list, not because it's specifically *selected* as it is in the HTML tags that produce Figure 8-6. The drop-down list produced by this program is in alphabetical order, as shown in Figure 8-8.

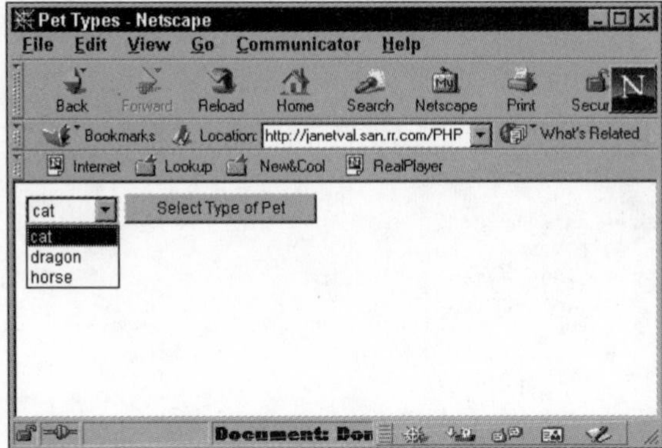

Figure 8-8: A selection field for the Pet Catalog produced by the program `buildSelect.php`.

You can also use PHP variables to set up which option is selected when the selection box is displayed. For instance, suppose you want the user to select a date from month, day, and year selection lists. You believe that most people will select today's date, so you want today's date to be selected, by default, when the box is displayed. Listing 8-7 shows the program `dateSelect.php`, which displays a form for selecting a date and selects today's date automatically.

Listing 8-7: Program to Build a Date Selection List

```
<html>
<head><title>Select a date</title></head>
<body>
<?php

  /* create an array of months*/
  $monthName = array(1=> "January", "February", "March", "April",
                         "May", "June", "July", "August",
                         "September", "October", "November",
                         "December");

  $today = Time();                       //stores today's date
  $f_today = date("M-d-Y",$today);       //formats today's date
```

```
    echo "<div align='center'>\n";
    /* display today's date */
    echo "<p> <h3>Today is $f_today</h3><hr>\n";

    /* create form containing date selection list */
    echo "<form action='processform.php' method='post'>\n";

    /* build selection list for the month */
    $todayMO = date("m",$today);            //get the month from $today
    echo "<select name='dateMO'>\n";
    for ($n=1;$n<=12;$n++)
    {
      echo "<option value=$n\n";
      if ($todayMO == $n)
      {
        echo " selected";
      }
      echo "> $monthName[$n]\n";
    }
    echo "</select>";

    /* build selection list for the day */
    $todayDay= date("d",$today);    //get the day from $today
    echo "<select name='dateDay'>\n";
    for ($n=1;$n<=31;$n++)
    {
      echo " <option value=$n";
      if ($todayDay == $n )
      {
        echo " selected";
      }
      echo "> $n\n";
    }
    echo "</select>\n";

    /* build selection list for the year */
    $startYr = date("Y", $today);         //get the year from $today
    echo "<select name='dateYr'>\n";
    for ($n=$startYr;$n<=$startYr+3;$n++)
    {
      echo " <option value=$n";
      if ($startYr == $n )
      {
        echo " selected";
      }
      echo "> $n\n";
    }
    echo "</select>\n";
    echo "</form>\n";
?>
</body>
</html>
```

The Web page produced by the program in Listing 8-7 is shown in Figure 8-9. The date appears above the form so that you can see that the select list shows the correct date. The selection list for the month shows all 12 months when it drops down. The selection list for the day shows 31 days when it drops down. The selection list for year shows four years.

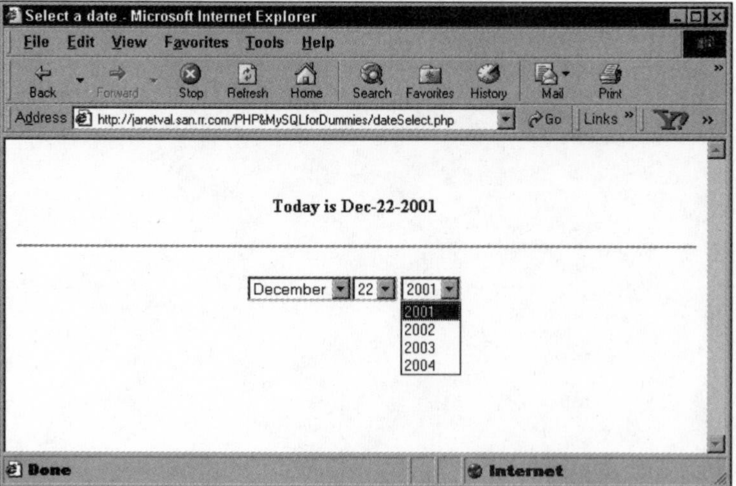

Figure 8-9: A selection field for the date with today's date selected.

The program in Listing 8-7 produces the Web page in Figure 8-9 by following these steps:

1. Creates an array containing the names of the months. The keys for the array are the numbers. The first month, January, starts with the key 1 so that the keys of the array match the numbers of the months.
2. Creates variables containing the current date. `$today` contains the date in a system format and is used in the form. `$f-today` is a formatted date that is used to display the date in the Web page.
3. Displays the current date at the top of the Web page.
4. Builds the selection field for the month.
    a. Creates a variable containing today's month.
    b. Echoes the select tag, which should be echoed only once.
    c. Starts a for loop that repeats 12 times.
    d. Inside the loop, echoes the option tag, using the first value from the `$monthName` array.
    e. If the number of the month being processed is equal to the number of the current month, adds the word `"selected"` to the option tag.
    f. Repeats the loop 11 more times.
    g. Echoes the closing select tag for the selection field, which should be echoed only once.
5. Builds the selection field for the day. Uses the procedure described in Step d. for the month. However, only numbers are used for this selection list. The loop repeats 31 times.

6. Builds the selection field for the year.
   a. Creates the variable `$todayYr`, containing today's year.
   b. Echoes the select tag, which should be echoed only once.
   c. Starts a for loop. The starting value for the loop is `$todayYr`. The ending value for the loop is `$todayYr+3`.
   d. Inside the loop, echoes the option tag, using the starting value of the for loop, which is today's year.
   e. If the number of the year being processed is equal to the number of the current month, adds the word `"selected"` to the option tag.
   f. Repeats the loop until the ending value equals `$todayYr+3`.
   g. Echoes the closing select tag for the selection field, which should be echoed only once.
7. Echoes the ending tag for the form.

Building lists of radio buttons

You may want to use radio buttons instead of selection lists. For instance, you can display a list of radio buttons for your Pet Catalog and have users select the button for the pet category they're interested in.

The format for radio buttons in forms is

```
<input type="radio" name="pets" value="Unicorn">
```

You can build a dynamic list of radio buttons representing all the pet types in your database in the same manner you build a dynamic selection list in the preceding section. Listing 8-8 shows the program `buildRadio.php`, which creates a list of radio buttons based on pet types.

Listing 8-8: Program to Build a List of Radio Buttons

```
<html>
<head><title>Pet Types</title></head>
<body>
<?php
  $user="catalog";
  $host="localhost";
  $password="";
  $database = "PetCatalog";

  $connection = mysql_connect($host,$user,$password)
       or die ("couldn't connect to server");
  $db = mysql_select_db($database,$connection)
       or die ("Couldn't select database");
  $query = "SELECT DISTINCT petType FROM Pet ORDER BY petType";
  $result = mysql_query($query)
       or die ("Couldn't execute query.");
```

(continued)

Listing 8-8 *(continued)*

```
   echo "<div style='margin-left: .5in'>
   <p> 
   <p><b>Which type of pet are you interested in?</b>
   <p>Please choose one type of pet from the following list:\n";


   /* create form containing radio buttons */
   echo "<form action='processform.php' method='post'>\n";

   while ($row = mysql_fetch_array($result))
   {
      extract($row);
      echo "<input type='radio' name='interest' value='$petType'>$petType\n";
      echo "<br>\n";
   }
 echo "<p><input type='submit' value='Select Type of Pet'>
         </form>\n";
?>
</div>
</body>
</html>
```

This program is very similar to the program in Listing 8-7. The Web page produced by this program is shown in Figure 8-10.

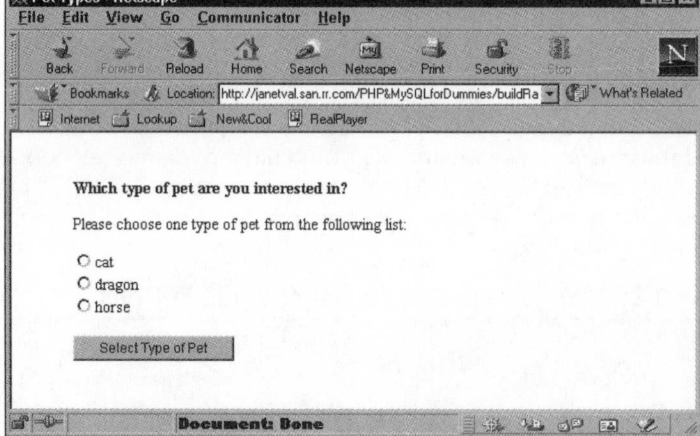

Figure 8-10: List of radio buttons produced by the program in Listing 8-8.

Building lists of check boxes

You may want to use check boxes in your form. Check boxes are different from selection lists and radio buttons because they allow users to select more than one option. For instance, if you display a list of pet categories using check boxes, a user can check two or three or more pet categories. The program `buildCheckbox.php` in Listing 8-9 creates a list of check boxes.

Listing 8-9: Program to Build a List of Check Boxes

```
<html>
<head><title>Pet Types</title></head>
<body>
<?php
  $user="catalog";
  $host="localhost";
  $password="";
  $database = "PetCatalog";

  $connection = mysql_connect($host,$user,$password)
       or die ("couldn't connect to server");
  $db = mysql_select_db($database,$connection)
       or die ("Couldn't select database");
  $query = "SELECT DISTINCT petType FROM Pet ORDER BY petType";
  $result = mysql_query($query)
       or die ("Couldn't execute query.");

  echo "<div style='margin-left: .5in'>
  <p> 
  <p><b>Which type of pet are you interested in?</b>
  <p>Choose as many types of pets as you want:\n";


  /* create form containing checkboxes */
  echo "<form action='processform.php' method='post'>\n";

  while ($row = mysql_fetch_array($result))
  {
     extract($row);
     echo "<input type='checkbox' name='interest[$petType]'
               value='$petType'>$petType\n";
     echo "<br>\n";
  }
echo "<p><input type='submit' value='Select Type of Pet'>
      </form>\n";
?>
</div>
</body>
</html>
```

This program is very similar to the program in Listing 8-8 that builds a list of radio buttons. However, notice that the input field uses a multidimensional variable `$interest` as the name for the field. This is because more than one check box can be selected. This program will create a multidimensional variable with a key/value pair for each check box that is selected. For instance, if the user selects both horse and dragon, the following array is created:

```
$interest[horse]=horse
$interest[dragon]=dragon
```

Figure 8-11 shows the Web page produced by `buildCheckbox.php`.

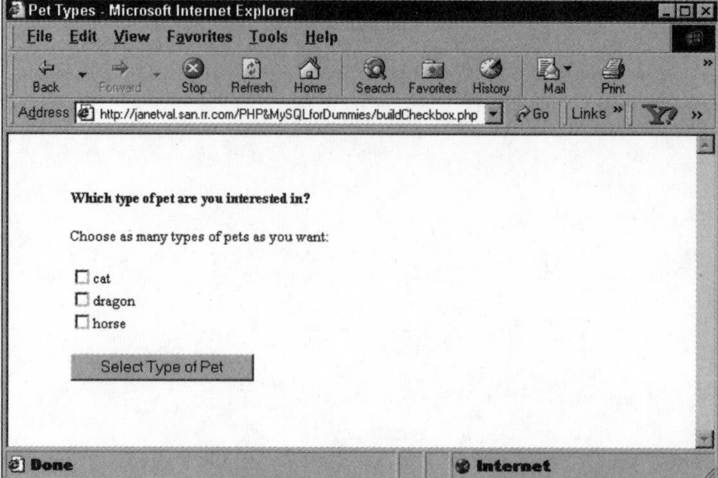

Figure 8-11: A list of check boxes produced by the program in Listing 8-9.

Using the information from the form

Joe Customer fills in an HTML form, selecting from lists and typing information into text fields. He clicks the submit button. You now have all the information you wanted. So where is it? How do you get it?

In the form tag, you tell PHP which program to run when the submit button is clicked. You do this by including `action="programname"` in the form tag. For instance, in most of the example listings in this chapter, I use `action="processform.php"`. When the user clicks the submit button, the program runs and receives the information from the form. Handling form information is one of PHP's best features. You don't need to worry about the form data — just use it.

The form data is available in the processing program in variables. The name of the variable is the name of the input field in the form. For instance, if you echo the following field in your form:

```
echo "<input type='text' name='firstName'>";
```

the processing program can use the variable `$firstName`, which contains the text the user typed into the field. The information the user selects from selection drop-down lists or radio buttons is similarly available for use. For instance, if your form includes the following list of radio buttons:

```
echo "<input type='radio' name='interest' value='dog'>dog\n";
echo "<input type='radio' name='interest' value='cat'>cat\n";
```

you can access the variable `$interest`, which contains either dog or cat, depending on what the user selected.

The information from the form is available in variables only if PHP has register_globals turned on. If it's not turned on, the information is only available in the array, `HTTP_POST_VARS`. (See the "Built-in arrays" sidebar and Table 8-2 for more on built-in arrays.) For instance, if your form has a text field with `name="first_name"`, the information the user typed is available in `$first_name` if register_globals is turned on, but is only available in `$HTTP_POST_VARS['first_name']` if register_globals is turned off. It's also available in `$_POST['first_name']` if PHP version 4.1.0 or later is installed. If you seem to be having problems getting information from form variables, check register_globals using `php_info()` and make sure it's turned on. It's turned on when PHP is installed unless the person installing it deliberately turns it off.

You handle check boxes in a slightly different way because the user can check more than one check box. As shown in Listing 8-9, the data from a list of check boxes can be stored in a multidimensional variable so that all the check boxes are available. For instance, if your form includes the following list of check boxes:

```
echo "<input type='checkbox' name='interest[dog]' value='dog'>dog\n";
echo "<input type='checkbox' name='interest[cat]' value='cat'>cat\n";
```

you can access the data using the multidimensional variable `$interest`, which contains the following:

```
$interest[dog] = dog
$interest[cat] = cat
```

Built-in arrays

PHP has several built-in arrays that you can use when writing PHP programs. PHP stores variables in these arrays and uses them to pass information from one Web page to the next. The variable names are the keys in these arrays.

In version 4.1.0, PHP introduced a new set of built-in arrays that contains the same information but can do additional things. The new arrays can be used anywhere, even in a function. The older arrays from previous versions of PHP need to be declared global before being accessed in a function. Functions and the use of variables inside functions are explained in Chapter 6.

Table 8-2 shows some useful built-in arrays. If you are using PHP 4.1.0 or newer, you can use the new built-in arrays. They are convenient when you write functions. I have written the programs in this book using the older arrays because they are available to everyone, even those using older versions of PHP.

Built-in arrays are available only if track-vars is enabled. As of PHP 4.0.3, track-vars is always enabled, unless the PHP administrator deliberately turned track-vars off. If the built-in arrays don't seem to be available, check with `phpinfo()` to make sure that track-vars is turned on.

In some cases, you may want to access all the fields in the form. Perhaps you want to check them all to make sure the user didn't leave any fields blank. PHP provides two arrays that contain all the fields in the form, including any hidden fields:

- `$HTTP_POST_VARS` contains all the variables passed by the *post* method.
- `$HTTP_GET_VARS` contains all the variables passed by the *get* method.

Most of the sample programs and statements in this book use the post method. The keys are the field names. See the sidebar "Post versus get" for more on the two methods.

Table 8-2 Handy Built-in Arrays

Array	*New in 4.1.0*	*Description*
`$GLOBALS`	No	Contains all the global variables. For instance, if you use the statement, `$testvar = 1`, you can then access the variable as `$GLOBALS['testvar']`.
`$HTTP_POST_VARS`	No	Contains all the variables passed in a form from a previous page if the form used `method="post"`.
`$_POST`	Yes	Same as `$HTTP_POST_VARS`.
`$HTTP_GET_VARS`	No	Contains all the variables passed from a previous page as part of the URL. This includes variables passed in a form using `method="get"`.
`$_GET`	Yes	Same as `$HTTP_GET_VARS`.
`$HTTP_COOKIE_VARS`	No	Contains all the cookie variables.
`$_COOKIE`	Yes	Same as `$HTTP_COOKIE_VARS`.
`$HTTP_SESSION_VARS`	No	Contains all the variables that are registered as session variables.
`$_SESSION`	Yes	Same as `$HTTP_SESSION_VARS`.
`$_REQUEST`	Yes	Contains all the variables together that are in `$_POST`, `$_GET`, and `$_SESSION`.

For instance, suppose your program includes the following statements to display a form:

```
echo "<form action='processform.php' method='post'>\n";
echo "<input type='text' name='lname' value='Smith'>\n";
echo "<input type='radio' name='interest' value='dog'>dog\n";
echo "<input type='radio' name='interest' value='cat'>cat\n";
echo "<input type='hidden' name='hidvar' value='3'>\n
echo "<input type='submit' value='Select Type of Pet'>
   </form>\n";
```

The program `processform.php` contains the following statements that will list all the variables received from the form:

```
foreach ($HTTP_POST_VARS as $key => $value)
{
   echo "$key, $value<br>";
}
```

The output from the foreach loop would be:

```
lname, Smith
interest, dog
hidvar, 3
```

The output shows three variables with these three values for the following reasons:

- **The user didn't change the text in the text field.** The value `"Smith"` that the program displayed is still the text in the text field.
- **The user chose the radio button for dog.** The user can select only one radio button.
- **The program passed a hidden field named *hidvar*.** The program sets the value for hidden fields. The user can't affect the hidden fields.

Checking the information

Joe Customer fills in an HTML form, selecting from lists and typing information into text fields. He clicks the submit button. You now have all the information you wanted. Well, maybe. Joe may have typed information that has a typo in it. Or he may have typed nonsense. Or he may even have typed in malicious information that can cause problems for you or for other people using your Web site. Before you use Joe's information or store it in your database, you want to check it to see that it is the information you asked for. Checking the data is called *validating* the data.

Validating the data includes the following:

- **Checking for empty fields:** You can require users to enter information in a field. If the field is blank, the user is told that the information is required, and the form is displayed again so the user can type the missing information.

- **Checking the format of the information:** You can check the information to see that it is in the correct format. For instance, *ab3&*xx* is clearly not a valid zip code.

Checking for empty fields

When you create a form, you can decide which fields are required and which are optional. Your decision is implemented in the PHP program. You check the fields that are required for information. If a required field is blank, you send a message to the user, indicating the field is required, and you redisplay the form.

The general format to check for empty fields is

```
if ($last_name == "")
{
    echo "You did not enter your last name.
          Last name is required.<br>\n";
    display the form;
    exit();
}
echo " Welcome to the Members Only club.
       You may select from the menu below.<br>\n";
display the menu;
```

Post versus get

You use one of two methods to submit form information. The methods pass the form data differently and have different advantages and disadvantages.

- **Get method:** The form data is passed by adding it to the URL that calls the form-processing program. For instance, the URL might look like this:

  ```
  processform.php?lname=Smith&fname=
    Goliath
  ```

  The advantages of this method are simplicity and speed. The disadvantages are that less data can be passed and the information is displayed in the browser, which can be a security problem in some situations.

- **Post method:** The form data is passed as a package in a separate communication with the processing program. The advantages of this method are unlimited information passing and security of the data. The disadvantages are the additional overhead and slower speed.

For CGI programs that are not PHP, the program that processes the form must find the information and put the data into variables. In this case, the get method is much simpler and easier to use. Many programmers use the get method for this reason. However, PHP does all this work for you. The get and post methods are equally easy to use in PHP programs. Therefore, when using PHP, it's almost always better to use the post method, because you have the advantages of the post method (unlimited data passing, better security) without its main disadvantage (more difficult to use).

Notice the exit statement. Exit statements end the program. Without the exit statement, the program would continue to the statements after the if statement. In other words, without the exit statement, the program would display the form and then continue to echo the welcome statement and the menu as well.

In many cases, you want to check all the fields in the form. You can do this by looping through the array `$HTTP_POST_VARS`. The following statements check the array for any empty fields:

```
foreach ($HTTP_POST_VARS as $value)
{
   if ( $value == "" )
   {
     echo "You have not filled in all the fields<br>\n";
     display the form;
     exit();
   }
}
echo "Welcome";
```

When you redisplay the Web form, make sure that it contains the information the user already typed. If users have to retype information they've already entered, they are likely to get frustrated and leave your Web site.

In some cases, you may require the user to fill in most of the fields but not all of them. For instance, you may request a fax number in the form or provide a field for middle name, but you don't really mean to restrict registration on your Web site to users with middle names and faxes. In this case, you can just make an exception for the fields that are not required, as follows:

```
foreach ($HTTP_POST_VARS as $key => $value)
{
   if ( $key != "fax" and $key != "middle_name" )
   {
      if ( $value == "" )
      {
        echo "You have not filled in all the fields<br>\n";
        display the form;
        exit();
      }
   }
}
echo "Welcome";
```

Notice that the outside if conditional statement is true only if the field is not the fax field and is not the middle name field. For those two fields, the program does not reach the inside if statement, which checks for blank fields.

In some cases, you may want to tell the user exactly which fields need to be filled in. The `checkBlank.php` program in Listing 8-10 processes a form with four fields: first_name, middle_name, last_name, and phone. All the fields are required except middle_name. In this case, the user didn't enter a first name. The error message when the form is processed tells the user which field was left blank.

Listing 8-10: Program That Checks for Blank Fields

```
<html>
<head><title>Empty fields</title></head>
<body>
<?php
  /* set up array of field labels */
  $label_array = array ( "first_name" => "First Name",
                         "middle_name" => "Middle Name",
                         "last_name" => "Last Name",
                         "phone" => "Phone");
  /* check each field except middle name for blank fields */
  foreach ($HTTP_POST_VARS as $key => $value)
  {
    if ($key != "middle_name")
    {
      if ( $value == "" )
      {
         $blank_array[$key] = "blank";
      }
    }
  }
  /* if any fields were blank, display error message and form */
  if (@sizeof($blank_array) > 0) //if any blank fields were found
  {
    echo "<b>You didn't fill in one or more required fields. You must
            enter:</b><br>";
    /* display list of missing information */
    foreach($blank_array as $key => $value)
    {
       echo "   {$label_array[$key]}<br>";
    }
    /* redisplay form */
    echo "<p><hr>
      <form action='checkBlank.php' method='post'>
      <center>
      <table width='95%' border='0' cellspacing='0' cellpadding='2'>
      <tr><td align='right'><B>{$label_array['first_name']}:</br></td>
        <td><input type='text' name='first_name' size='65' maxlength='65'
              value='$first_name' > </td>
      </tr>
      <tr><td align='right'><B>{$label_array['middle_name']}:</br></td>
        <td><input type='text' name='middle_name' size='65' maxlength='65'
              value='$middle_name' > </td>
      </tr>
      <tr><td align='right'><B>{$label_array['last_name']}:</B></td>
        <td> <input type='text' name='last_name' size='65' maxlength='65'
              value='$last_name'> </td>
      </tr>
      <tr><td align='right'><B>{$label_array['phone']}:</B></td>
        <td> <input type='text' name='phone' size='65' maxlength='65'
              value='$phone'> </td>
      </tr>
      </table>
      <p><input type='submit' value='Submit name and phone number'>
      </form>
      </center>";
    exit();
  }
  echo "Welcome";
?>
</body>
</html>
```

To check for blanks, the program does the following:

1. Sets up an array of field labels. These labels are used as labels in the form and are used to display the list of missing information.
2. Loops through all the variables passed from the form, checking for blanks. The variables are in the array `$HTTP_POST_VARS`. Any blank fields that are found are added to an array of blank fields `$blank_array`.
3. Checks to see if any blank fields were found. Checks the number of items in `$blank_array`.
4. If zero blank fields were found, jumps to Welcome message.
5. If one or more blank fields were found:
   a. Displays an error message. This message explains to the user that some required information is missing.
   b. Displays a list of missing information. Loops through `$blank_array` and displays the label(s).
   c. Displays the form. Because the form includes variable names in the value attribute, the information the user previously entered is displayed.
   d. Exits. Stops after the form displays. The user must click the submit button to continue.

Don't forget the exit statement. Without the exit statement, the program would continue and would display the Welcome message after displaying the form.

Figure 8-12 shows the Web page that results if the user didn't enter his or her first or middle name. Notice that the list of missing information doesn't include middle name because middle name is not required. Also, notice that the information the user typed into the form originally is still displayed in the form fields.

Checking the format of the information

Whenever users must type information in a form, you can expect a certain number of typos. You can detect some of these errors when the form is submitted, and then point out the error to the user and request that he or she type the information again. For instance, if the user types 8899776 in the zip code field, you know this is not correct. This information is too long to be a zip code and too short to be a zip+4 code.

You also need to protect yourself from malicious users — users who might want to damage your Web site or your database or steal information from you or your users. You don't want users to enter HTML tags into a form field, something that might have unexpected results when sent to a browser. A particularly dangerous tag would be a script tag that allows a user to enter a program into a form field.

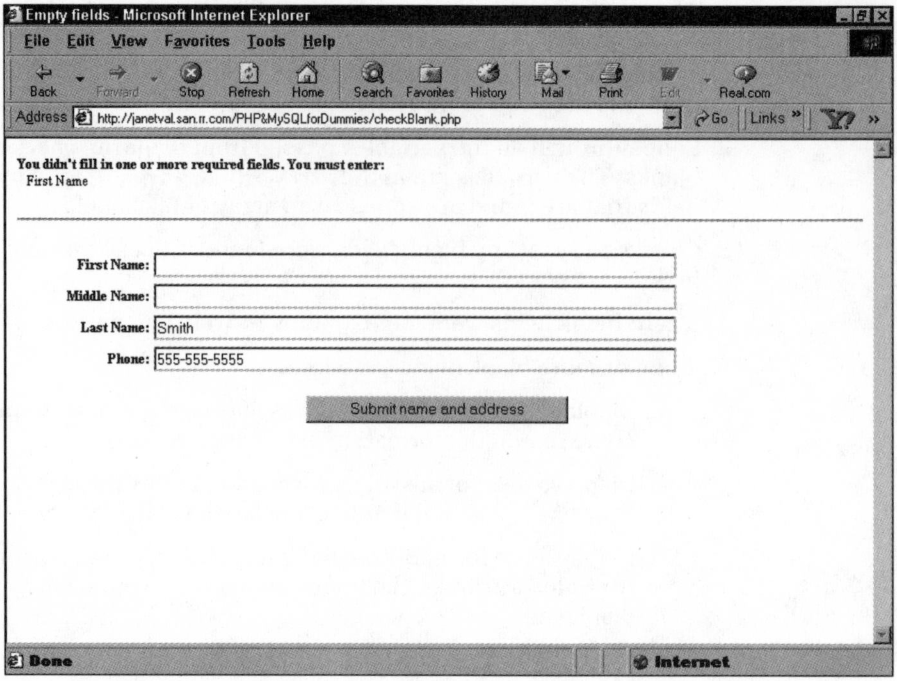

Figure 8-12: The result of processing a form with missing information.

If you check each field for its expected format, you can catch typos and prevent most malicious content. However, checking information is a balancing act. You want to catch as much incorrect data as possible, but you don't want to block any legitimate information. For instance, when you are checking a phone number, you might limit it to numbers. The problem with this check is that it would screen out legitimate phone numbers in the form 555-5555 or (888) 555-5555. So, you also need to allow hyphens (-), parentheses ( ), and spaces. You might limit the field to a length of 14 characters, including parentheses, spaces, and hyphens, but this screens out overseas numbers or numbers that include an extension. The bottom line: You need to think carefully about what information you want to accept or screen out for any field.

You can check field information by using *regular expressions.* Regular expressions are patterns. You compare the information in the field to the pattern to see if it matches. If it does not match, the information in the field is incorrect, and the user must type it over. (See Chapter 6 for more on regular expressions.)

In general, these are the statements you use to check fields:

```
if ( !ereg("pattern",$variablename) )
{
    echo error message;
    redisplay form;
    exit();
}
echo "Welcome";
```

Notice that the condition in the if statement is negative. That is, the ! (exclamation mark) means "not". So, the if statement actually says: If the variable does *not* match the pattern, execute the if block.

For example, suppose you want to check an input field that contains the user's last name. You can expect names to contain letters, not numbers, and possibly the punctuation characters' (O'Hara) and - (Smith-Jones). And also spaces (Van Dyke). Also, it's difficult to imagine a name longer than 50 characters. Thus, you can use the following statements to check a name:

```
if ( !ereg("[A-Za-z' -]{1,50}",$last_name)
{
    echo error message;
    redisplay form;
    exit();
}
echo "Welcome";
```

If you want to list a hyphen (-) as part of a set of allowable characters surrounded by square brackets ([ ]), you must list the hyphen at the beginning or at the end of the list. Otherwise, if you put it between two characters, the program will interpret it as the range between the two characters, such as *A-Z*.

In the preceding section, you find out how to check every form field to ensure it isn't blank. In addition to that, you will probably also want to check all the fields that have data to be sure the data is in an acceptable format. You can check the format by making a few simple changes to the program in Listing 8-10. Listing 8-11 shows the modified program, called `checkAll.php`.

Listing 8-11: Program That Checks All the Data in Form Fields

```
<html>
<head><title>Empty fields</title></head>
<body>
<?php
  /* set up array of field labels */
  $label_array = array ( "first_name" => "First Name",
                         "middle_name" => "Middle Name",
                         "last_name" => "Last Name",
                         "phone" => "Phone");
  foreach ($HTTP_POST_VARS as $key => $value)
  {
    /* check each field except middle name for blank fields */
    if ( $value == "" )
    {
      if ($key != "middle_name")
      {
        $blank_array[$key] = "blank";
      }
    }
    elseif ($key == "first_name" or $key == "middle_name"
             or $key == "last_name" )
    {
      if (!ereg("^[A-Za-z' -]{1,50}$",$HTTP_POST_VARS[$key]) )
      {
```

(continued)

Listing 8-11 *(continued)*

```
            $bad_format[$key] = "bad";
        }
    }
    elseif ($key == "phone")
    {
        if (!ereg("^[0-9)( -]{7,20}(([xX]|(ext)|(ex))?[ -]?[0-
              9]{1,7})?$",$phone) )
        {
            $bad_format[$key] = "bad";
        }
    }
  }
  /* if any fields were not okay, display error message and form */
  if (@sizeof($blank_array) > 0 or @sizeof($bad_format) > 0)
  {
    if (@sizeof($blank_array) > 0)
    {
        /* display message for missing information */
        echo "<b>You didn't fill in one or more required fields. You must
              enter:</b><br>";
        /* display list of missing information */
        foreach($blank_array as $key => $value)
        {
           echo "   {$label_array[$key]}<br>";
        }
    }
    if (@sizeof($bad_format) > 0)
    {
        /* display message for bad information */
        echo "<b>One or more fields have information that appears to be
              incorrect. Correct the format for:</b><br>";
        /* display list of bad information */
        foreach($bad_format as $key => $value)
        {
           echo "   {$label_array[$key]}<br>";
        }
    }
    /* redisplay form */
    echo "<p><hr>
      <form action='checkAll.php' method='post'>
      <center>
      <table width='95%' border='0' cellspacing='0' cellpadding='2'>
      <tr><td align='right'><B>{$label_array['first_name']}:</br></td>
        <td><input type='text' name='first_name' size='65' maxlength='65'
              value='$first_name' > </td>
      </tr>
      <tr><td align='right'><B>{$label_array['middle_name']}:</br></td>
        <td><input type='text' name='middle_name' size='65' maxlength='65'
              value='$middle_name' > </td>
      </tr>
      <tr><td align='right'><B>{$label_array['last_name']}:</B></td>
        <td> <input type='text' name='last_name' size='65' maxlength='65'
              value='$last_name'> </td>
      </tr>
      <tr><td align='right'><B>{$label_array['phone']}:</B></td>
        <td> <input type='text' name='phone' size='65' maxlength='65'
              value='$phone'> </td>
      </tr>
      </table>
      <p><input type='submit' value='Submit name and phone number'>
```

```
      </form>
      </center>";
    exit();
  }
  echo "Welcome";
?>
</body>
</html>
```

Here are the differences between this program and the program in Listing 8-10:

- **This program creates two arrays for problem data.** It creates `$blank_array`, as did the previous program. But this program also creates `$bad_format` for fields that contain information that is not in an acceptable format.
- **This program loops through `$bad_format` to create a separate list of problem data.** If any fields are blank, it creates one error message and list of problem fields, as did the previous program. If any fields are in an unacceptable format, this program also creates a second error message and list of problem fields.

The Web page in Figure 8-13 results when the user accidentally types his or her first name into the middle name field and also types nonsense for his or her phone number. Notice that two error messages appear, showing that the First Name field is blank and that the Phone field contains incorrect information.

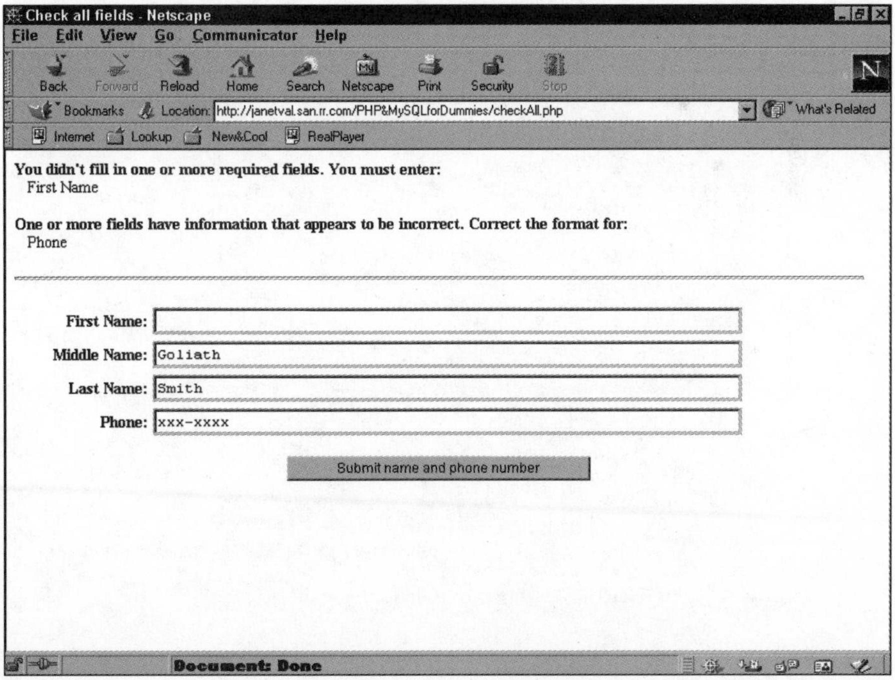

Figure 8-13: The result of processing a form with both missing and incorrect information.

Giving users a choice with multiple submit buttons

You can use more than one submit button in a form. For instance, in a customer order form, you might use a button that says *Submit Order* and a button that says *Cancel Order*. However, you can only list one program in the `action=programname` part of your form tag, meaning that the two buttons run the same program. PHP solves this problem. Using PHP, you can process the form differently, depending on which button the user clicked.

The following statements create a form with two submit buttons:

```
<form action="processform.php" method="post">
  <input type="text" name="last_name" maxlength="50"><br>
  <input type="submit" name="display_button" value="Show Address">
  <input type="submit" name="display_button" value="Show Phone Number">
</form>
```

Notice that the submit button fields have a name: `display_button`. The fields each have a different value. Whichever button the user clicks sets the value for `$display_button`. The program `twoButtons.php` in Listing 8-12 processes the preceding form.

Listing 8-12: Program That Processes Two Submit Buttons

```
 <html>
<head><title>Member Address or Phone Number</title></head>
<body>
<?php
  $user="admin";
  $host="localhost";
  $password="";
  $database = "MemberDirectory";
  $connection = mysql_connect($host,$user,$password)
       or die ("couldn't connect to server");
  $db = mysql_select_db($database,$connection)
       or die ("Couldn't select database");
  if ($display_button == "Show Address")
  {
     $query = "SELECT street,city,state,zip FROM Member WHERE
               lastName='$last_name'";
     $result = mysql_query($query)
       or die ("Couldn't execute query.");
     $row = mysql_fetch_array($result);
     extract($row);
     echo "$street<br>$city, $state  $zip<br>";
  }
  else
  {
     $query = "SELECT phone FROM Member WHERE lastName='$last_name'";
     $result = mysql_query($query)
       or die ("Couldn't execute query.");
```

```
$row = mysql_fetch_array($result);
     echo "Phone: {$row['phone']}<br>";
  }
?>
</body>
</html>
```

The program executes different statements, depending on which button is clicked. If the user clicks the button for the address, the program outputs the address for the name submitted in the form; if the user clicks the Show Phone Number button, the program outputs the phone number.

Putting Information into a Database

Your application probably needs to store data in your database. For example, your database may store information that a user typed into a form for your use — a Member Directory is a good example of this. Or your database may store data temporarily during the application. Either way, you store data by sending SQL queries to MySQL. (SQL queries are explained in detail in Chapter 4.)

Preparing the data

You need to prepare the data before storing it in the database. Preparing the data includes the following:

- Putting the data into variables
- Making sure the data is in the format expected by the database
- Cleaning the data

Putting the data into variables

You store the data by sending it to the database in an SQL query. You store the data in variables and include the variable names in the query. Using PHP, this process is simple. The user provides most of the data you want to store via a form. As discussed earlier in this chapter, PHP stores the data in a variable with the name of the form field, invisibly and automatically, without your having to store it yourself. You just use the variables that PHP provides. Occasionally, you want to store information that you generate yourself, such as today's date or a customer order number. You just need to store this information in a variable so that you can include it in a query.

Using the correct format

When you design your database, you set the data type for each column. The data you want to store must match the data type of the column you want to store it in. For instance, if the column expects a data type integer, the data sent must be numbers. Or if the column expects data that is a date, the data you send must be in a format that MySQL recognizes as a date. If you send incorrectly formatted data, MySQL still stores the data, but it may not store the value you expected. Here's a rundown of how MySQL stores data for the most frequently used data types:

- `CHAR` **or** `VARCHAR`**:** Stores strings. MySQL stores pretty much any data sent to a character column, including numbers or dates, as strings. When you created the column, you specified a length. For example, if you specified `CHAR(20)`, this means that only 20 characters can be stored. If you send a string longer than 20 characters, only the first 20 characters are stored. The remaining characters are dropped.

  Set the maxlength for any text input fields in a form to the same length as the column width in the database where the data will be stored. That way, the user can't enter any more characters than the database can store.

- `INT` **or** `DECIMAL`**:** Stores numbers. MySQL will try to interpret any data sent to a number column as a number, whether it makes sense or not. For instance, it might interpret a date as a number, and you could end up with a number like 2001.00. If MySQL is completely unable to interpret the data sent as a number, it stores 0 (zero) in the column.
- `DATE`**:** Stores dates. MySQL expects dates as numbers, with the year first, month second, and day last. The year can be two or four digits (2001 or 01). The date can be a string of numbers, or each part can be separated by a hyphen (-) or a period (.), or a forward slash (/). Some valid date formats are 20011203, 980103, 2001-3-2, and 2000.10.01. If MySQL cannot interpret the data sent as a date, it stores the date as 0000-00-00.
- `ENUM`**:** Stores only the values you allowed when you created the column. If you send data that is not allowed, MySQL stores a 0.

In many cases, the data is collected in a form and stored in the database as is. For instance, users type their names in a form, and the program stores them. However, in some cases, the data needs to be changed before you store it. For instance, if a user enters a date into a form in three separate selection lists for month, day, and year (as described in the section, "Building selection lists," earlier in this chapter), the values in the three fields must be put together into one variable. The following statement puts the fields together:

```
$expDate = $expYear."-".$expMonth."-".$expDay;
```

Another case in which you might want to change the data before storing it is when you're storing phone numbers. Users enter phone numbers in a variety of formats, using parentheses or dashes or dots or spaces. Rather than storing these varied formats in your database, you might just store the numbers. Then when you retrieve a phone number from the database, you can format the number however you want before you display it. The following statement removes characters from the string:

```
$phone = ereg_replace("[ )(.-]","",$phone);
```

The function ereg_replace uses regular expressions to search for a pattern. The first string passed is the regular expression to match. If any part of the string matches the pattern, it is replaced by the second string. In this case, the regular expression is [ )(.-], which means any one of the characters in the square brackets. The second string is "", which is a string with nothing in it. Therefore, any spaces, parentheses, dots, or hyphens in the string are replaced by nothing.

Cleaning the data

The earlier section "Getting Information from the User," which describes the use of HTML forms, discusses checking the data in forms. Users can type data into a text field, either accidentally or maliciously, that can cause problems for your application, your database, or your users. Checking the data and accepting only the characters expected for the information requested can prevent many problems. However, it is always possible to miss something. Also, in some cases, the information the user enters needs to allow pretty much anything. For instance, normally you wouldn't allow the characters < and > in a field. However, there might be a situation in which the user needs to enter these characters, perhaps the user needs to enter a technical formula or specification that requires them.

PHP provides two functions that can clean the data, rendering it harmless:

- strip_tags: This function removes all text enclosed by < and > from the data. It looks for an opening < and removes it and everything else, until it finds a closing > or reaches the end of the string. You can include specific tags that you want to allow. For instance, the following statement removes all tags from a character string except <b> and <i>:

```
$last_name = strip_tags($last_name,"<b><i>");
```

- htmlspecialchars: This function changes some special characters with meaning to HTML into an HTML format that allows them to be displayed without any special meaning. The changes are
  - < becomes <
  - > becomes >
  - & becomes &

  In this way, the characters < and > can be displayed on a Web page without being interpreted by HTML as tags. The following statement changes these special characters:

```
$last_name = htmlspecialchars($last_name);
```

If you are positive that you do not want to allow your users to type any < or > characters into a form field, use strip_tags. However, if you want to allow < or > characters, you can safely store them after they have been processed by htmlspecialchars.

Another function that you should use before storing data in your database is `trim`. Users often type spaces at the beginning or end of a text field without meaning to. `Trim` removes any leading or trailing spaces so they don't get stored. Use the following statement to remove these spaces:

```
$last_name = trim($last_name);
```

Adding new information

You use the `INSERT` query (described in Chapter 4) to add new information to the database. `INSERT` adds a new row to a database table. The general format is

```
$query = "INSERT INTO tablename (col,col,col...) VALUES ('var','var','var'...)";
$result = mysql_query($query)
       or die ("Couldn't execute query.");
```

For instance, the statements to store the name and phone number that a user entered in a form are

```
$firstName = "Goliath";        // from form field
$lastName = "Smith";           // from form field
$phone = "555-555-5555";       // from form field
$query = "INSERT INTO Member (lastName,firstName,phone) VALUES
              ('$lastName','$firstName','$phone')";
$result = mysql_query($query)
       or die ("Couldn't execute query.");
```

Listing 8-13 shows a program called `savePhone.php` that stores a name and a phone number from a form.

Listing 8-13: Program That Stores Data from a Form

```
<html>
<head><title>Member Phone Number</title></head>
<body>
<?php
  $user="admin";
  $host="localhost";
  $password="";
  $database = "MemberDirectory";
  $connection = mysql_connect($host,$user,$password)
       or die ("couldn't connect to server");
  $db = mysql_select_db($database,$connection)
       or die ("Couldn't select database");

  /* check information from the form */

  /* set up array of field labels */
  $label_array = array ( "first_name" => "First Name",
                         "middle_name" => "Middle Name",
                         "phone" => "Phone");
  foreach ($HTTP_POST_VARS as $key => $value)
```

```
{
  /* check each field for blank fields */
  if ( $value == "" )
  {
     $blank_array[$key] = "blank";
  }
  elseif ( ereg("(name)",$key) )       //if key includes "name"
  {
     if (!ereg("^[A-Za-z' -]{1,50}$",$HTTP_POST_VARS[$key]) )
     {
          $bad_format[$key] = "bad";
     }
  }
  elseif ($key == "phone")
  {
     if (!ereg("^[0-9)( -]{7,20}(([xX]|(ext)|(ex))?[ -]?[0-
            9]{1,7})?$",$phone) )
     {
          $bad_format[$key] = "bad";
     }
  }
}
/* if any fields were not okay, display error message and form */
if (@sizeof($blank_array) > 0 or @sizeof($bad_format) > 0)
{
  if (@sizeof($blank_array) > 0)
  {
     /* display message for missing information */
     echo "<b>You didn't fill in one or more required fields. You must
            enter:</b><br>";
     /* display list of missing information */
     foreach($blank_array as $key => $value)
     {
        echo "   {$label_array[$key]}<br>";
     }
  }
  if (@sizeof($bad_format) > 0)
  {
     /* display message for bad information */
     echo "<b>One or more fields have information that appears to be
            incorrect. Correct the format for:</b><br>";
     /* display list of bad information */
     foreach($bad_format as $key => $value)
     {
        echo "   {$label_array[$key]}<br>";
     }
  }
  /* redisplay form */
  echo "<p><hr>
    <form action='checkAll.php' method='post'>
    <center>
    <table width='95%' border='0' cellspacing='0' cellpadding='2'>
    <tr><td align='right'><B>{$label_array['first_name']}:</br></td>
      <td><input type='text' name='first_name' size='65' maxlength='65'
            value='$first_name' > </td>
    </tr>
    <tr><td align='right'><B>{$label_array['last_name']}:</B></td>
      <td> <input type='text' name='last_name' size='65' maxlength='65'
            value='$last_name'> </td>
    </tr>
    <tr><td align='right'><B>{$label_array['phone']}:</B></td>
```

(continued)

Listing 8-13 *(continued)*

```
        <td> <input type='text' name='phone' size='65' maxlength='65'
               value='$phone'> </td>
      </tr>
      </table>
      <p><input type='submit' value='Submit name and phone number'>
      </form>
      </center>";
    exit();
  }
  else   //if data is okay
  {
    $first_name = trim($first_name);
    $first_name = strip_tags($first_name);
    $last_name = trim($last_name);
    $last_name = strip_tags($last_name);
    $phone = trim($phone);
    $phone = strip_tags($phone);
    $phone = ereg_replace("[)( .-]","",$phone);

    $query = "INSERT INTO Member (lastName,firstName,phone) VALUES
               ('$last_name','$first_name','$phone')";
    $result = mysql_query($query)
       or die ("Couldn't execute query.");
    echo "New Member added to database<br>";
  }
?>
</body>
</html>
```

This program builds on the program in Listing 8-12. It checks the data from the form for blank fields and incorrect formats, asking the user to retype the data when it finds a problem. If the data is okay, the program trims the data, cleans it, and stores it in the database.

Your application may need to store data in several different places. A function that stores data from a form may be very useful. The following is a function that stores all the data in a form:

```
function storeForm($formdata,$tablename)
{
  $query = "INSERT INTO $tablename (";
  $query2 = " VALUES (";
  $counter = 0;
  foreach ($formdata as $key => $value)
  {
    $formdata[$key] = trim($formdata[$key]);
    $formdata[$key] = strip_tags($formdata[$key]);
    $counter++;
    if ($counter == sizeof($formdata) ) //if this is last field
    {
      $query = $query.$key;
      $query2 = $query2."'".$value."'";
    }
    else                               //if this is not the last field
    {
      $query = $query.$key.",";
      $query2 = $query2."'".$value."'".",";
    }
```

```
  }
  $query = $query.")";
  $query2 = $query2.")";
  $query=$query.$query2;
  $result = mysql_query($query)
       or die ("Couldn't execute query.");
}
```

Notice that this function works only if the field names in the form are the same as the column names in the database table. Also notice that this function assumes you are already connected to the MySQL server and have selected the correct database.

Using this function, here is the last part of the program in Listing 8-13:

```
else   //if data is okay
  {
    $stored = storeForm($HTTP_POST_VARS,"Member");
    echo "New Member added to database<br>";
  }
?>
</body>
</html>
```

Notice how much easier this program is to read with the majority of the statements in the function. Furthermore, this function works for any form, as long as the field names in the form are the same as the column names in the database table. If the function is unable to execute the query, it stops execution at that point and prints the error message `"Couldn't execute query"`. If there are circumstances in which the query might fail, you need to take these into consideration.

Updating existing information

You update existing information with the `UPDATE` query, as described in Chapter 4. Updating means changing data in the columns of rows that are already in the database, not adding new rows to the database table. The general format is

```
$query = "UPDATE tablename SET col=value WHERE col=value";
$result = mysql_query($query)
      or die ("Couldn't execute query.");
```

For instance, the statements to update the phone number for Goliath Smith are

```
$firstName = "Goliath";        // from form field
$lastName = "Smith";           // from form field
$phone = "555-555-5555";       // from  form field
$query = "UPDATE Member SET phone='$phone' WHERE lastName='$lastName' AND
              firstName='$firstName'";
$result = mysql_query($query)
      or die ("Couldn't execute query.");
```

If you don't use a WHERE clause in an UPDATE query, the field that is SET is set for all the rows. That is seldom what you want to do.

Listing 8-14 shows a program called updatePhone.php that stores a name and a phone number from a form.

Listing 8-14: Program That Updates Data

```
<html>
<head><title>Member Phone Number</title></head>
<body>
<?php
  $user="admin";
  $host="localhost";
  $password="";
  $database = "MemberDirectory";
  $connection = mysql_connect($host,$user,$password)
       or die ("couldn't connect to server");
  $db = mysql_select_db($database,$connection)
       or die ("Couldn't select database");

  /* check information from the form */

  /* set up array of field labels */
  $label_array = array ( "first_name" => "First Name",
                         "middle_name" => "Middle Name",
                         "phone" => "Phone");
  foreach ($HTTP_POST_VARS as $key => $value)
  {
    /* check each field for blank fields */
    if ( $value == "" )
    {
       $blank_array[$key] = "blank";
    }
    elseif ( ereg("(name)",$key) )       //if key includes "name"
    {
       if (!ereg("^[A-Za-z' -]{1,50}$",$HTTP_POST_VARS[$key]) )
       {
            $bad_format[$key] = "bad";
       }
    }
    elseif ($key == "phone")
    {
       if (!ereg("^[0-9)( -]{7,20}(([xX]|(ext)|(ex))?[ -]?[0-
              9]{1,7})?$",$phone) )
       {
            $bad_format[$key] = "bad";
       }
    }
  }
  /* if any fields were not okay, display error message and form */
  if (@sizeof($blank_array) > 0 or @sizeof($bad_format) > 0)
  {
    if (@sizeof($blank_array) > 0)
    {
       /* display message for missing information */
       echo "<b>You didn't fill in one or more required fields. You must
              enter:</b><br>";
       /* display list of missing information */
       foreach($blank_array as $key => $value)
```

```
            {
               echo "   {$label_array[$key]}<br>";
            }
        }
        if (@sizeof($bad_format) > 0)
        {
            /* display message for bad information */
            echo "<b>One or more fields have information that appears to be
                   incorrect. Correct the format for:</b><br>";
            /* display list of bad information */
            foreach($bad_format as $key => $value)
            {
               echo "   {$label_array[$key]}<br>";
            }
        }
        /* redisplay form */
        echo "<p><hr>
          <form action='checkAll.php' method='post'>
          <center>
          <table width='95%' border='0' cellspacing='0' cellpadding='2'>
          <tr><td align='right'><B>{$label_array['first_name']}:</br></td>
            <td><input type='text' name='first_name' size='65' maxlength='65'
                   value='$first_name' > </td>
          </tr>
          <tr><td align='right'><B>{$label_array['last_name']}:</B></td>
            <td> <input type='text' name='last_name' size='65' maxlength='65'
                   value='$last_name'> </td>
          </tr>
          <tr><td align='right'><B>{$label_array['phone']}:</B></td>
            <td> <input type='text' name='phone' size='65' maxlength='65'
                   value='$phone'> </td>
          </tr>
          </table>
          <p><input type='submit' value='Submit name and phone number'>
          </form>
          </center>";
        exit();
    }
    else   //if data is okay
    {
        $phone = trim($phone);
        $phone = strip_tags($phone);
        $phone = ereg_replace("[)( .-]","",$phone);

        $query = "UPDATE Member SET phone='$phone' WHERE lastName='$lastName' AND
                   firstName='$firstName'";
        $result = mysql_query($query)
           or die ("Couldn't execute query.");
        echo " Member phone number has been updated<br>";
    }
?>
</body>
</html>
```

The program in Listing 8-14, which updates the database, is almost identical to the program in Listing 8-13, which adds new data. Using an `UPDATE` query in this program, instead of the `INSERT` query you used to add new data, is the major difference. Both programs check the data and then clean it because both program store the data in the database.

Chapter 9

Moving Information from One Web Page to the Next

In This Chapter

- Moving your user from one page to the next
- Moving information from one page to the next
- Adding information to a URL
- Taking a look at cookies
- Using hidden form fields
- Discovering PHP sessions

Most Web sites consist of more than one Web page. This includes the static Web pages you may have developed in the past. With static Web pages, users click links to move from one page to the next. Users click a link in one Web page, and a new Web page appears in their browser. When users move from page to page this way, no information is transferred from the first page to the second. Each new page that is sent to the user's browser is independent of any other pages that the user may have seen previously. With dynamic Web pages, you may need to transfer information from one page to the next. If you are an advanced HTML developer, you may have some experience with limited methods for transferring information from one page to the next using HTML forms and CGI or cookies. However, PHP is much more powerful for passing information from Web page to Web page.

Moving Your User from One Page to Another

Using HTML only, you provide links so that a visitor can go from one page to another in your Web site. Using PHP, you have three options for moving your user from one page to the next:

- **Links:** You can echo the HTML tags that display a link. The general format of an HTML statement that displays a link is

  ```
  <a href="newpage.php">Text user sees as a link</a>
  ```

  When users click the link, the program `newpage.php` is sent to their browser. This method is used extensively in HTML Web pages. You can find out more about links in any HTML book, such as *HTML 4 For Dummies, Quick Reference*, by Deborah S. Ray and Eric J. Ray (Hungry Minds, Inc.).

- **Form submit buttons:** You can use an HTML form with one or more submit buttons. When the user clicks a submit button, the program in the form tag runs and sends a new Web page to the user's browser. You can create a form with no fields, only a submit button, but the user must click the submit button to move to the next page.

- **The `header` function:** You can send a message to the Web server that tells it to send a new page by using the PHP function `header`. Using this method, you can display a new page in the user's browser without the user having to click a link or a button.

You are familiar with creating links from your HTML experience. Forms and submit buttons are discussed thoroughly in Chapter 8. In the rest of this section, I explain how to use the PHP `header` function.

The PHP `header` function can be used to send a new page to the user's browser. The program uses a header statement and displays the new Web page without needing any user action. When the header statement is executed, the new page is displayed. The format of the `header` function that requests a new page is

```
header("Location: URL");
```

The file located at *`URL`* is sent to the user's browser. Either of the following statements are valid header statements:

```
header("Location: newpage.php");
header("Location: http://company.com/catalog/catalog.php");
```

The `header` function has a major limitation, however. The header statement can only be used *before* any other output is sent. You cannot send a message requesting a new page in the middle of a program, after you have echoed some output to the Web page. See the sidebar for a discussion of "Statements that must come before output."

In spite of its limitation, the `header` function can be useful. You can have as many PHP statements as you want before the `header` function, as long as they don't send output. Therefore, the following statements will work:

```
<?php
   if ($customer_age < 13)
   {
      header("Location: ToyCatalog.php");
```

```
    }
    else
    {
       header("Location: ElectronicsCatalog.php");
    }
?>
```

URLs

URL stands for Uniform Resource Locator. A URL is an address on the World Wide Web. Every Web page has its own URL or address. The URL is used by the Web server to find the Web page and send it to a browser.

The format of a URL is

```
HTTP://servername:portnumber/path#
    target?string=string
```

Here's a breakdown of the parts that make up the URL:

- **HTTP://servername:** This tells the server that the address is a Web site and gives the name of the computer where the Web site is located. Other types of transfer can be specified, such as FTP, but these aren't related to the subject of this book. If this part of the URL is left out, the Web server assumes that the computer is the same computer that the URL is typed on. Valid choices for this part are `HTTP://amazon.com` or `HTTP://localhost`. **Note:** HTTP doesn't have to be in uppercase letters.
- **:portnumber:** The Web server exchanges information with the Internet at a particular port on the computer. Most of the time, the Web server is set up to communicate via port 80. If the port number isn't specified, port 80 is assumed. In some unusual circumstances, a Web server may use a different port number, in which case the port number must be specified. The most common reason for using a different port number is to set up a test Web site on another port that's available only to developers and testers, not customers. When the site is ready for customers, it is made available on port 80.
- **path:** This is the path to the file, which follows the rules of any path. The root of the path is the main Web site directory. If the path points to a directory, rather than a file, the Web server searches for a default file name, such as `default.html` or `index.html`. The person who administers the Web site sets the default file name. The path `/catalog/show.php` indicates a directory called *catalog* that is in the main Web site directory and a file named `show.php`. The path `catalog/show.php` indicates a directory called catalog that is in the current directory.
- **#target:** An HTML tag defines a target. This part of the URL displays a Web page at the location where the target tag is located. For instance, if the tag `<a name="target"></a>` is in the middle of the file somewhere, the Web page will be displayed at the tag, rather than at the top of the file.
- **?string=string:** The question mark allows information to be attached to the end of the URL. The information in forms that use the get method is passed at the end of the URL in the format: fieldname=value. You can add information to the end of a URL to pass it to another page. PHP automatically gets information from the URL and puts it into variables. You can pass more than one string=string pair by separating each pair with an ampersand (&), for example, `?state=CA&city=home`.

Statements that must come before output

Some PHP statements can only be used before sending any output. Header statements, setcookie statements, and session functions, all described in this chapter, must all come before any output is sent. If you use one of these statements after sending output, you may see the following message:

```
Cannot add header information -
    headers already sent
```

The message will provide the name of the file and will indicate which line sent the previous output. Or you may not see a message at all; the new page may just not appear. (Whether you see an error message depends on what error message level is set in PHP; see Chapter 6 for details.) The following statements will fail because the header message is not the first output:

```
<html>
<head><title>testing
    header</title></head>
<body>
<?php
   header("Location:
    http://company.com");
?>
</body>
</html>
```

Three lines of HTML code are sent before the header statement. The following statements will work, although they don't make much sense:

```
<?php
   header("Location:
    http://company.com");
?>
<html>
<head><title>testing
    header</title></head>
<body>
</body>
</html>
```

The following statements will fail:

```
 <?php
   header("Location:
    http://company.com");
?>
<html>
<head><title>testing
    header</title></head>
<body>
</body>
</html>
```

The reason these statements fail is not easy to see, but if you look closely, you'll notice a single blank space before the opening PHP tag. This blank space is output to the browser although the resulting Web page looks empty. Therefore, the header statement fails because there is output before it. This is a common mistake and difficult to spot.

These statements run a program that displays a toy catalog if the customer's age is less than 13 and run a program that displays an electronics catalog if the customer's age is 13 or older.

Moving Information from Page to Page

HTML pages are independent from one another. When a user clicks a link, the Web server sends a new page to the user's browser, but the Web server doesn't know anything about the previous page. For static HTML pages, this process works fine. However, many dynamic applications need information to pass from page to page. For instance, you might want to store a user's name and refer to that person by name on another Web page.

Dynamic Web applications often consist of many pages and expect the user to view several different pages. The period beginning when a user views the first page and ending when a user leaves the Web site is called a *session.* Often you want information to be available for a complete session. The following are examples of sessions that necessitate sharing information among pages:

- **Restricting access to a Web site:** Suppose your Web site is restricted and users login with a password to access the site. You don't want users to have to login on every page. You just want them to login once and then be able to see all the pages they want. You want users to bring information with them to each page showing that they have logged in and are authorized to view the page. You want users to login and remain logged in for the whole session.
- **Providing Web pages based on browser:** Because browsers interpret some HTML features differently, you may want to provide different versions of your Web pages for different browsers. You want to check the user's browser when the user views the first page and then deliver all the other pages based on the user's browser type and version.

With PHP, you can move information from page to page by using any of the following methods:

- **Adding information to the URL:** You can add certain information to the end of the URL of the new page, and PHP will put the information into variables that you can use in the new page. This method is most appropriate when you need to pass only a small amount of information.
- **Storing information via cookies:** You can store *cookies* — small amounts of information containing `variable=value` pairs — on the user's computer. After the cookie is stored, you can get it from any Web page. However, users can refuse to accept cookies. Therefore, this method only works in environments where you know for sure that the user will have cookies turned on.
- **Passing information using HTML forms:** You can pass information to a specific program by using a form tag. When the user clicks the submit button, the information in the form is sent to the next program. This method is very useful when you need to collect information from users.

- **Using PHP session functions:** Beginning with PHP 4, PHP functions are available that set up a user session and store session information on the server; this information can be accessed from any Web page. This method is very useful for sessions in which you expect users to view many pages.

Adding information to the URL

A simple way to move information from one page to the next is to add the information to the URL. Put the information in the following format:

```
variable=value
```

The *`variable`* is a variable name, but do not use a dollar sign ($) in it. PHP will add the dollar sign when it gets the information from the URL. The *`value`* is the value to be stored in the variable. You can add the `variable=value` pairs anywhere you use a URL. You signal the start of the information with a question mark (?). The following statements are all valid ways of passing information in the URL:

```
<form action="nextpage.php?state=CA" method="post">
```

```
<a href="nextpage.php?state=CA">go to next page</a>
```

```
header("Location: nextpage.php?state=CA");
```

You can add several `variable=value` pairs, separating them with ampersands (&) as follows:

```
<form action="nextpage.php?state=CA&city=home" method="post">
```

Be careful with variable names. If variables in a form have the same name as variables in a URL, you may overwrite one variable with the next, and your variables in the new page may have unexpected values because of the order in which PHP processes the variables. See the sidebar "Variable processing order" for details.

Here are two reasons you may not want to pass information in the URL:

- **Security:** The URL is shown in the address line of the browser, which means that the information you attach to the URL is also shown. If the information needs to be secure, you don't want it shown so publicly. For instance, if you are moving a password from one page to the next, you probably don't want to pass it in the URL. Also, the URL can be bookmarked by the user. There may be reasons why you don't want your users to save the information you add to the URL.
- **Length of string:** There is a limit on the length of the URL. The limit differs for various browsers and browser versions, but there is always a limit. Therefore, if you are passing a lot of information, there may not be room for it in the URL.

Variable processing order

Using PHP, information from one page is available on the next page in variables, automatically, without your having to find it or process it. PHP sets up these variables in a specific order. Unless someone deliberately changes the order, the variables are created in the following order:

1. **GET:** Variables that are passed in the URL
2. **POST:** Variables that are passed from a form that uses the post method
3. **COOKIE:** Variables stored in cookies
4. **SESSION:** Variables that are registered as session variables

The variables' processing order is important because variables with the same name can overwrite one another. For instance, if a variable in a form has the same name as a variable passed in the URL, the variables on your new page might have unexpected values. PHP processes variables in the following way:

1. **Gets the string from the URL and then sets the variables.** For instance, if `state=CA` is in the URL, PHP sets `$state="CA"`.
2. **Gets data from the post form and then sets the variables.** For instance, if the form includes a text field named *state* and the user typed *WA* into that field, PHP sets `$state="WA"`.
3. **Gets data from the cookies and then sets up the variables.** For instance, if a cookie, `state=VA`, exists, PHP sets `$state="VA"`.
4. **Gets the session data and then sets up the variables.** For instance, if you registered a session variable named $state and set it to "MA", PHP sets `$state="MA"`.

As you can see, if a variable named state is sent in a URL, a form, a cookie, and stored as a session variable, `$state` ends up being equal to MA. When PHP performs the first step, `$state` equals CA. But in the second step, `$state` is set to WA. In the third step, `$state` is set to VA. And, finally, in the last step, `$state` is set to MA.

If you are the administrator for PHP, you can change the order in which the information is processed by changing the PHP configuration in the file `php.ini`. Find the setting for `"variables_order"` and change the order from `(GET,POST,COOKIE,SESSION)` to the order you prefer. You may need to restart the Web server before the change takes effect.

None of the information will be put into variables unless register_globals is turned on. If register_globals is not turned on, the variables are only available in the built-in arrays (as described in Chapter 8). At the present time, register_globals is turned on when PHP is installed unless the installer deliberately turns it off. However, future versions of PHP may have register_globals off when installed, as discussed on the PHP Web site (`www.php.net`).

You can see all your settings at any time, including the register_globals and the variable_order settings, in the output from the function `phpinfo()`.

Adding information to the URL is very useful for quick, simple data transfer. For instance, suppose you want to provide a Web page where users can update their phone numbers. You want the form to behave in the following way:

- When the user first displays the form, the phone number from the database is shown in the form so that the user can see what number is currently stored in the database.

- When the user submits the form, the program checks the phone number to see if the field is blank or if the field is in a format that could not possibly be a phone number.
- If the phone number checks out okay, the number is stored in the database.
- If the phone number is blank or has bad data, the program redisplays the form. However, this time you don't want to show the data from the database. Instead, you want to show the bad data that the user typed and submitted in the form field.

The `displayPhone.php` program in Listing 9-1 shows how to use the URL to determine if this is the first showing of the form or a later showing. The program shows the phone number for the user's login name and allows the user to change the phone number.

Listing 9-1: Program That Displays Phone Number in Form

```
<html>
<head><title>Display phone number</title></head>
<body>
<?php
  $host="localhost";
  $user="admin";
  $password="";
  $database="MemberDirectory";
  $loginName = "gsmith";      //login name passed from previous page
  $connection = mysql_connect($host,$user,$password)
       or die ("couldn't connect to server");
  $db = mysql_select_db($database,$connection)
       or die ("Couldn't select database");

  if (@$first == "no")
  {
    if (!ereg("^[0-9)( -]{7,20}(([xX]|(ext)|(ex))?[ -]?[0-9]{1,7})?$",$phone) or
             $phone == "")
    {
       echo "<p align='center'>Phone number does not appear to be valid.<br>";
    }
    else
    {
       $query = "UPDATE Member SET phone='$phone' WHERE
             loginName='$loginName'";
       $result = mysql_query($query)
            or die ("Couldn't execute query.");
       echo "Phone number has been updated.<br>";
       exit();
    }
  }
  else
  {
    $query = "SELECT phone FROM Member WHERE loginName='$loginName'";
    $result = mysql_query($query)
         or die ("Couldn't execute query.");
    $row = mysql_fetch_array($result);
    extract($row);
  }
```

```
   /* Display user phone in a form */
   echo "<br><p align='center'>
         <font size='+1'><b>Please check the phone number below and correct it if
               necessary.</b></font>
         <hr>
         <form action='displayPhone.php?first=no' method='post'>
          <div align='center'>
          <table width='50%' border='0' cellspacing='0' cellpadding='2'>
          <tr><td align='right'><B>$loginName</br></td>
             <td align='center'><input type='text' name='phone' size='20'
               maxlength='20' value='$phone' > </td>
          </tr>
          <tr><td></td><td align='center'>
             <br><input type='submit' value='Submit phone number'></td>
          </tr>
          </table>
         </form>";
?>
</body>
</html>
```

Notice the following key points about this program:

- **The same program displays and processes the form.** The name of this program is `displayPhone.php`. Notice that the form tag includes `action=displayPhone.php`, meaning that when the user clicks the submit button, the same program runs again.
- **Information is added to the URL.** The form tag includes `action=displayPhone.php?first=no`. When the user clicks the submit button and `displayPhone.php` runs the second time, a variable `$first` is set to `"no"`.
- **The variable `$first` is checked at the beginning of the program.** This is to see whether this is the first time the program has run.
- **If `$first` equals `"no"`, the phone number is checked.** `$first` only equals no if the form is being submitted. `$first` does not equal no if this is the first time through the program.
  - If the phone number is okay, it is stored in the database, and the program ends.
  - If the phone number is not okay, an error message is printed.
- **If `$first` does *not* equal `"no"`, the phone number is retrieved from the database.** In other words, if `$first` doesn't equal no, it *is* the *first* time the program has run. The program should get the phone number from the database.
- **If the program reaches the statements that display the form, the form is displayed.** If this is not the first time through the program and a phone number was submitted and was okay, the phone number is stored in the database, and the program *stops*. *It never reaches the statements that display the form*. In all other cases, the form is displayed.

The form displayed by the program in Listing 9-1 is shown in Figure 9-1. This shows what the Web page looks like the first time it's displayed. Notice that the URL in the browser address field doesn't have any added information.

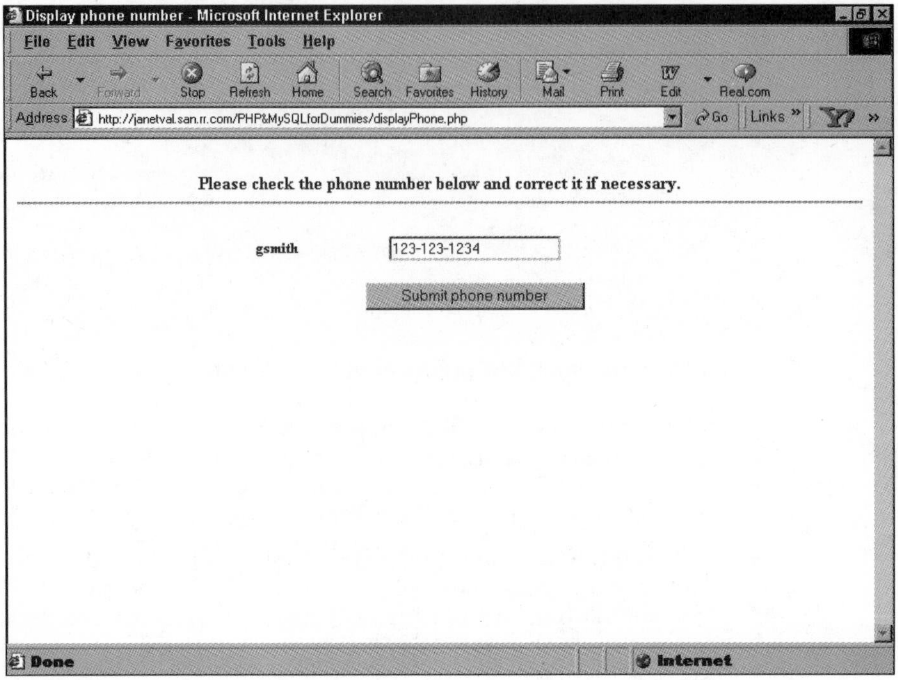

Figure 9-1: HTML form to update a phone number.

Figure 9-2 shows the results when a user types a nonsense phone number in the form in Figure 9-1. Notice that the URL in the browser address field now has `?first=no` added to the end of it.

Storing information via cookies

You can store information as cookies. *Cookies* are small amounts of information containing `variable=value` pairs, similar to the pairs you can add to a URL. The user's browser stores cookies on the user's computer. Your application can then get the cookie from any Web page. Why these are called cookies is one of life's great mysteries. Perhaps they're called cookies because they seem at first glance to be a wonderful thing, but on closer examination, you realize they aren't that good for you. For some people in some situations, cookies are not helpful at all.

At first glance, cookies seem to solve the entire problem of moving data from page to page. Just stash a cookie on the user's computer and get it whenever you need it. In fact, the cookie can be stored so that it remains there after the user leaves your site and will still be available when the user enters your Web site again a month later. Problem solved! Well, not exactly. Cookies are not under your control. They're under the user's control. The user can at any time delete the cookie. In fact, users can set their browsers to refuse to allow any cookies. And many users do refuse cookies or routinely delete them. Many users aren't comfortable with the whole idea of a stranger storing things on their computers, especially files that remain after they leave the stranger's Web site. It's an understandable attitude. However, it definitely limits the usefulness of cookies. If your application depends on cookies and the user has cookies shut off, your application won't work for that user.

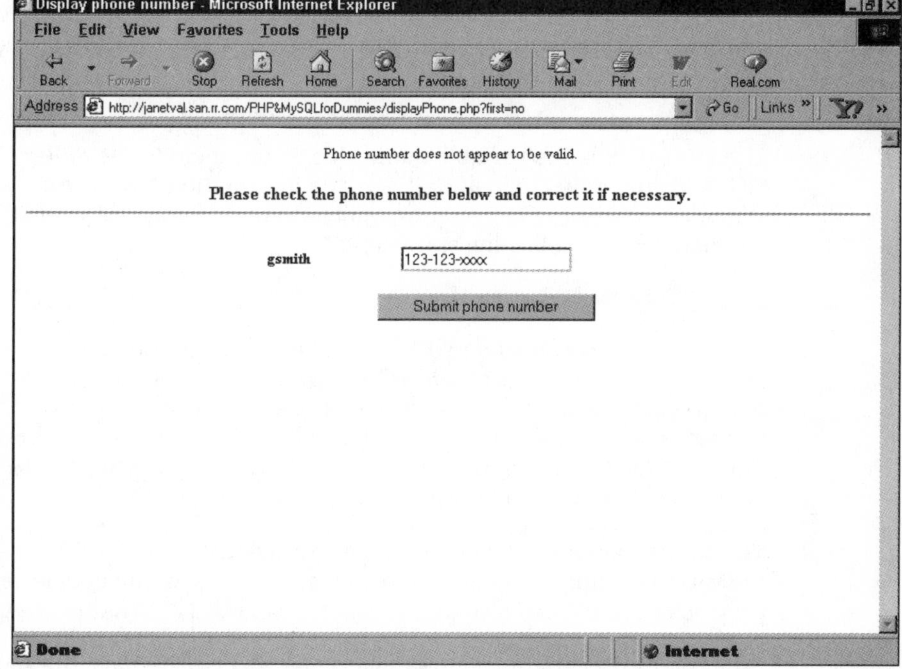

Figure 9-2: HTML form when a user submits a nonsense phone number.

Cookies were originally designed for storing small amounts of information for short periods of time. Unless you specifically set the cookie to last a longer period of time, the cookie will disappear when the user leaves your Web site. Although cookies are useful in some situations, you're unlikely to need them for your Web database application for the following reasons:

- **Users may set their browsers to refuse cookies.** Unless you know for sure that all your users will have cookies turned on or you can request that they turn on cookies and expect them to follow your request, cookies are a problem. If your application depends on cookies, it won't run if cookies are turned off.

- **PHP has features that work better than cookies.** Beginning with PHP 4, PHP includes functions that create sessions and store information that is available for the entire session. This session feature is more reliable and much easier to use than cookies for making information available to all the Web pages in a session. Sessions don't work for long-term storage of information, but PHP databases can be used for that.
- **You can store data in your database.** Your application includes a database where you can store and retrieve data, which is usually a better solution than a cookie. Users can't delete the data in your database unexpectedly. Because you're using a database in this application, you can use it for any data storage needed, especially long-term data storage. Cookies are more useful for applications that don't make use of a database.

You store cookies by using the `setcookie` function. The general format is

```
setcookie("variable","value");
```

The *variable* is the variable name, but do not include the dollar sign ($). PHP adds the dollar sign after it gets the information from the cookie. This statement stores the information only until the user leaves your Web site. For instance, the following statement:

```
setcookie("state","CA");
```

stores CA in a variable named `$state`. After you set the cookie, the information is available to your other PHP programs in the variable `$state`. You don't need to do anything to get the information from the cookie. PHP does this automatically. The cookie is not available in the program where it is set. The user must go to another page or redisplay the current page before the cookie information can be used.

The cookies are also available in an array called `$HTTP_COOKIE_VARS` with the variable names as keys. For instance, the value in the cookie set in the previous example can also be used as `$HTTP_COOKIE_VARS['state']`.

Be careful with variable names. If variables in a cookie have the same name as variables in a form, you may overwrite one variable with the next, and your variables in the new page may have unexpected values due to the order in which PHP processes the variables. See the sidebar "Variable processing order," earlier in this chapter.

If you want the information stored in a cookie to remain in a file on the user's computer after the user leaves your Web site, set your cookie with an expiration time, as follows:

```
setcookie("variable","value",expiretime);
```

The *expiretime* value sets the time when the cookie will expire. *Expiretime* is usually set using either the `time` or `mktime` function as follows:

- `time`: This function returns the current time in a format the computer can understand. You use the `time` function plus a number of seconds to set the expiration time of the cookie, as shown in the following statements:

```
setcookie("state","CA",time()+3600);      //expires in one hour
setcookie("Name",$Name,time()+(3*86400)) // expires in 3 days
```

- `mktime`: This function returns a date and time in a format that the computer can understand. You must provide the desired date and time in the following order: hour, minute, second, month, day, and year. If any value is not included, the current value is used. You use the `mktime` function to set the expiration time of the cookie, as shown in the following statements:

```
setcookie("state","CA",mktime(3,0,0,4,1,2003)); //expires at 3:00 AM on
          April 1, 2003.
setcookie("state","CA",mktime(12,0,0,,,)); //expires at noon today
```

You can remove a cookie by setting its value to nothing. Either of the following statements removes the cookie:

```
setcookie("name");
setcookie("name","");
```

The `setcookie` function has a major limitation, however. The `setcookie` function can only be used *before* any other output is sent. You *cannot* set a cookie in the middle of a program, after you have echoed some output to the Web page. See the sidebar "Statements that must come before output," earlier in this chapter.

Passing information using HTML forms

The most common way to pass information from one page to another is by using HTML forms. An HTML form is displayed with a submit button. When the user clicks the submit button, the information in the form fields is passed to the program included in the form tag. The general format is

```
<form action="processform.php" method="post">
    tags for one or more fields
<input type="submit" value="string">
</form>
```

The most common use of a form is to collect information from users (which I discuss in detail in Chapter 8). However, forms can also be used to pass other types of information using hidden fields, which are added to the form and sent with the information the user typed in. In fact, you can create a form that has only hidden fields. You always need a submit button, and the new page doesn't display until the user clicks the submit button, but you don't need to include any fields for the user to fill in.

For instance, the following statements pass the user's preferred background color to the next page when the user clicks a button that says *Next Page:*

```
<?php
   $color = "blue"; //passed via a user form
   echo "<form action='nextpage.php' method='post'>
         <input type='hidden' name='color' value='$color'>
         <input type='submit' value='Next Page'>
         </form>\n";
?>
```

The Web page shows a submit button that says Next Page, but it doesn't ask the user for any information. When the user clicks the button, `nextpage.php` runs and can use the variable `$color`, which contains `"blue"`.

Put the hidden field before the submit button field. If you put the hidden field after the submit button, it will not be sent.

Using PHP Sessions

A *session* is the time that a user spends at your Web site. Users may view many Web pages between the time they enter your site and leave it. Often you want information to follow the user around your site so that it's available on every page. PHP, beginning with version 4.0, provides a way to do this.

How PHP sessions work

PHP enables you to set up a session on one Web page and declare variables to be session variables. Then you open the session in any other page, and the session variables are available for your use. To do this, PHP does the following:

1. **Assigns a session ID number:** The number is a really long nonsense number that is unique for the user and that no one could possibly guess. The session ID is stored in a PHP system variable named `PHPSESSID`.
2. **Stores session variables in a file on the server:** The file is named with the session ID number. The file is stored in `\tmp` on Unix/Linux, and in Windows, it's stored in a directory called `sessiondata` under the directory where PHP is installed.

   If you are the PHP administrator, you can change the location where the session files are stored by editing the configuration file `php.ini`. Find the setting for `session.save_path` and change the path to the location where you want to store the files.
3. **Passes the session ID number to every page:** If the user has cookies turned on, PHP passes the session ID using cookies. If the user has cookies turned off, PHP passes the session ID in the URL for links or in a hidden variable for forms that use the post method.

4. **Gets the variables from the session file for each new session page:** Whenever a user opens a new page that is part of the session, PHP gets the variables from the file using the session ID number that was passed from the old page. You can use the variables, and they have the value that you assigned in the previous page.

Sessions do not work unless *track-vars* is enabled. As of PHP 4.0.3, track-vars is always turned on. For versions previous to 4.0.3, the option `--enable-track-vars` should be used when installing PHP.

If users have cookies turned off, sessions do not work unless *trans-sid* is turned on. PHP should be installed using the option `--enable-trans-sid`. You find out how to test whether trans-sid is turned on and how to use sessions when it is not turned on later in this chapter.

Opening sessions

You should open a session on each Web page. Open the session with the `session_start` function, as follows:

```
session_start();
```

The function first checks for an existing session ID number. If it finds one, it sets up the session variables. If it doesn't find one, it starts a new session by creating a new session ID number.

Because sessions use cookies if the user has them turned on, `session_start` is subject to the same limitation as cookies. That is, the `session_start` function must be called before any output is sent. For complete details, see the sidebar "Statements that must come before output," earlier in this chapter.

You can tell PHP that every page on your site should automatically start with a `session_start`. To do this, edit the configuration file `php.ini`. If you are the PHP administrator, you can edit this file; otherwise, ask the administrator to edit it. Look for the variable `session.auto_start` and set its value to 1. You may have to restart the Web browser before this takes effect. With `auto_start` turned on, you do not need to add a `session_start` at the beginning of each page.

Using PHP session variables

Register any variables you want to use throughout the session. Only the variables registered as session variables are available on later pages. To register a variable, use

```
session_register('varname');
```

The *varname* is the name of the variable you want to make a session variable, but do not use the dollar sign ($) in the name. You can include as many variables in session_register as you need, such as:

```
session_register('city','state','zip');
```

After this statement is executed, the variables are registered as session variables, but they are not given any value. If you were to echo a variable at this point, it would be empty. This statement just tells PHP to store this variable in the session file whenever its value is changed in the program. Thus, to store a value, you need to use these statements:

```
session_register('state');
$state = "CA";
```

After you have opened the session and registered the variables, the variables are available on any subsequent page in the session. When you start a session, PHP checks to see whether a session already exists, and if it does, it gets all the registered variables. Registered variables are also available in an array called $HTTP_SESSION_VARS.

Be careful with variable names. If variables in a form have the same name as variables in a URL, you might overwrite one variable with the next, and because of the order in which PHP processes the variables, your variables in the new page might have unexpected values. See the sidebar "Variable processing orders," earlier in this chapter.

If you want to stop storing any variable at any time, you can unregister the variable using the following statement:

```
session_unregister('varname');
```

The unregistered variable will no longer be available in future sessions. However, it is not removed from the current program. If you don't want it available in the current program, use these statements:

```
session_unregister('varname');
unset($varname);
```

You can unregister all the variables with one statement as follows:

```
session_unset();
```

This statements unregisters all the variables that are registered in the session.

The following two programs show how to use sessions to pass information from one page to the next. The first program, sessionTest1.php in Listing 9-2, shows the first page where the session begins. Listing 9-3 shows the program sessionTest2.php for the second page in a session.

Listing 9-2: Starting a Session

```
<?php
  session_start();
  session_register('session_var');
?>
<html>
<head><title>Testing Sessions page 1</title></head>
<body>
<?php
  $session_var = "testing";
  echo "This is a test of the sessions feature.
        <form action='sessionTest2.php' method='post'>
        <input type='text' name='form_var' value='testing'>
        <input type='submit' value='go to next page'>
        </form>";
?>
</body>
</html>
```

Notice that the variable `$session_var` is registered in the beginning of the program. However, its value is set later in the program. If the later statement that sets `$session_var` to equal `"testing"` were not included in the program, the value for `$session_var` would be empty.

Listing 9-3: The Second Page of a Session

```
<?php
  session_start();
?>
<html>
<head><title>Testing Sessions page 2</title></head>
<body>
<?php
  echo "session_var = $session_var<br>\n";
  echo "form_var = $form_var<br>\n";
?>
</body>
</html>
```

Point your browser at `sessionTest.php` and then click the submit button that says Go to Next Page. You will then see the following output from `sessionTest2.php`:

```
session_var = testing
form_var = testing
```

Because sessions work differently for users with cookies turned on and users with cookies turned off, you should test the two programs in both conditions. To turn off cookies in your browser, you change the settings for options or preferences.

To disable cookies in Internet Explorer, follow these steps:

1. **Choose Tools⇨Internet Options.**

   The Internet Options dialog box opens.

2. **Click the Security tab.**
3. **Click the Internet icon to highlight it.**
4. **Click the Custom Level button.**

   The Security Settings dialog box appears.
5. **Scroll down to the Cookies section and select Disable for each of the cookie settings.**
6. **Click OK.**

To disable cookies in Netscape Navigator, follow these steps:

1. **Choose Edit⇨Preferences.**
2. **Highlight Advanced.**
3. **Check Disable Cookies.**
4. **Click OK.**

If the output from `sessionTest2` shows a blank value for `$session_var` when you turn cookies off in your browser, it is probably because PHP wasn't installed using the option `—enable-trans-sid`. If you are the PHP administrator, you can reinstall PHP with trans-sid turned on to solve this problem. If you are not the administrator, you must ask the administrator to reinstall PHP. If you can't get this problem fixed, you can still use sessions, but you must pass the session ID number in your programming statements because PHP will not pass it automatically when cookies are turned off. For details on how to use sessions when trans-sid is not turned on, check out the next section.

Sessions without cookies

Many users turn off cookies in their browsers. PHP checks the user's browser to see whether cookies are allowed and behaves accordingly. If the user's browser allows cookies, PHP does the following:

- Sets the variable `$PHPSESSID` equal to the session ID number
- Uses cookies to move `$PHPSESSID` from one page to the next

If the user's browser is set to refuse cookies, PHP does the following:

- Sets a constant called `SID`. The constant contains a `variable=value` pair that looks like `PHPSESSID=`*`longstringofnumbers`*.

- May or may not move the session ID number from one page to the next, depending on whether trans-sid is turned on. If it is turned on, PHP passes the session ID number; if it is not turned on, PHP does not pass the session ID number. Trans-sid is turned on when PHP is installed using the option `—enable-trans-sid`.

Turning trans-sid on has advantages and disadvantages. The advantage is that sessions work seamlessly even when users turn cookies off. It also is much easier to program sessions with trans-sid turned on. The disadvantage is that the session ID number is often passed in the URL. In some situations, the session ID number should not be shown in the browser address. Also, when the session ID number is in the URL, it can be bookmarked by the user. Then, if the user returns to your site using the bookmark with the session ID number in it, the new session ID number from the current visit can get confused with the old session ID number from the previous visit and possibly cause problems.

Sessions with trans-sid turned on

When trans-sid is turned on and the user has cookies turned off, PHP automatically sends the session ID number in the URL or as a hidden form field. If the user moves to the next page using a link, a header function, or a form with the get method, the session ID number is added to the URL. If the user moves to the next page using a form with the post method, the session ID number is passed in a hidden field. PHP recognizes `$PHPSESSID` as the session ID number and handles the session without any special programming on your part.

The session ID number is only added to the URLs for pages on your own Web site. If the URL of the next page includes a server name, PHP assumes that the URL is on another Web site and doesn't add the session ID number. For instance, if your link statement is

```
<a href="newpage.php">
```

PHP will add the session ID number. However, if your statement is

```
<a href="HTTP://www.company.com/newpage.php">
```

PHP will *not* add the session ID number.

Sessions without trans-sid turned on

When trans-sid is *not* turned on, PHP does *not* send the session ID number to the next page when users have cookies turned off. Rather you must send the session ID number yourself.

Fortunately, PHP provides a constant that you can use to send the session ID yourself. A *constant* is a variable that contains information that can't be changed. (Constants are described in Chapter 6.) The constant that PHP provides is named `SID` and contains a `variable=value` pair that you can add to the URL, as follows:

```
<a href="nextpage.php?<?php echo SID?> > next page </a>
```

This link statement adds a question mark (?) and the constant `SID` to the URL. `SID` contains the session ID number formatted as `variable=value`. The output from `echo SID` looks something like this:

```
PHPSESSID=877c22163d8df9deb342c7333cfe38a7
```

Therefore, the URL that is sent is

```
<a href="nextpage.php?PHPSESSID=877c22163d8df9deb342c7333cfe38a7>
   next page </a>
```

For one of several reasons (which I discuss earlier in this chapter), you may not want the session ID number to appear on the URL shown by the browser. To prevent that, you can send the session ID number in a hidden field in a form by using the post method. First, get the session ID number. Then send it in a hidden field. The statements to do this are

```
<?php
  $PHPSESSID = session_id();
  echo "<form action='nextpage.php' method='post'>
        <input type='hidden' name='PHPSESSID' value='$PHPSESSID'>
        <input type='submit' value='Next Page'>
        </form>";
?>
```

These statements do the following:

1. Store the session ID number in a variable called `$PHPSESSID`. Use the function `session_id`, which returns the current session ID number.
2. Send `$PHPSESSID` in a hidden form field.

On the new page, PHP will automatically get `$PHPSESSID` without any special programming needed from you.

Making sessions private

PHP session functions are ideal for Web sites that are restricted and require users to login with a login name and password. Those Web sites undoubtedly have many pages, and you don't want the user to have to login to each page.

PHP sessions can keep track of whether the user has logged in and refuse access to users that aren't logged in. Using PHP sessions, you can do the following:

1. Show users a login page.
2. If a user logs in successfully, set and store a session variable.
3. Whenever a user goes to a new page, check the session variable to see if the user has logged in.
4. If the user has logged in, show the page.
5. If the user has not logged in, bring up the login page.

To check whether a user has logged in, add the following statements to the top of every page:

```
<?php
  session_start()
  if ( @$login != "yes" )
  {
    header("Location: loginPage.php");
    exit();
  }
?>
```

In these statements, `$login` is a session variable that is set to `"yes"` when the user logs in. The statements check to see if `$login` is equal to `"yes"`. If it is not, it means the user is not logged in, and the user is sent to the login page. If `$login` equals `"yes"`, the program proceeds with the rest of the statements on the Web page.

Closing PHP sessions

For restricted sessions that users log into, you often want users to logout when they're finished. To close a session, use the following statement:

```
session_destroy();
```

This statement gets rid of all the session variable information that is stored in the session file. PHP no longer passes the session ID number to the next page. However, the statement does *not* affect the variables currently set on the current page. They still equal the same values. If you want to remove the variables from the current page, as well as prevent them from being passed to the next page, unset them using this statement:

```
unset($variablename,$variablename,...);
```

Part IV
Applications

"The new technology has really helped me get organized. I Keep my project reports under the PC, budgets under my laptop, and memos under my pager."

In this part . . .

In this part, you find out how to take the planning and getting started information from Part I, the MySQL information from Part II, and the PHP information from Part III and put it all together into a whole Web database application. Chapters 11 and 12 present two sample applications, complete with their databases and all their PHP programs.

Chapter 10

Putting It All Together

In This Chapter

- Organizing your whole application
- Organizing individual programs
- Making your application secure
- Documenting your application

The previous chapters of this book provide you with the tools you need to build your Web database application. In Part I, you find out how PHP and MySQL work and how to get access to them. In addition, you discover what needs to be done to build your application and in what order to do it. In Part II, you find out how to build and use a MySQL database. In Part III, you discover what features PHP has and how to use them. In addition, this part also explains how to show information in a Web page, collect information from users, and store information in a database. Now you're ready to put it all together.

This chapter shows you how to put all the pieces together into a complete application. To do this, you need to

- Organize the application
- Make sure the application is secure
- Document the application

This chapter describes each of these steps in detail.

Organizing the Application

Organizing the application is for your benefit. As far as PHP is concerned, the application could be 8 million PHP statements all on one line of one computer file. PHP doesn't care about lines, indents, or files. However, humans write and maintain the programs for the application, and humans need organization. Applications require two levels of organization:

- **The application level:** Most applications need more than one program to deliver complete functionality. You must divide the functions of the application into an organized set of programs.
- **The program level:** Most programs perform more than one specific task. You must divide the tasks of the program into sections within the program.

Organizing at the application level

In general, Web database applications consist of one program per Web page. For instance, you might have a program that provides a form to collect information and a program that stores the information in a database and tells the user that the data has been stored.

Another basis for organization is one program per major task. For instance, you might have a program to present the form and a program that stores the data in a database. For Web applications, most major tasks involve sending a Web page. Collecting data from the user requires a Web page for the HTML form; providing product information to customers requires Web pages; and when you store data in a database, you usually want to send a confirmation page to the user that the data was stored.

One program per Web page or one program per major task is not a rule, merely a guideline. The only rule regarding organization is that it must be clear and easy to understand. And that's totally subjective. Still, the organization of an application such as the Pet Catalog need not be overly complicated. Suppose the Pet Catalog's design calls for the first page to list all the pet types — such as cat, dog, and bird — that the user can select from. Then, after the user selects a type, all the pets in the catalog for that type are shown on the next Web page. A reasonable organization would be two programs: one to show the page of pet types and one to show the pets based on the pet type that was chosen.

Here are a few additional pointers for organizing your programs:

- **Choose very descriptive names for the programs in your application.** Program names are part of the documentation that makes your application understandable. For instance, useful names for the Pet Catalog programs might be `ShowPetTypes.php` and `ShowPets.php`. It's usual, but not a requirement, to begin the program names with an uppercase letter. Case isn't important for program names on Windows computers, but it's very important on Unix/Linux computers. Pay attention to the upper/lowercase letters so that your programs can run on any computer if needed.
- **Put program files into subdirectories with meaningful names.** For instance, put all the graphic files into a directory called *images*. If you only have three files, you may be okay with only one directory, but looking through dozens of files for one specific file can waste a lot of time.

Organizing at the program level

A well-organized individual program is very important for the following reasons:

- **It's easier for you to write.** The better organized your program is, the easier it is for you to read and understand it. You can see what the program is doing and find and fix problems faster.
- **It's easier for others to understand.** Others may need to understand your program. After you claim that big inheritance and head off to the South Sea Island you purchased, someone else will have to maintain your application.
- **It's easier for you to maintain.** No matter how thoroughly you test it, your application is likely to have a problem or two. The better organized your program is, the easier it is for you to find and fix problems, especially six months later.
- **It's easier to change.** Sooner or later, you or someone else will need to change the program. The needs of the user may change. The needs of the business may change. The technology may change. The ozone layer may change. For one reason or another, the program will need to be changed. Figuring out what the program does and how it does it so that you can change it is much easier if it is well organized. I guarantee that you won't remember the details; you just need to be able to understand the program.

The following rules will produce well-organized programs. I hesitate to call them rules because there can be reasons in any specific environment to break one or more of the rules, but I strongly recommend thinking carefully before breaking any of the following rules:

- **Divide the statements into sections for each specific task.** Start each section with a comment describing what the section does. Separate sections from each other by adding blank lines. For instance, for the Pet Catalog, the first program might have three sections for three tasks:

  1. **Echo introductory text, such as the page heading and instructions.** The comment before the section might be `/* opening text */`. If the program echoes a lot of complicated text and graphics, you might make it into more than one section, such as `/* title and logo */` and `/* instructions */`.
  2. **Get a list of pet types from the database.** If this section is long and complicated, you can divide it into smaller sections, such as 1) connect to database; 2) execute `SELECT` query; and 3) put data into variables.
  3. **Create a form that displays a selection list of the pet types.** Forms are often long and complicated. It can be useful to have a section for each part of the form.

- **Use indents.** Indent blocks in the PHP statements. For instance, indent if blocks and while blocks as I have done in the sample code for this book. If blocks are nested inside other blocks, indent the nested block even further. It's much easier to see where blocks begin and end when they're indented, which in turn makes it easier to understand what the program does. It can also be helpful to indent the HTML statements. For instance, if you indent the lines between the open and close tags for a form or between the `<table>` tag and the `</table>` tag, you can more easily see what the statements are doing.
- **Use comments liberally.** Definitely add comments at the beginning that explain what the program does. And add comments for each section. Also, comment any statements that you think aren't obvious or statements where you think you may have done something in an unusual way. If it took you a while to figure out how to do it, it's probably worth commenting. Don't forget short comments on the end of lines; sometimes just a word or two can help.
- **Use simple statements.** Sometimes programmers get carried away with the idea of concise code to the detriment of readability. Nesting six function calls inside each other may save some lines and keystrokes, but it will also make the program more difficult to read.
- **Reuse blocks of statements.** If you find yourself typing the same ten lines of PHP statements in several places in the program, you can move that block of statements into another file and call it when you need it. One line in your program that says `getData()` is much easier to read than ten lines that get the data. Not only that, if you need to change something within those lines, you can change it in one external file, instead of having to find and change it a dozen different places in your program. There are two ways to reuse statements: functions and include statements. Chapter 7 explains how to write and use functions. The following two sections explain the use of functions and include statements in program organization.
- **Use constants.** If your program uses the same value many times, such as the sales tax for your state, you can define a constant in the beginning of the program that creates a constant called `CA_SALES_TAX` that is `.97` and use it whenever it's needed. Defining a constant that gives the number a name helps anyone reading the program understand what the number is, plus if you ever need to change it, you only have to change it in one place. Constants are described in detail in Chapter 6.

Using include statements

PHP allows you to put statements into an external file, a file separate from your program, and to insert the file wherever you want it in the program using an include statement. Include files are very useful for storing a block of statements that is repeated. You add an include statement wherever you want to use the statements, instead of adding the entire block of statements at several different locations. It makes your programs much shorter and easier to read. The format for an include statement is

```
include ("filename");
```

The file can have any name. I like to use the extension .inc. The statements in the file are included, as is, at the point where the include statement is used. The statements are included as HTML, not PHP. Therefore, if you want to use PHP statements in your include file, you must include PHP tags in the include file. Otherwise, all the statements in the include file are seen as HTML and output to the Web page as is.

Here are some ways to use include files to organize your programs:

- **Put all or most of your HTML into include files.** For instance, if your program sends a form to the browser, put the HTML for the form into an external file. When you need to send the form, use an include statement. Putting the HTML into an include file is a good idea if the form is shown several times. It is even a good idea if the form is shown only once because it makes your program much easier to read.
- **Store the information needed to access the database in a file separate from your program.** Store the variable names in the file as follows:

  ```
  <?php
  $host="localhost";
  $user="root";
  $password="";
  ?>
  ```

  Notice that this file needs the php tags in it because the include statement inserts the file as HTML. Include this file at the top of every program that needs to connect to the database. If any of the information, such as the password, changes, just change the password in the include file. You don't need to search through every program file to change the password. For a little added security, it's a good idea to use a misleading filename, rather than secret_passwords.inc.
- **Put your functions in include files.** You don't need the statements for functions in the program; you can put them in an include file. If you have a lot of functions, organize related functions into several include files, such as data_functions.inc and form_functions.inc. Use include statements at the top of your programs, reading in the functions that are used in the program.
- **Store statements that all the files on your Web site have in common.** Most Web sites have many Web pages with many elements in common. For instance, all Web pages start with <html>, <head>, and <body> tags. If you store the common statements in an include file, you can include them in every Web page, ensuring that all your pages look alike. For instance, you might have the following statements in an include file:

  ```
  <html>
  <head><title><?php echo $title ?></title></head>
  <body topmargin="0">
  <p align="center"><img src="logo.gif" width="100" height="200">
  <hr color="red">
  ```

> If you include this file in the top of every program on your Web site, you save a lot of typing, and you know that all your pages match. In addition, if you want to change anything about the look of all your pages, you only have to change it one place — in the include file.

You can use a similar statement as follows:

```
include_once("filename");
```

This statement prevents include files with similar variables from overwriting each other. Use `include_once` when you include your functions.

You can use a variable name for the file name as follows:

```
include ("$filename");
```

For instance, you might have different messages on different days:

```
$today = time("D");
include("$today"."inc");
```

You can use a path to include files from other directories, such as:

```
include("../../hidden/filename.inc");
```

In addition, PHP can assign a directory to be an include directory, a directory where PHP will look for files when no path is listed in the include statement. For security, you can set up an include directory outside your public Web space in a location that can't be reached by visitors from the Web. You can see the current include directory location by using the `phpinfo()` function. Check the value for `include_path`. If you're the PHP administrator, you can change the path for `include_path` in the `php.ini` configuration file. Setting more than one directory as an include directory is possible. If you can't set the path yourself, discuss your needs with the PHP administrator.

Using functions

Make frequent use of functions to organize your programs. (Chapter 7 discusses creating and using functions in detail.) Functions are useful when your program needs to perform the same task at repeated locations in a program or in different programs in the application. After you have written a function that does the task and you know it works, you can use it anywhere you need it.

Look for opportunities to use functions. Your program is much easier to read and understand with a line like this:

```
getMemberData();
```

than with 20 lines of statements that actually get the data.

In fact, after you've been writing PHP programs a while, you will have a stash of functions that you've written for various programs. Very often the program you're writing can use a function that you wrote for an application two jobs ago. For instance, I often have a need for a list of the states. Rather than include a list of all 50 states every time I need it, I have a function called `getStateNames()` that returns an array that holds the 50 state names in alphabetical order and a function called `getStateCodes()` that returns an array with all 50 two-letter state codes in the same order. These functions are frequently useful.

Name your functions very descriptively. The function calls in your program should tell you exactly what the function does. Long is okay. You don't want to see a line in your program that says:

```
function1();
```

This line isn't very informative. Even a line like the following is less informative than it could be:

```
getData();
```

You want to see a line like this:

```
getAllMemberNames();
```

Keeping It Private

You need to protect your Web database application. People out there may have nefarious designs on your Web site for purposes such as

- **Stealing stuff:** They hope to find a file sitting around full of valid credit card numbers or the secret formula for eternal youth.
- **Trashing your Web site:** Some people think this is funny. Some people do it to prove that they can.
- **Harming your users:** A malicious person can add things to your Web site that harm or steal from the people who visit your site.

This is not a security book. Security is a large, complex issue, and I am not a security expert. Nevertheless, I want to call a few issues to your attention and make some suggestions that might help. The following measures will increase the security of your Web site, but if your site handles really important, secret information, read some security books and talk to some experts:

- **Ensure the security of the computer that hosts your Web site.** This is probably not your responsibility, but you may want to talk to the people responsible and discuss your security concerns. You'll feel better if you know that someone is worrying about security.
- **Don't let the Web server display file names.** Users don't need to know the names of the files on your Web site.

- **Hide things.** Store your information so that it can't be easily accessed from the Web.
- **Don't trust information from users.** Always clean any information that you didn't generate yourself.
- **Use a secure Web server.** This requires extra work, but it's important if you have top-secret information.

Ensure the security of the computer

First, the computer itself must be secure. The system administrator of the computer is responsible for keeping unauthorized visitors and vandals out of the system. Security measures include such things as firewalls, encryption, password shadowing, scan detectors, and so on. In most cases, the system administrator is not you. If it is, you need to do some serious investigation into security issues. If you are using a Web hosting company, you may want to discuss security with those folks, to reassure yourself that they are using sufficient security measures.

Don't let the Web server display file names

You may have noticed that sometimes you get a list of file names when you point at a URL. If you point at a directory, rather than a specific file, and the directory doesn't contain a file with the default file name (such as `index.html`), the Web server may display a list of files for you to select from. You probably don't want your Web server to do this; your site won't be very secure if a visitor can look at any file on your site. On other Web sites, you may have seen an error message that says:

```
Forbidden
You don't have permission to access /secretdirectory on this server.
```

On those sites, the Web server is set so that it doesn't display a list of file names when the URL points to a directory. Instead, it delivers this error message. This is more secure than listing the file names. If the file name is being sent from your Web site, a setting for the Web server needs to be changed. If you aren't the administrator for your Web server, request a change. If you are the administrator, it's up to you to change this behavior. For instance, in Apache, this behavior is controlled by an option called Indexes, which can be turned on or off in the `httpd.conf` file as follows:

```
Options Indexes         // turns it on
Options -Indexes        // turns it off
```

See the documentation for your Web server to allow or not allow directory listings in the user's Web browser.

Hide things

Keep information as private as possible. Of course, the Web pages you want visitors to see must be stored in your public Web space directory. But, not everything needs to be stored there. For instance, you can store include files in another location altogether, in space on the computer that can't be accessed from the Web. Your database certainly isn't stored in your Web space, but it might be even more secure if it were stored on a totally different computer.

Another way to hide things is to give them misleading names. For instance, the include file containing the database variables shouldn't be called `passwords.inc`. A better name might be `UncleHenrysChickenSoupRecipe.inc`. I know this suggestion violates other sections of the book where I promote informative file names, but this is a special case. Malicious people sometimes do obvious things like typing `www.yoursite.com/passwords.html` into their browser to see what happens.

Don't trust information from users

Malicious users can use the forms in your Web pages to send dangerous text to your Web site. Therefore, never store information from forms directly into a database without checking it first. Check the information that you receive for reasonable formats and dangerous characters. In particular, you don't want to accept HTML tags, such as `<script>` tags, from forms. Using script tags, a user could enter an actual script, perhaps a malicious one. If you just accept the form field without checking it and store it in your database, you could have any number of problems, particularly if the stored script was sent in a Web page to a visitor to your Web site. For more on checking data from forms, see Chapter 8.

Use a secure Web server

Communication between your Web site and its visitors is not totally secure. When the files on your Web site are sent to the user's browser, someone on the Internet between you and the user can read the contents of these files as they pass by. For most Web sites, this isn't an issue, but if your site collects or sends credit card numbers or other secret information, use a secure Web server to protect this data.

Secure Web servers use SSL (Security Sockets Layer) to protect communication sent to and received from browsers. This is similar to the scrambled telephone calls you hear about in spy movies. The information is encrypted (translated into coded strings) before it is sent across the Web. The receiving software decrypts it into its original content. In addition, your Web site uses a certificate that verifies your identity. Using a secure Web server is extra work, but it's necessary for some applications.

You can tell when you are communicating using SSL. The URL begins with HTTPS, rather than HTTP.

Information about secure Web servers is specific to the Web server that you're using. To find out more about using SSL, look at the Web site for the Web server you are using. For instance, if you are using Apache, check out two open-source projects that implement SSL for Apache at `modssl.org` and `www.apache-ssl.org`. Commercial software is also available that provides a secure server based on the Apache Web server. If you're using Microsoft IIS, search for *SSL* on the Microsoft Web site at `www.microsoft.com`.

Completing Your Documentation

I'm making one last pitch here. Documenting your Web database application is essential. You started with a plan describing what the application is supposed to do. Based on your plan, you created a database design. Keep the plan and the design up-to-date. Often as a project moves along, changes are made. Make sure your documentation changes to match the new decisions.

Now, as you design your programs, associate the tasks in the application plan with the programs you plan to write. List the programs and what each one will do. If the programs are complicated, you may want to include a brief description of how the program will perform its tasks. If this is a team effort, list who is responsible for each program. When you have completed your application, you should have the following documents:

- **Application plan:** Describes what the application is supposed to do, listing the tasks it will perform
- **Database design:** Describes the tables and fields that are in the database
- **Program design:** Describes how the programs will do the tasks in the application plan
- **Program comments:** Describe the details of how the individual program works

Pretend it is five years in the future and you're about to do a major rewrite of your application. What will you need to know about the application in order to change it? Be sure that you include all the information you need to know in your documentation.

Chapter 11

Building an Online Catalog

In This Chapter

- Designing an online catalog
- Building the database for the Pet Catalog
- Designing the Web pages for the Pet Catalog
- Writing the programs for the Pet Catalog

Online catalogs are everywhere on the Web. Every business that has products for sale can use an online catalog. Some businesses use online catalogs to sell their products online, and some use them to show the quality and worth of their products to the world. Many customers have come to expect businesses to be online and provide information about their products. Customers often begin their search for a product online, researching its availability and cost through the Web.

In this chapter, you find out how to build an online catalog. I chose a pet store catalog for no particular reason except that it sounded like more fun than a catalog of socks or light bulbs. And looking at the pictures for a pet catalog was much more fun than looking at pictures of socks. I introduced the Pet Catalog example in Chapter 3 and use it for many of the examples throughout this book.

In general, all catalogs do the same thing: provide product information to potential customers. The general purpose of the catalog is to make it as easy as possible for customers to see information about the products. In addition, you want to make the products look as attractive as possible so that customers will want to purchase them.

Designing the Application

The first step in design is to decide what the application should do. The obvious purpose of the Pet Catalog is to show potential customers information about the pets. A pet store might also want to show information about pet products, such as pet food, cages, fish tanks, and catnip toys, but you decide not to include such items in your catalog. The purpose of your online catalog application is just to show pets.

For the customer, displaying the information is the sole function of the catalog. However, from your perspective, the catalog also needs to be maintained; you need to add items to the catalog. So you must include the task of adding items to the catalog as part of the catalog application. Thus, the application has two distinct functions:

- Show pets to the customers
- Add pets to the catalog

Showing pets to the customers

The basic purpose of your online catalog is to let customers look at pets. Customers can't purchase pets online, of course. Sending pets through the mail isn't feasible. But a catalog can showcase pets in a way that motivates customers to rush to the store to buy them.

If your catalog only has three pets in it, your catalog can be pretty simple — one page showing the three pets. However, most catalogs have many more items than that. Usually, a catalog opens with a list of the types of products — in this case, pets — that are available, such as cat, dog, horse, and dragon. Customers select the type of pet they want to see, and the catalog then displays the individual pets of that type. For example, if the customer selects dog, the catalog would then show collies, spaniels, and wolves. Some types of products might have more levels of categories before you see individual products. For instance, furniture might have three levels, rather than two. The top level might be the room, such as kitchen, bedroom, and so on. The second level might be type, such as chairs, tables, and so on. The third level would be the individual products.

The purpose of a catalog is to motivate those who look at it to make a purchase immediately. For the Pet Catalog, pictures are a major factor in motivating customers to make a purchase. Pictures of pets make people go ooooh and aaaah and say, "Isn't he cuuuute!" This generates sales. The main purpose of your Pet Catalog is to show pictures of pets. In addition, the catalog also should show descriptions and prices.

To show the pets to customers, the Pet Catalog will do the following:

1. Show a list of the types of pets and allow the customer to select a type.
2. Show information about the pets that match the selected type. The information includes the description, the price, and a picture of the pet.

Adding pets to the catalog

You can add items to your catalog several ways. However, the task of adding an item to the catalog is much easier if you use an application designed for adding your specific products. In many cases, you aren't the person who will be adding products to your catalog. One reason for adding maintenance functionality to your catalog application is so that someone else can do those boring maintenance tasks. The easier it is to maintain your catalog, the less likely that errors will sneak into it.

An application to add a pet to your catalog should do the following:

1. Prompt the user to enter a pet type for the pet. A selection list of possible pet types would eliminate many errors, such as alternate spellings (*dog* and *dogs*) and misspellings. The application also needs to allow the user to add new categories when needed.
2. Prompt the user to enter a name for the pet, such as *collie* or *shark.* A selection list of names would help prevent mistakes. The application also needs to allow the user to add new names when needed.
3. Prompt the user to enter the pet information for the new pet. The application should clearly specify what information is needed.
4. Store the information in the catalog.

The catalog entry application can check the data for mistakes and enter the data into the correct locations. The person entering the new pet doesn't need to know the inner workings of the catalog.

Building the Database

The catalog itself is a database. It doesn't have to be a database; it's possible to store a catalog as a series of HTML files that contain the product information in HTML tags and display the appropriate file when the customer clicks a link. However, it makes my eyes cross to think of maintaining such a catalog. Adding and removing catalog items manually. Finding the right location for each item by searching through many files. Ugh. For these reasons, it's better to put your Pet Catalog in a database.

The PetCatalog database contains all the information about pets. It uses three tables:

- Pet table
- PetType table
- Color table

The first step in building the Pet Catalog is to build the database. It's pretty much impossible to write programs without a working database to test the programs on. First you design your database; then you build it; then you add the data (or at least some sample data to use while developing the programs).

Some changes have been made to the database design developed in Chapter 3 for the Pet Catalog. Development and testing often result in changes. You find that you didn't take some factors into consideration in your design or that certain elements of your design don't work with real world data or are difficult to program. It's perfectly normal for the design to evolve as you work on your application. Just be sure to change your documentation when your design changes.

Building the Pet table

In your design for the Pet Catalog, the main table is the Pet table. It contains the information about the individual pets you sell. The following SQL query creates the Pet table:

```
CREATE TABLE Pet (
  petID          INT(5)        NOT NULL AUTO_INCREMENT,
  petName        CHAR(25)      NOT NULL,
  petType        CHAR(15)      NOT NULL DEFAULT "Misc",
  petDescription VARCHAR(255),
  price          DECIMAL(9,2),
  pix            CHAR(15)      NOT NULL DEFAULT "na.gif",
  PRIMARY KEY(petID) );
```

Each row of the Pet table represents a pet. The columns are as follows:

- **petID:** A sequence number for the pet. In another catalog, this might be a product number, a serial number, or a number used to order the product. The `CREATE` query defines the petID column in the following ways:
  - `INT(5)`**:** The data in the field is expected to be a numeric integer. The database won't accept a character string in this field.
  - `PRIMARY KEY(petID)`**:** This is the primary key, which is the field that must be unique. MySQL will not allow two rows to be entered with the same petID.
  - `NOT NULL`**:** This definition means that this field can't be empty. It must have a value. The primary key must always be set to `NOT NULL`.
  - `AUTO-INCREMENT`**:** This definition means that the field will automatically be filled with a sequential number if you don't provide a specific number. For example, if a row is added with 98 for a petID, the next row will be added with 99 for the petID unless you specify a different number. This is a useful way of specifying a column with a unique number, such as a product number or an order number. You can always override the automatic sequence number with a number of your own, but if you don't provide a number, a sequential number is stored.
- **petName:** The name of the pet, such as lion, collie, or unicorn. The `CREATE` query defines the petName column in the following ways:

  - `CHAR(25)`: The data in this field is expected to be a character string that's 25 characters long. The field will always take up 25 characters of storage, with padding if the actual string stored is less than 25 characters.
  - `NOT NULL`: This definition means that this field can't be empty. It must have a value. After all, it wouldn't make much sense to have a pet in the catalog without a name.
  - **No default value:** If you try to add a new row to the Pet table without a petName, it won't be added. It doesn't make sense to have a default name for a pet.
- **petType:** The type of pet, such as dog or fish. The `CREATE` query defines the petType column in the following ways:
  - `CHAR(15)`: The data in this field is expected to be a character string that's 15 characters long. The field will always take up 15 characters of storage, with padding if the actual string stored is less than 15 characters.
  - `NOT NULL`: This definition means that this field can't be empty. It must have a value. The online catalog application will show categories first and then pets within a category, so a pet with no category will never be shown on the Web page.
  - `DEFAULT "Misc"`: The value `"Misc"` is stored if you don't provide a value for petType. This ensures that a value is always stored for petType.
- **petDescription:** A description of the pet. The `CREATE` query defines the petDescription in the following way:
  - `VARCHAR(255)`: This data type defines the field as a variable character string that can be up to 255 characters long. The field is stored in its actual length.
- **price:** The price of the pet. The `CREATE` query defines price in the following way:
  - `DECIMAL(9,2)`: This data type defines the field as a decimal number that can be up to nine digits and has two decimal places. If you store an integer in this field, it will be returned with two decimal places, such as 9.00 or 2568.00.
- **pix:** The file name of the picture of the pet. Pictures on a Web site are stored in graphic files with names like `dog.jpg`, `dragon.gif`, or `cat.png`. This field stores the file name for the picture you want to show for this pet. The `CREATE` query defines pix in the following ways:
  - `CHAR(15)`: The data in this field is expected to be a character string that's 15 characters long. For some applications, the picture files might be in other directories or on other Web sites requiring a longer field, but for this application, the pictures are all in a

directory on the Web site and have short names. The field will always take up 15 characters of storage, with padding if the actual string stored is less than 15 characters.

- `NOT NULL`: This definition means that this field can't be empty. It must have a value. You need a picture for the pet. When a Web site tries to show a picture that can't be found, it displays an ugly error message in the browser window where the graphic would go. You don't want your catalog to do that, so your database should require a value. In this case, you define a default value so that a value will always be placed in this field.
- `DEFAULT "na.gif"`: The value `"na.gif"` is stored if you don't provide a value for pix. In this way, a value is always stored for pix The `na.gif` file might be a graphic that says something like: `"picture not available"`.

Notice the following points about this database table design:

- **Some fields are `CHAR`, and some are `VARCHAR`.** `CHAR` fields are faster, whereas `VARCHAR` fields are more efficient. Your decision will depend on whether disk space or speed is more important for your application in your environment.

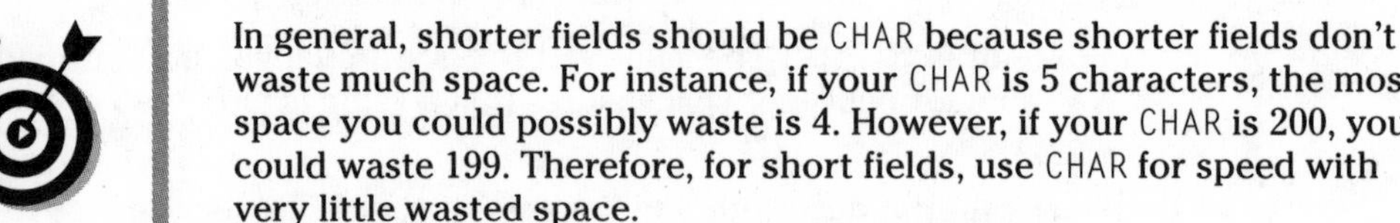

  In general, shorter fields should be `CHAR` because shorter fields don't waste much space. For instance, if your `CHAR` is 5 characters, the most space you could possibly waste is 4. However, if your `CHAR` is 200, you could waste 199. Therefore, for short fields, use `CHAR` for speed with very little wasted space.

- **The petID field means different things for different pets.** The petID field assigns a unique number to each pet. However, a unique number is not necessarily meaningful in all cases. For example, a unique number is meaningful for an individual kitten but not for an individual goldfish.

  There are really two kinds of pets. One is the unique pet, such as a puppy or a kitten. The customer buys a specific dog, not just a generic dog. The customer needs to see the picture of the actual animal. On the other hand, some pets are not especially unique, such as a goldfish or a parakeet. When customers purchase a goldfish, they see a tank full of goldfish and point at one. The only real distinguishing characteristic of a goldfish is its color. The customer doesn't need to see a picture of the actual fish in your catalog, just a picture of a generic goldfish, perhaps showing the possible colors.

  In your catalog, you have both kinds of pets. The catalog might contain several pets with the name *cat* but with different petIDs. The picture would show the individual pet. The catalog also contains pets that aren't individuals, but that represent generic pets, such as goldfish. In this case, there's only one entry with the name goldfish, with a single petID.

  I've used both kinds of pets in this catalog to demonstrate the different kinds of products that you might want to include in a catalog. The unique item catalog might include such products as artwork or vanity license plates. When the unique item is sold, it's removed from the catalog. Most products are more generic, such as clothing or automobiles. Although a picture shows a particular shirt, many identical shirts are available. You can sell the shirt many times without having to remove it from the catalog.

Building the PetType table

You assign each pet a type, such as dog or dragon. The first Web page of the catalog will list the types for the customer to select from. A description of each type would also be helpful to show. You don't want to put the type description in the main Pet table because the description would be the same for all pets with the same category. Repeating information in a table violates good database design.

The PetCatalog database includes a table called PetType that holds the type descriptions. The following SQL query creates the PetType table:

```
CREATE TABLE PetType (
  petType         CHAR(15)      NOT NULL,
  typeDescription VARCHAR(255),
  PRIMARY KEY(petType)  );
```

Each row of this table represents a pet type. These are the columns:

- **petType:** The type name. Notice that the petType column is defined the same in the Pet table (which I describe in the preceding section) and in this table. This makes table joining possible and makes matching rows in the tables much easier. However, the petType is the primary key in this table, but not in the Pet table. The `CREATE` query defines the petType column in the following ways:
  - `CHAR(15)`: The data in this field is expected to be a character string that's 15 characters long.
  - `PRIMARY KEY(petType)`: This definition sets the petType column as the primary key. This is the field that must be unique. MySQL will not allow two rows to be entered with the same petType.
  - `NOT NULL`: This definition means that this field can't be empty. It must have a value. The primary key must always be set to `NOT NULL`.
- **typeDescription:** A description of the pet type. The `CREATE` query defines the typeDescription in the following way:
  - `VARCHAR(255)`: The date in this field is expected to be a variable character string that can be up to 255 characters long. The field is stored in its actual length.

Building the Color table

When I discuss building the Pet table (see "Building the Pet table," earlier in this chapter), I discuss the different kinds of pets: pets that are unique, such as puppies and horses, and pets that are not unique, such as goldfish and turtles. For unique pets, the customer needs to see a picture of the actual pet. For pets that aren't unique, the customer only needs to see a generic picture.

In some cases, generic pets come in a variety of colors, such as blue parakeets and green parakeets. You might want to show two pictures for parakeets, a picture of a blue parakeet and a picture of a green parakeet. However, because most pets aren't this kind of generic pet, you don't want to add a color column to your main Pet table because it would be blank for most of the rows. Instead, you create a separate table containing only pets that come in more than one color. Then, when the catalog application is showing pets, it can check the Color table to see if there's more than one color available, and if there is, it can show the pictures from the Color table.

The Color table points to pictures of pets when the pets come in different colors so that the catalog can show pictures of all the available colors. The following SQL query creates the Color table:

```
CREATE TABLE Color (
  petName          CHAR(25)       NOT NULL,
  petColor         CHAR(15)       NOT NULL,
  pix              CHAR(15)       NOT NULL DEFAULT "na.gif",
  PRIMARY KEY(petName,petColor)  );
```

Each row represents a pet type. The columns are as follows:

- **petName:** The name of the pet, such as lion, collie, or Chinese bearded dragon. Notice that the petName column is defined the same in the Pet table and in this table. This makes table joining possible and makes matching rows in the tables much easier. However, the petName is the primary key in this table, but not in the Pet table. The `CREATE` query defines the petName in the following ways:
  - `CHAR(25)`: The data in this field is expected to be a character string that is 25 characters long.
  - `PRIMARY KEY(petName,petColor)`: The primary key must be unique. For this table, two columns together are the primary key — this column and the petColor column. MySQL won't allow two rows to be entered with the same petName *and* petColor.
  - `NOT NULL`: This definition means that this field can't be empty. It must have a value. The primary key must always be defined as `NOT NULL`.
- **petColor:** The color of the pet, such as orange or purple. The `CREATE` query defines the petColor in the following ways:

- `CHAR(15)`: This data type defines the field as a character string that's 15 characters long.
- `PRIMARY KEY(petName,petColor)`: The primary key must be unique. For this table, two columns together are the primary key — this column and the petName column. MySQL won't allow two rows to be entered with the same petName *and* petColor.
- `NOT NULL`: This definition means that this field can't be empty. It must have a value. The primary key must always be defined as `NOT NULL`.

- **pix:** The file name containing the picture of the pet. The `CREATE` query defines pix in the following ways:
  - `CHAR(15)`: This data type defines the field as a character string that is 15 characters long.
  - `NOT NULL`: This definition means that this field can't be empty. It must have a value. You need a picture for the pet. When a Web site tries to show a picture that can't be found, it displays an ugly error message in the browser window where the graphic would go. You don't want your catalog to do that, so your database should require a value. In this case, the `CREATE` query defines a default value so that a value will always be placed in this field.
  - `DEFAULT "na.gif"`: The value `"na.gif"` is stored if you don't provide a value for pix. In this way, a value is always stored for pix. The file `na.gif` might contain a graphic that says something like: `picture not available`.

Adding data to the database

You can add the data to the database many ways. You can use SQL queries to add pets to the database, or you can use the application that I describe in this chapter. My personal favorite during development is to add a few sample items to the catalog by reading the data from a file. Then, whenever my data becomes totally bizarre during development, as a result of programming errors or my weird sense of humor, I can re-create the data table in a moment. Just `DROP` the table, re-create it with the SQL query, and reread the sample data.

For example, the data file for the Pet table might look like this:

```
<TAB>Pekinese<TAB>Dog<TAB>Small, cute, energetic. Good alarm
          system.<TAB>100.00<TAB>peke.jpg
<TAB>House cat<TAB>Cat<TAB>Yellow and white cat. Extremely playful.
          <TAB>20.00<TAB>catyellow.jpg
<TAB>House cat<TAB>Cat<TAB>Black cat. Sleek, shiny. Likes children.
          <TAB>20.00<TAB>catblack.jpg
```

```
<TAB>Chinese Bearded Dragon<TAB>Lizard<TAB>Grows up to 2 feet long. Fascinating
             to watch. Likes to be held.<TAB>100.00<TAB>lizard.jpg
<TAB>Labrador Retriever<TAB>Dog<TAB>Black dog. Large, intelligent retriever.
             Often selected as guide dogs for the
             blind.<TAB>100.00<TAB>lab.jpg
<TAB>Goldfish<TAB>Fish<TAB>Variety of colors. Inexpensive. Easy care. Good first
             pet for small children.<TAB>2.00<TAB>goldfish.jpg
<TAB>Shark<TAB>Fish<TAB>Sleek. Powerful. Handle with
             care.<TAB>200.00<TAB>shark.jpg
<TAB>Asian Dragon<TAB>Dragon<TAB>Long and serpentine. Often gold or
             red.<TAB>10000.00<TAB>dragona.jpg
<TAB>Unicorn<TAB>Horse<TAB>Beautiful white steed with spiral horn on
             forehead.<TAB>20000.00<TAB>unicorn.jpg
```

These are the data file rules:

- The `<TAB>` tags represent real tabs, the kind you create by pushing the Tab key.
- Each line represents one pet and must be entered without pressing the Enter or Return key. The lines in the preceding example are shown wrapped to more than one line so that you can see the whole line. However, in the actual file, the data lines are one on each line.
- A tab appears at the beginning of each line because the first field is not being entered. The first field is the petID, which is entered automatically; you don't need to enter it. However, you do need to use a tab so that MySQL knows there's a blank field at the beginning.

You can then use an SQL query to read the data file into the Pet table:

```
LOAD DATA LOCAL INFILE "pets" INTO TABLE Pet;
```

Any time the data table gets odd, you can re-create it and read the data in again.

Designing the Look and Feel

After you know what the application is going to do and what information the database contains, you can design the look and feel of the application. The look and feel includes what the user sees and how the user interacts with the application. Your design should be attractive and easy to use. You can plan out this design on paper, indicating what the user sees, perhaps with sketches or with written descriptions. In your design, include the user interaction components, such as buttons or links, and describe their actions. You should include each page of the application in the design. If you're lucky, you have a graphic designer who can develop beautiful Web pages for you. If you're me, you just do your best with a limited amount of graphic know-how.

The Pet Catalog has two look and feel designs, one for the catalog that the customer sees and another, less fancy one for the part of the application that you or whoever is adding pets to the catalog uses.

Showing pets to the customers

The application includes three pages that customers see:

- **The storefront page:** This is the first page customers see. It states the name of the business and the purpose of the Web site.
- **The pet type page:** This page lists all the types of pets and allows customers to select which type of pet they want to see.
- **The pets page:** This page shows all the pets of the selected type.

Storefront page

The storefront page is the introductory page for the Pet Store. Because most people already know what a pet store is, this page doesn't need to provide much explanation. Figure 11-1 shows the storefront page. The only customer action available on this page is a link that the customer can click to see the Pet Catalog.

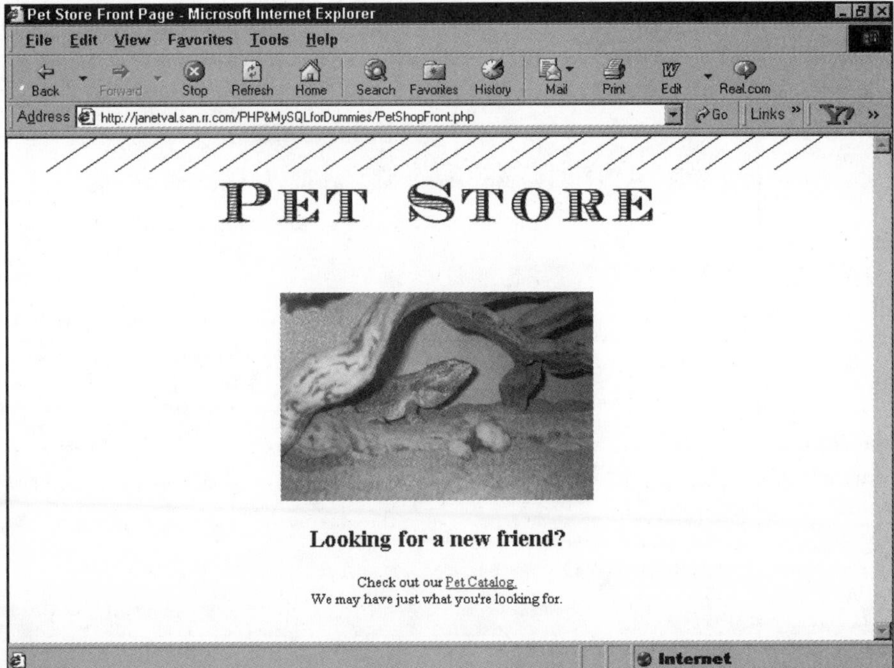

Figure 11-1: The opening page of the Pet Store Web site.

Pet type page

The pet type page lists all the types of pets in the catalog. Each pet type is listed with its description. Figure 11-2 shows the pet type page. Radio buttons appear next to each pet type so customers can select the type of pet they want to see.

Pets page

The pets page lists all the pets of the selected type. Each pet is listed with its petID, description, price, and picture. The pets page appears in a different format, depending on the information in the catalog database. Figures 11-3, 11-4, and 11-5 show some possible pets pages. Figure 11-3 shows a page listing three different dogs from the catalog.

Figure 11-4 shows that more than one pet can have the same pet name. Notice that the house cats have different petID numbers.

Figure 11-5 shows the output when pets are found in the Color table, showing more than one color is available.

On all of these pages, a line at the top says `Click on any picture to see a larger version.` If the customer clicks the picture, a larger version of the picture is displayed.

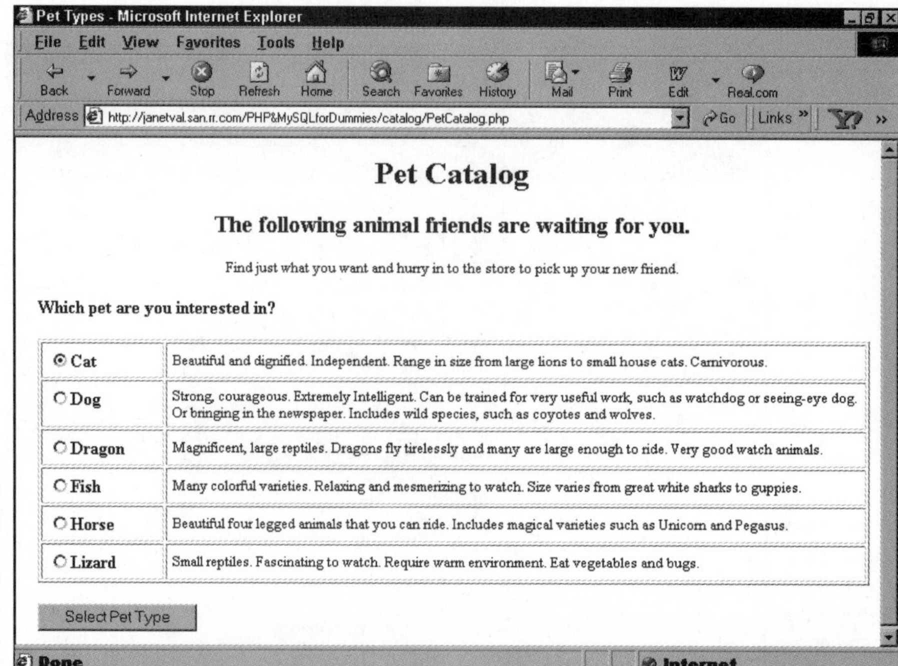

Figure 11-2: The pet type page of the Pet Store Web site.

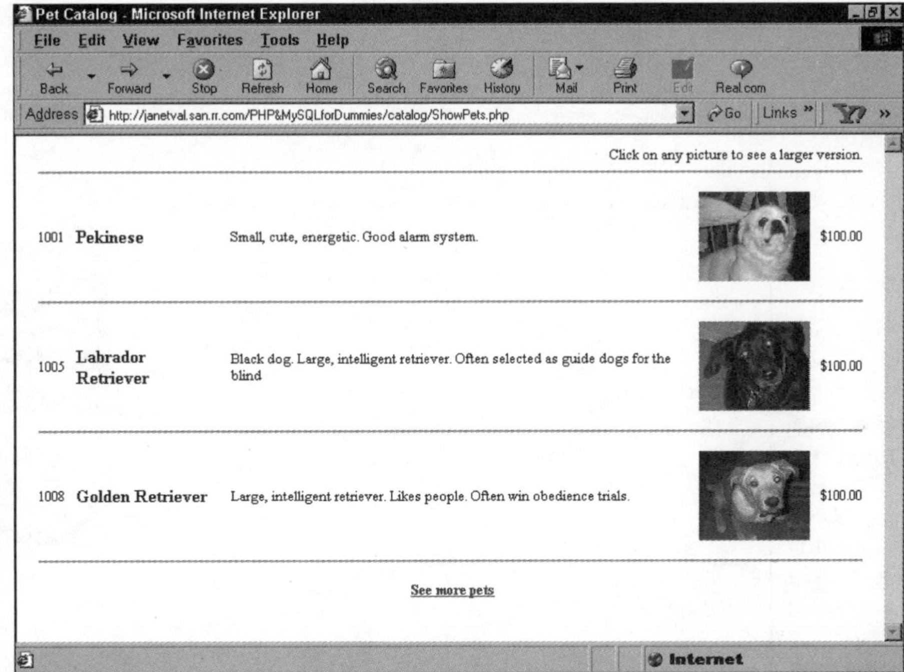

Figure 11-3: This pets page shows three different dogs.

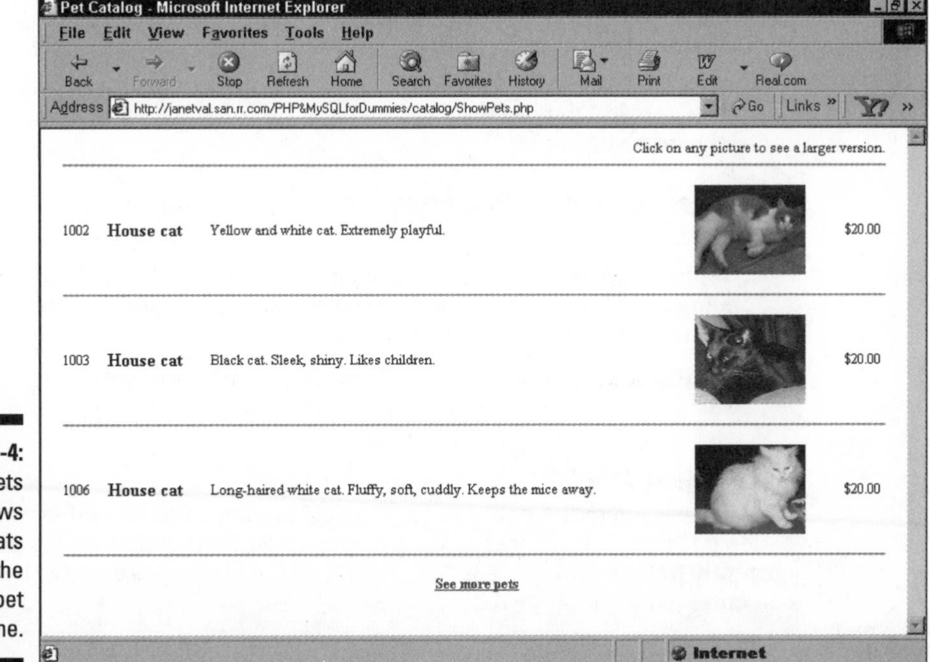

Figure 11-4: This pets page shows three cats with the same pet name.

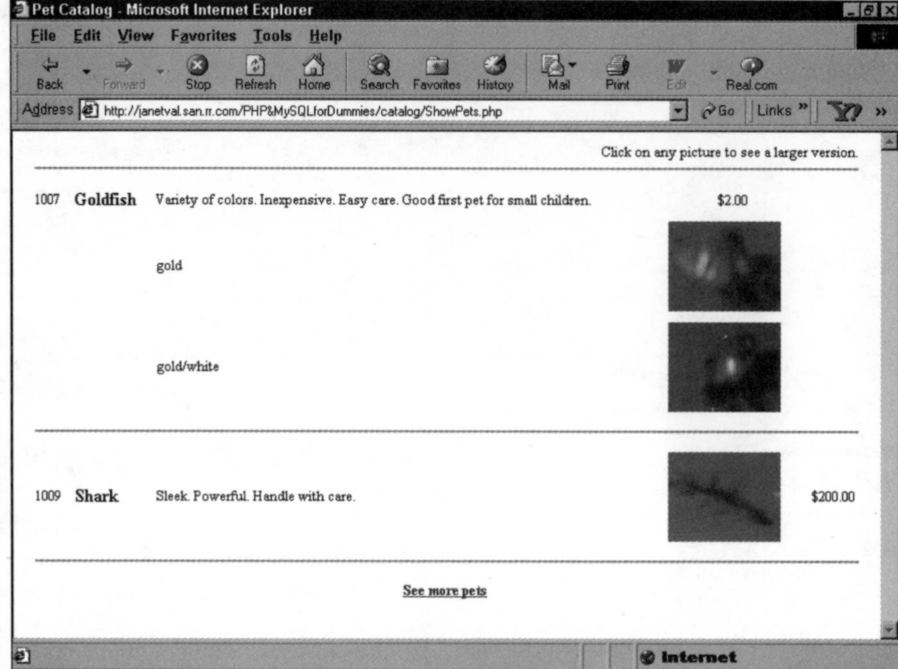

Figure 11-5: This pets page shows goldfish that are available in two colors.

Adding pets to the catalog

The application includes three pages that customers don't see; these are the pages used to add pets to the Pet Catalog. The three pages work in sequential order to add a single pet:

1. **Get pet type page.** The person adding a pet to the catalog selects the radio button for the pet type. The user can also enter a new pet type.
2. **Get pet information page.** The user selects the radio button for the pet being added and fills in the pet description, price, and picture file name. The user can also enter a new pet name.
3. **Feedback page.** A page is displayed showing the pet information that was added to the catalog.

Get pet type page

The first page gets the pet type for the pet that needs to be added to the catalog. Figure 11-6 shows the get pet type page. Notice that all the pet types currently in the catalog are listed, and a section is provided where the user can enter a new pet type if it's needed.

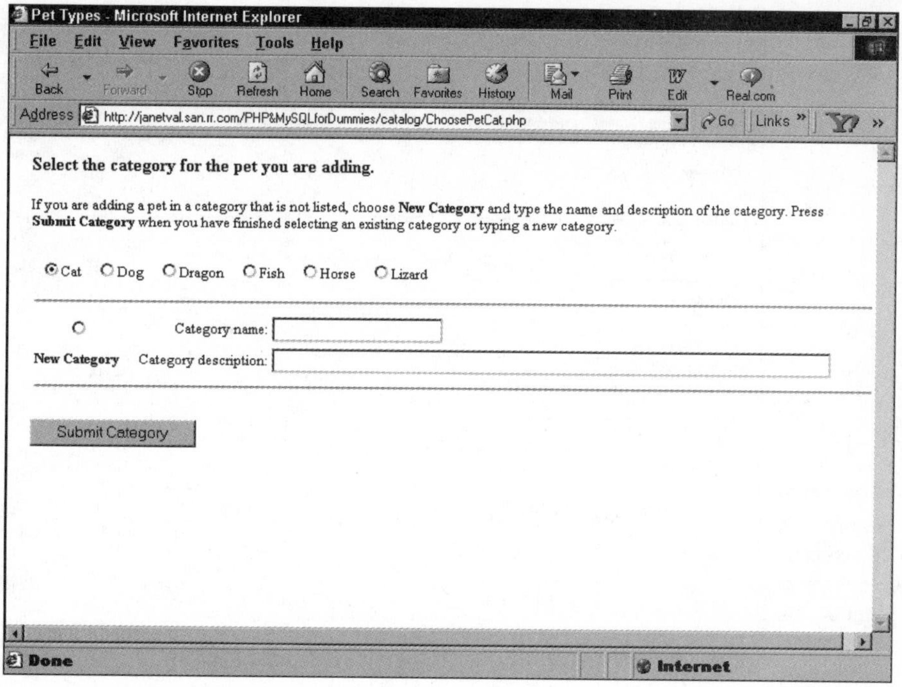

Figure 11-6: The first page for adding a pet to the catalog.

Get pet information page

Figure 11-7 shows the second page. This page lets the user type the information about the pet that goes in the catalog. This page lists all the pet names in the catalog for the selected pet type so the user can select one. It also provides a section where the user can type a new pet name if needed.

Feedback page

When the user submits the pet information, the information is added to the PetCatalog database. Figure 11-8 shows a page that verifies the information that was added to the database. The user can click a link to return to the first page and add another pet.

Get missing information page

The application checks the data to see that the user entered the required information and prompts the user for any information that isn't entered. For instance, if the user selects New Category on the first page, the user must type a category name and description. If the user doesn't type the name or the description, a page is displayed that points out the problem and requests the information. Figure 11-9 shows the page users see if they forget to type the category name and description.

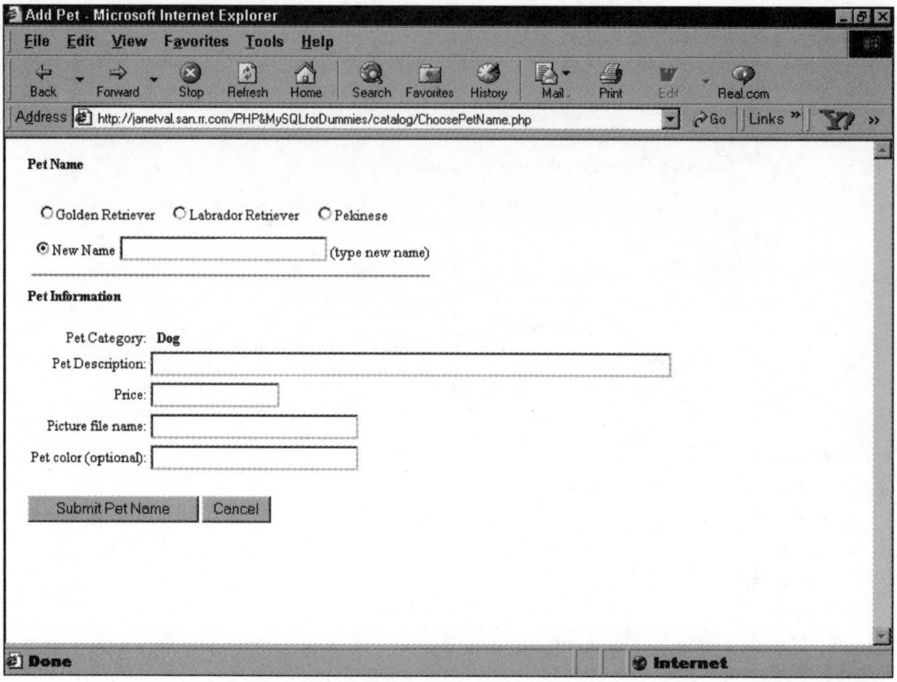

Figure 11-7: The second page asks for the pet name.

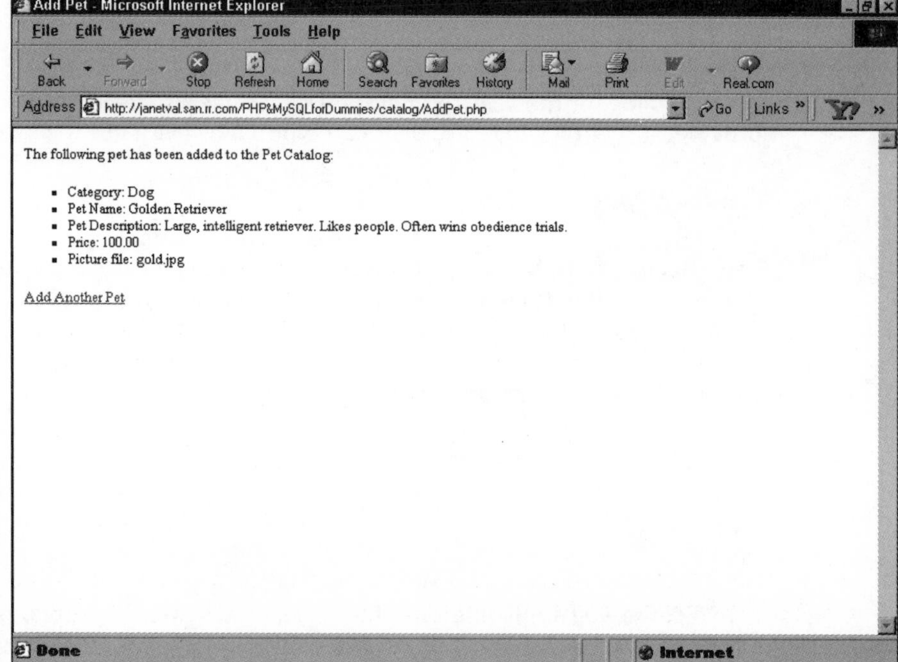

Figure 11-8: The last page provides feedback.

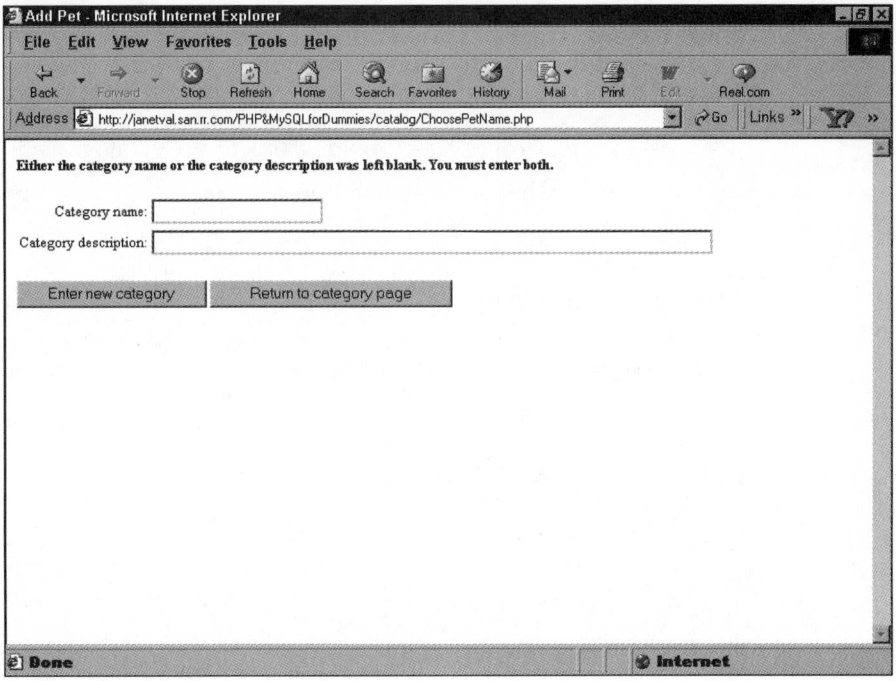

Figure 11-9: This page requests a new category and description.

Writing the Programs

After you know what the pages are going to look like and what they are going to do, you can write the programs. In general, you write a program for each page, although sometimes it makes sense to separate programs into more than one file or to combine programs on a page. (For details on how to organize applications, see Chapter 10.)

As I discuss in Chapter 10, keep the information needed to connect to the database in a separate file and include that file in all the programs that need to access the database. The file should be stored in a secure location, with a misleading name for security reasons. For this application, the following information is stored in a file named `misc.inc`:

```
<?php
  $user="root";
  $host="localhost";
  $password="";
  $database="PetCatalog";
?>
```

The Pet Catalog application has two independent sets of programs, one set to show the Pet Catalog to customers and one set to enter new pets into the catalog.

Showing pets to the customers

The application that shows the Pet Catalog to customers has three basic tasks:

- Show the storefront page. Provide a link to the catalog.
- Show a page where users select the pet type.
- Show a page with pets of the selected pet type.

Showing the storefront

The storefront page doesn't need any PHP statements. It simply displays a Web page with a link. HTML statements are sufficient to do this. Listing 11-1 shows the HTML file that describes the storefront page.

Listing 11-1: HTML File for the Storefront Page

```
<?php
  /* Program: PetShopFront.php
   * Desc:    Displays opening page for Pet Store.
   */
?>
<html>
<head><title>Pet Store Front Page</title></head>
<body topmargin="0" leftmargin="0" marginheight="0" marginwidth="0">
<table width="100%" height="100%" border="0"
       cellspacing="0" cellpadding="0">
  <tr>
    <td align="center" valign="top" height="30">
      <img src="images/awning-top.gif" alt="awning">
    </td>
  </tr>
  <tr>
    <td align="center" valign="top">
      <img src="images/Name.gif" alt="Pet Store">
      <p style="margin-top: 40pt">
      <img src="images/lizard-front.jpg" alt="animal picture"
        height="186" width="280">
      <p><h2>Looking for a new friend?</h2>
      <p>Check out our <a href="catalog/PetCatalog.php">Pet Catalog.</a>
        <br> We may have just what you're looking for.
    </td>
  </tr>
</table>
</body>
</html>
```

Notice that the link is to a PHP program, which is in a subdirectory called catalog. When the customer clicks the link, the Pet Catalog program (`PetCatalog.php`) begins.

Showing the pet types

The pet type page (refer to Figure 11-2) shows the customer a list of all the types of pets currently in the catalog. Listing 11-2 shows the program that produces the pet type Web page.

Listing 11-2: Program That Displays Pet Types

```
<?php
  /* Program: PetCatalog.php
   * Desc:    Displays a list of pet categories from the PetType table.
   *          Includes descriptions. User checks radio button.
   */
?>
<html>
<head><title>Pet Types</title></head>
<body>
<?php
  include("misc.inc");                                          // 11

  $connection = mysql_connect($host,$user,$password)            // 13
       or die ("couldn't connect to server");
  $db = mysql_select_db($database,$connection)                  // 15
       or die ("Couldn't select database");

  /* Select all categories from PetType table */
  $query = "SELECT * FROM PetType ORDER BY petType";            // 19
  $result = mysql_query($query)                                 // 20
       or die ("Couldn't execute query.");

  /* Display text before form */
  echo "<div style='margin-left: .1in'>
  <h1 align='center'>Pet Catalog</h1>
  <h2 align='center'>The following animal friends are waiting for you.</h2>
   <p align='center'>Find just what you want and hurry in to the store to pick
      up your new friend.
  <p><h3>Which pet are you interested in?</h3>\n";

  /* Create form containing selection list */
  echo "<form action='ShowPets.php' method='post'>\n";         // 34
  echo "<table cellpadding='5' border='1'>";
  $counter=1;                                                  // 36
  while ($row = mysql_fetch_array($result))                    // 37
  {
     extract($row);                                            // 39
     echo "<tr><td valign='top' width='15%'>\n";
     echo "<input type='radio' name='interest'                 // 41
             value='$petType'\n";
     if ( $counter == 1 )                                      // 43
     {
         echo "checked";
     }
     echo "><font size='+1'><b>$petType</b></font>             // 47
          </td>
          <td>$typeDescription</td>                            // 49
          </tr>";
     $counter++;                                               // 51
  }
  echo "</table>";
  echo "<p><input type='submit' value='Select Pet Type'>       // 54
        </form>\n";                                            // 55
?>
</div>
</body>
</html>
```

The program in Listing 11-2 has line numbers at the end of some of the lines. The line numbers are a reference so that I can refer to particular parts of the program. The numbers in the following list correspond to the line numbers in the listing. Here is a brief explanation of what the following lines do in the program:

11 The include statement brings in a file that contains the information necessary to connect to the database. I call it `misc.inc` because that seems more secure than calling it `passwords.inc`.

13 Connects to the MySQL server.

15 Selects the PetCatalog database.

19 A query that selects all the information from the PetType table and puts it in alphabetical order based on pet type.

20 Executes the query on line 19.

34 The opening tag for a form that will hold all the pet types. The action target is `ShowPets.php`, the program that shows the pets of the chosen type.

36 Creates a counter with a starting value of 1. The counter will keep track of how many pet types are found in the database.

37 Starts a while loop that will get the rows containing the pet type and pet description that were selected from the database on lines 19 and 20. The loop will execute once for each pet type that was retrieved.

39 Separates the row into two variables: `$petType` and `$petDescription`.

41 Echoes a form field tag for a radio button. The value is the value in `$petType`. This statement executes once in each loop, creating a radio button for each pet type. This statement echoes only part of the form field tag.

43 Starts an if block that executes only in the first loop. It echoes the word `"checked"` as part of the form field. This ensures that one of the radio buttons is checked in the form so that the form can't be submitted with no button checked, which would result in unsightly error messages or warnings. The counter was set up solely for this purpose.

Although adding `"checked"` to every radio button works in some browsers, it causes problems in other browsers. The extra programming required to add `"checked"` to only one radio button can prevent potential problems.

47 Echoes the remaining part of the form field tag for the radio button, the part that closes the tag.

49 Echoes the pet description in a second cell in the table row.

51 Adds 1 to the counter, to keep track of the number of times the loop has executed.

54 Adds the submit button to the form.

55 Closes the form.

When the user clicks a radio button and then clicks the submit button, the next program — named `ShowPets.php` in the form tag — runs, showing the pets for the selected pet type.

Showing the pets

The pets page (refer to Figures 11-3, 11-4, and 11-5) shows the customer a list of all the pets of the selected type that are currently in the catalog. Listing 11-3 shows the program that produces the pet Web page.

Listing 11-3: Program That Shows a List of Pets

```
<?php
  /* Program: ShowPets.php
   * Desc:    Displays all the pets in a category. Category is passed
   *          in a variable from a form. The information for each pet
   *          is displayed on a single line, unless the pet comes in
   *          more than one color. If the pet comes in colors, a single
   *          line is displayed without a picture and a line for each
   *          color, with pictures, is displayed following the single
   *          line. Small pictures are displayed, which are links to
   *          larger pictures.
   */
?>
<html>
<head><title>Pet Catalog</title></head>
<body topmargin="0" marginheight="0">
<?php
  include("misc.inc");

  $connection = mysql_connect($host,$user,$password)
       or die ("couldn't connect to server");
  $db = mysql_select_db($database,$connection)
       or die ("Couldn't select database");

  /* Select pets of the given type */
  $query = "SELECT * FROM Pet WHERE petType='$interest'";         // 25
  $result = mysql_query($query)
       or die ("Couldn't execute query.");

  /* Display results in a table */
  echo "<table cellspacing='10' border='0' cellpadding='0'
             width='100%'>";
  echo "<tr><td colspan='5' align='right'>
             Click on any picture to see a larger
             version.<br><hr>
          </td></tr>\n";
  while ( $row = mysql_fetch_array($result,MYSQL_ASSOC) )         // 36
  {
    $f_price = number_format($row['price'],2);//format as dollars

    /* check whether pet comes in colors */
    $query = "SELECT * FROM Color
                  WHERE petName='{$row['petName']}'";             // 42
    $result2 = mysql_query($query);                                 // 43
    $ncolors = mysql_num_rows($result2);                            // 44

    /* display row for each pet */
    echo "<tr>\n";
```

(continued)

Listing 11-3 *(continued)*

```
    echo "<td>{$row['petID']}</td>\n";
    echo "<td><font size='+1'><b>{$row['petName']}</b></font></td>\n";
    echo "<td>{$row['petDescription']}</td>\n";
    /* display picture if pet does not come in colors */
    if ( $ncolors <= 1 )                                        // 52
    {
       echo "<td><a href='../images/{$row['pix']}' border='0'>
            <img src='../images/{$row['pix']}' border='0'
              width='100' height='80'></a></td>\n";
    }
    echo "<td align='center'>\$$f_price</td>\n
          </tr>\n";
    /* display row for each color if pet comes in colors */
    if ($ncolors > 1 )                                          // 61
    {
       while ($row2 = mysql_fetch_array($result2,MYSQL_ASSOC))  // 63
       {
         echo "<tr><td colspan=2> </td>
              <td>{$row2['petColor']}</td>
              <td><a href='../images/{$row2['pix']}' border='0'>
             <img src='../images/{$row2['pix']}' border='0'
              width='100' height='80'></a></td>\n";
       }
    }
       echo "<tr><td colspan='5'><hr></td></tr>\n";
  }
  echo "</table>\n";
  echo "<div align='center'>
       <a href='PetCatalog.php'><b>See more pets</b></a></div>";
?>
</body>
</html>
```

The following numbers correspond to the line numbers shown as comments at the end of lines in Listing 11-3. I document only some of the lines in this program in the following list. Many of the tasks in the listing are also in most of the programs in this application, such as connecting to the database, creating forms, and executing queries. Because I document these common tasks for Listing 11-2, I don't repeat them here. Here is a brief explanation of what some of the other lines do in the program:

25 This query selects all the pets in the catalog that match the chosen type, which was passed in a form from the previous page.

36 Sets up a while loop that runs once for each pet selected. The loop creates a line of information for each pet found.

42 Lines 42, 43, and 44 check to see if there are any entries in the Color table for the pet. Notice that the query results are put in `$result2`. They could not be put in `$result` because this variable name is already in use. `$ncolors` stores the number of rows found in the Color table for the pet. Every pet name is checked for colors when it's processed in the loop.

52 Starts an if block that is executed only if zero or one rows for the pet were found in the Color table. The if block displays the picture of the pet. If the program found more than one color for the pet in the Color table, it means that the pet is available in more than one color and the picture

shouldn't be shown here. Instead, a picture for each color will be shown in later lines. Refer to Figures 11-3 and 11-4 for pet pages that display the pictures and information on a single row, as done in this if block.

61 Starts an if block that's executed if more than one color was found for the pet. The if block echoes a row for each color found in the Color table.

63 Sets up a while loop, within the if block, that runs once for each color that was found in the Color table. The loop displays a line, including a picture, for each color. Refer to Figure 11-5 for a pet page that displays separate lines with pictures for each color.

The page has a link to more pets at the bottom. The link points to the previous program that displays the pet types.

Adding pets to the catalog

The application that adds a new pet to the catalog should do the following tasks:

1. Create a form that asks for a pet category. The person adding the pet can choose one of the existing pet types or create a new one. To create a new type, the user needs to type a category name and description.
2. If a new type is created, check that the name and description were typed in.
3. Create a form that asks for pet information — name, description, price, picture file name, and color. The person adding the pet can choose one of the existing pet names for the selected category or create a new name. To create a new pet name, the user needs to type a pet name.
4. If new is selected for pet name, check that the name was typed in.
5. Store the new pet in the PetCatalog database.
6. Send a feedback page that shows what information was just added to the catalog.

The tasks are performed in three programs:

- `ChoosePetCat.php`: Creates the pet type form (task 1)
- `ChoosePetName.php`: Checks the pet category data and creates the pet information form (tasks 2 and 3)
- `AddPet.php`: Checks the pet name field, stores the new pet in the catalog database, and provides feedback (tasks 4, 5, and 6)

Writing ChoosePetCat

The first program produces a Web page with an HTML form where the person adding a pet can select a pet type for the pet. To make the program easier to read and maintain, as discussed in Chapter 10, keep some of the HTML statements used by the program in a separate file that you bring into the program using an include statement. Listing 11-4 shows `ChoosePetCat.php`.

Listing 11-4: Program That Lets User Select a Pet Type

```
<?php
  /* Program: ChoosePetCat.php
   * Desc:    Allows users to select a pet type. All the existing pet
   *          types from the PetType table are displayed. A section to
   *          enter a new pet type is provided. Selections are provided
   *          as radio buttons, with text fields for new category name
   *          and description.
   */
?>
<html>
<head><title>Pet Types</title></head>
<body>
<?php
  include("misc.inc");
  $connection = mysql_connect($host,$user,$password)
       or die ("couldn't connect to server");
  $db = mysql_select_db($database,$connection)
       or die ("Couldn't select database");

  /* gets pet types from PetType table in alphabetical order */
  $query = "SELECT petType FROM PetType ORDER BY petType";        // 21
  $result = mysql_query($query)
       or die ("Couldn't execute query.");

  /* Display text before form */
  echo "<div style='margin-left: .1in'>
  <p><h3>Select the category for the pet you are adding.</h3>
        If you are adding a pet in a category that is not
        listed, choose <b>New Category</b> and type the name
        and description of the category. Press <b>Submit Category</b>
        when you have finished selecting an existing category
        or typing a new category.\n";

  /* Create form containing selection list */
  echo "<form action='ChoosePetName.php' method='post'>\n";
  echo "<table cellpadding='5' border='0'>\n";
  echo "<tr>";
  $counter=0;                                                      // 38
  while ($row = mysql_fetch_array($result))                        // 39
  {
     extract($row);
     echo "<td>
      <input type='radio' name='category' value='$petType'";      // 43
            if ($counter == 0)                                     // 44
            {
               echo "checked";
            }
     echo ">$petType </td>\n";                                     // 48
     $counter++;                                                   // 49
  }
  echo "</tr></table>\n";

  include("NewCat_table.inc");                                     // 53
```

```
   echo "<p><input type='submit' value='Submit Category'>\n";
   echo "</form>\n";
?>
</div>
</body>
</html>
```

The following numbers correspond to the line numbers shown as comments at the end of lines in Listing 11-4. Only some of the lines are documented in the following list. Many of the tasks in the listing, such as connecting to the database, creating forms, and executing queries, are found in most of the programs in this application; refer to Listing 11-2 for an explanation. The following list provides a brief explanation of what the following lines do in the program:

21 A query that selects all the pet types from the PetType table and sorts them in alphabetical order.

38 Creates a counter with a starting value of 1. The counter will keep track of how many pet types are found in the database.

39 Starts a while loop that executes once for each pet type. The loop creates a list of radio buttons for the pet types, with one button checked. Here are the details of the while loop:

  43 Echoes a form field tag for a radio button with the value equal to `$petType`. This statement executes once in each loop, creating a radio button for each pet type. This statement echoes only the first part of the form field tag.

  44 An if block that executes only in the first loop. It echoes the word `"checked"` as part of the form field. This ensures that one of the radio buttons is checked when displayed so that the form can't be submitted with no button checked, which would result in unsightly error messages or warnings. The counter was set up solely for this purpose.

  Although adding `"checked"` to every radio button works in some browsers, it causes problems in other browsers. The extra programming required to add `"checked"` to only one radio button can prevent problems.

  48 Echoes the remaining part of the form field tag for the radio button, the part that closes the tag.

  49 Adds 1 to the counter, to keep track of the number of times the loop has executed. This is the last line in the while loop.

53 Creates a table that asks for the new pet type name and description. The HTML for the table is read in from another file called `NewCat_table.inc`. As discussed in Chapter 10, the HTML, especially HTML that describes a form, is often kept in a separate file to make the main program easier to read and to make the form easier to modify when necessary. This file is shown in Listing 11-5.

Listing 11-5: File Containing New Type Form

```
<?php
  /* Program:  NewCat_table.inc
   * Desc:     HTML code that displays a table for input of a
   *           new category
   */
?>
<table width='100%'>
  <tr><td colspan=3><hr></td></tr>
  <tr>
    <td align='center'>
      <input type='radio' name='category' value='new'> 
    </td>
    <td align='right'>Category name:</td>
    <td><input type='text' name='newCat' size='20' maxlength='20'></td>
  </tr>
  <tr><td><b>New Category</b></td>
    <td align='right'>Category description:</td>
    <td><input type='text' name='newDesc' size='70%' maxlength='255'>
    </td>
  </tr>
  <tr><td colspan=3><hr></td></tr>
</table>
```

This file is all HTML, except for a section of PHP in the top that holds the header as comments. I could actually have done this with HTML comments, but I like the PHP comment style better.

Writing ChoosePetName

This second program accepts the data from the form in the first program. It checks the information and asks for missing information. After the pet type information is received correctly, the program creates a form where a user can select a pet name for the new pet being added to the catalog and type the information for the pet. This program, as in the preceding program, brings in some of the HTML forms and tables from separate files using the include statement. This program also calls a function that is in an include file. This program brings in two files. Listing 11-6 shows `ChoosePetName.php`.

Listing 11-6: Program That Asks User for Pet Name

```
<?php
  /* Program: ChoosePetName.php
   * Desc:    Allows the user to enter the information for the pet.
   *          First, the program checks for a new category and enters
   *          it into the petType table if it is new. Then, all pets
   *          in the selected category are displayed with radio
   *          buttons. The user can enter a new name. Fields are
   *          provided to enter the description, price, and picture
   *          file name.
   */
?>
<?php
  if (@$newbutton == "Return to category page" or           // 13
      @$newbutton == "Cancel")
```

```
  {
    header("Location: ChoosePetCat.php");
  }
?>
<html>
<head><title>Add Pet</title></head>
<body>
<?php
  include("misc.inc");
  include("functions.inc");

  $connection = mysql_connect($host,$user,$password)
       or die ("couldn't connect to server");
  $db = mysql_select_db($database,$connection)
       or die ("Couldn't select database");

  /* If new was selected for pet category, check if text fields
     were filled in. If they were not filled in, display them again
     for the user to enter the category name and category description.
     When the fields are filled in, store the new category in the
     PetType table.*/
  if ($category == "new")                                       // 36
  {
    if ($newCat == "" or $newDesc == "")                        // 38
    {
      include("NewCat_form.inc");                               // 40
      exit();                                                   // 41
    }
    /* add new pet type to PetType table */
    else                                                        // 44
    {
      addNewType($newCat,$newDesc);                             // 46
      $category = $newCat;                                      // 47
    }
   }                                                            // 49

  /* Select pet names from table with given category. If user entered a
     new category, it is searched for. */
  $query = "SELECT DISTINCT petName FROM Pet                   // 53
            WHERE petType='$category' ORDER BY petName";
  $result = mysql_query($query)
                 or die ("Couldn't execute query 3.");
  $nrow = mysql_num_rows($result);                              // 57

  /* create form */
  echo "<div style='margin-left: .1in'>";
  echo "<form action='AddPet.php' method='post'>\n";
  echo "<p><b>Pet Name</b></p>\n";
  if ($nrow < 1)                                                // 63
  {
    echo "<hr><b>No pet names are currently in the database
                for the category $category</b><hr>\n";
  }
  else                                                          // 68
  {
    echo "<table cellpadding='5' border='0'>";
    echo "<tr>";
    while ($row = mysql_fetch_array($result))                   // 72
    {
      extract($row);
      echo "<td>";
```

(continued)

Listing 11-6 *(continued)*

```
        echo " <input type='radio' name='petName' value='$petName'";
        echo ">$petName</td>\n";
      }
      echo "</tr></table>";
    }
    include ("NewName_table.inc");                              // 81

    $petDescription=" ";$price = "";$pix = "";$petColor = "";
    include("PetInfo_table.inc");                               // 84

    echo "<input type='hidden' name='category'                 // 86
              value='$category'>\n";
    echo "<p><input type='submit' value='Submit Pet Name'>
          <input type='submit' name='newbutton' value='Cancel'>
          </form>\n";
?>
</div>
</body>
</html>
```

The following numbers correspond to the line numbers shown as comments at the end of lines in Listing 11-6. Only some of the lines are documented in the following list because many of the tasks in the listing are found in most of the programs in this application. The common tasks are documented for Listing 11-2 and explained in other parts of the book, so I don't repeat them here. Here is a brief explanation of what the following lines do in the program:

13 Checks whether the user clicked the submit button labeled *Cancel* or *Return to category page*. If so, it returns to the first page.

36 Starts an if block that executes only if the user selected the radio button for New Category in the form from the previous program. This block checks whether the new category name and description are filled in. If the user forgot to type them in, he or she is asked for the pet type name and description again. After the name and description are filled in, the program calls a function that adds the new category to the PetType table. The following lines describe this if block in more detail:

  38 Starts an if block that executes only if the category name and/or the category description are blank. Because this if block is inside the if block for a new category, this block executes only if the user selected New Category for pet type but did not fill in the new category name *and* description.

  40 Creates a form that asks for the category name and description. The HTML for the form is included from a file. This executes only when the if statement on line 38 is true — that is, if the category is new and the category name and/or description are blank.

  41 Stops the program after displaying the form on line 39. The program can't proceed until the category name and description are typed in. This block will repeat until a category name and description are filled in.

44 Starts an else block that executes only if both the category name and description are filled in. Because this block is inside the if block for the new radio button, this block executes when the user selected new and filled in the new category name and description.

46 Calls a function that adds the new category to the PetType table.

47 Up to this point, `$category` equals `"new"`. This line sets `$category` to the new category name.

49 This line ends the if block. If the user selected one of the existing pet types, the statements between line 36 and this line did not execute.

53 A query that selects one of each pet name with the chosen pet type and sorts them alphabetically.

57 Checks whether any pet names were found for the chosen pet type.

63 Starts an if block that executes only if *no* pets were found for the pet type. The block echoes a message to the user that no pets were found for the pet type.

68 Starts an else block that executes if pets *were* found for the pet type. The else block creates a list of radio buttons for the pet names found. The list is created with a while loop (starting on line 72) in the same manner that the list of categories was created, as explained in Listing 11-4.

81 Lines 81 and 84 create tables that ask for the new pet name and information, bringing the HTML in from separate files using include statements.

This program brings in three files containing HTML using include statements. Listing 11-7, 11-8, and 11-9 show the three files that are included: `NewCat_form.inc`, `NewName_table.inc`, and `PetInfo_table.inc`.

Listing 11-7: HTML Code That Creates New Pet Type Form

```
<?php
  /* Program: NewCat_form.inc
   * Desc:    Displays a form to collect a category name and
   *          description.
   */
?>
<b>Either the category name or the category description was
left blank. You must enter both.</b>
<form action="ChoosePetName.php" method="post">
  <table>
   <tr>
    <td align="right">Category name:</td>
    <td><input type="text" name="newCat" value="<?php echo $newCat ?>"
          size="20" maxlength="20">
    </td></tr>
   <tr>
    <td align="right">Category description:</td>
    <td><input type="text" name="newDesc"
          value="<?php echo $newDesc ?>"
          size="70%" maxlength="255">
```

(continued)

Listing 11-7 *(continued)*

```
    </td></tr>
  </table>
  <input type="hidden" name="category" value="new">
  <p><input type="submit" name="newbutton" value="Enter new category">
  <input type="submit" name="newbutton" value="Return to category page">
</form>
```

This program is almost all HTML code. Notice the following points about this form:

- This form is created only when the user selects the radio button for New Category on the pet type Web page, but does not type in the pet type name or description. This form is displayed to give the user a second chance to type the name or description.
- Most of the file is HTML, with only two small PHP sections that echo values for the two fields.
- The form returns to the program that generated it for processing. It is processed in the same manner as the form that was sent from the first page. The field names are the same and are checked again to see if they are blank.
- A hidden field is included that sends `$category` with a value of `"new"`. If this form didn't send `$category`, the program that processes it — the same program that generated it — wouldn't know that the pet type was new and wouldn't execute the if block that should be executed when `$category` equals `"new"`.

Listing 11-8: HTML File That Creates Table for New Name

```
<?php
  /* Program: NewName_table.inc
   * Desc:    Displays table to enter new pet name
   */
?>
<table border="0">
   <tr><td>
        <input type="radio" name="petName"
               value="new" checked >New Name</td>
      <td><input type="text" name="newName" size="25"
               maxlength="25"> (type new name)</td>
  </tr>
  <tr><td colspan=2><hr></td></tr>
</table>
```

This file is all HTML, no PHP. It displays the section of the pet name Web page where the user can enter a new pet name.

Listing 11-9: HTML That Creates Table for Pet Info

```
<?php
  /* Program: PetInfo_form.inc
   * Desc:    Displays table to collect pet information
   */
?>
<b>Pet Information</b><br>
 <p><table>
  <tr><td align="right">Pet Category:</td>
    <td><b>  <?php echo $category ?></b></td>
  </tr>
  <tr><td align="right">Pet Description:</td>
    <td><input type="text" name="petDescription"
            value="<?php echo $petDescription ?>"
            size="65" maxlength="255">
    </td></tr>
  <tr><td align="right">Price:</td>
    <td><input type="text" name="price"
            value="<?php echo $price ?>" size="15" maxlength="15">
    </td></tr>
  <tr><td align="right">Picture file name:</td>
    <td><input type="text" name="pix"
            value="<?php echo $pix ?>" size="25" maxlength="25">
    </td></tr>
  <tr><td align="right">Pet color (optional):</td>
    <td><input type="text" name="petColor"
            value="<?php echo $petColor ?>" size="25" maxlength="25">
    </td></tr>
 </table>
```

This file includes small PHP sections for the variable values. Otherwise, it is HTML.

In addition to HTML for tables and forms, the `ChoosePetName.php` program in Listing 11-6 called a function. The function is stored in a file named `functions.inc` and included in the beginning of the program. Listing 11-10 shows the function.

Listing 11-10: Function AddNewType()

```
<?php
 /* Function addNewType
  * Desc     Adds a new pet type and description to the PetType table.
  *          Checks for the new pet type first and does not add it to
  *          the table if it is already there.
  */
 function addNewType($petType,$typeDescription)
{
  /* Prepare data */
  $petType = ucfirst(strip_tags(trim($petType)));
  $typeDescription = ucfirst(strip_tags(trim($typeDescription)));

  /* Check whether new category is already in PetType table. If it
    is not in table, add it to table. */
  $query = "SELECT petType FROM PetType WHERE petType='$petType'";
  $result = mysql_query($query) or
                    die ("Couldn't execute query ");
```

(continued)

Listing 11-10 *(continued)*

```
  $ntype = mysql_num_rows($result); //
  if ($ntype < 1)  // if new type is not in table
  {
     $query = "INSERT INTO PetType (petType,typeDescription)
                          VALUES ('$petType','$typeDescription')";
     $result = mysql_query($query)
                 or DIE ("Couldn't execute query ");
  }
  return;
}
?>
```

The function cleans the data first. Then, it checks whether the pet type is already in the PetType table. If it is not, the function adds it to the table.

Writing AddPet

This last program accepts the data from the form in the second program. If new was selected for the pet name, it checks to see that a new name was typed in and prompts for it again if it was left blank. After the pet name is filled in, the program stores the pet information from the previous page. Notice that it does not check the other information because the other information is optional. This program, as in the previous program, brings in some of the HTML forms and tables from two separate files using the include statement. Listing 11-11 shows `AddPet.php`.

Listing 11-11: Program That Adds New Pet to Catalog

```
<?php
  /* Program: AddPet.php
   * Desc:    Add new pet to the database. A confirmation screen
   *          is sent to the user.
   */

  if (@$newbutton == "Cancel")                                    // 7
  {
     header("Location: ChoosePetCat.php");
  }
  if ($petName == "new")                                          // 11
  {
    if ($newName == "")                                           // 13
    {
       include("NewName_form.inc");
       exit();
    }
    else                                                          // 18
    {
       $petName = ucfirst(strtolower(strip_tags(trim($newName))));
    }
  }
  if ($pix == "")                                                 // 23
       $pix = "na.gif";
?>
<html>
<head><title>Add Pet</title></head>
<body>
```

```
<?php
  include("misc.inc");                                          // 30
  $connection = mysql_connect($host,$user,$password)
       or die ("couldn't connect to server");
  $db = mysql_select_db($database,$connection)
       or die ("Couldn't select database");
  /* Clean the data */
  $petDescription = strip_tags(trim($newName));
  $price = strip_tags(trim($price));
  $pix = strip_tags(trim($pix));
  $petColor = strip_tags(trim($petColor));

  $query = "INSERT INTO Pet (petName,petType,petDescription,price,pix)
           VALUES
          ('$petName','$category','$petDescription','$price','$pix')";
  $result = mysql_query($query)
       or die ("Couldn't execute query.");
  $petID = mysql_insert_id();                                   // 46

  echo "The following pet has been added to the Pet Catalog:<br> // 48
        <ul>
         <li>Category: $category
         <li>Pet Name: $petName
         <li>Pet Description: $petDescription
         <li>Price: $price
         <li>Picture file: $pix \n";

  if ($petColor != "")                                         // 56
  {
    if ($petName == "Goldfish" or $petName == "Parakeet")
    {
       $query = "SELECT petName FROM Color
                   WHERE petName='$petName' AND petColor='$petColor'";
       $result = mysql_query($query)
                  or die ("Couldn't execute query.");
       $num = mysql_num_rows($result);
       if ($num < 1)
       {
         $query = "INSERT INTO Color (petName,petColor,pix) VALUES
                  ('$petName','$petColor','$pix')";
         $result = mysql_query($query)
                  or die ("Couldn't execute query.");
         echo "<li>Color: $petColor\n";
       }
    }
  }                                                            // 74
  echo "</ul>";
  echo "<a href='ChoosePetCat.php'>Add Another Pet</a>\n";
?>
</body>
</html>
```

Notice the line numbers shown as comments at the end of lines in Listing 11-11. The numbers in the following list correspond to the line numbers in the listing. I document only some of the lines in the following list because many of the most common tasks, such as connecting to the database, have been documented for the previous programs in this chapter.

7 Checks whether the user clicked the Cancel button. If so, returns to the first page.

11 Starts an if block that executes only if the user selected New for the pet name. If the new name is blank, it creates a form that asks for the new pet name repeatedly until the user types one in. After the new name is filled in, `$petName` is set to the new name.

23 If the picture file name was not typed in, it is set to the default picture.

30 Lines 30–46 add the new pet to the database. The data is cleaned before it's added.

48 Starts echoing the feedback page.

56 Starts an if block that executes only if the color was filled in. The color is only stored for parakeets and goldfish. The Color table is checked to see if the name and color are already there. If not, they are added to the Color table.

This program brings in an HTML file that creates the form to prompt the user for the pet name if the user forgot to type it in. Listing 11-12 shows the file that is included: `NewName_form.inc`.

Listing 11-12: HTML That Asks User for a New Pet Name

```
<?php
  /* Program: NewName_form.inc
   * Desc:    Displays form to collect a pet name
   */
?>
<b>You must type a pet name.</b>
<form action="AddPet.php" method="post">
 <table><tr>
   <td align="right">Pet name:</td>
   <td><input type="text" name="newName" value="<?php echo $newName ?>"
          size="25" maxlength="25">
   </td></tr>
 </table>
 <input type="hidden" name="category" value="<?php echo $category ?>">
 <input type="hidden" name="petName" value="<?php echo $petName ?>">
 <input type="hidden" name="petDescription" value="<?php echo $petDescription
             ?>">
 <input type="hidden" name="price" value="<?php echo $price ?>">
 <input type="hidden" name="pix" value="<?php echo $pix ?>">
 <input type="hidden" name="petColor" value="<?php echo $petColor ?>">
 <p><input type="submit" name="newbutton" value="Enter new pet name">
 <input type="submit" name="newbutton" value="Cancel">
</form>
```

This file creates the form that is displayed if the user forgets to type in the new pet name. It is very similar to the program in Listing 11-7 that's displayed when a user forgets to type in a new category. Notice that two hidden fields are used to keep the values for `$category` and `$petName`. When the form is filled in, the values for these two variables are needed to store the pet information.

At the end, this program provides a link to the first page so that the user can add another new pet to the catalog if desired.

Chapter 12

Building a Members Only Web Site

In This Chapter

- Designing the Members Only Web site
- Building the database for the member directory
- Designing the Web pages for the Members Only section
- Writing the programs for logging into the Members Only section

Many Web sites require users to log in. Users can't view any Web pages without entering a password. Sometimes just part of the Web page requires a login. Here are some reasons you may want to require a user login:

- **The information is secret.** You don't want anyone except a few authorized people to see the information. Or perhaps only your own employees should see the information.
- **The information or service is for sale.** The information or service your Web site provides is your product, and you want to charge people for it. For instance, you might have a corner on some survey data that researchers are willing to pay for. AAA Automobile Club offers some of its information for free, but you have to be a member to see its hotel ratings.
- **You can provide better service.** If you know who your customers are or have some of their information, you can make their interaction with your Web site easier. For instance, if you have an account with Barnes and Noble.com or the Gap and log into its site, it uses your stored shipping address, and you don't have to type it in again.
- **You can find out more about your customers.** Marketing would like to know who is looking at your Web site. A list of customers with addresses and phone numbers and perhaps some likes and dislikes is a useful thing. If your Web site offers some attractive features, customers may be willing to provide some information in order to access your site. For instance, a person might be willing to answer some questions in order to download some free software or to play a great online game.

Typically, a login requires the user to enter a user ID and a password. Often, users can create their own accounts on the Web site, choosing their own user ID and password. Sometimes users can maintain their accounts — for example, change their password or phone number — online.

In Chapter 11, you find out how to build an online catalog for your Pet Store Web site. Now, you want to add a section to your Web site that's for Members Only. You plan to offer special discounts, a newsletter, a database of pet information, and more in the Members Only section. You hope that customers will see the section as so valuable that they'll be willing to provide their addresses and phone numbers to get a member account that lets them use the services in the restricted section. In this chapter, you build a login section for the Pet Store.

Designing the Application

The first step in design is to decide what the application should do. Its basic function is to gather customer information and store it in a database. It offers customers access to valuable information and services to motivate them to provide information for the database. Because state secrets or credit card numbers aren't at risk, you should make it as easy as possible for customers to set up and access their accounts.

The application that provides access to the Members Only section of the Pet Store should do the following:

- Provide a means for customers to set up their own accounts with member IDs and passwords. This includes collecting the information from the customer that's required to become a member.
- Provide a page where customers type their member ID and password and then check to see they are valid. If so, the customer enters the Members Only section. If not, the customer can try another login.
- Show the pages in the Members Only section to anyone who is logged in.
- Refuse to show the pages in the Members Only section to anyone who is *not* logged in.
- Keep track of member logins. You want to know who logs in and how often.

Building the Database

The database is the core and purpose of this application. It holds the customer information that's the goal of the Members Only section. It also holds the Member ID and password so that the user can log into the Members Only section.

The Members Only application database contains two tables:

- Member table
- Login table

The first step in building the login application is to build the database. It's pretty much impossible to write programs without a working database to test the programs on. First design your database; then build it; then add some sample data for use while developing the programs.

Some changes have been made to the database design developed in Chapter 3 for the Members Only restricted section of the Pet Store Web site. Development and testing often result in changes. You find that you didn't take some factors into consideration in your design or that certain elements of your design don't work with real world data or are difficult to program. It's perfectly normal for the design to evolve as you work on your application. Just be sure to change your documentation when your design changes.

Building the Member table

In your design for the login application, the main table is the Member table. It holds all the information entered by the customer, including the customer's personal information (name, address, phone number, and so on) and the Member ID and password. The following SQL query creates the Member table:

```
CREATE TABLE Member (
  loginName     VARCHAR(20)     NOT NULL,
  createDate    DATE            NOT NULL,
  password      VARCHAR(255)    NOT NULL,
  lastName      VARCHAR(50),
  firstName     VARCHAR(40),
  street        VARCHAR(50),
  city          VARCHAR(50),
  state         CHAR(2),
  zip           CHAR(10),
  email         VARCHAR(50),
  phone         CHAR(15),
  fax           CHAR(15),
PRIMARY KEY(loginName) );
```

Each row represents a member. The columns are

- **loginName:** A Member ID for the member to use when logging in. The customer chooses and types in the login name. The CREATE query defines the loginName in the following ways:

- `CHAR(20)`: This data type defines the field as a character string that's 20 characters long. The field will always take up 20 characters of storage, with padding if the actual string stored is less than 20 characters. If a string longer than 20 characters is stored, any characters after 20 are dropped.
- `PRIMARY KEY(loginName)`: The primary key identifies the row and must be unique. MySQL will not allow two rows to be entered with the same loginName.
- `NOT NULL`: This definition means that this field can't be empty. It must have a value. The primary key must always be set to `NOT NULL`.

- **createDate:** The date when the row was added to the database — that is, the date when the customer created the account. The query defines createDate as:
  - `DATE`: This is a string that's treated as a date. Dates are displayed in the format YYYY-MM-DD. They can be entered in that format or some similar formats, such as YY/M/D or YYYYMMDD.
  - `NOT NULL`: This definition means that this field can't be empty. It must have a value. Because the program, not the user, creates the date and stores it, it won't ever be blank.
- **password:** A password for the member to use when logging in. The customer chooses and types in the password. The `CREATE` query defines the password in the following ways:
  - `VARCHAR(255)`: This statement defines the field as a variable character string that can be up to 255 characters long. The field is stored in its actual length. You don't expect the password to be 255 characters long. In fact, you expect it to be pretty short. However, you intend to use the MySQL password function to encrypt it, rather than store it in plain view. After it's encrypted, the string will be longer, so you're allowing room for the longer string.
  - `NOT NULL`: This statement means that this field can't be empty. It must have a value. You're not going to allow an empty password in this application.
- **lastName:** The customer's last name, as typed by the customer. The `CREATE` query defines the field as:
  - `VARCHAR(50)`: This data type defines the field as a variable character string that can be up to 50 characters long. The field is stored in its actual length.
- **firstName:** The customer's first name, as typed by the customer. The `CREATE` query defines the field as:

  - `VARCHAR(40)`: This data type defines the field as a variable character string that can be up to 40 characters long. The field is stored in its actual length.

- **street:** The customer's street address, as typed by the customer. The `CREATE` query defines the field as:
  - `VARCHAR(50)`: This data type defines the field as a variable character string that can be up to 50 characters long. The field is stored in its actual length.

- **city:** The city in the customer's address, as typed by the customer. The `CREATE` query defines the field as:
  - `VARCHAR(50)`: This data type defines the field as a variable character string that can be up to 50 characters long. The field is stored in its actual length.

- **state:** The state in the customer's address. The string is the two-letter state code. The customer selects the data from a drop-down list containing all the states. The `CREATE` query defines the field as:
  - `CHAR(2)`: This data type defines the field as a character string that's 2 characters long. The field will always take up 2 characters of storage, with padding if the actual string stored is less than 2 characters.

- **zip:** The zip code the customer types in. The `CREATE` query defines the field as:
  - `CHAR(10)`: This data type defines the field as a character string that's 10 characters long. The field will always take up 10 characters of storage, with padding if the actual string stored is less than 10 characters. The field is long enough to hold a zip+4 code, such as 12345-1234.

- **email:** The e-mail address the customer types in. The `CREATE` query defines the field as:
  - `VARCHAR(50)`: This data type defines the field as a variable character string that can be up to 50 characters long. The field is stored in its actual length.

- **phone:** The phone number the customer types in. The `CREATE` query defines the field as:
  - `CHAR(15)`: This data type defines the field as a character string that's 15 characters long. The field will always take up 15 characters of storage, with padding if the actual string stored is less than 15 characters.

- **fax:** The fax number the customer types in. The CREATE query defines the field as:
  - CHAR(15): This data type defines the field as a character string that's 15 characters long. The field will always take up 15 characters of storage, with padding if the actual string stored is less than 15 characters.

Notice that some fields are CHAR and some are VARCHAR. CHAR fields are faster, whereas VARCHAR fields are more efficient in using disk space. Your decision will depend on whether disk space or speed is more important for your application in your environment.

In general, shorter fields should be CHAR because shorter fields don't waste much space. For instance, if your CHAR is 5 characters, the most space that could possibly be wasted is 4 characters. However, if your CHAR is 200, you could waste 199 characters. Therefore, for short fields, use CHAR for speed with very little wasted space.

Building the Login table

The login table keeps track of member logins by recording the date and time every time a member logs in. Because each member has multiple logins, the login data requires its own table. The CREATE query that builds the Login table is

```
CREATE TABLE Login (
  loginName     VARCHAR(20) NOT NULL,
  loginTime     DATETIME    NOT NULL,
PRIMARY KEY(loginName,loginTime) );
```

The Login table only has two columns, as follows:

- **loginName:** The Member ID that the customer uses to login with. The loginName is the connection between the Member table (described in the preceding section) and this table. Notice that the loginName column is defined the same in the Member table and in this table. This makes table joining possible and makes matching rows in the tables much easier. The CREATE query defines the loginName in the following ways:
  - CHAR(20): This data type defines the field as a character string that's 20 characters long. The field will always take up 20 characters of storage, with padding if the actual string stored is less than 20 characters. If a string longer than 20 characters is stored, any characters after 20 are dropped.
  - PRIMARY KEY(loginName,loginTime): The primary key identifies the row and must be unique. For this table, two columns together are the primary key. MySQL will not allow two rows to be entered with the same loginName *and* loginDate.

- `NOT NULL`: This definition means that this field can't be empty. It must have a value. The primary key must always be set to `NOT NULL`.

- **loginTime:** The date and time when the member logged in. This field uses both the date and time because it needs to be unique. It's very unlikely that two users would login at the same second at the Pet Store Web site. However, in some very busy Web sites, two users might log in during the same second. At such a site, you might have to create a sequential login number to be the unique primary key for the site. The `CREATE` query defines the loginTime in the following ways:
  - `DATETIME`: This is a string that's treated as a date and time. The string is displayed in the format YYYY-MM-DD HH:MM:SS.
  - `PRIMARY KEY(loginName,loginTime)`: The primary key identifies the row and must be unique. For this table, two columns together are the primary key. MySQL will not allow two rows to be entered with the same loginName *and* loginDate.
  - `NOT NULL`: This definition means that this field can't be empty. It must have a value. The primary key must always be set to `NOT NULL`.

Adding data to the database

This database is intended to hold data entered by customers, not by you. It will be empty when the application is first made available to customers, until customers add data. However, to test the programs as you write them, you need to have at least a couple of members in the database. You need a couple of Member IDs and passwords to test the login program. You can add a couple of fake members for testing purposes, using an `INSERT` SQL query, and remove them when you're ready to go live with your Members Only application.

Designing the Look and Feel

Now that you know what the application is going to do and what information you want to get from customers and store in the database, you can design the look and feel. The look and feel includes what the user sees and how the user interacts with the application. Your design should be attractive and easy to use. You can create your design on paper, indicating what the user sees, perhaps with sketches or with written descriptions. You should also show the user interaction components, such as buttons or links, and describe their actions. Include each page of the application in the design.

The Pet Store Members Only application has three pages that are part of the login procedures. In addition, the application includes all the pages that are part of the Members Only section, such as the page that shows the special discounts and the pages that provide discussions of pet care. In this chapter, you only build the pages that are part of the login procedure. You don't build the pages that are part of the Members Only section, but I do discuss what needs to be included in them to protect them from viewing by non-members.

The login application includes three pages, plus the group of pages that comprise the Members Only section, as follows:

- **Storefront page:** The first page a customer sees. It provides the name of the business and the purpose of the Web site. A storefront page was included in Chapter 11, and in this chapter, you modify it to provide access to the Members Only section.
- **Login page:** Allows the customer to either log in or create a new member account. It shows a form for the customer to fill in to get a new account.
- **New Member Welcome page:** Welcomes the new users by name, letting them know that their accounts have been created. Provides any information they need to know. Provides a button so that users can continue to the Members Only section or return to the main page.
- **Members Only section:** A group of Web pages that contain the content of the Members Only section.

Storefront page

The storefront page is the introductory page for the Pet Store. Because most people know what a pet store is, the page doesn't need to provide much explanation. Figure 12-1 shows the storefront page. Two customer actions are available on this page: a link that the customer can click to see the pet catalog and a link to the Members Only section.

Login page

The login page allows the customer to log in or create a new member account. It includes the form that customers need to fill out to get a member account. Figure 12-2 shows the Login page. This page has two different submit buttons: one to log in with an existing member account and one to create a new member account.

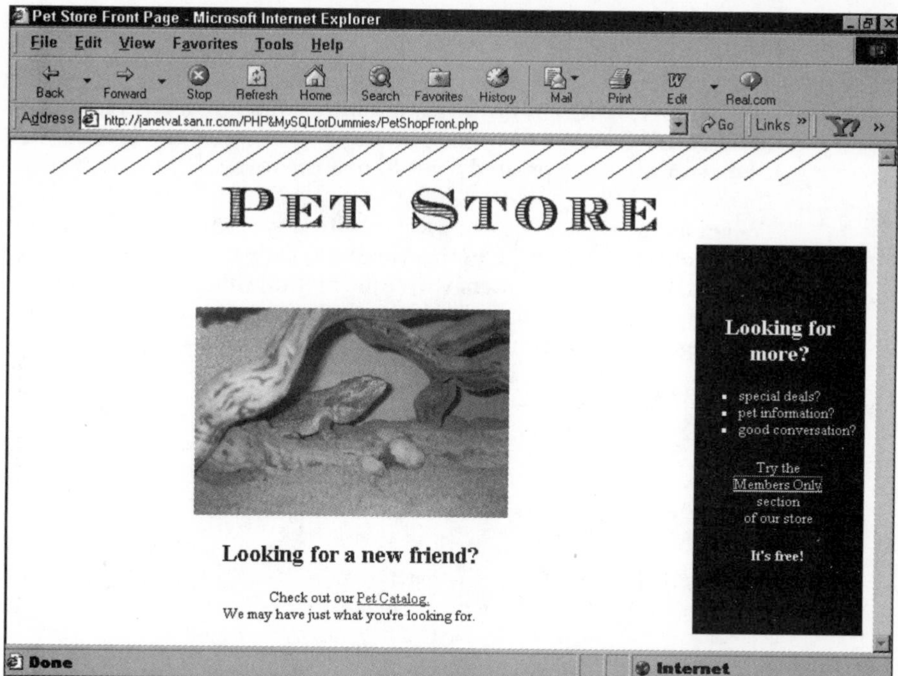

Figure 12-1: The opening page of the Pet Store Web site.

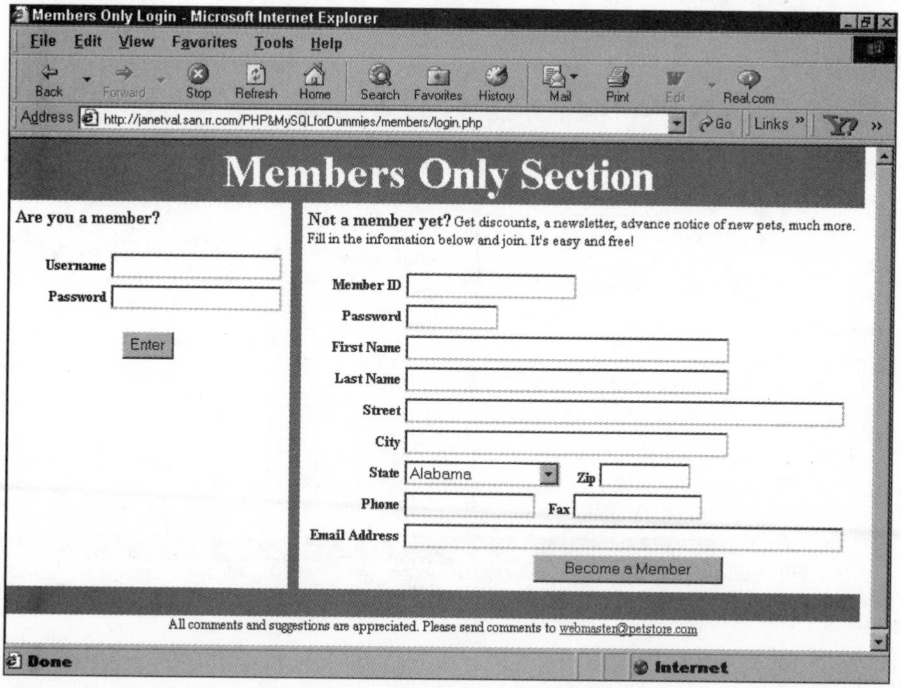

Figure 12-2: The page where customers log in or create a new member account.

If a customer makes a mistake on the login page, either in the login section or the new member section, the form is displayed again with an error message. For instance, say the customer made an error in typing his e-mail address. He forgot to type the *.com* at the end of the e-mail address. Figure 12-3 shows the screen that he sees after he submits the form with the mistake in it. Notice the error message printed right above the form.

When members successfully log in with a valid Member ID and password, they go to the first page of the Members Only section. When new members successfully submit a form with information that looks reasonable, they go to a new member welcome page (see the next section). In addition, an e-mail message is sent to the new member with the following contents:

```
A new Member Account has been setup for you. Your new Member ID
and password are:

gsmith
secret

We appreciate your interest in Pet Store at PetStore.com

If you have any questions or problems, send email
to webmaster@petstore.com
```

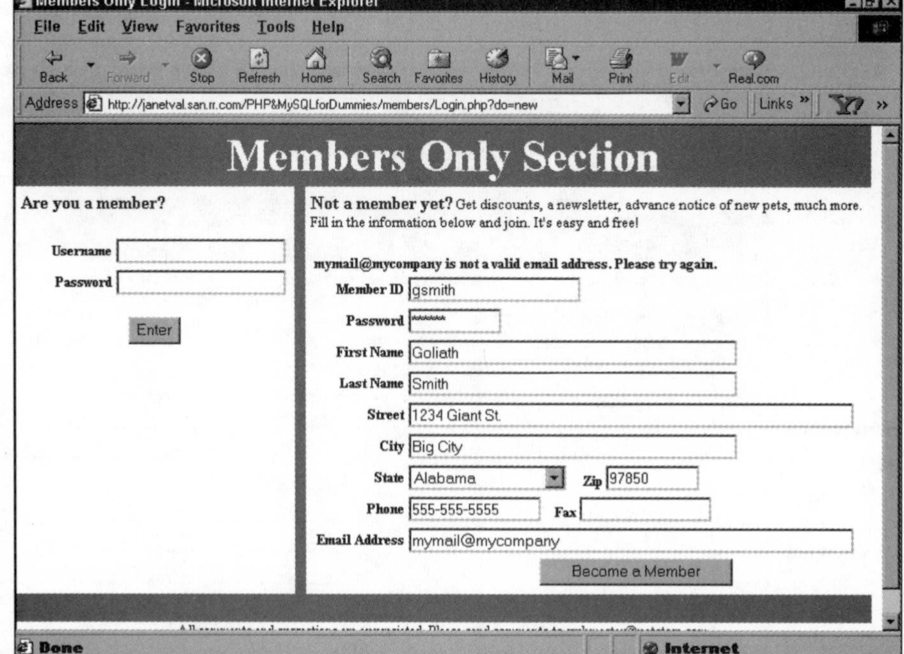

Figure 12-3: Page showing a message resulting from a mistake in the form.

This e-mail message contains the customer's password. I think it is very helpful to both the customer and the business to provide customers with a hard copy of their password. Customers *will* forget their password. It seems to be one of the rules. An e-mail message with their password might help them when they forget it, saving both them and you some trouble. Of course, e-mail messages aren't necessarily secure, so sending passwords via e-mail isn't a good idea for some accounts, such as an online bank account. But, for this Pet Store application, with only unauthorized discounts and pet care information at risk, sending the password via e-mail is a reasonable risk.

New Member welcome page

The New Member feedback page welcomes the customer and offers useful information. The customer sees that the account has been installed and can then enter the Members Only section immediately. Figure 12-4 shows a welcome page.

Members Only section

One or more Web pages make up the contents of the Members Only section. Whatever the content is, the pages are no different than any other Web pages or PHP programs, except for some PHP statements in the beginning of each file that prevent non-members from viewing the pages.

Writing the Programs

After you know what the pages are going to look like and what they are going to do, you can write the programs. In general, you create a program for each page, although sometimes it makes sense to separate programs into more than one file or to combine programs on a page. (See Chapter 10 for details on how to organize applications.)

As I discuss in Chapter 10, keep the information needed to connect to the database in a separate file and include it in all the programs that need to access the database. Store the file in a secure location, with a misleading name. For this application, the following information is stored in a file named `dogs.inc`:

```
<?php
  $user="root";
  $host="localhost";
  $password="";
  $database="MemberDirectory";
?>
```

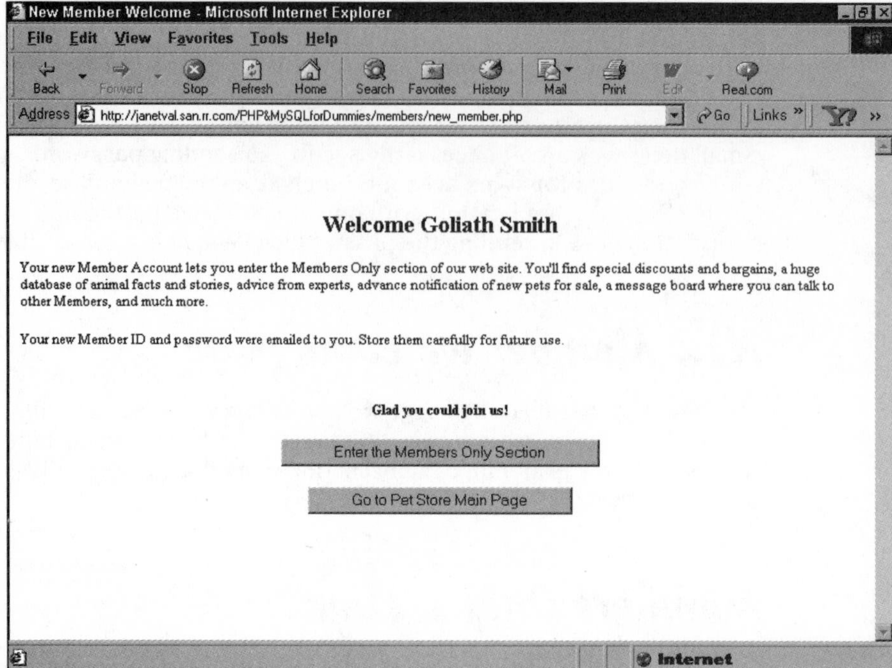

Figure 12-4: A page welcoming new members.

The member login application has several basic tasks:

1. Show the storefront page. Provide a link to the login page.
2. Show a page where customers can fill in a Member ID and a password to log in.
3. Check the Member ID and the password that the customer types against the Member ID and password stored in the database. If the ID and password are okay, the customer enters the Members Only section. If the ID and/or password are not okay, the customer is returned to the login page.
4. Show a page where customers can fill in the information needed to obtain a member account.
5. Check the information the customer typed in for blank fields or incorrect formats. If bad information is found, show the form again so the customer can correct the information.
6. When good information is entered, add the new member to the database.
7. Show a welcoming page to the new member.

The tasks are performed in three programs:

- `PetShopFront.php`: Shows the storefront page (task 1).
- `Login.php`: Performs both the login and create new member account tasks (tasks 2–6).
- `New_member.php`: Shows the page that welcomes the new member (task 7).

Writing PetShopFront

The storefront page doesn't need any PHP statements. It simply displays a Web page with two links — one link to the pet catalog and one link to the Members Only section of the Web site. HTML statements are sufficient to do this. Listing 12-1 shows the HTML file that describes the storefront page.

Listing 12-1: HTML File for the Storefront Page

```
<?php
  /* Program: PetShopFront.php
   * Desc:    Displays opening page for Pet Store.
   */
?>
<html>
<head><title>Pet Store Front Page</title></head>
<body topmargin="0" leftmargin="0" marginheight="0" marginwidth="0">
<table width="100%" height="100%" border="0"
       cellspacing="0" cellpadding="0">
  <tr>
    <td align="center" valign="top" height="30" colspan="2">
      <img src="images/awning-top.gif" alt="awning">
    </td>
  </tr>
  <tr>
    <td align="center" valign="top" colspan="2">
      <img src="images/Name.gif" alt="Pet Store">
    </td></tr>
  <tr>
    <td width="80%" align="center">
      <p style="margin-top: 40pt">
      <img src="images/lizard-front.jpg" alt="lizard picture"
        height="186" width="280">
      <p><h2>Looking for a new friend?</h2>
      <p>Check out our <a href="catalog/PetCatalog.php">Pet Catalog.</a>
        <br> We may have just what you're looking for.
    </td>
    <td width="20%" bgcolor="black">
       <div style="color: white; link: white">
       <p style="text-align: center; font-size: 15pt">
       <b>Looking for <br>more?</b></p>
       <ul>
        <li>special deals?
        <li>pet information?
        <li>good conversation?
```

(continued)

Listing 12-1 ***(continued)***

```
      </ul>
      <p style="text-align: center">Try the
      <br><a href="members/login.php" style="color: white">Members Only</a>
      <br>section <br>of our store
      <p style="text-align: center"><b>It's free!</b></p>
    </td>
  </tr>
</table>
</body>
</html>
```

Notice that there is a link to the login PHP program, which is in a subdirectory called members. When the customer clicks the link, the login page appears.

Writing Login

The Login page (refer to Figure 12-2) is produced by the program `Login.php`, shown in Listing 12-2. The program uses a switch to create two sections, one for the login and one for creating a new account. The program creates a session that's used in all the Members Only Web pages. The login form itself isn't included in this program; it's in a separate file called `login_form.inc`, which is called into this program, whenever the form is needed, using include statements.

Listing 12-2: Login Program

```
<?php
/* Program: Login.php
   Desc:    Login program for the Members Only section of the
            pet store. It provides two options: (1) login using an
            existing Login Name and (2) enter a new login name. Login
            Names and passwords are stored in a MySQL database.
 */
  session_start();                                             //  8
  session_register('auth');                                    //  9
  session_register('logname');
  include("dogs.inc");                                         // 11
  switch (@$do)                                                // 12
  {
    case "login":                                              // 14
      $connection = mysql_connect($host, $user,$password)      // 15
               or die ("Couldn't connect to server.");
      $db = mysql_select_db($database, $connection)
               or die ("Couldn't select database.");

      $sql = "SELECT loginName FROM Member                     // 19
              WHERE loginName='$fusername'";
      $result = mysql_query($sql)
                  or die("Couldn't execute query.");
      $num = mysql_num_rows($result);                          // 23
      if ($num == 1)  // login name was found                     24
      {
         $sql = "SELECT loginName FROM Member                  // 26
```

```
              WHERE loginName='$fusername'
              AND password=password('$fpassword')";
        $result2 = mysql_query($sql)
                 or die("Couldn't execute query.");
        $num2 = mysql_num_rows($result2);
        if ($num2 > 0)  // password is correct                  // 32
        {
          $auth="yes";                                          // 34
          $logname=$fusername;                                  // 35
          $today = date("Y-m-d h:m:s");                         // 36
          $sql = "INSERT INTO Login (loginName,loginTime)
                  VALUES ('$logname','$today')";
          mysql_query($sql) or die("Can't execute query.");
          header("Location: Member_page.php");                  // 40
        }
        else    // password is not correct                      // 42
        {
          unset($do);                                           // 44
          $message="The Login Name, '$fusername' exists,        // 45
                    but you have not entered the correct
                    password! Please try again.<br>";
          include("login_form.inc");                            // 48
        }
      }                                                         // 50
      elseif ($num == 0)  // login name not found               // 51
      {
        unset($do);                                             // 53
        $message = "The Login Name you entered does not
                    exist! Please try again.<br>";
        include("login_form.inc");
      }
    break;                                                      // 58

    case "new":                                                 // 60
      foreach($HTTP_POST_VARS as $key => $value)                // 61
      {
        if ($key != "fax")                                      // 63
        {
          if ($value == "")                                     // 65
          {
            unset($do);
            $message_new = "Required information is missing.
                Please try again.";
            include("login_form.inc");
            exit();
          }
        }
        if (ereg("(Name)",$key))                                // 74
        {
         if (!ereg("^[A-Za-z' -]{1,50}$",$key))
         {
           unset($do);
           $message_new = "$lastName is not a valid name.
                          Please try again.";
           include("login_form.inc");
           exit();
         }
        }
        $$key = strip_tags(trim($value));                       // 85
      }
```

(continued)

Listing 12-2 *(continued)*

```
if (!ereg("^[0-9]{5,5}(\-[0-9]{4,4})?$",$zip))             // 87
{
  unset($do);
  $message_new = "$zip is not a valid zip code.
                  Please try again.";
  include("login_form.inc");
  exit();
}
if (!ereg("^[0-9)(xX -]{7,20}$",$phone))                   // 95
{
  unset($do);
  $message_new = "$phone is not a valid phone number.
                  Please try again.";
  include("login_form.inc");
  exit();
}
if ($fax != "")                                           // 103
{
  if (!ereg("^[0-9)(xX -]{7,20}$",$fax))
  {
    unset($do);
    $message_new = "$fax is not a valid phone number.
                    Please try again.";
    include("login_form.inc");
    exit();
  }
}
if (!ereg("^.+@.+\\..+$",$email))                         // 114
{
  unset($do);
  $message_new = "$email is not a valid email address.
                  Please try again.";
  include("login_form.inc");
  exit();
}
/* check to see if login name already exists */
$connection = mysql_connect($host,$user,$password)       // 123
          or die ("Couldn't connect to server.");
$db = mysql_select_db($database, $connection)
          or die ("Couldn't select database.");
$sql = "SELECT loginName FROM Member
          WHERE loginName='$newname'";
$result = mysql_query($sql)
          or die("Couldn't execute query.");
$num = mysql_numrows($result);
if ($num > 0)                                            // 132
{
  unset($do);
  $message_new = "$newname already used. Select another
                  Member ID.";
  include("login_form.inc");
  exit();
}
else                                                     // 140
{
  $today = time("Y-m-d");
  $sql = "INSERT INTO Member (loginName,createDate,password,
             firstName,lastName,street,city,state,zip,phone,
             fax,email) VALUES
           ('$newname','$today',password('$newpass'),
```

```
                '$firstName', '$lastName','$street','$city','$state',
                '$zip','$phone','$fax','$email')";
      mysql_query($sql);
      $auth="yes";                                          // 150
      $logname = $newname;                                  // 151
      /* send email to new member */                        // 152
      $emess1="A new Member Account has been setup for you. ";
      $emess2="Your new Member ID and password are: ";
      $emess3="\n\n\t$newname\n\t$newpass\n\n";
      $emess4="We appreciate your interest in Pet Store ";
      $emess5="at PetStore.com\n\n";
      $emess6="If you have any questions or problems, email ";
      $emess7="webmaster@petstore.com";
      $emess =
         $emess1.$emess2.$emess3.$emess4.$emess5.$emess6.emess7;
      $ehead="From: member-desk@petstore.com\r\n";          // 162
      $subject = "Your new Member Account from Pet Store";
      $mailsend=mail("$email","$subject","$emess","$ehead");// 164
      header("Location: New_member.php");                   // 165
    }
  break;                                                    // 167

  default:                                                  // 169
      include("login_form.inc");
}
?>
```

Some of the lines in Listing 12-2 have line numbers at the ends of the lines. The following list refers to the line numbers in the listing to discuss the program and how it works:

8 Starts a session. The session has to be started at the beginning of the program, even though the user hasn't logged in yet.

9 Registers two variables, `$auth` and `$logname`. `$auth` is used to keep track of whether the member has logged in. `$logname` holds the member's login name (Member ID). However, at this point, the variables are just registered. They are not set to any value yet. They are just named as session variables, and if they are later set to a value, the value will be stored in the session file and will be available in later pages in the session.

11 Reads in the file that sets the variables needed to connect to the database. The program is called `dogs.inc`, a misleading name that seems more secure than calling it `mypasswords.inc`.

12 Starts a switch statement. The switch statement contains three sections. The first section runs when `$do` equals login, the second section runs when `$do` equals new, and the third section is the default that runs if `$do` doesn't equal either login or new. The third section just creates the login page and only runs when the customer first links to the login page.

14 Starts the case block for the login section — the section that runs when the customer logs in. The login section of the form sends `do=login` in the URL, which causes this section of the switch statement to run.

15 Lines 15–18 connect to MySQL and select the database.

19 Lines 19–22 look in the database table Member for a row with the login name typed by the customer.

23 Checks to see whether a row was found with a loginName field containing the Member ID typed by the customer. `$num` will equal 0 or 1, depending on whether the row was found.

24 Starts an if block that executes if the Member ID was found. That means that the user submitted a Member ID that *is* in the database. This block then checks to see whether the password submitted by the user is correct for the given Member ID. This block is documented in more detail in the following list:

> 26 Creates a query that looks for a row with both the Member ID and the password submitted by the customer. Notice that the password submitted in the form (`$fpassword`) is encrypted using the MySQL function, `password()`. Passwords in the database are encrypted, so the password that you're trying to match must also be encrypted, or it won't match.
>
> 29 Lines 29–31 execute the query and check to see whether a match was found. `$num2` equals 1 or 0, depending on whether a row with both the Member ID and the password is found.
>
> 32 Starts an if block that executes if the password is correct. This is a successful login. Lines 32–40 are executed, performing the following tasks: 1) The two session variables, `$auth` and `$logname`, are set. Because these variables are registered as session variables, these values are stored in the session file. 2) `$today` is created with today's date and time in the correct format expected by the database table. 3) A row for the login is entered into the Login table 4) The first page of the Members Only section is sent to the member.
>
> 42 Starts an if block that executes if the password is not correct. This is an unsuccessful login. Lines 44–48 are executed, performing the following tasks: 1) Unset the form variable `$do`. This prevents any confusion later. 2) Set the appropriate error message into `$message`. 3) Show the login page again. The login page will show the error message.

Notice that the loop starting on line 42 lets the user know when they have a real login name but the wrong password. If the security of your data is very important, you may want to write this loop differently. Providing that information may be helpful to someone who is trying to break in. The cracker now only needs to find the password. For more security, just have one condition that gives the same error message whenever either the login name or the password is incorrect. In this example, I prefer to provide the information because it is helpful to the legitimate member (who may not remember whether he or she installed an account at all), and I'm not protecting any vital information.

50 Ends the block that executes when the Member ID is found in the database.

51 Starts an if block that executes when the Member ID is *not* found in the database. This could actually be an else, instead of an elseif, but I think it is clearer to humans with the if condition in the statement. This block unsets the form variable `$do`, creates the appropriate error message, and shows the login page again, which includes the error message.

58 Ends the case block that executes when the customer submits a Member ID and password to log in. The login block extends from line 14 to this line.

60 Starts the case block that executes when the customer fills out the form to get a new member account. The form sends `do=new` in the URL, causing the program to jump to this section of the switch statement.

61 Starts a foreach loop that loops through every field in the new member form. The loop checks for empty required fields and checks the first and last name for acceptable characters. The statements in the loop are documented in more detail in the following list:

63 Checks whether the field is the fax field. The fax field is not required. The fax field isn't checked to see if it is blank because it's okay for it to be blank.

65 Checks whether the field is blank. If it is, the if block performs the following tasks: 1) unsets `$do`; 2) creates an error message that explains the problem; 3) shows the login form again, including the error message; 4) stops the program and waits for the user to submit the form again with the field filled in.

74 Checks whether the field is the last name or first name field. If so, it checks the field format for allowed characters. If any characters that are not allowed are found, it performs the following tasks: 1) unsets `$do`; 2) creates an error message that explains the problem; 3) shows the login form again, including the error message; 4) stops the program and waits for the user to submit the form again with the correct format.

85 Trims extra spaces from all the fields after they are checked in line 65 to be sure they aren't blank. Removes any HTML tags that are in any of the fields. Creates a variable for each of the fields in the following way. Suppose in the first loop of the foreach loop, the variable is `$HTTP_POST_VARS[loginName] = gsmith`. The foreach loop sets `$key="loginName"` and `$value="gsmith"`. Therefore, the statement in line 85 is equivalent to: `$loginName=strip_tags (trim("gsmith"))`. The `$$key` is `$loginName` because `$key= loginName`.

86 Ends the foreach loop.

87 Lines 87–121 are a series of if blocks that check the fields for the correct format. If any of the fields checked doesn't have the correct format, the block performs the following tasks; 1) unsets `$do`; 2) creates an error message that explains the problem; 3) shows the login form again, including the error message; 4) stops the program and waits for the user to submit the form again with the correct format.

123 Lines 123–131 check to see if the Member ID submitted by the customer is already a loginName in the database table Member. The loginName must be unique. `$num` equals 0 or 1, depending on whether the loginName is found in the database.

132 Starts an if block that executes if the loginName is already in the database. The new member cannot be added if the Member ID is not unique. The block performs the following tasks: 1) unsets `$do`; 2) creates an error message that explains the problem; 3) shows the login form again, including the error message; 4) stops the program and waits for the user to submit the form again with a different Member ID.

140 Starts an else block if the loginName is *not* already in the database. This is a successful application for a member account. The block inserts a new row in the Member table for the new member account and sends an e-mail message to the customer about the new account. The statements in the block are documented in more detail in the following list:

 142 Sets `$today` to today's date in the correct format for the createDate field in the Member table.

 143 Creates an `INSERT` query to add the new member row. Notice that the password is encrypted as `password('$newpass')` when it is entered. This is a security method so that no one who looks in the database can see the password. If you're totally sure that no one will see the database that shouldn't, encryption isn't really necessary.

 149 Executes the `INSERT` query.

 150 In lines 150 and 151, the two session variables, `$auth` and `$logname`, are set. Because these variables are registered as session variables, these values are stored in the session file.

 152 Lines 152–164 send an e-mail to the new member, verifying the Member ID and password. Notice that the e-mail message is created in several variables (emess1, emess2 . . .) and combined on line 161 into `$emess`. This is to make it easier for humans to read, not because PHP needs this. Unlike HTML content that ignores extra spaces and line ends, extra spaces and other things have an effect on an e-mail message. For instance, if I created one long message, with extra spaces to indent it so I could read it, those spaces would show up in the e-mail. So, I set the message in several variable statements that I can indent for readability in the program. Line 164 uses the PHP function `mail` to send the e-mail message. The `mail` function is documented in Chapter 14.

165 Sends the customer to the New Member page.

166 Ends the else block for a successful new member account application.

167 Ends the case block for the new member section of the login page.

169 Starts the case block for the default condition. If `$do` is not set to either `"login"` or `"new"`, the program skips to this block. Because both the forms on the login page set `$do`, this block only executes the first time this program runs — when the user links to it from the storefront page and has not yet submitted either form. This section has only one statement, a statement that displays the login page.

This program shows the login page in many places. This is done with include statements that call the file `login_form.inc`. This file includes the HTML that produces the login page. The program `Login.php` does *not* produce any output at all. All the output is produced by `login_form.inc`. This type of application organization is discussed in Chapter 10. This is a good example of the use of include files. Just imagine this program, which is long enough, if the statements in `login_form.inc`, shown in Listing 12-3, were included in the Login program at each place where `login_form` is included. Whew, that would be a mess that only a computer could understand.

Listing 12-3: File That Creates the Login Page

```
<?php
 /* File: login_form.inc
  * Desc: Displays login page. Page displays two forms--one form for
  *       entering an existing login name and password and another
  *       form for the information needed to apply for a new account.
*/
include("functions.inc");                                        // 7
?>
<html>
<head><title>Members Only Login</title></head>
<body topmargin="0" leftmargin="0" marginheight="0" marginwidth="0">
<table border="0" cellpadding="5" cellspacing="0">
 <tr><td colspan="3" bgcolor="gray" align="center">
  <font color="white" size="+10">
       <b>Members Only Section</b></font></td></tr>
 <tr>
  <td width="33%" valign="top">
   <font size="+1"><b>Are you a member?</b></font>
   <p>
   <!-- form for customer login -->
   <form action="Login.php?do=login" method="post">              // 21
   <table border="0">
    <?php                                                        // 23
      if (isset($message))
          echo "<tr><td colspan='2'>$message </td></tr>";
    ?>
    <tr><td align=right><b>Username</b></td>
     <td><input type="text" name="fusername" size="20" maxsize="20">
     </td></tr>
```

(continued)

Listing 12-3 *(continued)*

```
    <tr><td width="120" align="right"><b>Password</b></td>
     <td><input type="password" name="fpassword"
              size="20" maxsize="20"></td></tr>
    <tr><td align="center" colspan="2">
      <br><input type="submit" name="log" value="Enter"></td></tr>
   </table>
   </form>
  </td>
  <td width="1" bgcolor="gray"></td>
  <td width="67%">
    <p><font size="+1"><b>Not a member yet?</b></font> Get discounts,
     a newsletter, advance notice of new pets, much more. Fill
     in the information below and join. It's easy and free! </b>
   <!-- form for new member to fill in -->
   <form action="Login.php?do=new" method="post">                     // 44
   <p>
   <table border="0" width="100%">
    <?php
      if (isset($message_new))                                          // 48
           echo "<tr><td colspan='2'><b>$message_new</b></td></tr>";
    ?>
    <tr><td align="right"><b>Member ID</b></td>
     <td><input type="text" name="newname"
              value="<?php echo @$newname ?>"
              size="20" maxlength="20"></td></tr>
    <tr><td align="right"><b>Password</b></td>
     <td><input type="password" name="newpass"
          value="<?php echo @$newpass ?>"
            size="10" maxlength="8"></td></tr>
    <tr><td align="right"><b>First Name</b></td>
     <td><input type="text" name="firstName"
            value="<?php echo @$firstName ?>"
            size="40" maxlength="40"></td></tr>
    <tr><td align="right"><b>Last Name</b></td>
     <td><input type="text" name="lastName"
            value="<?php echo @$lastName ?>"
            size="40" maxlength="40"></td></tr>
    <tr><td align="right"><b>Street</b></td>
     <td><input type="text" name="street"
            value="<?php echo @$street ?>"
            size="55" maxlength="50"></td></tr>
    <tr><td align="right"><b>City</b></td>
     <td><input type="text" name="city" value="<?php echo @$city ?>"
            size="40" maxlength="40"></td></tr>
    <tr><td align="right"><b>State</b></td>
     <td>
      <select name="state">                                             // 76
      <?php
        $stateName=getStateName();                                      // 78
        $stateCode=getStateCode();                                      // 79
        for ($n=1;$n<=50;$n++)
        {
          $state=$stateName[$n];
          $scode=$stateCode[$n];
          echo "<option value='$scode'";
          if ($scode== "AL")
             echo " selected";
             echo ">$state\n";
        }
```

```
      ?>
      </select>
          <b>Zip</b>
      <input type="text" name="zip" value="<?php echo @$zip ?>"
             size="10" maxsize="10">
     </td></tr>
    <tr><td align=right><b>Phone</b></td>
     <td><input type="test" name="phone" value="<?php echo @$phone ?>"
             size="15" maxlength="20">
           <b>Fax</b>
        <input type="text" name="fax" value="<?php echo @$fax ?>"
             size="15" maxlength="20"></td></tr>
    <tr><td align=right><b>Email Address</b></td>
     <td><input type="test" name="email" value="<?php echo @$email ?>"
             size="55" maxlength="67"></td></tr>
    <tr><td> </td>
     <td align="center">
       <input type="submit" value="Become a Member"></td>
    </tr>
   </table>
   </form>
  </td>
 </tr>
 <tr><td colspan="3" bgcolor="gray"> </td></tr>
</table>
<div align="center"><font size="-1">
All comments and suggestions are appreciated. Please send comments
to <a href="mailto:webmaster@petstore.com">webmaster@petstore.com</A>
</font></div>
</body>
```

Notice the following points about `login_form`:

- Most of the statements are HTML, with a few small PHP sections here and there.
- The two forms that start on lines 21 and 44 set action to the same program, but add a different string to the URL — `do=login` or `do=new`.
- The error messages are shown on the login page using small PHP sec-ions. Each form has its section, and the message has different names for the two forms: `$message` and `$message_new`. On line 23, the variable `$message` is tested. If it has a value, the message is shown, but not if it has no value. If there was no error in the form, the message was never set, and no message is displayed. A similar statement on line 48 shows error messages for the new member form.
- A selection drop-down list (started on line 76) is provided for the customer to select the state, guarding against typing errors by the customer. Notice that lines 78 and 79 call functions. These functions are not PHP functions; they're my functions. The functions are included in the program on line 7. The functions make arrays from a list of state names and a list of two-letter state codes. By using functions, you don't need the two lists of 50 states in the program. The functions can be used repeatedly for many programs. The `function.inc` file contains the two functions as follows:

```
function stateCode ()
{
  $stateCode = array(1=> "AL" ,
      "AK" ,
      "AZ" ,
      ...
      "WY" );
  return $stateCode;
}

function getStateName()
{
  $stateName = array(1=> "Alabama",
      "Alaska",
      "Arizona",
      ...
      "Wyoming" );
  return $stateName;
}
```

A for loop then creates 50 options for the select list, using the two state arrays.

After running `Login.php`, if the user is successful with a login, the first page of the Members Only section is displayed. If the user is successful in obtaining a new user account, the `New_member.php` program is run.

Writing New_member

The New Member feedback page greets new members by name and provides information about their accounts. Members then have the choice of entering the Members Only section or returning to the main page. Listing 12-4 shows the program that displays the page that new members see.

Listing 12-4: Program That Welcomes New Members

```
<?php
 /* Program: New_member.php
  * Desc:    Displays the new member welcome page. Greets member by
  *          name and gives user choice to enter restricted section
  *          or go back to main page.
  */
  session_start();                                              // 7
  if (@$auth != "yes")                                           // 8
  {
     header("Location: login.php");
     exit();
  }
  include("dogs.inc");
  $connection = mysql_connect($host, $user,$password)           // 13
               or die ("Couldn't connect to server.");
  $db = mysql_select_db($database, $connection)
               or die ("Couldn't select database.");
  $sql = "SELECT firstName,lastName FROM Member                 // 17
                WHERE loginName='$logname'";
```

```
  $result = mysql_query($sql)
             or die("Couldn't execute query 1.");
  $row = mysql_fetch_array($result,MYSQL_ASSOC);
  extract($row);
  echo "<html>
        <head><title>New Member Welcome</title></head>
        <body>
        <h2 align='center' style='margin-top: .7in'>
        Welcome $firstName $lastName</h2>\n";
?>                                                          // 28
<p>Your new Member Account lets you enter the Members Only
section of our web site. You'll find special discounts and
bargains, a huge database of animal facts and stories, advice
from experts, advance notification of new pets for sale, a
message board where you can talk to other Members, and much more.
<p>Your new Member ID and password were emailed to you. Store them
carefully for future use.<br>
<div align="center">
<p style="margin-top: .5in"><b>Glad you could join us!</b>
<form action="member_page.php" method="post">               // 38
  <input type="submit" value="Enter the Members Only Section">
</form>
<form action="../PetShopFront.php" method="post">           // 41
  <input type="submit" value="Go to Pet Store Main Page">
</form>
</div>
</body>
</html>
```

Notice the following points about `New_member.php`:

- A session is started on line 7. This makes the session variables registered in `Login.php` available to this program.
- The program checks, beginning on line 8, to see if the customer is logged in. `$auth` is set to yes in `Login.php` when the customer successfully logs in or creates a new account. If `$auth` doesn't equal yes, then the customer isn't logged in. If a customer tries to run the `New_member.php` program without running the `Login.php` program first, `$auth` won't equal yes, and the user will be sent to the login page.
- The program gets the customer's first and last name from the database, beginning with the database connection statement on line 13. In line 17, the query is created using `$logname` to search for the member's information. `$logname` is a session variable that contains the Member ID set in the login program.
- The PHP section ends on line 28. The remainder of the program is HTML.
- The program uses two different forms to provide two different submit buttons. The form statements on lines 38 and 41 start different programs.

The customer controls what happens next. If the customer clicks the button to return to the main page, the `PetShopFront.php` programs runs. If the customer clicks the Members Only Section submit button, the first page of the Members Only section is shown.

Writing the Members Only section

The Web pages in the Members Only section are no different than any other Web pages. You just want to restrict them to members who are logged in. To do this, you start a session and check whether they're logged in at the top of every page. The statements for the top of each program are

```
session_start();
if (@$auth != "yes")8
{
   header("Location: Login.php");
   exit();
}
```

When `session_start` executes, PHP checks for an existing session. If one exists, it sets up the session variables. One of the session variables is `$auth`. When the user logs in, `$auth` is set to yes. If `$auth` doesn't equal yes, the user is not logged in, and the program takes the user to the login page.

Planning for Growth

The original plan for an application usually includes every wonderful thing the user might want it to do. Realistically, it's usually important to make the application available to the users as quickly as possible. Consequently, applications usually go public with a subset of the planned functionality. More functionality is added later. That's why it's important to write your application with future growth in mind.

Looking at the login application in this chapter, I'm sure you can see many things that could be added to it. Here are some possibilities:

- **E-mail a forgotten password.** Users often forget their passwords. Many login applications have a link that users can click to have their passwords e-mailed to them.
- **Change the password.** Members might want to change their password. The application could offer a form for password changes.
- **Update information.** Members might move or change their phone number or e-mail address. The application could provide a way for members to change their own information.
- **Create member list.** You might want to output a nicely formatted list of all the members in the database. This probably isn't something you want to make available to other members, just for yourself, although in some situations, you might want to make the list available to all members.

You can easily add any of these abilities to the application. For instance, you can add a button to the login form that says *Forgot my password* that e-mails the password to the e-mail address in the database. The button can run the login program with a section for e-mailing the password or run a different program that e-mails the password. In the same manner, you can add buttons for changing the password or updating the customer information. You don't need to wait until an application has all its bells and whistles to let your customers use it. You can write it one step at a time.

Part V
The Part of Tens

"DO YOU WANT ME TO CALL THE COMPANY AND HAVE THEM SEND ANOTHER REVIEW COPY OF THEIR DATABASE SOFTWARE SYSTEM, OR DO YOU KNOW WHAT YOU'RE GOING TO WRITE?"

In this part . . .

The three chapters in this part contain hints, tips, and warnings based on my experience. Perhaps they can serve as a shortcut for you on your journey to becoming a confident Web developer. I sincerely hope so.

Chapter 13

Ten Tips for Database Design

In This Chapter

- Making the data in your database as error free as possible
- Avoiding some database design mistakes
- Designing your database to fit the data

Designing a database for the first time can be a little daunting. Don't worry; you'll get the hang of it pretty quickly. Here are a few lessons I've learned the hard way that perhaps you can learn without making my mistakes.

Ask Everyone

When you start planning your database, think of all the information you might possibly want to know. Ask everyone who might ever be interested in the information in your database — whether they will ever use it themselves or not — what questions they might want to ask it. I guarantee that they'll think of questions that never occurred to you. If you didn't talk to the marketing manager, would you think to ask the customer's birthday so that the company could send birthday cards? If you didn't talk to the CEO, would you think to ask employees' hobbies so that the company would know which activities to sponsor? If you didn't talk to human resources, would you think to ask customers where they went on their last vacation so the company could offer a trip to a popular place as a prize in a contest? You may not be able to collect all the information, but you want to consider it all before deciding what to save. You can synthesize, organize, and compress a set of realistic, affordable, and useful information from the total wish list. However, if you start out with a set of information that's too small with too narrow a viewpoint, your database is going to be incomplete and less useful than it could be.

Identify a Unique Identifier for the Primary Key

This sounds obvious, but it's more difficult than it sounds. For instance, you might be tempted to use the customer's name as the unique identifier for a customer table. That's not a good idea, even if you know that in your environment, no two customers have the same name. The identifier must remain the same for the entire life of the database. A customer could change his or her name for a variety of reasons, in a variety of ways. Or what if you misspelled the customer's name when you added it. This is why social security numbers are popular as unique identifiers — they're unique, and they don't change. In most tables, you need to invent an identifier — such as a customer number — to be sure it's unique and won't change.

Primary Keys Can Be Links

Many tables are linked by including the primary key from one table as a column in the other table. This is the one-to-many relationship that is the most common relationship between tables. For instance, a customer can be linked to his or her order by including a column containing the customer's unique ID, such as customer number, in the order table. Many rows in the order table can have the same customer number because one customer can place many orders.

Store Information in the Smallest Reasonable Chunks

Storing data in small chunks is more flexible for future, unexpected uses. You can put two data fields together much easier than you can separate two pieces of data stored together in a field. For instance, storing a customer's first and last names in one long field is a problem if you need the last name only. A better idea is to put a first name field and a last name field together when you need the complete name.

Avoid Repeating Information

Information should not be repeated in a table. If the information changes, you have to change it in several places, introducing an opportunity for errors to creep into the database and cause problems. If you find you're storing the same information repeatedly in a table row, you need to make another table or reorganize the data in another way. For instance, if you have a table of people that contains their addresses and you discover the same address stored for several people, you can store the addresses in a separate table, called household. Then you can link the people to the household by including the unique identifier for the household in the table row for each person who lives at that address.

One Piece of Information per Column

Store only one piece of information in a column. For instance, a table called *movie* with a column called *actors* that lists all the actors in the movie is not a good idea. What you probably need to do is create a separate table called *actor* that has a row for each actor and link the actor row to the movie table.

Use Descriptive Names

Descriptive database names, table names, and column names can make your database easy to understand by anyone who needs to use it. The names should describe clearly what's stored there. For example, Table1 is not a descriptive name; Person is a little better, and Customer is even better than that. Date is not a great name, but birth_date or purchase_date or closing_date or manufactured_date or first_gray_hair_date is much better.

Most Numbers Are Really Character Strings

Numbers should be stored as numbers only if you plan to do something mathematical with them. Phone numbers, zip codes, and social security numbers are never going to be added together, so they should be stored as character strings.

Make Columns as Wide as Necessary

This should go without saying, but I've made a column too narrow more than once. Think carefully about the widths of columns and do some research. What's the longest name in the phone book? What's the longest city name? Zip codes are five characters — oh wait, nine characters, if you consider zip+4 numbers. Phone numbers are just ten numbers? What about international numbers? What about extension numbers? Is *supercalifragilisticexpialidocious* really the longest possible word?

Use ENUM Fields

Use ENUM fields whenever possible to reduce data entry errors. ENUM fields only accept certain values, which keeps the number of typos in a database to a minimum. Even if the number of possible values is fairly high, it's worth the effort to specify them in an ENUM field to keep the database more accurate. MySQL allows 65,535 different values in an ENUM field, which is probably more than you want to handle.

Chapter 14

Ten Things You Might Want to Do Using PHP Functions

In This Chapter

- Finding out about many useful functions
- Understanding what functions can do

One of the strongest aspects of PHP is its many built-in functions. In this chapter, I list the PHP functions that I use most often. I describe some of them elsewhere in this book, and some I only mention in passing or not at all. These are not all the functions, by any means. There are many hundreds of functions in the PHP language. For a complete list of all the functions, see the PHP documentation at `www.php.net`.

Communicate with MySQL

PHP has many functions designed specifically for interacting with MySQL. The following MySQL functions are described thoroughly in this book, particularly in Chapter 8:

```
mysql_connect();     mysql_select_db();     mysql_fetch_array()
mysql_close();       mysql_num_rows();      mysql_query()
```

The following functions may be useful, but they are not discussed or are discussed only briefly in the previous chapters:

- **`mysql_insert_id()`:** For use with an `AUTO-INCREMENT` MySQL column. This function gets the last number inserted into the column.
- **`mysql_fetch_row($result)`:** Gets one row from the temporary results location. The row is put into an array with numbers as the keys. It's the same as `mysql_fetch_array($row,MYSQL_NUM)`.

- mysql_affected_rows($result): Returns the number of rows that were affected by a query — for instance, the number of rows deleted or updated.
- mysql_num_fields($result): Returns the number of fields in a result.
- mysql_field_name($result, N): Returns the name of the row indicated by N. For instance, mysql_field_name($result,1) returns the name of the second column in the result. The first column is 0.

Send E-Mail

PHP provides a function that sends e-mail from your PHP program. The format is

```
mail(address,subject,message,headers);
```

These are the values you need to fill in:

- *address*: The e-mail address that will receive the message.
- *subject*: A string that goes on the subject line of the e-mail message.
- *message*: The content that goes inside the e-mail message.
- *headers*: A string that sets values for headers. For instance, you might have a headers string as follows:

  ```
  "From: member-desk@petstore.com\r\nbcc: mom@hercompany.com"
  ```

  The header would set the From header to the given e-mail address, plus send a blind copy of the e-mail message to mom.

Sometimes you might have a problem with your e-mail. PHP has a configuration setting that must be correct before the mail function can connect to your system e-mail software. The default is usually correct, but if your e-mail doesn't seem to be getting to its destination, check the PHP configuration setting with your system administrator. It may be set incorrectly. If you're running PHP on Windows, the setting in the PHP configuration file must be set for the e-mail server that you're using. You should be able to find the name of the outgoing mail server you're using in your e-mail software. For instance, in Microsoft Outlook Express, choose Tools⇨Accounts⇨Properties and then select the Servers tab. Look for the name of your outgoing mail server. The value for SMTP in your PHP.ini file should be set to the name of your outgoing server. For Unix/Linux, the default SENDMAIL command is usually correct.

Use PHP Sessions

The functions to open or close a session or to register variables in a session follow. All of these functions are explained in Chapter 9.

```
session_start();     session_destroy()
session register()   session_unregister()
```

Stop Your Program

Sometimes you just want your program to stop, cease, and desist. There are two functions for this: `exit()` and `die()`. Actually, these are two different names for the same function. Exit is probably accurate, but sometimes it's just more fun to say die. Both functions will print a message when they stop if you provide one. The format is

```
exit("message string");
```

When `exit` executes, the message string is output.

Handle Arrays

Arrays are very useful in PHP. They are particularly useful for getting the results from database functions and for form variables. The following array functions are explained elsewhere in the book, mainly in Chapter 7:

```
array();     extract();     sort();     asort();
rsort();     arsort();      ksort();    krsort();
```

Here are some other useful functions:

- `array_reverse($varname)`: Returns an array with the values in reverse order.
- `array_unique($varname)`: Removes duplicate values from an array.
- `in_array("string",$varname)`: Looks through an array `$varname` for a string `"string"`.
- `range(value1,value2)`: Creates an array containing all the values between `value1` and `value2`. For instance, `range('a','z')` creates an array containing all the letters between *a* and *z*.

- `explode("sep","string")`: Creates an array of strings in which each item is a substring of *string*, separated *sep*. For example, `explode(" ",$string)` creates an array in which each word in `$string` is a separate value.
- `implode("glue",$array)`: Creates a string containing all the values in *$array* with *glue* between them. For instance, `implode(", ",$array)` creates a string: value1, value2, value3, and so on.

And there are many more useful array functions. PHP can do almost anything you can think of that you want to do with an array.

Check for Variables

Sometimes you just need to know whether a variable exists. The following functions can be used to test whether or not a variable is currently set:

```
isset($varname);  // true if variable is set
!isset($varname); // true if variable is not set
empty($varname);  // true if value is 0 or is not set
```

Format Values

Sometimes you need to format the values in variables. Chapter 6 explains how to format numbers into dollar format using `number_format()` and `sprintf()`. Chapter 6 also discusses `unset()`, which removes the values from a variable. In this section, I describe additional capabilities of `sprintf()`.

The function `sprintf()` allows you to format any string or number, including variable values. The general format is

```
$newvar = sprintf("format",$varname1,$varname2,...);
```

where *format* gives instructions for the format and *$varname* contains the value(s) to be formatted. *format* can contain both literals and instructions for formatting the values in the *$varname*. Actually, the format can contain only literals. The following statement is valid:

```
$newvar = sprintf("I have a pet");
```

This statement outputs the literal string. However, you can also add variables, using the following statements:

```
$ndogs = 5;
$ncats = 2;
$newvar = sprintf("I have %s dogs and %s cats",$ndogs,$ncats);
```

The `%s` is a formatting instruction that tells `sprintf` to insert the variable value as a string. Thus, the output is: `I have 5 dogs and 2 cats.` The `%` character signals `sprintf` that a formatting instruction starts here. The formatting instruction has the following format:

```
%pad-width.dectype
```

These are the components of the formatting instructions:

- **%:** Signals the start of the formatting instruction.
- *pad*: A padding character that's used to fill out the number when necessary. If you don't specify a character, a space is used. `pad` can be a space, a 0, or any character preceded by a single quote ('). For instance, it's common to pad numbers with 0 — for example, `01` or `0001`.
- -: A symbol meaning to left justify the characters. If this isn't included, the characters are right justified.
- *width*: The number of characters to use for the value. If the value doesn't fill the width, then the padding character is used to pad the value. For instance, if the width is 5, the padding character is 0, and the value is 1, the output is `00001`.
- *.dec*: The number of decimal places to use for a number.
- *type*: The type of value. Use *s* for most values. Use *f* for numbers that you want to format with decimal places.

Some possible `sprintf` statements are

```
sprintf("I have $%03.2f. Does %s have any?",$money,$name);
sprintf("%'.-20s%3.2f",$product,$price);
```

The output of these statements is

```
I have $030.00. Does Tom have any?
Kitten.............. 30.00
```

Compare Strings to Patterns

Previous chapters in this book use regular expressions as patterns to match strings. (Regular expressions are explained in Chapter 6.) The following functions use regular expressions to find and sometimes replace patterns in strings:

- `ereg("`*`pattern`*`",$`*`varname`*`)`: Checks whether the *pattern* is found in *$varname*. `eregi` is the same function, except that it ignores upper- and lowercase.

- `ereg_replace("pattern","string",$varname)`: Searches for the *pattern* in *$varname* and replaces it with the *string*. `eregi_replace` is the same function, except that it ignores upper- and lowercase.

Find Out about Strings

Sometimes you need to know things about a string, such as how long it is or whether the first character is an uppercase *O*. PHP offers many functions for checking out your strings:

- `strlen($varname)`: Returns the length of the string.
- `strpos("string","substring")`: Returns the position in `string` where `substring` begins. For instance, `strpos("hello","el")` returns 1. Remember, the first position for PHP is 0. `strrpos()` finds the *last* position in `string` where `substring` begins.
- `substr("string",n1,n2)`: Returns the substring from *string* that begins at *n1* and is *n2* characters long. For instance, `substr("hello",2,2)` returns `ll`.
- `strtr($varname,"str1","str2")`: Searches through the string *$varname* for *str1* and replaces it with *str2* every place it's found.
- `strrev($varname)`: Returns the string with the characters reversed.

Many, many more string functions exist. See the documentation at `www.php.net`.

Change the Case of Strings

Changing uppercase letters to lowercase and vice versa is not so easy. Bless PHP for providing functions to do this for you:

- `strtolower($varname)`: Changes any uppercase letters in the string to lowercase letters
- `strtoupper($varname)`: Changes any lowercase letters in the string to uppercase letters
- `ucfirst($varname)`: Changes the first letter in the string to uppercase
- `ucwords($varname)`: Changes the first letter of each word in the string to uppercase

Chapter 15

Ten PHP Gotchas

In This Chapter

- Recognizing common PHP errors
- Interpreting error messages

I guarantee that you will do all of the things that I mention in this chapter. It's not possible to write programs without making these mistakes. The trick is to learn to recognize them, roll your eyes and say "Not again," and fix them. One error message you will see many times is

```
Parse error: parse error in c:\test.php on line 7
```

This is PHP's way of saying "Huh?" It means it doesn't understand something. This message helpfully points to the file and the line number where PHP got confused. Sometimes it's directly pointing at the error, but sometimes PHP's confusion results from an error earlier in the program.

Missing Semicolons

Every PHP statement ends with a semicolon (;). PHP doesn't stop reading a statement until it reaches a semicolon. If you leave out the semicolon at the end of a line, PHP continues reading the statement on the following line. For instance, consider the following statement:

```
$test = 1
echo $test;
```

Of course, the statement doesn't make sense to PHP when it reads the two lines as one statement, so it complains with an error message, such as the annoying

```
Parse error: parse error in c:\test.php on line 2
```

Before you know it, you'll be writing your address with semicolons at the end of each line.

Not Enough Equal Signs

When you ask whether two values are equal, you need two equal signs. Using one equal sign is a common mistake. It's perfectly reasonable because you have been using one equal sign to mean equals since the first grade when you learned that 2 + 2 = 4. This is a difficult mistake to recognize because it doesn't cause an error message. It just makes your program do odd things, like infinite loops or if blocks that never execute. I'm continually amazed at how long I can stare at

```
$test = 0;
while ( $test = 0 )
{
   $test++;
}
```

and not see why it's looping endlessly.

Misspelled Variable Names

This is another PHP gotcha that doesn't result in an error message, just odd program behavior. If you misspell a variable name, PHP considers it a new variable and does what you ask it to do. Here's another clever way to write an infinite loop:

```
$test = 0;
while ( $test == 0 )
{
   $Test++;
}
```

Missing Dollar Signs

A missing dollar sign in a variable name is really hard to see, but at least it usually results in an error message so that you know where to look for the problem. It usually results in the old familiar parse error:

```
Parse error: parse error in test.php on line 7
```

Troubling Quotes

You can have too many, too few, or the wrong kind of quotes. You have too many when you put quotes inside of quotes, such as:

```
$test = "<table width="100%">";
```

PHP will see the second double quote (") — before `100` — as the ending double quote (") and read the `1` as an instruction, which makes no sense. *Voilà!* Another parse error. The line must be either

```
$test = "<table width='100%'>";
```

or

```
$test = "<table width=\"100%\">";
```

You have too few quotes when you forget to end a quoted string, such as

```
$test = "<table width='100%'>;
```

PHP will continue reading the lines as part of the quoted string until it encounters another double quote ("), which might not occur for several lines. This is one occasion when the parse error pointing to where PHP got confused is not pointing to the actual error. The actual error occurred some lines previously, when you forgot to end the string.

You have the wrong kind of quotes when you use a single quote (') when you meant a double quote (") or vice versa. The difference between single and double quotes is sometimes important, and I explain it in Chapter 6.

Invisible Output

Some statements, such as the header statement, must execute before the program produces any output. If you try to use such statements after sending output, they fail. The following statements will fail because the header message isn't the first output:

```
<html>
<?php
   header("Location: http://company.com");
?>
```

`<html>` is not in a PHP section and is therefore sent as HTML output. The following statements will work:

```
<?php
   header("Location: http://company.com");
?>
<html>
```

The following statements will fail:

```
 <?php
   header("Location: http://company.com");
?>
<html>
```

because there's one single blank space before the opening PHP tag. The blank space is output to the browser, although the resulting Web page looks empty. Therefore, the header statement fails because there is output before it. This is a common mistake and difficult to spot.

Numbered Arrays

PHP believes the first value in an array is numbered zero (0). Of course, humans tend to believe that lists start with the number one (1). This fundamentally different way of viewing lists results in us humans believing an array isn't working correctly when it's working just fine. For instance, consider the following statements:

```
$test = 1;
while ( $test <= 3 )
{
   $array[] = $test;
   $test++;
}
echo $array[3];
```

No output results. I leap to the conclusion that there's something wrong with my loop. Actually, it's fine. It just results in the following array:

```
$array[0]=1
$array[1]=2
$array[2]=3
```

And doesn't set anything into `$array[3]`.

Including PHP Statements

When a file is read in using an include statement in a PHP section, it seems reasonable to me that the statements in the file will be treated as PHP statements. After all, PHP adds the statements to the program at the point where I include them. However, PHP doesn't see it my way. If a file named `file1.inc` contains the following statements:

```
if ( $test == 1 )
      echo "Hi";
```

and I read it in with the following statements in my main program:

```
<?php
$test = 1;
include ("file1.inc");
?>
```

I expect the word `Hi` to appear on the Web page. However, the Web page actually displays this:

```
if ( $test == 1 ) echo "Hi";
```

Clearly, the file that is included is seen as HTML. To send `Hi` to the Web page, `file1.inc` needs to contain the following statements:

```
<?php
if ( $test == 1 )
       echo "Hi";
?>
```

Missing Mates

Parentheses and curly brackets come in pairs and must be used that way. Opening with a `(` that has no closing `)` or a `{` without a `}` will result in an error message. One of my favorites is using one closing parenthesis where two are needed, as in the following statement:

```
if ( isset($test)
```

This statement needs a closing parenthesis at the end. It's much more difficult to spot that one of your blocks didn't get closed when you have blocks inside of blocks inside of blocks. For instance, consider the following:

```
while ( $test < 3 )
{
if ( $test2 != "yes" )
{
if ( $test3 > 4 )
{
echo "go";
}
}
```

You can see there are three opening curly brackets and only two closing ones. Imagine that 100 lines of code are inside these blocks. It can be difficult to spot the problem — especially if you think the last closing bracket is closing the while loop, while PHP sees it as closing the if loop for `$test2`. Somewhere later in your program, PHP might be using a closing bracket to close the while loop that you aren't even looking at. It can be difficult to trace the problem in a large program.

Indenting blocks makes it easier to see where closing brackets belong. Also, I often use comments to keep track of where I am, such as:

```
while ( $test < 3 )
{
 if ( $test2 != "yes" )
 {
  if ( $test3 > 4 )
  {
   echo "go";
  } // closing if block for $test3
 } // closing if block for $test2
```

Confusing Parentheses and Brackets

I'm not sure if this is a problem for everyone or just a problem for me because I refuse to admit that I can't see as well as I used to. While PHP has no trouble distinguishing between parentheses and curly brackets, my eyes are not so reliable. Especially while staring at a computer screen at the end of a 10-hour programming marathon, I can easily confuse `(` and `{`. Using the wrong one gets you a parse error message.

Part VI

Appendixes

The 5th Wave
By Rich Tennant
WANDA HAD THE DISTINCT FEELING HER HUSBAND'S NEW SOFTWARE PROGRAM WAS ABOUT TO BECOME INTERACTIVE.
MANUAL

In this part . . .

This part provides instructions for installing MySQL and PHP. Appendix C describes the software that is provided on the CD that comes with this book.

Appendix A

Installing MySQL

Although MySQL runs on many platforms, I describe how to install it on Linux, Windows, and Unix, which together account for the majority of Web sites on the Internet. Be sure to read the instructions all the way through before beginning the installation.

On Linux and Unix, MySQL can be installed from precompiled, ready-to-install packages, called RPMs (Linux) or binary files (Linux or Unix). These packages are set up for specific versions of Linux and Unix. If such a package is available for your operating system, use it; it is much easier to install MySQL this way. However, if no package works for your operating system, you can still install MySQL from source code.

On Linux Using RPM

MySQL can be installed on Linux using RPM. RPM stands for *Red Hat Package Manager,* but RPM is available on most flavors of Linux, not just Red Hat. Using RPM is the easiest way to install on Linux. If installing from an RPM file doesn't work for you, try using a ready-to-install package called a binary, which is also easy to install; for installation instructions, see the section, "On Linux/Unix from Binary Files." If neither of these methods works for you, you can always install MySQL from source files. To do this, follow the instructions in the section, "On Linux/Unix from Source Files."

You can download the RPM file using the following instructions. However, the RPM file may already be on the CD that your Linux operating system came on. Installing the RPM file from a CD saves you the trouble of downloading (you can skip Steps 1 through 9 in the following list), but if the version of MySQL on your CD is not the most recent, you may want to download an RPM file anyway. It's best not to install any version prior to 3.23.

To install MySQL on Linux from an RPM file, follow these steps:

1. **Point your Web browser to `www.mysql.com`, the MySQL home page.**
2. **Click Downloads.**

3. **Under MySQL Database, click the link to the newest stable release.**

   As of this writing, MySQL 3.23 is the newest stable release.

4. **Scroll down the screen until you come to the heading Linux Downloads.**

   This section lists several downloads for Linux.

5. **Scroll down to the list of Red Hat Packages, and locate the correct package for your version of Linux.**

   In most cases, Server (i386) is the correct version for you.

6. **Click the download link for the version you need.**

   A page shows a list of locations from which you can download.

7. **Click the HTTP or FTP link for the location closest to you.**

   A dialog box opens.

8. **Select the option to save the file.**

   A box opens that lets you select where you want to save the file.

9. **Navigate to where you want to save the RPM (for example, `/usr/src/mysql`). Then click Save.**

10. **Repeat Steps 6 through 9 to download the RPM file for Client Programs (i386) into the same download location.**

11. **Change to the directory where you saved the download.**

    For instance, type `cd /usr/src/mysql`. You see two files in the directory — one file named `MySQL-`, followed by the version number and `.i386.rpm`, and a second file named similarly with `client` embedded in its name. For example: `MySQL-3.23.47-1.i386.rpm` and `MySQL-client-3.23.47-1.i386.rpm`.

12. **Install the RPM by entering this command:**

    ```
    rpm -i listofpackages
    ```

    For instance, using the example in Step 11, the command would be this:

    ```
    rpm -i MySQL-3.23.47-1.i386.rpm MySQL-client-3.23.47-1.i386.rpm
    ```

    This command installs the MySQL packages. It sets the MySQL account and group name that you need, and creates the data directory at `/var/lib/mysql`. It also starts the MySQL server and creates the appropriate entries in `/etc/rc.d` so that MySQL starts automatically whenever your computer starts.

13. **To test that MySQL is running okay, type this:**

    ```
    bin/mysqladmin --version
    ```

    You should see the version number of your MySQL server.

On Windows

In most cases, when you download and install MySQL, the server is started automatically. If it isn't or if you need to stop and start it for another reason, you can start it manually using a utility called WinMySQLadmin that is installed with MySQL, as described in the upcoming section, "Starting the MySQL server." You can also use WinMySQLadmin to set up MySQL so that it starts every time your computer starts.

Downloading and installing MySQL

To install MySQL on Windows, follow these steps:

1. **Point your Web browser to `www.mysql.com`, the MySQL home page.**
2. **Click Downloads.**
3. **Under the heading MySQL Database, click the link to the newest stable release.**

   As of this writing, MySQL 3.23 is the newest stable release.
4. **Scroll down the screen until you come to the heading Windows Downloads.**
5. **Click the download link by the MySQL version name in the Windows section.**

   A page appears, listing the locations from which you can download.
6. **Click the HTTP or FTP link for the location closest to you.**

   A dialog box opens.
7. **Select the option to save the file.**

   A dialog box opens that lets you select where you want the file saved.
8. **Navigate to where you want to save the file (for example, `c:\downloads`). Then click Save.**

   After the download, you see a zip file in the download location (for example, `c:\downloads`) containing the MySQL files. The file is named `mysql-`, followed by the version number and `-win.zip` — for instance, `mysql-3.23.47-win.zip`.
9. **Use your favorite zip utility to unzip the files and save them in a temporary location (for example, `c:\downloads\mysql`).**

   Two popular zip utilities are PKZIP at `www.pkware.com`, and WinZip at `www.winzip.com`.

10. **Navigate to the temporary directory where the unzipped files are stored. Then double-click** `setup.exe`.

    Note: If you're installing from a Windows NT/2000/XP system, be sure that you're logged into an account with administrative privileges.

    The opening screen shown in Figure A-1 is displayed.

11. **Click Next.**

    The license is displayed.

12. **Click the I Agree button to continue.**

    You see a screen showing the directory where MySQL will be installed.

13. **If you want to install MySQL in the default directory,** `c:\mysql`, **click Next. If you want to install MySQL in a different directory, click Browse, select a directory, and click OK; then click Next.**

    You see a screen in which you can choose the type of installation.

14. **Check Typical and then click Next.**

    The installation of MySQL begins. A message appears when the installation is complete.

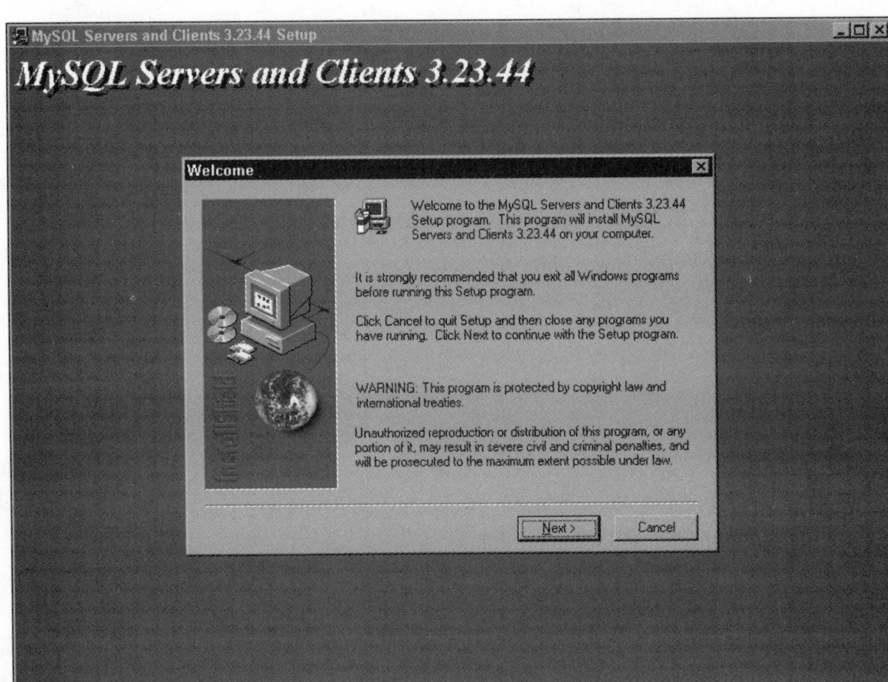

Figure A-1: The opening screen of the MySQL setup program.

The server may or may not have been started during installation. If it is running, you should see a traffic signal in your system tray with a green light showing. If it isn't running, check out the next section.

Starting the MySQL server

You can start and stop your server manually with WinMySQLadmin, a program that was installed with MySQL.

First, start WinMySQLadmin. You may be able to start WinMySQLadmin from your StartUp menu: Choose Start⇨Programs⇨Startup⇨WinMySQLadmin. If you can't find it on your StartUp menu, use Windows Explorer to navigate to the bin directory in the directory where MySQL is installed (for example, `c:\mysql\bin`) and double-click WinMySQLadmin.

To start the MySQL server using WinMySQLadmin, follow these steps:

1. **Right-click in the WinMySQLadmin window.**

   You see a short menu.

2. **Select your operating system: Windows 9x or Windows NT.**
3. **Click Start the Server.**
4. **Exit WinMySQLadmin by right-clicking in the WinMySQLadmin window and then clicking Hide Me.**

Setting up the server to start when the computer starts

If you want to set up your MySQL server so that it starts every time your computer starts, start WinMySQLadmin as described in the previous section and then follow these steps:

1. **Click the my.ini Setup tab.**
2. **Click Create ShortCut on Start Menu in the bottom-left corner of the screen.**
3. **Exit WinMySQLadmin by right-clicking in the WinMySQLadmin window and then choosing Hide Me.**

On Linux/Unix from Binary Files

Ready-to-use, compiled binary files are available for several flavors of Linux and Unix. If none of the flavors work for your Linux/Unix machine, you can install MySQL from source files, but it's better to use a binary if at all possible. As of this writing, MySQL binary files were available for the following flavors of Unix, but more may be made available at any time:

- Solaris
- HP-UX
- AIX
- SCO
- SGI Irix
- Dec OSF
- BSDi
- FreeBSD

To install a binary file version of MySQL on Linux or Unix, follow these steps:

1. **Point your Web browser to `www.mysql.com`, the MySQL home page.**
2. **Click Downloads.**
3. **Under the heading MySQL Database, click the link to the newest stable release.**

   As of this writing, the newest stable release is MySQL 3.23.
4. **Scroll down the screen until you come to the heading for Linux or for your version of Unix (for example, Solaris Downloads).**

   Each section lists several downloads for that operating system.
5. **Locate the correct package for your version of operating system.**

   For Linux, you probably want the Intel libc6 binary version. For Unix, select the correct version of the Unix system — for example, Solaris 2.8 (Sparc).
6. **Click the download link for the version you need.**

   A page appears, listing locations from which you can download.
7. **Click the HTTP or FTP link for the location closest to you.**

   A dialog box opens.
8. **Select the option to save the file.**

   A box opens that lets you select where you want to save the file.

9. **Navigate to where you want to install MySQL. Then click Save.**

   The standard location is /usr/local; it's best to use this location if possible.

10. **After the download is complete, change to the download directory — for instance,** cd-/usr/local.

    You see a file named mysql-, followed by the version number, the name of the operating system, and .tar.gz — for instance, mysql-3.23.47-sun-solaris2.8-sparc.tar.gz. This file is called a *tarball.*

11. **Create a user and group ID for MySQL to run under by using these commands:**

    ```
    groupadd mysql
    useradd -g mysql mysql
    ```

    The syntax for the commands may differ slightly on different versions of Unix, or they may be called adduser and addgroup.

    Note: You must be using an account that is authorized to add users and groups.

12. **Unpack the tarball by typing this:**

    ```
    gunzip -c filename | tar -xvf -
    ```

    For example:

    ```
    gunzip -c mysql-3.23.47-sun-solaris2.8-sparc.tar.gz | tar -xvf -
    ```

    Note: You must be using an account that is allowed to create files in /usr/local.

13. **Create a link to the new directory so that you can refer to it by a shorter name, rather than its current, difficult-to-type name. Type the following:**

    ```
    ln -s newdirectoryname mysql
    ```

    For example:

    ```
    ln -s mysql-3.23.47-sun-solaris2.8-sparc mysql
    ```

    Now you can refer to the directory as mysql, instead of by its long name.

14. **Change to the new directory by typing** cd mysql.

    You should see several subdirectories, including /bin and /scripts.

15. **Add the path to the bin directory (for example,** /usr/local/mysql/bin**) to your system path so that the MySQL programs can be accessed by any programs that need to access MySQL.**

    You should do this by editing the file that sets the system variables when your computer starts up.

16. **Type the following:**

    ```
    scripts/mysql_install_db
    ```

    This command runs a script that initializes your MySQL databases.

17. **Make sure that the ownership and group membership of your MySQL directories are correct. Set the ownership with these commands:**

    ```
    chown -R root  /usr/local/mysql
    chown -R mysql /usr/local/mysql/data
    chgrp -R mysql /usr/local/mysql
    ```

    These commands make `root` the owner of all the MySQL directories except data and make `mysql` the owner of data. All MySQL directories belong to group `mysql`.

18. **Set up your computer so that MySQL starts automatically when your machine starts by copying the file `mysql.server` from `/usr/local/mysql/support-files` to the location where your system has its startup files.**

19. **To test MySQL, you can start your server manually, without restarting your computer, by typing the following:**

    ```
    bin/safe_mysqld --user=mysql &
    ```

20. **To test that MySQL is running okay, type**

    ```
    bin/mysqladmin --version
    ```

    You should see the version number of your MySQL server.

On Linux/Unix from Source Files

Before you decide to install MySQL from source files, check for binary files for your operating system. MySQL binary files are precompiled, ready-to-install packages for installing MySQL. MySQL binary files are very convenient and reliable.

You install MySQL by downloading source files, compiling the source files, and installing the compiled programs. This process sounds terribly technical and daunting, but it's not. Read all the way through the following steps before you begin the installation procedure.

To install MySQL from source code, follow these steps:

1. **Point your Web browser to `www.mysql.com`, the MySQL home page.**
2. **Click Downloads.**
3. **Under the heading MySQL Database, click the link to the newest stable release.**

   As of this writing, the newest stable release is MySQL 3.23.

4. **Scroll to the bottom of the screen to the heading Source Downloads.**

   This section lists several downloads.

5. **Locate the tarball version and then click the download link next to it.**

   A page appears, listing locations from which you can download.

6. **Click the HTTP or FTP link for the location closest to you.**

   A dialog box opens.

7. **Select the option to save the file.**

   A box opens that lets you select where the file will be saved.

8. **Navigate to where you want to install MySQL and then click Save.**

   The standard location is `/usr/local`. It is best to use the standard location if possible.

9. **After the download is complete, change to the download directory — for instance,** `cd-/usr/local`.

   You see a file named `mysql-`, followed by the version number and `.tar.gz.` — for instance, `mysql-3.23.47.tar.gz`. This file is called a *tarball.*

10. **Create a user and group ID for MySQL to run under by using the following commands:**

    ```
    groupadd mysql
    useradd -g mysql mysql
    ```

    The syntax for the commands may differ slightly on different versions of Unix, or they may be called `adduser` and `addgroup`.

    Note: You must be using an account that is authorized to add users and groups.

11. **Unpack the tarball by typing:**

    ```
    gunzip -c filename | tar -xvf -
    ```

    For example:

    ```
    gunzip -c mysql-3.23.44.tar.gz | tar -xvf -
    ```

    You see a new directory named `mysql-version` — for instance, `mysql-3.23.44`.

    You must be using an account that is allowed to create files in `/usr/local`.

12. **Change to the new directory.**

    For instance, type `cd mysql-3.23.44`.

13. **Type the following:**

    ```
    ./configure --prefix=/usr/local/mysql
    ```

    You see several lines of output. The output will tell you when configure is done. This may take some time.

14. **Type** `make`**.**

    You see many lines of output. The output will tell you when make is done. Make may run for some time.

15. **Type** `make install`**.**

    Make install will finish quickly.

    Note: You might need to run this command as `root`.

16. **Type the following:**

    ```
    scripts/mysql_install_db.
    ```

    This command runs a script that initializes your MySQL databases.

17. **Make sure that the ownership and group membership of your MySQL directories are correct. Set the ownership with these commands:**

    ```
    chown -R root  /usr/local/mysql
    chown -R mysql /usr/local/mysql/data
    chgrp -R mysql /usr/local/mysql
    ```

    These commands make `root` the owner of all the MySQL directories except data and make `mysql` the owner of data. All MySQL directories belong to group `mysql`.

18. **Set up your computer so that MySQL starts automatically when your machine starts by copying the file** `mysql.server` **from** `/usr/local/mysql/support-files` **to the location where your system has its startup files.**

19. **To test MySQL, you can start your server manually, without restarting your computer, by typing the following:**

    ```
    bin/safe_mysqld --user=mysql &
    ```

20. **To test that MySQL is running okay, type:**

    ```
    bin/mysqladmin --version
    ```

    You should see the version number of your MySQL server.

Appendix B
Installing PHP

Although PHP runs on many platforms, I describe installing it on Unix/ Linux and Windows, which includes the majority of Web sites on the Internet. PHP runs with several Web servers, but these instructions focus mainly on Apache and IIS because together they power almost 90 percent of the Web sites on the Internet. If you need instructions for other operating systems or Web servers, see the PHP Web site (`www.php.net`).

On Unix/Linux with Apache

You can install PHP as an Apache module or as a stand-alone interpreter. If you're using PHP as a scripting language in Web pages to interact with a database, you want to install it as Apache module. PHP is faster and more secure as a module. I do not discuss PHP as a stand-alone interpreter in this book.

You install PHP by downloading source files, compiling the source files, and installing the compiled programs. This process isn't as technical and daunting as it may appear. I provide step-by-step instructions in the next few sections. Read all the way through the steps before you begin the installation procedure.

For Linux users only: PHP for Linux is available in an RPM, as well as in source files. It may be in RPM format on your distribution CD. However, when you install PHP from an RPM, you cannot control the options that PHP is installed with. For instance, you need to install PHP with MySQL support enabled, but the RPM may or may not have MySQL support enabled. MySQL is popular, so many RPMs enable support for it, but it is out of your control. Also, an RPM usually enables all the most popular options, so an RPM may enable options you don't need. Consequently, the simplest and most efficient way to install PHP may be from the source. If you're familiar with RPMs, by all means feel free to find an RPM and install it. RPMs are available. However, I am providing steps for source code installation, not RPMs.

Before installing

Before beginning to install PHP, check the following:

- **The Apache module mod_so is installed.** It usually is. To display a list of all the modules, type the following:

  ```
  httpd -l.
  ```

  You may have to be in the directory where httpd is located before the command will work. The output usually shows a long list of modules. All you need to be concerned with for PHP is mod_so. If mod_so is not loaded, Apache must be reinstalled.
- **The apxs utility is installed.** Apxs is installed when Apache is installed. You should be able to find a file called apxs. If Apache was installed on Linux from an RPM, apxs may not have been installed. Some RPMs for Apache consist of two RPMs, one for the basic Apache server and one for Apache development tools. Possibly the RPM with the development tools, which installs apxs, needs to be installed.
- **Apache version is 1.3.0 or newer.** To check the version, type the following:

  ```
  httpd --v
  ```

  You may have to be in the directory where httpd is located before the command will work.

Installing

To install PHP on Unix/Linux with an Apache Web server, follow these steps:

1. **Point your Web browser to `www.php.net`, the PHP home page.**
2. **Click Downloads.**
3. **Click the latest version of the PHP source code, which is version 4.1.1 as of this writing.**

   A dialog box opens.
4. **Select the option to save the file.**

   A dialog box opens that lets you select where the file will be saved.
5. **Navigate to where you want to save the source code (for example, `/usr/src`). Then click Save.**
6. **After the download, change to the download directory (for instance, `cd-/usr/src`).**

   You see a file named `php-`, followed by the version name and `tar.gz`. This file is called a *tarball*.

7. **Unpack the tarball. The command for PHP version 4.1.1 is**

```
gunzip -c php-4.1.1.tar.gz | tar -xf -
```

   A new directory called php-4.1.1 is created with several subdirectories.

8. **Change to the new directory that was created when you unpacked the tarball. For example:**

```
cd php-4.1.1
```

9. **Type the configure command:**

```
./configure --with-mysql --with-apxs --enable-trans-id
```

   The configure command expects to find MySQL installed in its default location at `/usr/local`. If MySQL is installed in a different location on your system, include the path to MySQL in the option. For example:

```
--with-mysql=/home/local
```

   You will see many lines of output. Wait until the configure command has completed. This may take a few minutes.

   If the apxs utility is not installed in the expected location, you will see an error message, indicating that apxs could not be found. If you get this message, check the location where apxs is installed (`find / -name apxs`) and include the path in the `with-apxs` option of the configure command: `—with-apxs=/usr/sbin/apxs`.

10. **Type `make`.**

   You will see many lines of output. Wait until it is finished. This may take a few minutes.

11. **Type `make install`.**

Alternative method for installing

Occasionally, you can't install PHP using apxs. This section provides an alternative method of installation for situations in which apxs isn't available or refuses to work. The preceding installation method is easier and usually works fine. This section is just here to provide an alternative in case the first section fails you. Follow these steps:

1. **Point your Web browser to `www.php.net`, the PHP home page.**
2. **Click Downloads.**
3. **Click the latest version of the PHP source code — version 4.1.1 as of this writing.**

   A dialog box opens.

4. **Select the option to save the file.**

   A dialog box opens that lets you select where the file will be saved.

5. **Navigate to where you want to save the source code (for example, `/usr/src/php`). Then click Save.**
6. **After the download is complete, change to the download directory (for instance, `cd-/usr/src/php`).**

   You see a file named `php-`, followed by the version number and `tar.gz`. This file is called a *tarball.*
7. **Unpack the tarball. The command to unpack the tarball for the current PHP version 4.1.1 is**

   ```
   gunzip -c php-4.1.1.tar.gz | tar -xf -
   ```

   A new directory called php-4.1.1 is created with several subdirectories.
8. **Repeat Steps 1 through 5, but this time, download the Apache source code into the directory where the PHP source code was unpacked. You can find the Apache source code at `httpd.apache.org`.**

   For the rest of this example, I use the current version, 1.3.22. By the time you read this, a later version may be available.
9. **Unpack the Apache tarball. For the current version, the command is**

   ```
   gunzip -c apache_1.3.22.tar.gz | tar -xf -
   ```

   Now there are two directories: `php-4.1.1` and `apache_1.3.22`. Each has several subdirectories.
10. **Type `cd apache_1.3.22`.**
11. **Type `./configure`.**

    The options do not matter for this command. This is a preliminary configuration of Apache that should be done before you configure PHP. The Apache configure will be run again in a later step with the appropriate options. Wait until the configure has completed. This may take a while.
12. **Type `cd ../php-4.1.1`.**
13. **Type the following:**

    ```
    ./configure --with-mysql --enable-trans-id --with-apache=../apache_1.3.22
    ```

    You can type this command on one line. If you type it on two lines, type a `\` at the end of the first line.
14. **Type `make`.**

    You see many lines of output. You will be informed when it is finished running. It may take some time.
15. **Type `make install`.**

    This finishes quickly.
16. **Type `cd ../apache_1.3.22` to return to the Apache directory tree.**

17. **Type the following command to configure Apache again:**

```
./configure --prefix=/www
    --activate-module=src/modules/php4/libphp4.a
```

You can type this command on one line. If you type it on two lines, type a `\` at the end of the first line.

18. **Type** `make`**.**

You see many lines of output. You will be informed when it is finished running. It may take some time.

19. **This final step depends on whether Apache is already installed on your system or whether this is the first install of Apache.**

For a first installation of Apache, type `make install`**.**

If Apache is currently installed and running, do the following:

1. **Shut down Apache.**

   You can stop the Apache Web server by using a script that was installed on your system during installation. This script is usually called apachectl. It may be located in the bin directory in the directory where Apache was installed — for example, `/usr/local/apache/bin` or in `/sbin` or in `/usr/sbin`. You also may be able to find it in the directory on your system where startup scripts are located — for example, `/etc/rc.d/init.d`. For example, you may be able to stop the server by typing **apachectl stop**. You may need to be in the directory with the script in order to use it.

2. **Find the new file named httpd that you just created.**

   This file will be somewhere under the apache directory tree that you just created — for example, `/usr/src/php/apache_1.3.22/bin/httpd`.

3. **Find the existing file named httpd.**

   This file will be somewhere on your disk, possibly in `/usr/local/apache/bin` or `/sbin` or `/usr/sbin`.

4. **Copy the new file named httpd over the old one — that is, replace the old one with the new one.**

You may want to make a backup copy of the old one before you copy over it.

Advanced installing

The previous sections give you steps to quickly install PHP with the options needed for the applications in this book. However, you may want to install PHP differently. For instance, all the PHP programs and files are installed in their default locations, but you may need to install PHP in different locations.

Or you may be planning applications using additional software. You can use additional command line options if you need to configure PHP for your specific needs. Just add the options to the command shown in Step 13 of the preceding section. In general, the order of the options in the command line doesn't matter. Table B-1 shows the most commonly used options for PHP. To see a list of all possible options, type `configure —help`.

Table B-1 PHP Configure Options

Option	*Tells PHP to . . .*
`prefix=`*`PREFIX`*	Set main PHP directory to *`PREFIX`*. Default *`PREFIX`* is `/usr/local`.
`exec-prefix=`*`EPREFIX`*	Install architecture dependent files in *`EPREFIX`*. Default *`EPREFIX`* is *`PREFIX`*.
`bindir=`*`DIR`*	Install user executables in *`DIR`*. Default is *`EPREFIX`*`/bin`.
`sbindir=`*`DIR`*	Install system administration executables in *`DIR`*. Default is `EPREFIX/sbin`.
`infodir=`*`DIR`*	Install info documentation in *`DIR`*. Default is *`PREFIX`*`/info`.
`mandir=`*`DIR`*	Install man files in *`DIR`*. Default is *`PREFIX`*`/man`.
`with-config-file-path=`*`DIR`*	Look for the configuration file (`php. ini`) in *`DIR`*. Without this option, PHP looks for the configuration file in a default location, usually `/usr/local/lib`.
`enable-debugger`	Enable support for internal debugger.
`enable-ftp`	Enable FTP support.
`enable-magic-quotes`	Enable automatic escaping of quotes with a backslash.
`enable-trans-id`	Enable PHP to pass session variables transparently.
`enable-url-includes`	Allow the `include()` function to get files from HTTP and FTP locations, as well as from the include directory.

Option	*Tells PHP to . . .*
`with-apxs=`*`FILE`*	Build a shared Apache module using the apxs utility located at *`FILE`*. Default *`FILE`* is apxs.
`with-apxs2=`*`FILE`*	Build a shared Apache 2 module using the apxs utility located at *`FILE`*. Default *`FILE`* is apxs.
`with-msql=`*`DIR`*	Enable support for mSQL databases. Default *`DIR`* where mSQL is located is `/usr/local/Hughes`.
`with-mysql=`*`DIR`*	Enable support for MySQL databases. Default *`DIR`* where MySQL is located is `/usr/local`.
`with-openssl=`*`DIR`*	Enable OpenSSL support for a secure server. Requires OpenSSL version 0.9.5 or later.
`with-oracle=`*`DIR`*	Enable support for Oracle. Default *`DIR`* is contained in the environmental variable, `ORACLE_HOME`.
`with-pgsql=`*`DIR`*	Enable support for PostgreSQL databases. Default *`DIR`* where PostgreSQL is located is `/usr/local/pgsql`.
`with-servlet=`*`DIR`*	Include servlet support. *`DIR`* is the base install directory for the JSDK. The Java extension must be built as a shared dl.
`with-regex=`*`TYPE`*	regex library type: system, apache, php.
`with-xml`	Enable XML support.

Configuring

You must configure Apache to recognize PHP files, as well as configure PHP itself. Follow these steps to configure your system for PHP:

1. **An Apache configuration file, called `httpd.conf`, is on your system, possibly in `/etc` or in `/usr/local/apache/conf`. You must edit this file before PHP can run properly. Make the following changes:**

   - **LoadModule:** You need to tell Apache to load the PHP module. Find the list of LoadModule statements. You load the PHP module with the line:

     ```
     LoadModule php4_module libexec/libphp4.so.
     ```

     Check to be sure that this line is there. If it is not there, add it. If it is there with a pound sign (#) at the beginning of the line, remove the pound sign.

   - **AddType:** You need to tell Apache which files might contain PHP code. Look for a section describing AddType. You may see one or more AddType lines for other software. The AddType line for PHP is

     ```
     AddType application/x-httpd-php .php
     ```

     Look for this line. If you find it with a pound sign (#) at the beginning of the line, remove the pound sign (#). If you don't find this line, add it to the list of AddType statements. This line tells Apache to look for PHP code in all files with a `.php` extension. You can specify any extension or series of extensions.

2. **A default configuration file is also provided for PHP. Copy the file** `php.ini-dist` **to** `/usr/local/lib/php.ini`**.**

   You can edit this file if necessary, but in most cases the defaults are okay.

3. **Start (if it is not running) or restart (if it is running) the Apache httpd server.**

   You can start or restart the server by using a script that was installed on your system during installation. This script may be apachectl or httpd.apache, and it may be located in `/bin` or in `/usr/local/apache/bin`. For example, you may be able to start the server by typing `apachectl start` or restart it using `apachectl restart` or stop it using `apachectl stop`. Sometimes restarting is not sufficient; you must stop the server first and then start it. In addition, your computer is undoubtedly set up so that Apache will start whenever the computer starts. Therefore, you can shut down and then start your computer to restart Apache.

On Windows

PHP runs on Windows 95/98/ME and Windows NT/2000. It is expected to run on Windows XP, but as I'm writing this, it has not yet been tested for XP. It does not run on Windows 3.1.

Installing

To install PHP on Windows, follow these steps:

1. **Point your Web browser at** `www.php.net`**.**
2. **Click Download.**
3. **Go to the Windows Binaries section. Click the download link for the installer for the most recent version of PHP (as of this writing, 4.1.1).**

   A dialog box opens.
4. **Select the option to save the file.**

   A dialog box opens that lets you select where the file will be saved.
5. **Navigate to where you want the file to be downloaded. Then click Save.**

   After the download is complete, you see a file in the download location containing all the files needed. The file is named `php`, followed by the version number without the dots and `-installer.exe`. For the current version, the file is named `php411-installer.exe`.
6. **If you're not using IIS or PWS for your Web server and you currently have your Web server running, shut it down.**
7. **Navigate to the directory where you downloaded php and double-click** `php411-installer.exe`**.**

   The installer software starts with the screen shown in Figure B-1.
8. **Click Next.**

   The license is displayed.
9. **Click I Agree to continue.**

   You see a screen in which you can choose the type of installation.

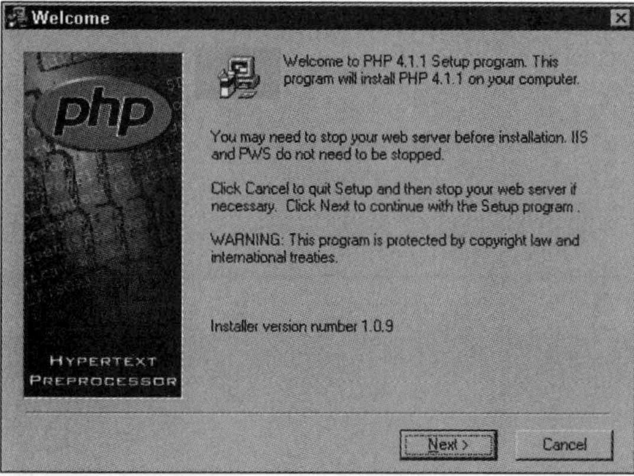

Figure B-1: The opening screen of the PHP installer.

10. **Select Standard and then click Next.**

    You see a screen showing the directory where PHP will be installed.

11. **If you want to install PHP in the default directory,** `c:\php`**, click Next. If you want to install PHP in a different directory, click Browse, select a directory, and click OK; then click Next.**

    You see a mail configuration screen.

12. **Mail configuration is not important for the scripts in this book. Just leave the defaults selected and click Next.**

    If you need to, you can change this later by editing the PHP configuration file.

    You see the screen shown in Figure B-2. It shows a list of servers that PHP can be installed with.

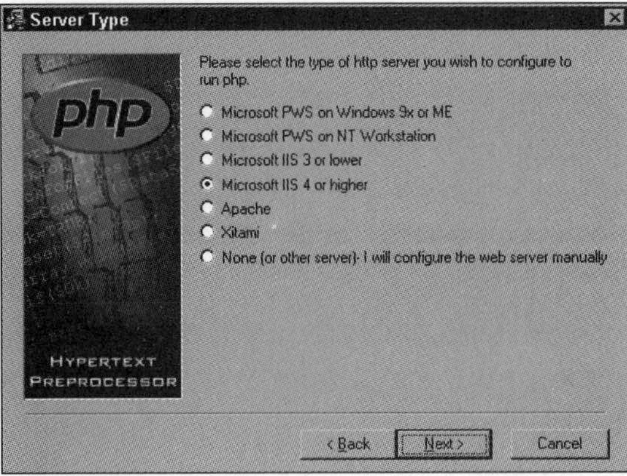

Figure B-2: The Server Type screen in the PHP installer program.

13. **Select the server that you're using. If the server you're using is not listed, select None. Then click Next.**

    You see the ready screen. The installer is now ready to install.

14. **Click Next to start the installation.**

    You see a confirmation message after PHP 4.1.1 has been installed. Any information you need will be displayed, such as whether you need to reboot or restart your server. For instance, when I selected Apache, I saw the screen in Figure B-3.

    This message doesn't mean that Apache was not installed. It just means that it wasn't automatically configured, so I have to configure it myself, as described in the next section. Perhaps by the time you install PHP, the configuration for Apache will also be automated, saving you the trouble.

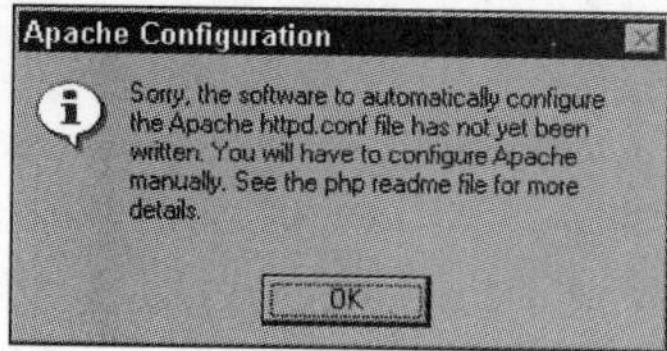

Figure B-3: An installer message about Apache.

Configuring

Your Web server needs to be configured to recognize PHP files, and PHP itself needs to be configured. If your Web server is IIS or PWS, it was automatically configured during the installation procedure. If your Web server is Apache, you may need to do the configuration yourself. Just follow these steps:

1. **You configure Apache by editing a file called `httpd.conf`.**

   You may be able to edit it by choosing Start➪Programs➪Apache Web Server➪Management➪Edit Configuration.

   If Edit Configuration isn't on your Start menu, find the `httpd.conf` file on your hard disk, usually in the directory where Apache is installed, in a subdirectory called conf (for example, `c:\program files\Apache group\Apache\conf`). Open this file in an editor, such as Notepad or WordPad.

2. **Your `httpd.conf` file must instruct Apache to send PHP code to the PHP program. Two statements work together to do this:**

   - **ScriptAlias:** A ScriptAlias statement is used to set up a name for the directory where PHP is installed. Look for ScriptAlias statements in the `httpd.conf` file. You may see some for other software. If you do not see one for PHP, add the following:

     ```
     ScriptAlias /php/ "c:/php/"
     ```

     The first argument is the name, and the second argument is what it represents. In this statement, the name `/php/` is used to mean `c:/php/`.

   - **Action:** An Action statement is used to tell Apache where to find PHP. If you don't find an Action statement for PHP, add the following:

     ```
     Action application/x-httpd-php /php/php.exe
     ```

     Notice that the Action statement uses the name defined in the ScriptAlias statement. It locates `php.exe` in `/php/` which means `c:/php/`. If you change the ScriptAlias statement to say `c:/php27/`, the Action statement would then look for `php.exe` in `c:/php27`.

Don't worry whether you should use forward or backward slashes. Apache can handle either kind.

3. **You need to tell Apache which files might contain PHP code.**

   In the `httpd.conf` file, look for a section describing AddType. This section may contain one or more AddType lines for other software. The AddType line for PHP is

   ```
   AddType application/x-httpd-php .php
   ```

   Look for this line. If you find it with a pound sign (#) at the beginning of the line, remove the pound sign. If you don't find the line, add it to the list of AddType statements. This line tells Apache to look for PHP code in all files with a `.php` extension. You can specify any extension or series of extensions.

4. **PHP also has a configuration file named `php.ini`, which should be located in `Windows\System` for Windows 95/98/ME or `Windows\System32` for Windows NT/2000. You can edit this file if necessary, but in most cases the defaults are okay.**

5. **The file called `php4ts.dll` should be installed in your System or System32 directory. If it is not there, copy it over from the directory where PHP was installed (for example, `c:\php\php4ts.dll`).**

6. **Start (if it is not running) or restart (if it is running) Apache.**

   You can start it as a service on Windows NT/2000 by choosing Start➪Programs➪Apache Web Server➪Apache as a Service.

   Or you can start it on Windows 95/98/ME by choosing Start➪Programs➪Apache Web Server➪Management.

   Sometimes restarting Apache is not sufficient; you must stop it first and then start it. In addition, your computer is undoubtedly set up so that Apache will start whenever the computer starts. Therefore, you can shut down and then start your computer to restart Apache.

Appendix C

CD Contents

System Requirements

Make sure that your computer meets the minimum system requirements shown in the following list. If your computer doesn't match up to most of these requirements, you may have problems using the software and files on the CD. For the latest and greatest information, please refer to the ReadMe file located at the root of the CD-ROM.

For Windows

- A PC with a Pentium or faster processor
- Microsoft Windows 95 or later
- At least 32MB of total RAM installed on your computer; for best performance, I recommend at least 64MB
- A CD-ROM drive
- A sound card for PCs
- A monitor capable of displaying at least 256 colors or grayscale
- A modem with a speed of at least 14,400 bps

For Linux

- PC with a Pentium processor running at 90 MHz or faster
- At least 32MB of total RAM installed on your computer; for best performance, I recommend at least 64MB
- Ethernet network interface card (NIC) or modem with a speed of at least 28,800 bps
- A CD-ROM drive

If you need more information on the basics, check out these books published by Hungry Minds, Inc.: *PCs For Dummies,* by Dan Gookin; *Windows 95 For Dummies, Windows 98 For Dummies, Windows 2000 Professional For Dummies,* and *Microsoft Windows Me Millennium Edition For Dummies,* all by Andy Rathbone.

Using the CD with Microsoft Windows

To install items from the CD to your hard drive, follow these steps:

1. **Insert the CD into your computer's CD-ROM drive.**

   Give your computer a moment to take a look at the CD.

2. **When the light on your CD-ROM drive goes out, double-click the My Computer icon. (It's probably in the top-left corner of your desktop.)**

   This action opens the My Computer window, which shows you all the drives attached to your computer, the Control Panel, and a couple other handy things.

3. **Double-click the icon for your CD-ROM drive.**

   Another window opens, showing you all the folders and files on the CD.

Using the CD with Linux

To install the items from the CD to your hard drive, follow these steps:

1. **Log in as root.**
2. **Insert the CD into your computer's CD-ROM drive.**
3. **If your computer has Auto-Mount enabled, wait for the CD to mount; otherwise, do one of the following:**

   - **Command-line instructions:**

     At the command prompt, type:

     ```
     mount /dev/cdrom /mnt/cdrom
     ```

     This will mount the `cdrom` device to the `mnt/cdrom` directory. If your device has a different name, then exchange `cdrom` with that device name — for instance, `cdrom1`.

   - **Graphical:**

     Right-click the CD-ROM icon on the desktop and choose Mount CD-ROM from the selections. This will mount your CD-ROM.

4. **Browse the CD and follow the individual installation instructions for the products listed in the next section.**
5. **To remove the CD from your CD-ROM drive, do one of the following:**
   - **Command-line instructions:**

     At the command prompt, type:

     ```
     unmount /mnt/cdrom
     ```
   - **Graphical:**

     Right-click the CD-ROM icon on the desktop and choose Unmount CD-ROM from the selections. This will unmount your CD-ROM.

What You'll Find on the CD

The following sections are arranged by category and provide a summary of the software and other goodies you'll find on the CD. If you need help with installing the items provided on the CD, refer to the installation instructions in the preceding section.

Shareware programs are fully functional, free, trial versions of copyrighted programs. If you like particular programs, register with their authors for a nominal fee and receive licenses, enhanced versions, and technical support. *Freeware programs* are free, copyrighted games, applications, and utilities. You can copy them to as many PCs as you like — for free — but they offer no technical support. *GNU software* is governed by its own license, which is included inside the folder of the GNU software. There are no restrictions on distribution of GNU software. See the GNU license at the root of the CD for more details. *Trial, demo,* or *evaluation* versions of software are usually limited either by time or functionality (such as not letting you save a project after you create it).

Apache

Open source Web server

The source code can be compiled on almost every system. Software is also provided for Windows.

```
source/apache_1.3.23.tar.gz
windows/apache_1.3.23-win32-x86.exe
```

Apache is used on about 60 percent of Web sites, according to Web surveys at Netcraft (`www.netcraft.com/survey/`). Apache runs on almost every operating system. It's reliable, fast, and free. For more information, see `httpd.apache.org`.

MySQL

Open source relational database management system (RDBMS)

Binaries are provided for many operating systems, and source code is provided that can be compiled on almost every system. The versions provided are

```
linux/MySQL-3.23.49-1.i386.rpm
linux/MySQL-client-3.23.49-1.i386.rpm
linux/MySQL-3.23.49-1.src.rpm
linux/mysql-3.23.49-pc-linux-gnu-i686.tar.gz
source/mysql-3.23.49.tar.gz
windows/mysql-3.23.49-win.zip
```

For more information, see www.mysql.com.

PHP

Open source scripting language

Source files are provided that can be compiled on almost every system except Windows. A file is provided that will install PHP on Windows.

```
windows/php411-installer.exe
source/php-4.1.1-tar.gz
```

For more information, see www.php.net.

Author-created material

All the examples provided in this book are located in the Author directory on the CD and work with Macintosh, Linux, Unix, and Windows 95/98/NT and later computers. These files contain much of the sample code from the book.

Troubleshooting

I tried my best to compile programs that work on most computers with the minimum system requirements. Alas, your computer may differ, and some programs may not work properly for some reason.

The two likeliest problems are that you don't have enough memory (RAM) for the programs you want to use, or you have other programs running that are affecting the installation or running of a program. If you get an error message such as `Not enough memory` or `Setup cannot continue`, try one or more of the following suggestions and then try using the software again:

- **Turn off any antivirus software running on your computer.** Installation programs sometimes mimic virus activity and may make your computer incorrectly believe that it's being infected by a virus.
- **Close all running programs.** The more programs you have running, the less memory is available to other programs. Installation programs typically update files and programs; so if you keep other programs running, installation may not work properly.
- **Have your local computer store add more RAM to your computer.** This is, admittedly, a drastic and somewhat expensive step. However, if you have a Windows 95 PC, adding more memory can really help the speed of your computer and allow more programs to run at the same time. This may include closing the CD interface and running a product's installation program from Windows Explorer.

If you still have trouble installing the items from the CD, please call the Hungry Minds, Inc. Customer Service phone number at 800-762-2974 (outside the U.S.: 317-572-3994) or send e-mail to `techsupdum@wiley.com`.

Index

Symbols

• A •

• E •

• F •

• I •

• T •

• U •

• V •

• W •

• X Y Z •

Hungry Minds, Inc.
End-User License Agreement

READ THIS. You should carefully read these terms and conditions before opening the software packet(s) included with this book ("Book"). This is a license agreement ("Agreement") between you and Hungry Minds, Inc. ("HMI"). By opening the accompanying software packet(s), you acknowledge that you have read and accept the following terms and conditions. If you do not agree and do not want to be bound by such terms and conditions, promptly return the Book and the unopened software packet(s) to the place you obtained them for a full refund.

1. **License Grant.** HMI grants to you (either an individual or entity) a nonexclusive license to use one copy of the enclosed software program(s) (collectively, the "Software") solely for your own personal or business purposes on a single computer (whether a standard computer or a workstation component of a multi-user network). The Software is in use on a computer when it is loaded into temporary memory (RAM) or installed into permanent memory (hard disk, CD-ROM, or other storage device). HMI reserves all rights not expressly granted herein.

2. **Ownership.** HMI is the owner of all right, title, and interest, including copyright, in and to the compilation of the Software recorded on the disk(s) or CD-ROM ("Software Media"). Copyright to the individual programs recorded on the Software Media is owned by the author or other authorized copyright owner of each program. Ownership of the Software and all proprietary rights relating thereto remain with HMI and its licensers.

3. **Restrictions on Use and Transfer.**

   (a) You may only (i) make one copy of the Software for backup or archival purposes, or (ii) transfer the Software to a single hard disk, provided that you keep the original for backup or archival purposes. You may not (i) rent or lease the Software, (ii) copy or reproduce the Software through a LAN or other network system or through any computer subscriber system or bulletin-board system, or (iii) modify, adapt, or create derivative works based on the Software.

   (b) You may not reverse engineer, decompile, or disassemble the Software. You may transfer the Software and user documentation on a permanent basis, provided that the transferee agrees to accept the terms and conditions of this Agreement and you retain no copies. If the Software is an update or has been updated, any transfer must include the most recent update and all prior versions.

4. **Restrictions on Use of Individual Programs.** You must follow the individual requirements and restrictions detailed for each individual program in Appendix C of this Book. These limitations are also contained in the individual license agreements recorded on the Software Media. These limitations may include a requirement that after using the program for a specified period of time, the user must pay a registration fee or discontinue use. By opening the Software packet(s), you will be agreeing to abide by the licenses and restrictions for these individual programs that are detailed in Appendix C and on the Software Media. None of the material on this Software Media or listed in this Book may ever be redistributed, in original or modified form, for commercial purposes.

5. **Limited Warranty.**

   (a) HMI warrants that the Software and Software Media are free from defects in materials and workmanship under normal use for a period of sixty (60) days from the date of purchase of this Book. If HMI receives notification within the warranty period of defects in materials or workmanship, HMI will replace the defective Software Media.

   (b) **HMI AND THE AUTHOR OF THE BOOK DISCLAIM ALL OTHER WARRANTIES, EXPRESS OR IMPLIED, INCLUDING WITHOUT LIMITATION IMPLIED WARRANTIES OF MERCHANTABILITY AND FITNESS FOR A PARTICULAR PURPOSE, WITH RESPECT TO THE SOFTWARE, THE PROGRAMS, THE SOURCE CODE CONTAINED THEREIN, AND/OR THE TECHNIQUES DESCRIBED IN THIS BOOK. HMI DOES NOT WARRANT THAT THE FUNCTIONS CONTAINED IN THE SOFTWARE WILL MEET YOUR REQUIREMENTS OR THAT THE OPERATION OF THE SOFTWARE WILL BE ERROR FREE.**

   (c) This limited warranty gives you specific legal rights, and you may have other rights that vary from jurisdiction to jurisdiction.

6. **Remedies.**

   (a) HMI's entire liability and your exclusive remedy for defects in materials and workmanship shall be limited to replacement of the Software Media, which may be returned to HMI with a copy of your receipt at the following address: Software Media Fulfillment Department, Attn.: *PHP & MySQL For Dummies*, Hungry Minds, Inc., 10475 Crosspoint Blvd., Indianapolis, IN 46256, or call 1-800-762-2974. Please allow four to six weeks for delivery. This Limited Warranty is void if failure of the Software Media has resulted from accident, abuse, or misapplication. Any replacement Software Media will be warranted for the remainder of the original warranty period or thirty (30) days, whichever is longer.

   (b) In no event shall HMI or the author be liable for any damages whatsoever (including without limitation damages for loss of business profits, business interruption, loss of business information, or any other pecuniary loss) arising from the use of or inability to use the Book or the Software, even if HMI has been advised of the possibility of such damages.

   (c) Because some jurisdictions do not allow the exclusion or limitation of liability for consequential or incidental damages, the above limitation or exclusion may not apply to you.

7. **U.S. Government Restricted Rights.** Use, duplication, or disclosure of the Software for or on behalf of the United States of America, its agencies and/or instrumentalities (the "U.S. Government") is subject to restrictions as stated in paragraph (c)(1)(ii) of the Rights in Technical Data and Computer Software clause of DFARS 252.227-7013, or subparagraphs (c) (1) and (2) of the Commercial Computer Software - Restricted Rights clause at FAR 52.227-19, and in similar clauses in the NASA FAR supplement, as applicable.

8. **General.** This Agreement constitutes the entire understanding of the parties and revokes and supersedes all prior agreements, oral or written, between them and may not be modified or amended except in a writing signed by both parties hereto that specifically refers to this Agreement. This Agreement shall take precedence over any other documents that may be in conflict herewith. If any one or more provisions contained in this Agreement are held by any court or tribunal to be invalid, illegal, or otherwise unenforceable, each and every other provision shall remain in full force and effect.